U.S. Foreign Policy
in a Changing World

U.S. Foreign Policy
in a Changing World

THE NIXON
ADMINISTRATION,
1969-1973

Edited by Alan M. Jones, Jr.
University of California, Davis

DAVID McKAY COMPANY, INC., NEW YORK

Acknowledgments

The editor gratefully acknowledges the permission of authors and publishers in reprinting the following articles:

"Moscow's Options in a Changing World," by Vernon V. Aspaturian, published in *Problems of Communism*, July–August 1972, a periodical edited at the United States Information Agency, Washington, D.C. Reprinted by permission of the author.

"Weighing the Balance of Power," by Stanley Hoffmann. Copyright 1972 by the Council on Foreign Relations, Inc., New York. Reprinted by permission from *Foreign Affairs*, July 1972.

*For my parents
and my wife*

Preface

This volume of essays on American foreign policy under the Nixon administration grew out of a series of lectures presented by members of the political science faculty at the Davis campus of the University of California in the spring of 1972. In preparing these lectures, many members were struck by the paucity of published analysis of policy since the Johnson years. Much had been written about the substance and formulation of American actions abroad during the 1960s, and many proposals for future initiatives and redirections had been advanced. Specific decisions of the Nixon administration had been described and sometimes analyzed, but generally as isolated incidents, unrelated to the overall policies pursued by Washington either simultaneously or in the past. The picture of American foreign policy under Nixon available to interested readers was one of disorder, with ill-fitting bits and pieces scattered about. Nowhere had these pieces been brought together to produce a cohesive and coherent pattern, either overall or in the principal areas of American concern.

The essays in this volume are attempts, individually and collectively, to set forth and analyze the foreign policy actions of the first Nixon administration in this broader framework. As such, they are first attempts only. Writing on contemporary affairs permits neither the greater objectivity nor the beneficial hindsight of works claiming to provide definitive analyses of the past. Nonetheless, these essays do provide a view of Nixon policy as it evolved during the four years of its self-proclaimed attempt to shift American policy onto a new basis. These four years saw the end of the American military role in Vietnam, the establishment of high-level contacts and understandings with the two great Communist powers, and the readjustment of relations with allied countries in Europe and East Asia. For these reasons and others developed in the essays that follow, the years 1969–73 may be seen, as they came to be seen by the Nixon administration itself, as a relatively self-contained transitional period from two decades of cold war confrontation to a future "structure of peace" whose general features had been sketched but whose specific content remained only vaguely defined. American policy in the remainder of the 1970s would be devoted, not to a further redirection of basic policy, but rather to the elaboration of the framework already established. One may well question whether the years of the Nixon first term were in fact the most important period of adjustment in foreign policy since the post-World War II transformation from Soviet-American alliance to hostility. But, through these essays, it should become clear that the late 1960s and early 1970s was a time when many of the assumptions and policies of the United States were recast to meet the demands of a changing world.

Any collection of essays necessarily reflects the strengths and styles of the contributors. The result of a series of individual efforts, its unity and comprehensiveness are both less and more than a single author could provide: less because of greater diversity, more because of greater collective expertise. Differences of approach have meant shifting emphases on Nixon policy in the contexts of past U.S. policy and the international politics of the areas described. The essays do not deal solely with American foreign policy under President Nixon, nor do they attempt to assess all the aspects of that policy in their subject areas. Collective expertise also has its limits. As a glance at the contents will demonstrate, some parts of the world have received more attention than others, while still other areas have been omitted entirely from separate treatment. An attempt at universality would have increased substantially the size and complexity of the project, with the likelihood of disparate and unwieldy results. Instead the collection reflects the knowledge and interests of a relatively small number of scholars, nearly all affiliated with one academic institution. Like all but the most encyclopedic discussions, the views presented here are partial ones.

These limitations having been stated, the value of the collection remains. As indicated at the outset, it represents one of the first scholarly attempts to assess the significance of Nixon foreign policy over its four-year evolution. Second, while most of the contributors are departmental colleagues, they are also recognized scholars in their fields, several with national and international reputations. Third, although the subjects discussed reflect individual areas of concentration, they are also broadly ones of basic importance to the United States and in which the Nixon administration has been confronted with far-reaching policy challenges. While the views presented below are partial, they are not superficial, idiosyncratic, or irrelevant to American policy concerns.

The years 1969–73 are likely to be best remembered in American foreign policy for President Nixon's summit meetings in Moscow and Peking. The opening of high-level contacts with the Chinese Communist regime, the accords reached with the Soviet Union, lay at the heart of the Nixon "strategy for peace." These developments must be given primacy of place in any survey, and they are treated here by John Starr (China) and Vernon Aspaturian (Soviet Union). Related to the Soviet détente are the changes taking place in Central and Eastern Europe, raising the prospect of an end to the cold war division of the European continent. Alexander Groth analyzes the Nixon efforts to promote and control this movement toward rapprochement. A different type of coming together has occurred in Western Europe, with British entry into the Common Market. Robert Lieber examines the background of this reversal of British and European policies and its implications for the future of American relations with its Atlantic allies. Nearly half the essays in this collection are devoted to United States policy toward the Communist powers and to Europe, reflecting the importance assigned to them by the Nixon administration.

The President frequently expressed his view that, in the early 1970s, the Middle East was the world's most dangerous crisis area, because of the possibility of collision there between Washington and Moscow. Shahrough Akhavi describes Nixon's policy toward the area in the context of Arab-Israeli rivalry and the Soviet-American confrontation which it produced. Beyond its Middle Eastern focus and a diminishing legacy in Indochina (culminating in the Paris cease-fire agreements ending the American involvement in Vietnam), the administration devoted relatively little attention to the problems of the Third World. Donald Rothchild discusses the course and consequences of Washington's seeming indifference on U.S. relations with African nations, especially the last strongholds of white rule in Southern Africa. Relative disinterest on the part of the Nixon administration extended to the United Nations as well. Geoffrey Wandesforde-Smith examines the growing American concern with problems of the international environment and the role of the United Nations in dealing with them.

Bringing together these and other aspects of American policy during the first Nixon administration, Alan Jones provides an introductory overview of their role in the development of the Nixon grand design and its place in broader perspectives of American foreign policy. In the concluding essay, Stanley Hoffmann contrasts the assumptions of the Nixon strategy with the realities of contemporary world politics.

More than most academic works, this volume is the collective product of many efforts. In addition to those contributors whose essays appear below, Richard Gable, Kenneth Hanf, Lloyd Musolf, and Paul Zinner joined in earlier stages of the project. Their efforts in the critical initial phases are greatly appreciated. Of the contributors, Donald Rothchild guided the project from its inception, enabling the present editor to assume responsibility at a later date and providing helpful advice throughout. Without his continuing support, this collection could not have appeared. Alexander Groth was no less generous in helping to see the volume through the trials of publication. At an equally important level, Mrs. Roberta Kenney succeeded in the tedious and often frustrating task of transcribing the original lectures, while Mrs. Dottie Larsen and Mrs. Linda Eernisse transformed the pastework revisions of these drafts into polished and

coherent manuscripts. This multiple assistance greatly eased the
work of the present editor while still providing a valuable lesson in
the rewards and tribulations of editorship.

Alan M. Jones, Jr.

Davis, California
April 1973

Contributors

Shahrough Akhavi (Ph.D., Columbia) is assistant professor of international studies at the University of South Carolina. Recent publications include "The Egyptian Political Elite," in Frank A. Tachau, ed., *Modernization in the Middle East* (Cambridge, Mass.: Schenkman, 1973). A larger study of Egyptian socialism is to be published by Columbia University Press.

Vernon V. Aspaturian (Ph.D., UCLA) is research professor of political science and director of the Slavic and Soviet Language and Area Center, at the Pennsylvania State University, College Park. Recent publications include *Process and Power in Soviet Foreign Policy* (Boston: Little, Brown, 1971). He has contributed to leading journals in political science and Soviet studies.

Alexander J. Groth (Ph.D., Columbia) is professor of political science at the University of California, Davis. Recent publications include *Comparative Politics: A Distribution Approach* (New York: Macmillan, 1971), *Major Ideologies* (New York: Wiley, 1972), and *People's Poland* (San Francisco: Chandler, 1972). He has also contributed to *American Political Science Review, Comparative Politics, Slavic Review, Political Science Quarterly, Orbis,* and other journals.

Stanley Hoffmann (Ph.D., Paris) is professor of government and chairman of West European Studies at Harvard University. Recent publications include *Gulliver's Troubles* (New York: McGraw-Hill, 1968), and numerous other books and articles in leading journals.

Alan M. Jones, Jr., (Ph.D., MIT) is assistant professor of political science at the University of California, Davis.

Robert J. Lieber (Ph.D., Harvard) is associate professor of political science at the University of California, Davis. Recent publications include *British Politics and European Unity* (Berkeley: University of California, 1970), and *Theory and World Politics* (Cambridge, Mass.: Winthrop, 1972). He has contributed to the *American Political Science Review, International Affairs,* and other journals.

Donald Rothchild (Ph.D., Johns Hopkins) is professor of political science at the University of California, Davis. Recent publications include *Government and Politics in Kenya* (Nairobi, Kenya: East African Publishing, 1969), and *Politics of Integration* (Nairobi, Kenya: East African Publishing, 1968). He has contributed to the *American Political Science Review, World Politics, Journal of Modern African Studies, Race,* and other journals.

John B. Starr (Ph.D., Berkeley) is assistant professor of political science at the University of California, Berkeley. Recent publications include *Ideology and Culture: An Introduction to the Dialectics of Contemporary Chinese Politics* (New York: Harper & Row, 1973). He has contributed to *Asian Survey* and other journals.

Geoffrey Wandesforde-Smith (Ph.D., University of Washington) is assistant professor of political science at the University of California, Davis. Recent publications include *Environmental Watchdogs* (Davis, Calif.: Institute of Governmental Affairs, University of California, Davis, 1972), and *Congress and the Enviroment* (Seattle, Wash.: University of Washington, 1970; co-editor). He has contributed to the *Stanford Law Review* and other journals.

Contents

U.S. Foreign Policy
in a Changing World

Alan M. Jones, Jr.

Nixon and the World

The four years of the first Nixon administration were marked simultaneously by White House efforts to reshape American foreign policy and by mounting domestic opposition to most of the legacies of that policy. The parallel development of these two trends transformed the presidential election of 1972 into a contest of opposing approaches to American foreign policy. Despite Senator Barry Goldwater's insistence in 1964 that he offered "A Choice, Not an Echo," he advocated an intensification of the cold war emphasis of existing policy, an insistence on more and better weapons (especially nuclear) and the will to use them, rather than a reversal of that emphasis.[1] The Democrats of 1972, however, saw recent foreign entanglements (especially the war in Indochina) as the culmination of more than a decade of flawed premises and policies producing a whole series of disastrous defeats and missed opportunities. And like the Eisenhower Republicans of twenty years before, the McGovern Democrats pledged their new administration (if elected) to basic changes in foreign policy.

1972: The Competition of Grand Designs

The principal change called for by the Democratic opponents of the Nixon policy was well summarized in the theme of Senator George McGovern's July 13, 1972, acceptance speech, culminating in his appeal to "Come Home, America."

[W]e will call America home to the founding ideals that nourished us in the beginning.

From secrecy and deception in high places, come home, America.

From a conflict in Indochina which maims our ideals as well as our soldiers, come home, America.

From military spending so wasteful that it weakens our nation, come home, America.[2]

As McGovern indicated in his speech, "coming home" involved a return both to the primacy of domestic needs over foreign concerns and to the traditional role of American idealism and morality as a principal criterion by which policy is measured. The Democratic candidate went far toward repudiating a course centered upon Great Power rivalry, alliance systems, and military strength, instead proposing greater cooperation among major states, renewed support for the United Nations, increased responsiveness to the needs of less-developed countries, and added respect for the rule of law.[3] This call for redirection of national priorities received authoritative support by the *New York Times* and by prominent authors in *Foreign Affairs*, the most prestigious American journal on foreign issues, as well as in other quarters.[4] For large numbers of Americans, the focus had shifted from competition to collaboration, from America's mission in the world at large to achievement of essential goals at home.

In contrast to Democratic demands for fundamental change, the Nixon administration appealed for a continuation of the President's "strategy for peace," which it claimed had been strikingly successful in adjusting American policies to the new situations produced by the transformation of world politics since the days of bilateral Soviet-American confrontation shortly after World War II.

As the 1972 Republican platform proclaimed with satisfaction:

> In only four years, we have fashioned foreign policies based on a new spirit of effective negotiation with our adversaries and a new sense of real partnership with our allies. Clearly, the prospects for lasting peace are greater today than at any time since World War II.
>
> From one sector of the globe to another, a sure and strong America, in partnership with other nations, has once again resumed her historic mission—the building of lasting peace.[5]

For all his efforts to emphasize successful new departures, President Nixon was careful to place his administration within (and, by implication, to exclude Senator McGovern from) the post-1945 mainstream of American foreign policy. In his acceptance speech at the Republican convention in late August 1972, Nixon briefly described his conception of this heritage and his commitment to it.

These five Presidents [Franklin Roosevelt to Lyndon Johnson] were united in their total opposition to isolation for America and in their belief that the interest of the United States and the interest of world peace required that America be strong enough and intelligent enough to assume the responsibilities of leadership in the world.

They were united in the conviction that the United States should have a defense second to none in the world. They were all men who hated war and were dedicated to peace.

But not one of these five men and no President in our history believed that America should ask an enemy for peace on terms that would betray our allies and destroy respect for the United States all over the world.

And as your President, I pledge that I shall always uphold that proud bipartisan tradition.[6]

The corollary of these widely differing views on the basic direction of American foreign policy for the mid- and late-1970s was an equally wide and fundamental disagreement over the nature and functioning of the processes by which American foreign policy is made. The Democrats pledged themselves to "return to Congress, and to the people, a meaningful role in decisions on peace and war."[7] Behind this pledge was a conviction that, under Johnson and Nixon, the White House had usurped the power of Congress to affect foreign policy. The Johnson pattern of relying upon a small circle of senior advisers had been succeeded by the intimate confidences of Nixon and Dr. Henry Kissinger, his special assistant for national security affairs. To these critics of recent practice, the concentration of decision-making authority in the executive branch had been largely responsible for the massive American military involvement in Indochina which began in 1965 and for the major reescalations of that in-

volvement by the Nixon administration in sending American troops
into Cambodia in June 1970 and in renewing large-scale bombing of
North Vietnam (coupled with the mining of North Vietnamese waters) in the spring of 1972.[8] The latter action, for example, produced
a sharp exchange between Secretary of State William P. Rogers and
Senator J. William Fulbright, chairman of the Senate Foreign Relations Committee.

> THE CHAIRMAN: Why was the Congress not consulted in any
>   fashion, and I don't think it was, in advance of this major
>   reescalation of the war?
> SECRETARY ROGERS: I think the reason was, of course, Mr.
>   Chairman, that the secrecy of this type of thing is very im-
>   portant. Now the Congress knew, and the President has
>   told the Congress from time to time, that if the enemy . . .
>   mounted a major offensive, he would take whatever retalia-
>   tory action he thought was necessary. . . . To that extent
>   the Congress has been informed. The Congress was not in-
>   formed precisely of the military actions involved.[9]

In protest against what many regarded as the usurpation of its
foreign policy prerogatives by the administration, the Senate (and, to
a lesser degree, the House) adopted a policy of active resistance to
proposals submitted by the President and has sought to advance its
own claims to greater responsibility for and participation in foreign
policy decisions. That Congress could no longer be counted on to
support the President's initiatives overseas was made clear early in
the Nixon administration when the Senate overwhelmingly adopted
the National Commitments Resolution of June 1969. This resolution
lacked the force of law. But it did make clear the view of the legislative body principally charged with foreign affairs "that a national
commitment by the United States results only from affirmative action taken by the Legislative and Executive Branches of the United
States Government by means of a treaty, statute, or concurrent resolution of both Houses of Congress specifically providing for such
commitment." [10]

More recently, congressional attention has shifted to the War

Powers Act, an attempt to translate the sentiment of the National Commitments Resolution into binding authority. On March 13, 1972, the Senate overwhelmingly (by a vote of 68–16) passed a bill limiting the President's power to commit American forces to combat without congressional approval. "In the absence of a declaration of war by the Congress," the bill restricted presidential command of the military to cases involving direct attack on American territory, or U.S. forces and citizens located abroad, and to a period of no more than thirty days. Unless "special legislation" were enacted by Congress to extend this time limit, the President's authority would lapse, and the forces be required to cease fighting.[11]

These Senate restrictions were drastically reduced in the House version of the bill, passed even more overwhelmingly (344–13) in mid-August 1972. Like its action of the year before, the House simply required the President to make a formal report of any decision to engage American forces overseas, without seeking to limit the circumstances or duration of their use. Rather than being made dependent on congressional support for major foreign military action, the President could satisfy congressional sensibilities with an account of that action.[12] The differences between the provisions of the House and Senate bills meant that, as so often before when the Senate had tried to curb the administration's foreign activities, the stronger language and greater limitations of the Senate version would be discreetly buried in the graveyard of the conference committee formed to reconcile the conflicting views of the two houses. In the rush toward election-year adjournment and the focus on the presidential campaign, the war-powers legislation was forgotten. Despite some anxious moments, the Nixon administration reached the end of its first term substantially unscathed by congressional attempts to intrude on its control over the nation's foreign policy.

President Nixon's determination to maximize his personal direction of foreign policy free from congressional restrictions and from the pressures of the professional bureaucracies was made clear at the beginning of his tenure. In his first Report to the Congress on U.S. foreign policy (popularly referred to as the "State of the World" message), the President set forth his plans for a revitalized "National Security Council system" providing for a more "rigorous and systematic process of policy making." [13] In successive reports, this system was more fully elaborated until it encompassed a network of committees and study groups extending from the White House and the Executive Office into the senior levels of the competing foreign policy departments and agencies scattered around Washington.[14] While these committees were intended to "summon and gather the best ideas, the best analyses, and the best information available" for presidential assessment,[15] they also provided a new and far-reaching vehicle of White House control over the detailed conduct of U.S. policies abroad (as clearly shown in the leaked documents tracing Washington's reaction to the Indo-Pakistani war of December 1971).[16] It was wholly in keeping with this centralization of decision making in the White House that the President's reports allocated no place for Congress in this foreign policy scheme.

In addition to offering sharply conflicting overviews of the contents of future policy and its formulation, the two parties were also at odds over the specific means by which these broad plans would be put into action. For Senator McGovern and his supporters, immediate disengagement from the war in Indochina was the first order of business for a new president. Opposition to the war was the original McGovern theme—his first claim to national attention. As American participation in the war dragged on through the Nixon years, he joined with other senators in sponsoring legislation to restrict American activities in Laos and Cambodia and to set a firm deadline for the withdrawal of all U.S. forces from the area. McGovern's acceptance speech as presidential candidate repeated his conviction that the war was a moral as well as physical tragedy for the United States, and he reaffirmed his determination to stop it.

> In 1968, Americans voted to bring our sons home from Vietnam—and since then, twenty thousand have come home in coffins.
>
> I have no secret plans for peace. I have a public plan.
>
> As one whose heart has ached for 10 years over the agony of Vietnam, I will halt the senseless bombing of Indochina on Inauguration Day. . . .

Within 90 days of my inauguration, every American soldier and every American prisoner will be out of the jungle and out of their cells and back home in America where they belong.

And then let us resolve that never again will we shed the precious young blood of this nation to perpetuate an unrepresentative client abroad.[17]

Refuting charges that such a precipitate removal of U.S. forces would be judged a defeat for the United States, the Democrats maintained that disengagement would "enable us to heal domestic divisions and to end the distortion of our international priorities." [18]

Having campaigned successfully for the Presidency in 1968 in part on a promise to end the Vietnam war, Nixon had all but erased the American presence on the ground in Vietnam (reducing it from 543,000 in January 1969 to 27,000 in December 1972).[19] But American planes dominated the skies of Indochina at the end of his term as they had at its beginning. The North Vietnamese offensive of March 1972—the largest military action since the Viet Cong attacks during the Tet holidays four years earlier—had triggered a massive reintroduction of naval and air forces into the Indochina theater, so that the small number of Americans in Vietnam itself was belied by the much larger and infinitely more powerful presence which enveloped it.

For none of this did the President apologize. Nor would he follow his predecessor into political oblivion. Instead, he attacked the Democrats as the party of surrender. Their pledge of complete withdrawal within ninety days

might be good politics, but it would be disastrous to the cause of peace in the world. If at this time we betray our allies, it will discourage our friends abroad and it will encourage our enemies to engage in aggression.

To our friends and allies . . . I say the United States will continue its great bipartisan tradition—to stand by our friends and never desert them.[20]

Refusing to isolate Vietnam, Nixon treated it as the test by which American strength of purpose would be judged in the years to come.

Defending his April 1972 decision to expand the use of American airpower in the wake of the North Vietnamese offensive, the President declared: "If the Communists win militarily in Vietnam, the risk of war in other parts of the world would be enormously increased." [21] The war had become Nixon's own.

The other major issue on which Republican and Democratic conceptions of foreign policy clashed was, in effect, an extrapolation of their disagreement over Vietnam. As a senator, McGovern had long resisted large defense budgets, regarding the forces they purchased as redundant and provocative—and tempting for policy makers faced with difficulty or failure. The resources consumed by the military could be better used to ease the plight of the urban and rural poor at home and to feed the hungry abroad.[22] (McGovern directed the Food-for-Peace Program under John F. Kennedy and had later become its Senate champion.)[23] At the beginning of his campaign for his party's nomination, he presented an "alternative defense posture" calling for a $30 billion reduction in the military budget. Under this plan, the existing American strategic nuclear forces would be maintained at their present levels but efforts to increase the number of warheads they could deliver would be curtailed. Administration plans for a new intercontinental bomber (the B-1) and a new series of missile-carrying submarines (the latter to cost at least $1 billion apiece) were rejected by McGovern as enormously costly and more likely to hinder the arms limitation talks with the Soviets than aid in their success. These weapons would only perpetuate

> Mr. Nixon's "poker game" theory of arms control, an approach that has already moved the arms race to a more deadly level, at the same time as it has postponed an agreement that could have been had years ago.[24]

Even greater changes were contemplated for the nonstrategic ("general purpose") forces. American troops would be withdrawn not only from Southeast Asia but from all of the Far East, with the naval-air forces there reduced by more than two-thirds. American ground forces stationed in Europe would be cut in half, but naval

strength in the Mediterranean would be maintained to fulfill Mc-
Govern's strong pledge to the defense of Israel. Air Force strength
would also be curbed. The intent of these major alterations in the
size and location of the bulk of the American military was spelled
out by the senator.

> I propose that we stop spending our limited resources:
> To maintain extra military forces that can have no other pur-
> pose than to repeat our experience in Vietnam . . . a monstrous
> national blunder . . . and
> To react to a world of old discredited myths, made up of
> blocs, puppets and dominoes, instead of the real world of today
> and the future, with multiple ideologies and interests.[25]

To these proposals, the administration reacted with massive
scorn. The Democrats were offering a "white-flag budget" reflecting
a "slash-now, beg-later approach to defense policy" which "would
undercut our defenses and have America retreat into virtual isolation." [26] In contrast, Nixon pledged that the United States would
"always have a defense second to none," so that an American president would never "negotiate from weakness." [27] Declaring that "a
strong America" was "the guardian of peace," Nixon returned to the
theme of peace-through-strength contained in his 1972 "State of the
World" report.

> American strength is essential if we are to move from an era of
> confrontation toward an era of negotiation. As the world's
> strongest power, this nation has important responsibilities to its
> friends as well as unique opportunities for improving global sta-
> bility. American weakness would make no contribution to
> peace. On the contrary it would undermine prospects for
> peace.[28]

Republican and Democratic conceptions of the proper foreign
policy for the United States to pursue in the late 1970s were thus in
sharp contrast on each of these major points: overall approach, policy making, the most important single issue (Indochina), and the
level of military power. There were areas of agreement as well. Both
parties pledged added support for Israel in its conflict with the Arab

states, and both dedicated themselves to expanding ties with Moscow and Peking. But the basic differences remained, affecting even the priority of attention given to foreign policy issues. While these questions appeared first and foremost in the Republican platform, they were allocated to the rear of the Democratic program, appended to a far more extensive treatment of domestic needs, GOP failures, and Democratic remedies.[29]

All these statements and issues were aimed at the general electorate far more than at the other party or at foreign governments. For months, the candidates and their staffs had inundated the media in search of popular attention. As the campaign drew to a close, Senator McGovern returned to the Vietnam war as his main theme, charging that the administration's assertions of an imminent cease-fire constituted "cruel political deception" designed to win votes but with no basis in fact. McGovern claimed that peace in Vietnam was "not even in sight" because of the President's warlike policies.[30] While Senator McGovern stepped up his attacks on the Nixon regime, the President retained his previous low-key approach, making few statements of his own and relying on a variety of party and government officials to rebuff McGovern's challenges. Like previous Presidents seeking reelection, Nixon sought to identify himself with the Presidency as an institution transcending partisan differences to encompass the nation as a whole. Republican strategists intended the calm efficiency of the White House incumbent to contrast with the shrill rhetoric of his opponent.

Early in November the electorate passed judgment, its verdict apparent from the outset and never in doubt. Nixon had been returned as Chief Executive by "the largest margin ever given a President" in popular votes. It was, especially for the highly partisan leader of the minority party, an extraordinary personal victory. Winning over 60 percent of the popular vote and capturing all but one of the states, Richard Nixon placed himself in the ranks of Warren Harding, Franklin Roosevelt, and Lyndon Johnson by the massive proportions of his electoral triumph. Despite his victory, however, Nixon failed to carry with him enough Republican candidates to win control of either house of Congress. In fact, the alignments of the two parties in the Congress changed only marginally, while Republican gubernatorial aspirants were defeated in states giving overwhelming support to the GOP presidential ticket.[31] Nixon's victory, then, was his alone, independent of party and isolated from the remainder of the American political landscape.

The Nixon landslide highlighted the extent to which the presidential campaign had become a separate arena of competition between two individuals. In this highly personalized contest, the strengths and weaknesses of the candidates themselves tended to overshadow questions of party affiliation and policy. The outcome became primarily an expression of confidence in one individual over another rather than a vote of approval or rejection of positions on specific issues. The choice made at the polls could not, therefore, be regarded as a definitive referendum on recent foreign policy or as a national mandate to continue the course charted abroad by the first Nixon administration.

In retrospect, Senator McGovern attributed his defeat to the attempted assassination of Governor Wallace of Alabama in May 1972, removing Wallace from presidential contention and forcing his followers to choose Nixon's relative conservatism as a second-best alternative over McGovern's liberal views.[32] Another factor was the dropping of Senator Thomas Eagleton of Missouri as the Democratic vice-presidential nominee after publicity over his previous treatments for emotional problems. Others cited the dispute at the Democratic convention over the meaning and extent of reforms to make the delegates more representative of the national population.[33] Beyond these specific problems was the view that the electorate did not believe Senator McGovern to be "competent enough, credible enough, Presidential enough to do the job." [34]

Yet the divison between the two candidates on foreign policy issues was a real one, affecting the nature of the November results. In retrospect, both candidates agreed that the campaign had centered on the extent to which Senator McGovern's stands, especially on foreign policy, were reflected in the country as a whole. President Nixon clearly felt that they were not: "This election was decided the day [McGovern] was nominated. The issue in this election was his views . . . and his views simply turned off the solid majority of the American people."[35] In Nixon's view, McGovern's "extreme position on issues" had ensured his defeat from the outset, and no amount of effort by either candidate could change the inevitability of the verdict at the polls.

Responding to this reflection, Senator McGovern agreed to a surprising extent:

> The President may have been right. He may have had his thumb closer to the public pulse than I did. . . . I held views that the country was not prepared to accept right now. I'm convinced that they'll come to those views, very quickly. But I was incapable of suppressing the moral outrage I felt against the war because that was the issue that catapulted me into the national picture in the first place. That's how we won the nomination.[36]

This was McGovern's foreign policy dilemma: his antiwar views enabled him to rally supporters throughout the country against opponents in his own party but those same views, expressed repeatedly in the fall campaign, found no similar echo in the general electorate. Indeed, a Gallup poll taken shortly after the election suggested that opinion on the Vietnam issue was divided along lines nearly identical to the split in the presidential voting, with 59 percent favoring the President's handling of the war and 33 percent opposed.[37]

On the eve of the election, Nixon indicated the direction which U.S. foreign policy would take in the second term which seemed assured. Arms control discussions would occupy much of his attention, both the continued strategic arms limitations talks with the Soviet Union and proposals to reduce the size of the forces which confronted each other in Central Europe. The United States would continue its "dialogue" with Peking, "although this is a long-term process. Nothing sudden is going to happen." In addition, "the Middle East will have a very high priority because . . . it can explode at any time." Finally, reacting to criticism of Washington's neglect of Latin America and Africa, Nixon promised to reexamine U.S. policies toward those regions. Overall, the President stressed continuity with his earlier policies. His first term had laid the bases of his policies abroad; his second term would see the unfolding of his policies from those bases.

So I would say that while the next four years will not be as spectacular as the year 1972, where we had the opening to Peking, the first summit with the Russians [for his administration] and the August 15th [1971, *sic*] international monetary moves, that the next four years will build on those and will really accomplish more, because those were basically the first steps which opened the way for much bigger steps in the future.[38]

Abroad, Mr. Nixon's reelection was received with the customary congratulatory messages from allied and friendly governments. In NATO, where Senator McGovern's call to reduce American troop strength in Europe had caused concern, the news of the Nixon victory brought widespread relief. Perhaps the most significant foreign reaction, however, came from the Soviet Union. Claiming that the President owed much of his electoral success to "the improvement of Soviet-American relations," Soviet President Podgorny indicated Moscow's satisfaction with the results and went on to "express the confidence that in the coming period, Soviet-American relations will be further favorably developed in the interests of the Soviet and American peoples, in the interest of insuring international security and strengthening world peace." [39]

Korea and Vietnam: Similarities and Differences

What was behind the change of position by the Democratic party which produced this posing of sharp alternatives at the polls, a time when parties and candidates have traditionally moved close together and transformed the election campaign into a fight over middle ground? It was only slightly more than a decade before that another Democratic standard-bearer had stood on the Capitol steps in the bitter cold and proclaimed:

Let every nation know, whether it wishes us well or ill, that we shall pay any price, bear any burden, meet any hardship, support any friend, oppose any foe to assure the survival and success of liberty.[40]

The price had proved too great, and the burden too heavy. It had been harder to tell friend from foe than had seemed possible on the threshold of the New Frontier. As the conflict progressed, it seemed less and less a struggle for liberty than a dispute between dictatorships. The party's last President was now isolated, repudiated, insofar as possible forgotten—not because of the Great Society he envisaged at home but for the greater catastrophe he had brought forth abroad.

This transformation of attitudes is well illustrated by the shifting views of Senator Fulbright, the previously cited chairman of the Senate Foreign Relations Committee. With an interest in foreign affairs dating from his days as a Rhodes Scholar in the 1920s, Fulbright had been Lyndon Johnson's choice for secretary of state in 1960, had he won nomination and election. He had urged the American invasion of Cuba and the overthrow of Fidel Castro during the 1962 missile crisis. In May 1964 the senator had written:

> Until and unless they [responsible officials in the Executive branch of our government] conclude that the military situations in South Vietnam, and the political situation in Southeast Asia, warrant the expansion of the war, or that the overall situation has changed sufficiently to establish some basis for a successful negotiation, it seems to me that we have no choice but to support the South Vietnamese Government and Army by the most effective means available. It should be clear to all concerned that the United States will continue to defend its vital interests with respect to Vietnam.[41]

This support for Vietnam policy and reliance on the President's judgment was confirmed in his sponsorship of the Tonkin Gulf Resolution in August 1964. Despite charges that Congress was misled and the resolution railroaded through the Senate under extreme pressure from the Johnson administration, the record at the time indicates an awareness of the stakes involved.

> MR. [John Sherman] COOPER: . . . [A]re we now giving the President advance authority to take whatever action he may deem necessary respecting South Vietnam and its defense . . . ?

Mr. Fulbright: I think that is correct.

Mr. Cooper: Then, looking ahead, if the President declared that it was necessary to use such force as would lead to war, we will give that authority by this resolution?

Mr. Fulbright: That is the way I would interpret it.[42]

It was only after the President had in fact taken this action, involving U.S. troops directly in the war, that Senator Fulbright became an outspoken critic not only of the administration's Vietnam policy but of American foreign policy generally. He characterized this policy as governed by an "arrogance of power"—"the tendency for great nations to equate power with virtue and major responsibilities with a univeral mission." A lifelong champion of greater American involvement in world affairs, he now warned:

> An excessive preoccupation with foreign relations over a long period of time is more than a manifestation of arrogance; it is a drain on the power that gave rise to it, because it diverts a nation from the sources of its strength, which are in its domestic life.[43]

Vietnam and its reaction had brought Fulbright from support for American policy and Executive leadership in foreign affairs to fundamental criticism of both policy and leadership and a focus on problems at home. Many other prominent men have undergone similar transformations in the years since 1965.

What is being suggested here is that the agonizing reappraisal of U.S. foreign policy that produced the foreign policy division of 1972 was almost entirely a reaction to American involvement in the Vietnam war. This reaction to war and its effects in producing dramatic changes in foreign policy was not unique to the present disaffection over Vietnam. Most of the major shifts of direction that marked American foreign policy in this century resulted from the experience of war. The Spanish-American War of 1898 is generally taken as the beginning of the "modern" era of American foreign policy and it was followed by a twenty-year period of active American participation in world affairs beyond the Western Hemisphere. World War I and its reaction led to a basic reversal of policy, repudiating American responsibilities abroad and attempting to prevent a recurrence of American sacrifice to win someone else's fight. After Pearl Harbor, this doctrine of isolation was itself repudiated, being replaced by acceptance of the role of world policeman (an image frequently used by Franklin D. Roosevelt)—first in collaboration with the Soviet Union against Germany and later to limit Soviet expansion when the war against the Axis was over.

The Korean conflict in 1950 brought about a series of no less significant changes. It transformed American policy in East Asia from one of reluctant acceptance of the newly established Communist regime in China to active opposition to it. As a result, the cold war was extended full-scale from Europe to other areas of the world, and American defense treaties and commitment were expanded from the Western Hemisphere and Europe to Asia as well. The war also intensified the European struggle between Washington and Moscow, resulting in the armed confrontation of the superpowers which has underscored the division of Germany and Europe ever since.

With Vietnam, the outlines of policy established during the Korean war began to become unstuck. American commitments in East Asia were being questioned, a rapprochement was started with Peking, and the withdrawal of American forces from Europe, either unilaterally or in conjunction with a similar Soviet pullback, was seriously debated. The basic reorientation of policies and attitudes which took place in World War II had not generally been challenged, but the specific forms taken, especially during and after Korea, were subjected to intensely critical scrutiny. Whatever the outcome of these debates, the direction of future change was fairly clear: a restricted view of American commitments, the reduction or withdrawal of the American forces which guaranteed the fulfillment of these commitments, and a shifting of the focus of policy away from East Asia and the Third World generally and toward the Western Hemisphere, Europe, and Japan. The result was less likely to be a revival of isolationism than a rearrangement of overseas policy to emphasize those areas which, for reasons of military and economic security, were considered vital to American well-being.

Whether or not the ultimate reaction to the Vietnam experience took approximately this form, there was one "lesson" clear to all: no more Vietnams. The United States was not prepared to see its forces engaged in another land war, particularly in Asia, but probably also anywhere else in the Third World. It was this sentiment above all which led to the formulation of the Nixon Doctrine as the basis of the current administration's foreign policy.

It is worth noting the extraordinary parallels here with the aftermath of Korea. That war was, after all, the other Asian land war fought by the United States. (Washington's conflict with Japan in World War II was waged across the Pacific rather than on the Asian mainland.) Like Vietnam, Korea was undeclared by Congress, although it too had initial congressional and public support. It also was seen as a prolonged and costly stalemate, and popular approval of the war and the President fell even further and more sharply than in Vietnam. The same charges of Executive usurpation of authority were raised in the Congress when Truman dispatched American combat forces to Europe to guard against a possible Soviet attack there. Senator Robert A. Taft, in terms reminiscent of those used by current congressional critics, declared: "The commitment of a land army to Europe is a program never approved by Congress. . . . The policy of secret executive agreements has brought us to danger and disaster. It threatens the liberties of our people." [44] Truce talks dragged on interminably with the prisoner issue a central public concern. "No more Koreas" was the lesson brought away, and the Democratic administration that had led the country into war had its nominee rejected at the polls in favor of a Republican committed to ending the war. For a decade afterward, Korea remained the most unpopular war in recent American history. In view of so many parallels, it is not surprising that Korea's place in popular disfavor has since been taken by Vietnam.

Nixon and Dulles

To argue that voters were faced with the greatest foreign policy choice in twenty years is not to suggest that the programs advanced

were substantially similar to those offered the electorate of a generation before. Nonetheless, the parallels between the Nixon-Kissinger
and Eisenhower-Dulles brands of foreign policy are so great as to
make comparison alluring. Both policies were drafted in reaction to
unpopular Asian land wars by administrations committed to ending
those wars and preventing their repetition. Moreover, as vice-president, Nixon sat in on National Security Council sessions and received much of his foreign policy education from President Eisenhower and his Secretary of State, John Foster Dulles. The military
retrenchment in East Asia begun by Nixon, with its reliance on
naval air forces, bears a more-than-passing resemblance to the Eisenhower "New Look" in its deemphasis of American ground forces and
reliance on naval air power for areas outside the Western Hemisphere and Europe. Dr. Richard J. Barnet of the Institute of Policy
Studies in Washington, D.C., has written:

> The "Nixon Doctrine" is really an exercise in nostalgia. It is a
> throwback to the calmer days of the Eisenhower era when John
> Foster Dulles suggested that we "let Asians fight Asians" and
> "back them up" with nuclear weapons. The effect of the Nixon
> Doctrine, if it is taken seriously, is to increase the reliance on
> nuclear weapons around the world.[45]

While this identification with the past is easy and attractive, re-
calling to mind forgotten debates and that specter which Dulles cast
over the 1950s, it is also basically mistaken. Dulles's "Massive Retaliation" policy was centered principally on the threat of nuclear
weapons—and on a wall of treaties to back up that threat. The
Nixon policy has been focused neither on nuclear forces nor on formalized obligations. It is almost a mirror image of the Dulles program—the same elements are present, but their positions have been
reversed.

On nuclear weapons, Dulles wrote:

> The free world must devise a better strategy for its defense,
> based on its own special assets. Its assets include, especially, air
> and naval power and atomic weapons which are now available
> in a wide range. . . . The free world must make imaginative use

of the deterrent capabilities of these new weapons. . . . Properly used, they can produce defensive power able to retaliate at once and effectively against any aggression.[46]

Compare this statement of the centrality of nuclear weapons with the 1971 Nixon report's careful delineation of the circumstances under which American nuclear power might be brought into play in Europe and Asia. Quoting the President's November 1969 speech, it began:

> "We shall provide a shield if a nuclear power threatens the freedom of a nation allied with us or of a nation whose survival we consider vital to our security." Nuclear power is the element of security that our friends cannot provide or can provide only with great and disruptive efforts. Hence, we bear special obligations toward non-nuclear countries. Their concern would be magnified if we were to leave them defenseless against nuclear blackmail or conventional aggression backed by nuclear power.[47]

The United States would use its nuclear power solely to counter nuclear threats by others, not "against any aggression." The atomic umbrella would ease the fears giving rise to nuclear proliferation, since "the spread of nuclear capabilities would be inherently destabilizing." Hence for Nixon, American nuclear weapons were intended as much to discourage nuclear arming by allies and friends as threatened attacks by enemies.

To make the nuclear deterrent effective, Dulles relied on a global network of American commitments. Bilateral and multilateral mutual defense treaties were extended from the Western Hemisphere, Europe, and the western Pacific, to include as much of the Third World as was willing to join. This girdling of Communist borders with alliance systems was partially a means of ensuring forward basing for the American strategic bomber force, but it was also a substitute for more tangible American interests in the protection of these countries against Communist aggression.

In Europe, deterrence could be secured by the presence of large numbers of American troops stationed on a relatively permanent basis. The troops would act as a "tripwire," triggering an American nuclear response. Behind these troops was a large-scale military organization whose strategy was centered on nuclear weapons and whose direction was primarily in the hands of American commanders. Overhanging this commitment "on the ground" were the North Atlantic treaty and American military intervention in Europe during the world wars. If the nuclear deterrent was "credible" anywhere outside North America, Western Europe was that place.

None of these conditions applied to Asia and the Third World. Except for the U.S. forces left in Japan and Korea, there were no large American troop concentrations. The American record had been one of broad neglect punctuated by brief periods of intense involvement tied to European affairs. World War II in the Pacific had been a Japanese-American duel, from which the Asian mainland was essentially excluded. Korea was a war to forget, not a basis for future planning. Hence in the "gray areas" where the challenge of Communist aggression seemed greatest, the American deterrent rested not upon present forces or historical precedent but upon the pledged word of the United States. The stronger this pledge could be made, the more automatic the American nuclear reaction to attack would appear. The greater would be the prospect (however irrational it might otherwise seem) of "the power of the free community to retaliate with great force by mobile means at places of its own choice." [48] The greater also would be the chance of convincing a potential aggressor that attack could only be a costly failure.

In place of commitments, the Nixon policy has stressed interests:

> Our objective, in the first instance, is to support our interests over the long run with a sound foreign policy. The more that policy is based on a realistic assessment of our and others' interests, the more effective our role in the world can be. [49]

Dulles had declared: "The cornerstone of security for the free nations must be a collective system of defense . . . a system in which local defensive strength is reinforced by more mobile deterrent power." [50] The Nixon policy took a much less clear-cut view of the need for collective action and the indivisibility of security.

It is no longer natural or possible in this age to argue that security or development around the globe is primarily America's concern. The defense and progress of other countries must be first their responsibility, and second, a regional responsibility. Without the foundations of self-help and regional help, American help will not succeed. The United States can and will participate, where our interests dictate, but as *a* weight—not *the* weight—in the scale.[51]

The one area where American commitment to collective defense was specifically reaffirmed was in Europe. Here the administration effort has been to bend American policy sufficiently to meet European objections to American dominance of the alliance without either relinquishing American influence on policy or encouraging sentiment for a withdrawal of American forces. The 1970 report declared: "We must change the pattern of American predominance."[52] However, the 1971 report cautioned against letting the administration's goal of partnership get out of hand:

Our allies' new spirit of independence, reflecting as it does their vitality as nations, can be source of strength. But our cohesion, too, is a source of strength. . . . We must learn to reconcile autonomy and unity.[53]

The limits of divergence were indicated by the administration's warning regarding independent initiatives toward Eastern Europe.

Thus, Western cohesion must be the bedrock of our pursuit of detente. We and our allies have a responsibility to consult together in sufficient depth to ensure that our efforts are complementary and that our priorities and broad purposes are essentially the same.[54]

Predominance was to yield to partnership, but the expected results were to be basically unchanged from before.

A similar attitude of commitment combined with confidence in the mutuality of American interest was expressed with regard to Japan.

Japan is our most important ally in Asia. It is our second greatest trading partner. It is an essential participant, if a stable

world peace is to be built. Our security, our prosperity, and our
global policies are therefore intimately and inextricably linked
to the U.S.–Japanese relationship. The well-being of both
countries requires cooperation and a shared commitment to the
same fundamental goals.[55]

The Nixon "shocks" of mid-1971 confirmed the "need to adjust our
relationship . . . in a way that serves the interests of both of our
countries." [56]

The basis of Nixon policy was the accommodation of national
interest: a recognition by each major state of the need to formulate
its foreign policy goals and practices based on respect for those of
other countries. This theme appeared in the 1970 report: "Any nation today must define its interest with special concern for the interests of others." And the "others" to be included were not only principal allies in Europe and Asia but *all* the major states. It was power
far more than attitude that determined the priority of Washington's
foreign attention. Thus, a major aim of Nixon policy was the reaching of some overall understanding with past adversaries, Peking and
especially Moscow. The China initiative was more dramatic because
of its background of total Chinese-American hostility and because it
was an effort to recognize Peking's legitimate voice after two decades
of enforced silence.

It is in America's interest, and the world's interest, that the People's Republic of China play its appropriate role in shaping international arrangements that affect its concern.[57]

But Peking's role was not yet that of one of "the nuclear superpowers
on whose decisions the survival of mankind may well depend." [58]
Only through Soviet-American collaboration could "the issue of war
and peace . . . be solved." [59]

Hence the most important effort of the administration was the
fundamental altering of relations between Washington and Moscow.
In the words of the 1972 report:

It has been the purpose of this Administration to transform the
U.S.–Soviet relationship so that a mutual search for a stable
peace and security becomes its dominant feature and its driving

force. If the ultimate prospect for stable world peace requires accommodation between China and the United States, both the immediate and the long-term hopes for world stability rest on a more decent and mutually beneficial relationship between ourselves and the Soviet Union.[60]

This process rested upon mutual agreement "that the general improvement in our relationship transcends in importance the kind of narrow advantages which can be sought only by imperiling the cooperation between our two countries." [61]

As for the rest of the world, it was treated to a series of "do-it-yourself" formulas designed to encourage the growth of regional ties and forces within a series of frameworks promoting stability and order. Where one or more major states was or became involved, it too was expected to act as a stabilizing influence, channeling national aspirations away from possible violence and toward peaceful change to mutual advantage. To cite but one of many similarly phrased passages making this point:

> We believe that the stability of the Middle East requires establishing a balance in the activities of the various outside powers involved there. Each must be free to pursue its own legitimate interests, but within the limits imposed by respect for the legitimate interests of others and the sovereignty of the nations of the area.[62]

Upon these regional arrangements was to be erected the global "structure of peace" which the administration has been designing, "building," and "emerging" in its three reports. That structure was to be based not only on mutual recognition of "the right of each state to be secure within its own borders and to be free from intimidation." It was also based upon a pooling of efforts for the betterment of all. Laying out his ultimate objective, President Nixon declared:

> Essentially, peace is rooted in a sense of community, in a recognition of the common destiny of mankind, in a respect for the common dignity of mankind and in the patterns of cooperation that make common enterprises possible.[63]

The Role of Commitments

Perhaps the greatest change of the Nixon policy from that of Dulles (and from that of Secretary of State Dean Rusk in the 1960s) was the reduction in importance of formal commitments—especially mutual defense treaties—which, in effect, required the United States not only to preserve the physical existence of scores of foreign countries but also to adhere to the decisions of the governments of those countries. Alliance with, and military equipment provided by, Washington had given these governments far greater capacity than before to pursue their own foreign policy objectives with regard to neighboring states. When the policies adopted interfered with U.S. aims in a given area, Washington found that its aid had, if anything, reduced the influence it could exert on recipient governments. On the contrary, American assistance became a vehicle by which foreign regimes gained American support or acquiescence for plans and actions distasteful to the United States. The tail wagged the dog. All too often, the undertakings fostered by Dulles and continued by Rusk became the ties that bound Washington against its will to the destinies of others.

To break out of this self-inflicted servitude, the Nixon administration sought to deemphasize the role of formal obligations and to emphasize instead the limited nature of American involvement.

> This is the message of . . . the "Nixon Doctrine." Its central thesis is that the United States will participate in the defense and development of allies and friends, but that America cannot —and will not . . . undertake *all* the defense of the free nations of the world. We will help where it makes a real difference and is considered in our interest.[64]

The focus was on flexibility. The administration would treat each case on its merits, deciding what action to take, how much, and when, based on its careful calculations of the relative consequences of action or inaction upon the interests and objectives of the United States. Where the conclusions of this analysis pointed to a policy in keeping with that of Washington's ally, then previous commitments would take on real meaning and the direction of American policy would be like what had gone before. But if this process suggested a different course of action, Washington would not be barred from taking it by the orthodoxy of the past and obligations designed to meet situations which had long since changed. The choice of options, then, would be Nixon's and no others. As the first "State of the World" message made clear:

> It is misleading . . . to pose the fundamental question so largely in terms of commitments. . . . We are not involved in the world because we have commitments; we have commitments because we are involved. Our interests must shape our commitments, rather than the other way around.[65]

This attitude of skepticism regarding the value of formal ties per se did not mean that the administration was determined not to enter into any new obligations. The lesson it drew from the decade-long military involvement in Indochina was indeed "no more Vietnams" in the sense of the massive commitment of American troops. Nixon and his advisers also took away the conviction that further undertakings should be made cautiously and selectively. Above all, once made, the commitments should not be open-ended or allowed to become so. American interests were bound to be limited, and new agreements and pledges should reflect those limitations. As the initial report also emphasized:

> We will view new commitments in the light of a careful assessment of our own national interests and those of other countries, of the specific threats to those interests, and of our capacity to counter those threats at an acceptable risk and cost.[66]

Perhaps the best example of President Nixon's determination not to be hamstrung by previous policy and past obligations was his policy toward Taiwan. The 1972 foreign policy report stressed that the President's trip to Peking would not affect "our friendship, our diplomatic ties, and our defense commitment" with Taiwan.[67] Discussing the final Nixon-Chou communiqué, Kissinger reaffirmed this position. "Nothing has changed . . ."[68] The 1954 mutual defense treaty, like the other commitments which the United States has made since 1945, does not *formally* require any specific action by the United States. Article V declares that in the event of "armed attack" (interpreted by the Senate as "external armed attack"), each party "would act to meet the common danger in accordance with its constitutional processes"—powers delegated wholly to the President by the 1955 congressional joint resolution.[69] The presumption of both the treaty and the resolution is that American forces would be used, but their use is authorized (by the resolution), not required, and the texts do not commit the United States to other actions in support of Taiwan.

The importance of these undertakings for the Nixon administration was that they did not commit the United States to the support of Taiwan's position in the international community or even to the independent existence of the Republic of China. During the latter 1950s and 1960s, the treaty became a symbol of Washington's promotion of the Taipei regime as *the* legitimate government of China, its provision of massive military and economic aid, and its pledge of an unchanging China policy. (The treaty and resolution had other immediate objects in 1954–55: underscoring Washington's strong but ambiguous commitment in the Offshore Islands crisis, "leashing" Chiang's forces by the stipulation for joint action lest Taipei involve Washington in a war with Peking.[70])

The treaty no longer carried this additional baggage. The United States *did* fight hard to keep Taiwan in the United Nations in October 1971, but as the effective government of a small state. In the UN debate, U.S. Ambassador George Bush characterized Taiwan as "a Government representing over 14 million people, served here by decent men, with no Charter violations" in contrast to "the representatives of the People's Republic of China with its enormous territory and population." [71] Furthermore, he specifically disclaimed any attempt to preserve Taiwan's sovereignty. The American-sponsored resolution "is simply founded on the reality of the present situation, but it does not seek to freeze this situation for the future." [72] In the Nixon-Chou communiqué in February 1972, the United States pledged to "progressively reduce its forces and military installations on Taiwan as the tension in the area diminishes." [73]

In the communiqué and the 1972 foreign policy report, Washington indicated its disinterest in the form of a settlement between Peking and Taipei—even if it meant Taiwan's incorporation into Communist China. "The ultimate relationship between Taiwan and the mainland is not a matter for the United States to decide. We are not . . . urging either party to follow any particular course." [74] Even the peaceful nature of a settlement, obviously critical to the treaty commitment with Taiwan, was urged in relatively mild and passive tones. "A peaceful resolution of this problem by the parties would do much to reduce tension in the Far East." [75] "[The United States] reaffirms its interest in a peaceful settlement of the Taiwan question by the Chinese themselves." [76] In part, these statements were a recognition by Washington that any resolution of the Taiwan question was likely to prove difficult and that its status might remain uncertain for some time, heightening tensions and hindering the development of regularized U.S.–Peking relations. But they also indicated that Washington was likely to take a restrictive view of what its commitment to the Republic of China entailed.

Results of the Nixon Policy

The most spectacular events of the Nixon first term were clearly the establishment of high-level contacts with the People's Republic of China and the negotiation of a series of accords with the Soviet Union. This was, equally importantly, also the President's assessment of his foreign policy performance.

> And when the history of this period is written, I believe it will be recorded that our most significant contributions to peace resulted from our trips to Peking and Moscow. The dialogue that we have begun with the People's Republic of China has reduced the danger of war and has increased the chance for peaceful cooperation between two great peoples.
>
> And, within the space of four years in our relations with the Soviet Union, we have moved from confrontation to negotiation and then to cooperation in the interest of peace.[77]

The emphasis on Peking and Moscow was wholly in accord with the basic conception of world politics contained in the Nixon reports cited above. Communist China and the Soviet Union received highest priority in these years as the most important potential partners of the United States in constructing and implementing a global system of international politics in which the strongest states would band together to advance and protect the "legitimate national interests" of all nations.[78] That Washington's attentions led to major overt results suggested that the aims of China and Russia were also served. That those results occurred during the year in which the Nixon administration made its bid for reelection was not only a tribute to the artful orchestration of initiatives by the administration. It was also an indication that the Soviet and Chinese leaders regarded the gains achieved as sufficiently valuable to overshadow any attempt to influence the American political process.

Indeed, it is possible to argue that both governments saw an advantage in furthering Nixon's electoral prospects. The Republican party had never publicly accepted Franklin Roosevelt's acquiescence to Soviet designs in Eastern Europe or Truman's "loss" of China. The Eisenhower administration (with which Nixon continued to be identified by inheritance) had come into office pledged to "liberate" these areas and "roll back" the iron and bamboo curtains. Nixon's own earlier career had established his unimpeachable anti-Communist credentials, from the Alger Hiss case which first won him national attention to his 1959 debates with Soviet leaders and his 1960 affirmation of the American commitment (however ambiguous) to Nationalist Chinese control of the Offshore Islands. Precisely because the rapprochements with Peking and Moscow were Republican achievements, the result of Republican initiatives, the Soviet and Chinese leaders had "reconciled the irreconcilables." By his trips to the two principal Communist capitals—the first American President to visit either one, Nixon formally linked the Republican party with the Soviet and Chinese conceptions of themselves as the legitimate governments of major states, rightfully extending their influence into immediate areas and throughout the world. The old partisan division over policy toward the two countries was thus erased, and neither Peking nor Moscow needed to fear that a future Republican victory would automatically entail a policy of complete and unremitting hostility to their basic objectives.

THE TRIP TO PEKING On February 21, 1972, the President of the United States alighted from his plane and shook hands with the Premier of the People's Republic of China. It was a handshake seen around the world, momentous in its implications, for it epitomized the symbolic coming together of two long-time enemies.[79] As the Chinese premier, Chou En-lai, was quick to note, a previous American secretary of state, John Foster Dulles, had refused any form of greeting when both had attended the 1954 Geneva conference charged with bringing peace to Indochina in the aftermath of French defeats there. For over two decades, China had been Washington's great adversary in Asia, the threat against which the American alliance system had been constructed and nuclear-armed American forces deployed. The verbal clashes in which the two countries had engaged intensified the bitterness of mutual antagonism and lent to their hostility an evangelical air, as if each government were the incarnation of everything the other hated and feared.

In the changed atmosphere of the 1970s, this paraded enmity was gradually eroded, to be replaced by a reciprocal movement toward reassessment. Nixon had made the reexamination of China policy an initial aim of his administration, supplementing the beginning steps taken by Kennedy and Johnson which had been overshadowed by the Vietnam war and the turmoil resulting from China's Cultural Revolution. Now American troops were being withdrawn from the war, and the new President pledged a much altered and reduced American role in Asia. Now, too, the Cultural Revolution had spent its force, giving way to a period of relative moderation at home and renewed interest in state-to-state relations abroad. For both Washington and Peking, the removal of these sources of hostility and the adoption of new positions in foreign policy generally were prerequisites to bilateral progress. After these changes in the first year of the Nixon term, each side indicated its willingness to explore some form of direct contacts. In July 1970

Nixon indicated his belief, in response to a question, that regular diplomatic relations with Peking were in the U.S. interest. In April 1971 an American table-tennis team became the first Americans since 1950 to visit China with Washington's consent. Given extensive press coverage and received by Chinese leaders, this team was seen as the harbinger of a wide range of Sino-American exchanges permitted by the elimination of barriers on both sides. Then in mid-July came the announcement that, as a result of secret meetings in Peking between presidential adviser Kissinger and Chou En-lai, President Nixon would soon make a "journey for peace" to China to "seek the normalization of relations between the two countries and to exchange views on questions of concern to both sides." [80]

Despite these hopeful words, the Peking trip was marked more by correctness than cordiality. Unlike other major visitors to China, Nixon was not greeted by vast, cheering crowds. There were no placards proclaiming Sino-American solidarity in the quest for peace. The reception was official, not popular, resplendent with the trappings of formal visits between heads of state but lacking any significant opportunity for contact with the Chinese populace at large. Indeed, with few exceptions (and those mainly for the benefit of disgruntled newsmen), the Nixon trip was taken up with protracted and wholly secret high-level discussions. The purpose of these talks (including a lengthy meeting between Nixon and Mao) was not principally to negotiate specific differences but to identify areas of common interest, explain divergent positions, and establish personal rapport. These aims, in turn, highlighted the preparatory nature of the Nixon visit as the prelude to more extensive contacts. The joint communiqué issued at the end of the President's tour proclaimed the commitment of both parties to increased exchanges, reduction of military conflict, and opposition to East Asian hegemony by any state or coalition. But beyond these generalized professions of goodwill, the statement dealt at length with Chinese-American differences on virtually every major world issue. The Peking summit, spectacular and precedent-breaking as it was, marked the beginning of reconciliation between the two countries, not the final phase of a new era in their relations.[81]

Beyond the erosion of Republican opposition to the Peking government's existence, the Chinese leaders achieved other gains from the Nixon trip—in undermining the rival Taiwan regime of Chiang Kai-shek, in raising doubts about the policies toward Peking pursued by Japan and other Asian countries, and in demonstrating to Moscow that China was not isolated and open to Soviet military pressure. These gains for the Chinese had come from the *fact* of high-level contact with the United States. By contrast, most of Washington's aims of a new mutuality of interests in East Asia would have to come from the future *substance* of Sino-American contacts. Despite the beginnings of significant Sino-American trade in grain and high-technology equipment, the year that followed the Peking summit was devoted to the establishment of sustained diplomatic contacts rather than to the achievement of political agreements. "Normalization" between Peking and Washington increasingly became an exercise in the approximation of governments lacking formal mutual recognition and possessing sharply contrasting world views. How real the gains for American foreign policy would be from these expanded liaisons remained very much an open question.[82]

The potential difficulties for the United States implicit in the attempt to reverse twenty years of opposition to and obstruction of the Chinese Communists were indicated by developments in Japan. The election in early July 1972 of Kakuei Tanaka as leader of the ruling Liberal-Democratic party and consequently as prime minister of Japan was nothing less than a revolution in Japanese politics and had before the year was out produced the beginnings of a no less fundamental change in Japanese foreign policy. In winning his victory, Tanaka successfully opposed the university-business-government elite of the party which (in various incarnations) had exercised exclusive control of Japan's destiny since the end of American military occupation following World War II.[83] That elite had tied Japan's foreign policy inseparably to the United States, both as the principal source of its renewed economic prosperity and as its sole protector against the possibly aggressive intentions of its militarily superior Soviet and Chinese neighbors. So great was this reliance on and identification with U.S. policy that in the late 1960s Japan found itself to be the only major Asian country supporting American involvement in Indochina, a steadfastness rewarded by the return of Japanese rule over Okinawa in May 1972, after the bulk of American forces which that base served had been withdrawn.[84] Indeed, Japan was the only major country in the United Nations to follow the American lead of keeping Taiwan a separate member of the organization after Peking had acceded to China's place.[85] The defeat of this proposal was thus a humiliation not only for the United States but for the Japanese government as well. Coming on top of the twin "Nixon shocks" of midsummer (announcement of the trip to Peking and of U.S. import surcharges), this blow revealed to Tokyo the penalties of its reliance on Washington and the position of isolation in Asia to which this dependence had led.

Tanaka came to power committed to enhance Japan's standing in Asia, promising especially to "set about the task of normalizing relations with China." [86] The September 1972 visit to Peking of Tanaka and other Japanese leaders to fulfill this pledge bore a more than superficial resemblance to the Nixon journey of seven months before. But the outcome produced a far greater change in policy. Publicly expressing regret for past aggressions, Tanaka established diplomatic ties with the Communist Chinese regime and severed relations (and a prior peace treaty) with the Nationalists.[87] Japan thus went significantly beyond Washington's lead in reversing its China policy and setting the stage for further changes as Japan sought to redefine its role in East Asia and its relationships with its two powerful neighbors as well as with the United States.

These changes in foreign policy contributed to the outcome of the December 1972 parliamentary elections in Japan. Premier Tanaka appealed for continued support for the Liberal-Democratic party, stressing his commitment to a good life for the Japanese people and emphasizing his intention of increasing Tokyo's independence from Washington in foreign policy, although promising to retain the alliance with the United States upon which Japanese defense policy was based. The elections returned Tanaka to power, but with a slightly reduced majority and without the clear-cut mandate for his policies he had desired. Within his own party, the electoral results favored the more conservative forces which he had defeated in his July bid for the leadership. Among these voters at least, his new policies were less popular than ones based on closer Japanese-American relations.

Indeed, the shifts at home and abroad seemed to favor other parties at Tanaka's expense. The Socialist party regained most of its earlier losses while the Japanese Communist party more than tripled its previous seats in its greatest triumph in postwar Japanese history. The importance of these results should not be exaggerated. The Liberal-Democrats continued to enjoy a comfortable majority in the Diet, and Communist candidates gained only 10 percent of the total votes cast. As always, domestic factors played their part. Nonetheless, the election suggested that Tanaka's efforts to alter Japan's foreign policies were likely to have internal consequences as well. And, given the predominance of the Liberal-Democrats, those consequences would likely be at the expense of that party and of its long-standing commitment to cooperation with the United States.[88]

Another major development in the Far East after the Nixon trip was the beginning of relations between the two Korean regimes. The South Korean government was initially an American creation, as that of North Korea was a result of Soviet occupation at the end of World War II. The United States rescued and reinstated its protégé during the Korean war and continued for twenty years thereafter to maintain not only its firm commitment to the defense of Korea but also two American divisions as a symbol of that commitment. Like Japan, South Korea supported American policy in Vietnam, dispatching a force there whose size was curiously coincidental to that of the U.S. military presence in Korea. Seoul thus became the largest Asian contributor to the war in Indochina. Perhaps in consequence, the North Korean government emerged as the staunchest Asian supporter of Hanoi, chastizing both Moscow and Peking for their limited aid. This sign of continued enmity between North and South was affirmed by continuous skirmishes along the 1953 armistice line and by Northern attempts to assassinate the Southern leaders.[89]

Given this record of unremitting opposition, the announcement in July 1972 that secret talks had begun and would continue to take

place designed to reunite the divided country, came as a major surprise to foreign governments, not least the United States.[90] Establishing a hot line linking the two capitals to ease communications and
resolve disputes, the two sides agreed that they would not let "external imposition or interference" stand in the way of peaceful reunification "transcending differences in ideas, ideologies, and systems." [91] Nonetheless, Seoul sought to enhance its bargaining
position in its talks with the North by assuring the continued presence of American troops in the South through mid-1974, despite reports of Washington's desire to withdraw them. The administration
agreed to retain the 40,000-man force in exchange for Seoul's pledge
to withdraw its similarly sized contingent from South Vietnam only
as part of the removal of foreign troops provided by the January
1973 cease-fire.[92] Rather than a means of physical protection, the
U.S. force in South Korea had become a pawn which Seoul hoped to
trade for concessions from Pyongyang.

Equally dramatic changes occurred in Australia and New Zealand as the result of parliamentary elections in both countries in No-
vember and December 1972. Tied by heritage and trade to their
British motherland, these two nations had turned to the United
States for protection in the war against Japan, an alliance cemented
by the ANZUS treaty of 1951 during the Korean war and by the
SEATO pact of 1954. For two decades thereafter, their policies toward Asia had been inexorably entwined with that of the United
States. They had strongly opposed any dealings with Communist
China, and their military support of American efforts in the Viet-
nam war was second only to that of South Korea and Thailand
among Asian nations.[93]

These two governments, strongly committed to the United
States, were both removed from office within a week of one another.
In each case, the Labour party, which had been in opposition for
most of the postwar period, came to power with a large majority and
claiming a mandate for massive change. While substantial redirections of domestic policies by Labour seemed nearly certain after such
a long period out of power, the immediate effects of these elections
occurred in foreign policy. No sooner had the new regimes taken

control than conscription was ended, draft resisters amnestied, arrangements made to withdraw remaining forces from Vietnam, and steps taken to recognize Peking instead of Taipei. By the end of December 1972, all these actions had been completed. Moreover, each new government threatened to renounce its defense ties with the United States by questioning the value of SEATO and announcing its intention to reexamine ANZUS in favor of nonmilitary cooperation with Washington. In following months, both governments adopted more restrained positions on these military ties, pledging adherence to current commitments while resisting further entanglements. Despite the modifications of their initial positions, the Australian and New Zealand regimes seemed intent upon ending their countries' reliance on powerful but distant supporters, instead finding their own paths through a rapidly changing Asian environment.[94]

These developments, in and of themselves, were not inimical to the policies pursued by the United States under the Nixon administration. Washington could hardly object to the aim of "normalization" in Northeast Asia expressed by Japan's recognition of Peking or the movement toward Korean unity. Similarly, the actions of the new governments in Australia and New Zealand were not unexpected given the parties' campaigns and followed American actions in withdrawing its forces from Vietnam, curtailing the draft, and enlarging contacts with Communist China. Nonetheless, the initiatives toward Peking did exceed the limits of American policy and took place at the expense of the Nationalist regime in Taiwan to whose support Washington remained committed despite the Peking summit. That these intitiatives could mean the end of trade with Taiwan (large in the case of Japan) and would further intensify the pariah status assigned to the Taipei government by much of the world community—these were consequences that Washington could only regard as regrettable.[95]

Beyond these questions of specific policy, the actions of the Asian governments amounted to a declaration of foreign policy independence from the United States. As if in response to the surprise July 1971 announcement of the President's China journey, none of the governments consulted Washington in advance of its unilateral initiative.[96] Instead, the Nixon administration was reminded that other regimes could also present seemingly abrupt policy changes as faits accomplis without notice. Faced with these decisions, Washington had no choice but to accept them with good grace, proclaiming in the communiqué at the end of the Tanaka-Nixon talks in late August 1972 that the Japanese and Korean actions "serve to further the trend for the relaxation of tension in Asia." [97] Unofficial reports indicated a less formal understanding between the two leaders by which Japan would go its separate way in China policy and, ultimately, on other issues as well.[98] As Tanaka remarked at his meeting with Nixon, it was "the beginning of a new era" in Japanese-American relations, reflecting "an increasingly multipolarized world where Japan has come to assume greater responsibilities in the international community commensurate with her increased national strength." [99] As the new era and Japan's power continued to grow, the prospect of greater divergence between Tokyo and Washington over questions of equal importance seemed likely to increase as well.

THE MOSCOW SUMMIT   If the gains which Washington expected from the journey to China lay in the ill-seen future, the accomplishments of President Nixon's visit to Moscow in May 1972 were multiple and concrete. Agreements for Soviet-American cooperation ranged from cancer research to environmental preservation to joint space projects. New rules were laid down to govern Soviet and American surveillance of each other's naval activities, so that the harassment and near-collisions of earlier maneuvers would be curtailed. Negotiations to expand Soviet-American trade were intensified. But by far the most important accords resulted from the strategic arms limitation talks (SALT) which the two countries had conducted since late 1969 in utmost secrecy.[100]

The first of these SALT pacts was a treaty between Washington and Moscow, restricting the numbers and types of antiballistic missiles (ABMs) that could be developed and deployed by each side. These weapons were designed to seek out and destroy (or nullify by radiation) the incoming thermonuclear warheads of missiles fired

from land or sea thousands of miles away. They thus seemed to provide, for the first time, some effective means of protection from a surprise nuclear attack. Based apparently on this reasoning, the Soviet
Union had begun to station a series of ABMs around Moscow in
1964, increasing the size of this force in 1967 and thereafter. Some
authorities argued that a 1966 Soviet deployment around Leningrad, intended primarily for defense against incoming bombers,
might also be effective against missiles.[101] Meanwhile, the United
States engaged in a public debate on the effectiveness and utility of
its own newly developed version of the antimissile missile. After
much soul-searching, Defense Secretary Robert McNamara announced in September 1967 Washington's approval of a system providing broad protection of the United States against attack by a
small but growing force of Chinese nuclear-tipped rockets predicted
for the mid-1970s, arguing that the American ABM would be unable
to blunt a much larger and more advanced Soviet attack.[102] Upon
taking office, the Nixon administration disagreed with this assessment of the ABM's limited value. While the program was kept relatively small, its emphasis was reversed to stress defense of land-based
missiles against a possible Soviet effort to destroy them and thus reduce Washington's ability to strike back. Since this revised plan
could easily be expanded to encompass larger portions of the American land retaliatory forces, the controversy over ABM escalated, further stimulated by partisan opposition. As a result, the Senate narrowly approved the new ABM in mid-1969, largely on the basis of
Nixon's assurance that this system was an important "bargaining
chip" in the SALT negotiations with Moscow scheduled to begin the
following November.[103]

Thus in the late 1960s both countries found themselves with
ABM systems of different types and deployments, designed for different threats. Moscow's off-and-on increases in its system around
Moscow indicated uncertainty as to the value of the undertaking,
particularly since it contrasted with the rapid and steady growth of
Soviet offensive missile capacity in this period.[104] Widespread debates and the administration's paper-thin victory in the Senate
(where Vice-President Spiro Agnew cast the tie-breaking vote for a

total of 51–50 to continue ABM) affirmed even greater skepticism in
the United States. This mutual discomfort with ABM provided the
basis for proposals to limit or abolish it, although differences continued on the size, location, and capability of whatever ABM forces
were to be retained.[105]

The agreement reached provided that each country could deploy two small ABMs, one around the national capital (as the Soviets had done at Moscow) and the other at a substantial distance from
the national capital (as the Americans had done at the completed
missile-defense site in North Dakota). Neither of these locations was
to have more than one hundred ABMs and limited radars, meaning
that the sites in both countries would probably be of little value in
stopping an attack by the other (since it would be massive and sophisticated) but that they might still be able to protect against an accidental firing or an attack by a country possessing only a small missile force (such as China). In purpose if not in form, the strategic
defensive systems of the two superpowers had reverted to the McNamara formulation of 1967. Each side had ensured that the weapons
deployed would not be a threat to itself and had thereby renounced
their use against the other. This was as close to bilateral disarmament by major states as the post-1945 world had come. As President
Nixon declared to Congress upon his return from Moscow: "We took
the first step toward a new era of mutually agreed restraint and arms
limitation between the two principal nuclear powers." [106]

The ABM treaty had other provisions as well. Each country
promised that it would not subvert the spirit of the agreement by developing new and better ABMs, which might be employed against
the other signatory. Each pledged not to interfere with the other's
"national technical means of verification," by which Soviet and
American space satellites would satisfy their masters that the treaty
was indeed being kept. Each agreed not to provide ABMs to other
countries or to deploy them "outside its national territory," as the
United States had once contemplated through a sea-based system.
Finally, each agreed that the treaty should be maintained for the indefinite future, ensuring that the ABM would not again become a
factor in the arms race and a source of mutual concern. Either

country could renounce the treaty, however, withdrawing from it six months thereafter, if it was convinced that "extraordinary events" had "jeopardized its supreme interests." [107] Thus while the treaty was designed to eliminate ABM from strategic calculations, it was not an irrevocable commitment by either side. The pact dealt solely with matters central to the "supreme interests" of both signatories, and any major change in the global nuclear balance (such as the rise of a third large-scale nuclear force in China or Western Europe) would call into question the ABM accord and indeed the whole concept of bilateral Soviet-American agreements limiting nuclear arms. With these precautionary clauses in mind, the Senate overwhelmingly approved the treaty in early August 1972 (by a vote of 88–2), and President Nixon formally signed it in White House ceremonies in early October.[108]

The delay between Senate passage and the final ratification procedure was the result of a drawn-out Senate fight over the other strategic arms product of the Moscow meetings. This was an "interim agreement" between the United States and the Soviet Union not to increase the size of their major nuclear forces during the five-year period from July 1972 through July 1977 while further SALT negotiations took place to establish a more permanent limitation on the two sides' strategic arsenals. The agreement was thus the first step in an attempt to restrict the *offensive* nuclear forces of the superpowers, just as the ABM treaty had curbed their strategic *defensive* forces. In this short-term pact, however, unlike the ABM treaty, there was no attempt to curtail technological advances in the forces affected (such as multiple guided warheads or MIRVs) or to limit specifically the explosive power of the weapons (although an undefined distinction between "heavy" and "light" missiles was made).[109]

The controversy which this agreement stirred in Congress centered around what was referred to as the "Jackson amendment," after Senator Henry M. Jackson of Washington, a former Democratic presidential aspirant. The Jackson amendment took exception to the number of offensive missiles allocated to each side by the protocol to the interim pact and, potentially, by a future treaty as well.

These numbers, in turn, reflected the different postures of the two sides during the SALT bargaining. The United States figures reflected the force levels which had been reached in 1967: 1,054 land-based missiles (ICBMs) and 656 submarine-based missiles (SLBMs). These forces were the result of a substantial buildup of American missile strength in the early 1960s, as well as continual qualitative changes in the missiles. While the numbers were the same as in 1967, the capability of the missiles to destroy more targets, more accurately, had increased greatly.[110]

The Soviet Union, on the other hand, was in the midst of a massive expansion of its force levels for land- and sea-based missiles as the 1970s began, a buildup that had commenced in the mid-1960s. As a result, when the SALT accords were being hammered out, Moscow held a quantitative lead in land forces (having 1,618 missiles) and claimed an advantage in sea-based forces (48 submarines with 740 missiles).[111] This latter claim was particularly disputed by Senator Jackson, who asserted that Moscow had, at best, 42 submarines completed and should thus be held to the same level as that of the United States.[112] The discrepancy in part reflected the difficulty of determining the status of submarines "under construction," which the Russians insisted should be counted with their forces. Rather than reveal its own intelligence data or jeopardize the chances for reaching agreement, Washington acceded to this figure.[113]

Even greater potential differences in the size of offensive forces grew out of another clause in the interim pact by which both Washington and Moscow could replace "old" missiles built before 1964 with more advanced sea-based weapons of roughly similar magnitude. The United States had previously phased out most of its older systems as obsolete, retaining only 54 *Titan II* weapons because of their relatively large warheads. Moscow, by contrast, had over 200 of its earlier missiles still on hand, as added protection during its recent expansion. This meant that while the United States could bring its submarine force level to no more than 710 missiles during the five-year moratorium, the Soviet Union was allowed an increase to 950 missiles.[114] Since much of current strategic argument maintained that land-based forces were becoming ever more vulnerable to surprise attack (because of their fixed location, improved accuracy, and multiple warheads), the greater invulnerability of sea-based forces (because of the difficulties of detection) made them appear more valuable to possess.[115] Thus, not only could the Soviets legitimately augment their missile capacity to a wide numerical margin over the American levels, but Moscow would also be able to concentrate this growth in the forces considered most important for future military power.

Jackson regarded this prospect as intolerable and led a Senate group seeking not to reject the accord but to qualify it through reservations. The first of these warned that failure to negotiate a formal treaty limiting strategic arms within the five years provided by the interim agreement "could jeopardize the supreme national interests of the United States"—language so close to the wording of the ABM treaty that the clear intention was to press for U.S. withdrawal from that pact if Moscow reneged in the SALT-II talks begun in fall 1972 at Geneva.[116] The other reservation affected the substance of the future agreement:

> [T]he Congress recognizes the principle of United States-Soviet Union equality reflected in the anti-ballistic missile treaty, and urges and requests the President to seek a future treaty that, *inter alia,* would not limit the United States to levels of intercontinental strategic forces inferior to the limits provided for the Soviet Union.[117]

So stated, the amendment won the support of the Nixon administration and large numbers of Republican senators, after having been rejected by the Foreign Relations Committee. After a protracted fight on the Senate floor between groups led by Jackson and Senator Fulbright, the interim agreement with the Jackson provisos attached was passed by a lopsided majority (87–2) in mid-September 1972.[118] The agreement (unlike the ABM treaty) was submitted to both houses of Congress, and the House approved it equally overwhelmingly (329–7) in mid-August, avoiding a Jackson-type addition and possible delays.[119] The Jackson reservations were retained in the final joint resolution worked out by the two houses in late September and signed by President Nixon. More than one-third of the Senate had cosponsored these reservations, and this was more than the number needed to defeat a new arms limitation treaty requiring Senate ratification. The Senate, in a move backed by the White House, had gone on record warning the Soviet Union that the final agreement reached would have to be more favorable to the United States than the interim accord signed at Moscow had been. That done, the interim agreement was formally put into force with the ABM treaty in the October 1972 ceremonies.[120]

Despite the number and scope of these bilateral undertakings and the similarity of views contained in the May 1972 statement of basic principles and joint communiqué,[121] the Nixon experience with the Soviet Union was not uniformly successful. Sharp differences remained on Vietnam, and Moscow refused either to curtail its aid to Hanoi (which had enabled the North Vietnamese to launch their March 1972 offensive) or to pressure it to reach agreement with Washington. Soviet President Nicolai Podgorny had gone to Hanoi in the wake of the Moscow summit, but the trip seemed intended rather to reassure the North Vietnamese of continued Russian support than to insist upon messages conveyed from the American President.[122] While Moscow did not directly challenge the American mining of North Vietnamese ports in May 1972, it did reroute its supplies to Hanoi through China and Laos.[123]

The buildup of Soviet naval strength in the Mediterranean and the Indian Ocean was also a major source of concern to the Nixon administration. Soviet military aid undermined American efforts at arms stability in the Middle East. Although Soviet advisers were withdrawn from Egypt in August 1972, the Soviet mutual-defense pact with Cairo of May 1971 remained in force, and Moscow established a further military presence in Syria.[124] In South Asia, Soviet and American policies and objectives were also at odds. Having bound India to a "friendship" treaty in August 1971, Moscow proceeded to give New Delhi unstinting support in her war with Pakistan over Bengal in December 1971.[125] Washington, on the contrary, denounced India as an aggressor and led a successful fight in the UN General Assembly against her.[126] India readily defeated Pakistan, and Soviet prestige on the subcontinent grew while that of the United States diminished. Despite later efforts to moderate this outcome, the basic Soviet-American clash persisted.

In Europe, the policies of the two superpowers seemed more likely to coincide. Both governments favored talks (begun in Helsinki in late 1972) to improve communications between the divided halves of Europe and to bring about a generalized reduction of tensions on the continent. Agreement on these aims had been incorporated into the Moscow communiqué.[127] With such developments, Moscow wished to gain formal recognition of the border revisions and of its predominance in the East stemming from World War II. Washington, on the other hand, hoped that greater Western contact and self-assurance would enable the East European countries to exercise greater independence of the Soviet Union and move gradually away from its tutelage, as Rumania had already done.

But the proposals for mutual and balanced force reductions (MBFR) in Central Europe revealed greater basic differences. There was no consensus that talks on this question should be merged with the European Security Conference at Helsinki. Washington insisted that the preliminary discussions be bilateral between representatives of the two opposing alliances, NATO and the Warsaw Pact—a view upheld by the other active members of the North Atlantic pact. Moscow and its allies rejected this approach, favoring a generalized forum open to all members and neutrals as well. The Western powers stressed the importance of prior ratification of the September 1971 treaty governing access to Berlin, long a cold war trouble-spot. The East ignored it, pointing instead to the 1970 German nonaggression accords with Poland and the Soviet Union. Moscow denounced NATO plans to supplement its forces in the 1970s, claiming this action to be incompatible with a serious intent to achieve European arms reductions. NATO rejected these charges and reproached the Soviets for their own military additions.[128] The lack of concrete progress indicated by such divergences emphasized the depth of division between the two sides, despite the opening of formal talks in early 1973.

The Moscow summit, therefore, achieved important but limited results. It increased and underscored the extent of Soviet-American agreement on issues of mutual interest. Negotiations with the Russians on important questions could lead to mutually satisfactory conclusions. A start was made toward regulation of the principal military forces of both countries, agreements which, more than any other, affected the basic national security of each and demonstrated a degree of confidence and mutual respect (if not yet trust) unprecedented in twenty-five years of Soviet-American antagonism. As Nixon had declared in his address to Congress, confrontation had given way to negotiation. It had yet to be demonstrated that negotiation would provide the way to cooperation. As the 1972 "State of the World" report cautioned:

> Our series of conversations in Moscow cannot be expected to end two decades' accumulation of problems. For a long period of time, competition is likely to be the hallmark of our relationship with the Soviet Union. We will be confronted by ambiguous and contradictory trends in Soviet policy. The continuing buildup of Soviet military power is one obvious source of deep concern. Soviet attitudes during the crisis in South Asia have dangerous implications for other regional conflicts. . . . Similarly, the USSR's position in the Middle East reflects a mixture of Soviet interest in expansionist policies and Soviet recognition of the dangers of confrontation.[129]

Problems of the Nixon Policy

The consequences of the Peking and Moscow summits illustrate the difficulties of the Nixon foreign policy. Attempts to revise relations with one country affect others, producing a chain reaction of redirections whose ultimate forms may be opposed to American desires. Attempts to negotiate bilateral differences omit clashes of policy in other areas and are themselves open to challenge once made. Efforts to reason together do not always produce incentives to reason alike. These difficulties were particularly evident in the Nixon administration's efforts to achieve "peace with honor" in Vietnam and in its attempts to bring about basic agreement on the future course of international politics through a global "structure of peace."

VIETNAM: THE SEARCH FOR A SETTLEMENT   The war in Indochina continued to haunt the first Nixon administration in its closing
days. Despite the withdrawal of nearly all American forces from Vietnam, U.S. participation in the conflict remained high. Peace,
which had seemed near in the fall, was engulfed in a winter mael-
strom of renewed conflict, emerging in the cease-fire accords of late
January and February 1973. Until that time, from the beginning of
large-scale American involvement in 1965, attempts had been made
to bring about a negotiated settlement. For nearly seven years, often
frenetic activity had ended in futility.[130] At the root of this failure
was Washington's determination not to see the Saigon regime collapse during fighting or in its immediate aftermath. However cam-
ouflaged, the fall of its ally was regarded by Washington as spelling
the failure of its years of blood and treasure and was therefore unacceptable. Yet Hanoi seemed equally determined to continue its own
military actions until a government was established around the National Liberation Front (later the Provisional Revolutionary Government) as a prelude to unification with North Vietnam through
Communist leadership.

Despite the enormity of these differences, the Nixon administration had come into office convinced of the necessity of a negotiated
settlement and placing high hopes in the Paris peace talks which had
begun at the end of the Johnson years.[131] As the talks dragged on
without result, the administration turned increasingly to the revival
of the South Vietnamese army under American tutelage and with
massive air and naval support. While the war continued, and American ground forces began to be withdrawn in large numbers, Washington also changed its peace terms and stepped up its efforts at private talks between Dr. Henry Kissinger and Le Duc Tho, a member
of the North Vietnamese Politburo and "adviser" to Hanoi's delegation to the public peace talks. By the beginning of 1972, these two
representatives had met a dozen times, only to find their positions as
far apart as ever. President Nixon's disclosure of the American terms
in January 1972 showed the United States was willing to accept the
continued presence of North Vietnamese forces in the South after a

cease-fire and the withdrawal of all American troops from Vietnam. But it was also an admission that both public and secret talks were hopelessly deadlocked and that the American efforts at negotiation had failed.[132]

The talks had indeed failed. Hanoi denounced the United States for violating the secrecy of the private talks while repudiating the President's call for a cease-fire, insisting that Washington terminate all aid to South Vietnam and replace the regime of President Nguyen Van Thieu with one centered around its own southern ally.[133] The public Paris talks went on in desultory fashion, with the American delegation seeming to follow delaying tactics and harden the mutual vituperation which already existed. In late March, the Nixon administration declared that the talks would be indefinitely suspended since Hanoi was insisting upon "conditions we can never accept." [134] These charges notwithstanding, the North Vietnamese indicated their willingness to resume the talks at any time, an offer Washington summarily rejected.[135]

Then at the end of March 1972, North Vietnam launched a full-scale offensive seemingly designed to capture the former Vietnamese capital of Hue, cut South Vietnam in half, and threaten Saigon. None of these goals was achieved. The South Vietnamese retreated, sometimes broke, but generally contained the Northern assaults, largely as the result of heavy American air support. Hanoi's main offensive penetrated twenty-five miles below the DMZ, capturing a provincial capital (Quang Tri), but failed to take Hue. The effort to bisect the South stalled in the Central Highlands, while the assault on Saigon was halted on the Cambodian border. Meanwhile, the United States mounted an air attack on North Vietnam of unprecedented severity, producing (according to Hanoi) extensive civilian damage.[136]

The North Vietnamese invasion and the strong American response had the seemingly paradoxical effect of reviving hopes in the peace negotiations. Despite the massive bombing of its territory, North Vietnam early indicated its willingness to resume the talks, perhaps hoping that victories on the battlefield would bolster its position at the bargaining table.[137] At the same time, Washington seems to have believed that the American reaction would convince Hanoi of its inability to accomplish its goals militarily and thus make the North Vietnamese more willing to agree to a settlement of the war acceptable to the United States.[138] Undoubtedly also, with most of the Democratic presidential aspirants highly critical of the talks' suspension and renewed bombing, the Nixon administration felt itself under heavy domestic pressure to resume negotiations. Thus the formal talks began again in Paris at the end of April with the secret Kissinger-Tho meetings resuming in early May. But the hopes of the two sides were quickly dashed when the negotiators discovered themselves as far apart as ever, the new fighting having widened rather than reduced the chasm separating their positions. The talks broke down only a week after they had been renewed.[139] The American reaction was now to expand its military efforts against the North through the closing of all North Vietnamese ports (the source of 80 percent of Hanoi's imports, including all its heavy military equipment) while at the same time repeating Washington's offer of a "stand-still" cease-fire in which American forces would be wholly withdrawn from Indochina but North Vietnamese troops would remain in possession of the territory they were occupying as a result of their attacks.[140]

This carrot-stick approach produced results. By the end of June, Washington and Hanoi had agreed to meet again in Paris in mid-July.[141] The public and secret sessions continued thereafter throughout the summer and fall, despite North Vietnamese charges that American bombers were deliberately attacking the vast system of dikes upon which the Northern population depended for food and protection against flooding. Then in early October, according to versions released later by Hanoi and Washington, the North Vietnamese reversed their previous insistence that the Thieu regime be dismantled before any kind of settlement could be reached and agreed to a cease-fire, prisoner exchange, and American troop withdrawal as the first stage of a process whose ultimate political form would be resolved among the groups in the South without further military action. Since these terms were essentially the same as those proposed by President Nixon in May, the way seemed clear for a quick settlement of the war. By the end of October, when Hanoi's disclosure of its new plan forced Washington to respond, Kissinger could declare that "peace is at hand." The October sessions had produced a virtually completed draft, with a few minor changes necessary to make it fully acceptable.[142]

Why had North Vietnam changed the views it had held so strongly over the previous years? No official explanation was offered by either side, but speculation suggested two reasons. First, the war in the South had not gone well for Hanoi. The massive use of American air power (especially the concentrated bombing of the B-52s) had inflicted enormous losses on the North Vietnamese forces and destroyed much of the heavy equipment upon which they had counted to spearhead their attacks. Moreover, the offensive had failed to halt or even slow the American withdrawal of ground forces, which took no active combat role in the fighting. Washington was able to demonstrate that the Northern offensive could be halted without the continual presence of U.S. troops in large numbers and carrying the main burden of the war. Indeed, heavily supported by American (and increasingly, South Vietnamese) bombers, Saigon's forces gradually pushed back the North Vietnamese, regaining the major losses of the spring attacks by the end of September 1972, despite bitter enemy resistance. Thus the Northern offensive had failed, Washington proving able and willing to react with massive force and Saigon demonstrating its ability to carry on the ground war under the American air umbrella.

By late September also, a second factor was probably coming into play in Hanoi's calculations. The Northern leaders, impressed by the role of French politics in bringing about the 1954 settlement ending the first Indochina war, seemed more than once to have attempted to take advantage of the American political process. The largest Northern attacks of the war, the 1968 Tet offensive and the March 1972 assaults, had both taken place in presidential election years, a time when domestic political considerations become of paramount importance both to the incumbent administration and to its potential rivals. Both offensives were launched in the spring, perhaps to influence the choice of presidential nominees in the primary campaigns, as well as because of weather conditions in Vietnam. Whatever their intent, there can be no doubt that the two offensives had important effects on the 1968 and 1972 presidential campaigns, boosting the prospects of such antiwar candidates as Eugene McCarthy (and, later, Robert Kennedy) and George McGovern. Senator McGovern's victory at the July 1972 Democratic convention and his commitment to withdrawal from the war may have encouraged Hanoi to believe that the Nixon administration's opposition to its objectives could be removed at the November elections. As the campaign developed, however, McGovern's prospects of victory became increasingly remote, and by early October, with barely a month to go, it may have seemed to the North Vietnamese that the Nixon terms were the best they were likely to receive. If Hanoi had become convinced of a Nixon victory, then it may have wished to conclude a settlement while the campaign was still underway and the President's opponents still able to attract national attention to their demands for an immediate end to the fighting. In short, Hanoi may have concluded (as the administration had argued before) that it could achieve a better settlement by dealing with Nixon "while the heat was on" than by waiting until after the President had been returned to office.

Whatever Hanoi's motivations in changing its terms, it now placed great pressure on the United States to sign the nearly completed draft agreement by the end of October (and before the presidential elections). This the administration refused to do, asserting that, while the alterations required were minor, further negotiations would be necessary. The North Vietnamese denounced the U.S. for its delaying tactics but nonetheless agreed to continue the Kissinger-Tho talks.[143] At first, it was maintained (at least by the administration) that one more series of meetings would be sufficient to harmonize the English and Vietnamese texts and draft technical addenda to implement the settlement.[144] Additional sessions were held, however, and the talks dragged on through November into mid-December. Various reasons were given for this delay. It became increasingly clear that Washington and Saigon had differing positions on crucial issues, such as the continued presence of North Vietnamese forces in the South, the nature of the demarcation between the two parts of Vietnam, and the extent of participation by the Provisional Revolutionary Government in establishing a new political structure in the South and administering new elections there.[145] At the time, these differences seemed to be the main obstacle, and speculation was raised that the United States had changed its terms (repudiating the draft agreement) to meet Saigon's objections. Washington, however, rejected this explanation, placing the blame on Hanoi for reraising in the new talks issues which, according to the United States, had been resolved earlier. Instead of insisting on a new agreement, Washington portrayed itself as defending the earlier accord against incessant attempts by Hanoi to back away from its terms.[146]

By mid-December 1972, the administration had become convinced that Hanoi was engaged in delaying tactics at the Paris talks the main purpose of which was to conceal its preparations for a new offensive in South Vietnam to expand the area under its control before a cease-fire could take effect. This, in turn, was seen as bolstering the position of its Southern ally in dealing with the Thieu regime on political questions and as making an effective North Vietnamese withdrawal more difficult than before, should Saigon insist upon it as a prelude to a political settlement. Moreover, in Washington's view, Hanoi was out to sabotage the implementation of a cease-fire through its insistence upon a relatively small multinational observer force dependent upon its hosts for supplies and equipment. (The U.S. conception, by contrast, called for a much larger force with its own resources and complete freedom of movement throughout the South.) As a result of its beliefs, the Nixon administration decided in mid-December 1972 to curtail the Kissinger-Tho talks and to increase the military pressure on the North to accept Washington's version of the October agreement.[147] American air attacks over North Vietnam were accordingly intensified, with the first large-scale use of B-52 bombers in the Hanoi-Haiphong area. The United States indicated its willingness to continue the public discussions as well as private technical negotiations but Hanoi refused while the bombing continued. As 1972 ended, peace in Vietnam seemed as distant as it had ever been.

New hope came with the New Year. At first it was a small hope, stunted offspring of the ebullience of October, blighted by the disappointments of December. On the next-to-last day of 1972, the White House announced an end to the massive waves of bombing over the major populated areas of North Vietnam. Until further notice, the air armada would be restricted to the lower portion of the North and to South Vietnam, although this redirected bombing would continue with undiminished force. In exchange for this limitation, "serious negotiations" would resume in Paris in early January, both at the senior level of Kissinger and Tho and among the expert delegations of the two sides.[148] Implicit in the announcement was the threat that, if the revived talks proved less than "serious" in Washington's definition of that term, aerial attacks above the 20th parallel might be resumed. By its reference to "serious negotiations," the administration also recalled its statements during mid-December placing virtually all the blame for the breakdown of the peace talks on Hanoi's continual dilatory tactics. In indirect response to the domestic and foreign condemnations of "terror bombing" which its actions had provoked, Washington implied that the renewed devastation was North Vietnam's own fault, the virtually inevitable consequence of its policies in Paris.

Another probable reason for the administration's decision was the foreign and domestic protest which renewed bombing had aroused. Soviet leader Leonid Brezhnev warned that the development of Soviet-American relations along the hopeful lines laid down at the Moscow summit would depend in large part "on what kind of turn is taken on the issue of ending the war in Vietnam." [149] Denunciations of the American actions were voiced in Peking.[150] The most extreme criticism, however, came from Swedish Prime Minister Olof Palme. In contrast to the measured phrases of the Communist leaders, he compared the bombing of Hanoi with the worst Nazi atrocities of World War II.[151] Of more immediate concern for the President were the increasingly ominous signs of congressional opposition and of a further clash on the war issue once the newly elected Congress convened in early January. Particularly significant was the fact that criticism came not only from partisan opponents and antiwar legislators but from Republicans who had previously supported the President's positions.[152]

The resumption of the Paris talks failed to still the mounting discontent on Capitol Hill. By overwhelming margins, Senate and House Democrats voted to support the withholding of future funding for all military operations in Indochina and urged that "such operations be terminated immediately," providing arrangements could be made to "insure the safe withdrawal of American troops and the return of American prisoners of war." [153] The resolutions adopted had no direct impact on the war or the negotiations. But they did express the unusual degree of congressional discontent over inability to influence the administration's policies, especially regarding Vietnam. Speaking on the Senate floor, the chairman of the Foreign Relations Committee, J. W. Fulbright, attempted to present the President with an ultimatum by warning that unless a peace agreement were signed before "the inauguration, it will be Congress' responsibility to take immediate action to end the war by cutting off funds for its prosecution." [154] For all these fiery words, Congress was left in frustration, unable to force action and dependent for its information upon the press and occasional administration briefings. Summing up his colleagues' position, Senate Majority Leader Mike Mansfield noted: "We can make resolutions, but we can't end the war. We shouldn't fool ourselves." [155]

Now as before, hopes for a settlement centered on the secret talks in Paris. In contrast to the easy optimism of October, the new session was cloaked in caution and mutual intimations of bad faith, as much to lay the groundwork for failure as to prepare for possible success. President Nixon indicated that the U.S. position would depend on "whether the North Vietnamese, as they claimed, are ready to seriously negotiate the three major issues of the October agreement": release of American prisoners, implementation of a cease-fire, and arrangements for the future of the Saigon regime. This, he said, Washington "should know fairly quickly." [156] For its part, Hanoi questioned Washington's "goodwill" and "serious attitude," calling this "the decisive moment" for a settlement and asserting that the responsibility for war or peace "rests entirely with the United States." [157]

The initial meetings of the negotiators were as chilly as these words. The technical talks produced only restatements of earlier antagonism. Missing was the public cordiality that had marked the comings and goings of delegates the month before. As before, nothing of the substance of the talks was revealed, and the "atmospherics" surrounding the sessions came to stand for the progress or stalemate occurring within. As the sessions continued however, hints of movement began to appear. The meetings became longer, extended into the weekend, and experts joined the principals. By these outward signs at least, "serious negotiations" seemed to be taking place on the detailed provisions of a cease-fire document. [158]

Authoritative confirmation of progress came when, in mid-January, the Nixon administration ended bombing, shelling, and mining affecting all of North Vietnam. This cessation of all acts of war by the United States meant that, in effect, Washington had removed itself from the military struggle in Vietnam and begun to assume the role of nonbelligerent which a settlement would require. It was the first time since March 1972 that bombing had been halted over the whole of North Vietnam for more than brief periods. In addition, the President's order ruled out "armed reconnaissance" flights over the North, flights previously used as the basis for the "protective reaction" raids which Washington had undertaken sporadically during the Nixon years. Instead, aerial reconnaissance missions would still be flown, but without armament and without expected opposition from Hanoi. The United States was thus returning to the tacit "understanding" regarding American overflights of North Vietnam which was said to exist in late 1968, after the Johnson administration had halted its bombing campaign against the North. [159]

As the President's second inaugural approached, peace again seemed "at hand" in Vietnam. After previous disappointments, the high hopes of October were now revived. The end of the bombing triggered new speculation that agreement had been reached on nearly all outstanding issues. Meeting soon after Inauguration Day,

Kissinger and Tho ironed out final details of the complex cease-fire agreement and protocols by which it would be implemented.[160] Thus after a little more than four years of grappling with Vietnam, the Nixon administration had brought the country to peace. Rebuffing pressures to set deadlines on American involvement and seemingly oblivious to massive demonstrations for immediate withdrawal, Nixon had moved cautiously toward a settlement which, he believed, would enable an American withdrawal under conditions faithful to his earlier aims of preserving South Vietnamese independence from internal subversion or Northern attack.

It quickly became evident that the Paris agreements had changed the nature of the Vietnam war but had not ended it. Fighting continued when the cease-fire went into effect and in the months that followed. In the initial period at least, the conflict consisted of a multitude of low-level clashes throughout the country, as both sides jockeyed for position in the delineation of occupation zones to be prescribed by the revived control commission. Over time, however, the nonwar seemed to become a prolonged test of military strength between the two Vietnamese parties.

In this fighting, American forces took no part. Whatever the other effects of the Paris agreements, they marked the end of the American ground combat role which had begun (originally disguised as an advisory capacity) a decade before. U.S. forces left in installments as American prisoners of war were released in Hanoi and the South. By late March 1973, this process had been completed. At least 7,000 Americans still remained in South Vietnam, but most were Defense Department civilians recruited to supply and service the huge South Vietnamese military establishment which "Vietnamization" had created. Subject to congressional approval, American economic and military aid to the Saigon government would continue for several years to come (as promised in the Nixon-Thieu communiqué of April 1973), but as South Vietnamese President Thieu had pledged during that same month, Saigon would "never, never" request the return of American troops. It seemed even more certain that such a request, if made, would not be granted.[161]

Nonetheless, the Paris agreements did not mark the end of U.S.

participation in the Indochina war. Those agreements had provided for the arrangement of cease-fires in Laos and Cambodia but had failed to ensure that such provisions would in fact be implemented. In contrast to the pervasive but low-level conflict in Vietnam, major offensives were conducted, particularly in Cambodia. While these wars continued, American bombing continued as well, including the use of B-52s based in Thailand. Even after a formal Laotian cease-fire had been proclaimed in late February 1973, the bombing went on unabated. Prospects for a similar truce (however artificial) seemed remote in Cambodia, and intensified Communist attacks on the Lon Nol government in March and April 1973 triggered a correspondingly increased American response.[162]

The President's willingness to retain an American air role in Indochina after the withdrawal of U.S. ground forces was sharply challenged in the Congress as exceeding presidential authority and violating the Paris agreements. To the administration, however, this action was designed to promote the objectives of the cease-fire accords and to serve notice to North Vietnam and its allies that the United States would not tolerate a renewed Communist effort at military victory anywhere in Indochina. Reports of North Vietnamese infiltration of heavy weapons into the South at an unprecedented rate were variously interpreted (as matching Saigon's preagreement buildup or as preparation for a new major offensive like that of the year before), but they drew strong if ambiguous warnings from the President that Washington might once again resort to the massive application of force if the Paris terms were violated in a substantial and public way. Thus the peace won by the administration seemed both partial and precarious, dependent not on the pledged word of the participants or the elaborate mechanisms created by the agreements but rather on the threat of renewed involvement in a war from which most Americans assumed the United States had now finally and permanently withdrawn.[163]

The month-long bombing campaign over North Vietnam after the U.S. withdrawal from the secret talks underscored the President's determination not to allow a Communist victory in South Vietnam, at least not initially or by force. This same conviction lay behind the

American use of air power in Laos and Cambodia in the months following the cease-fire, as Washington attempted to bolster the positions of pro-Western regimes in those countries. As Nixon had warned in November 1971,

> Air power, of course, will continue to be used longer than our ground forces . . . and we will continue to use it in support of the South Vietnamese until there is a negotiated settlement or, looking further down the road, until the South Vietnamese have developed the capability to handle the situation themselves.[164]

At the heart of this determination was a generalized opposition to violent change threatening existing borders and the viability of existing governments. The administration's underlying view was clearly stated by the President in April 1972. Defending the use of American air and naval forces against North Vietnam, he warned (in terms reminiscent of those used by President Truman regarding American intervention in Korea) that successful aggression in one part of the world would breed aggression elsewhere.

> Let us look at what the stakes are—not just for South Vietnam but for the United States and for the cause of peace in the world. If one country, armed with the most modern weapons by other countries, can invade another nation and succeed in conquering it, other countries will be encouraged to do exactly the same thing—in the Mideast, in Europe, and in other international danger spots. If the Communists win militarily in Vietnam, the risk of war in other parts of the world would be enormously increased.[165]

POLICING THE GLOBAL PEACE   More than the President might care to admit, this statement of policy in Vietnam reflected the Nixon administration's basic plan for world peace. That plan was based on the assumption of compatability of "legitimate national interests" among different countries, especially the major states. In the words of the first "State of the World" message in February 1970,

> The United States, like any other nation, has interests of its own, and will defend those interests. But any nation today must

define its interests with special concern for the interests of others. If some nations define their security in a manner that means insecurity for other nations, then peace is threatened and the security of all diminished. This obligation is particularly great for the nuclear superpowers on whose decisions the survival of mankind may well depend.[166]

The success of mutual self-interest depended on mutual self-restraint. Discussing the upcoming summit in Moscow, the 1972 foreign policy report stated:

> We do not, of course, expect the Soviet Union to give up its pursuit of its own interests. We do not expect to give up pursuing our own. We do expect, and are prepared ourselves to demonstrate, self-restraint in the pursuit of those interests. We do expect a recognition of the fact that the general improvement in our relationship transcends in importance the kind of narrow advantages which can be sought only by imperiling the cooperation between our two countries.[167]

The formula for stability adopted by the administration was not a new one. It dates back to the precepts of European diplomacy— particularly in the eighteenth and nineteenth centuries—founded on a balance of power among the major states. Those precepts were directly related to present American policy by Dr. Kissinger, both through his own writings and through those of his "model statesman," Metternich, the Austrian foreign minister during the restoration of Europe following the upheavals of the Napoleonic wars. According to Kissinger:

> Stability has commonly resulted not from a quest for peace but from a generally accepted legitimacy. Legitimacy implies the acceptance of the framework of the international order by all major powers, at least to the extent that no state is so dissatisfied that . . . it expresses its dissatisfaction in a revolutionary foreign policy. A legitimate order does not make conflicts impossible but it limits their scope.[168]

Legitimacy and hence stability were, in Metternich's terms, based on a common "recognition of the true interests of *all* states."

It is in the general interests that the guarantee of existence is
to be found, while particular interests—the cultivation of which
is considered political wisdom by restless and short-sighted men
—have only a secondary importance.[169]

It may be useful to recall that the European order established
by Metternich, which was based on great-power agreement to oppose revolution as the greatest threat to peace, broke down fairly
quickly when the reemergence of other values led some of the major
states to support a particular revolt (that of the Greeks against Turkish rule in the 1820s) while others continued to oppose it.[170] In the
1970s as well, the success of a policy of major-state cooperation centered on adherence to higher principles depended on the existence of
real and substantial shared objectives and mutual interests. The economic and military interdependence of Western Europe and Japan
with the United States was likely to mean continued general cooperation, although surprises were to be expected on both sides, as the
Tanaka visit to Peking made clear. The Nixon "shocks" of the summer of 1971 were momentarily successful, but they put Europe and
Japan on notice that cooperation did not exclude major unilateral
shifts of policy. It was a lesson they were unlikely to forget.

No such degree of interdependence existed between the United
States and the Soviet Union or the People's Republic of China. The
President's trip to Peking marked a beginning of formal communication that was long overdue. But communication was not understanding, and understanding was not agreement. Despite the Moscow accords, cooperation with the Soviet Union in establishing stability was
not likely to be quick or easy. The fact that Washington and Moscow
had conflicting policies bilaterally and in many areas of the world in
part reflected fundamentally different *perceptions* of their interests.
Washington was simply not able to set the terms by which Soviet-
American competition would be replaced by collaboration. As if to
emphasize this point, the 1972 foreign policy report plaintively summarized the difficulties of collaboration with a recalcitrant partner.

The United States, under the Nixon Doctrine, has struck a new
balance between our international commitments and the in-

creasing self-reliance of our friends; the Soviet Union in the
1970's is projecting a political and military presence without
precedent in many new regions of the globe. Over the past three
years, we have sought to encourage constructive trends in U.S.–
Soviet relations. It would be dangerous to world peace if our
efforts to promote a detente between the superpowers were interpreted as an opportunity for the strategic expansion of Soviet
power. If we failed to take a stand, such an interpretation could
only have been encouraged, and the genuine relaxation of tensions we have been seeking could have been jeopardized.[171]

This basic inability to impose general-interest principles applied
to other countries as well as the great powers. The failure of Washington to bring about a settlement in the Middle East was an indication of this problem. The defeat of Washington's efforts was not only
due to Soviet support of Egypt but equally to Israeli refusal of and
resentment at American terms. Israel particularly made clear that,
even if the great powers could agree, it would not accept a solution
imposed by them. The President's remarks in his 1970 report were to
prove unusually prophetic:

I believe that the time has passed in which powerful nations
can or should dictate the future to less powerful nations. The
policy of this Administration is to help strengthen the freedom
of other nations to determine their own futures. Any effort by an
outside power to exploit local conflict for its own advantage or
to seek a special position of its own would be contrary to that
goal.[172]

The process of strengthening others, of course, makes them less ame-
nable to outside pressure, and makes it even more difficult for the
United States or a combination of major states to resolve local conflicts by defining for those nations what their "legitimate interests"
should and should not be.

American frustrations in its dealings with India and Pakistan
constituted a case in point. Washington's policy toward these South
Asian protagonists had fluctuated considerably over the score of
years since their independence. At first, American attitudes were

friendly but remote, with both countries looking mainly to Britain and secondly to China. As cold war hostility intensified and became global during the 1950s, however, the United States turned mainly to Pakistan, building up its army in exchange for Pakistani accession to Western treaties aimed against Moscow and Peking which India refused to join. Such neutralism was regarded as immoral by Washington, and Indo-American relations deteriorated accordingly. In the latter 1950s, as perceptions changed, Washington came to see India as China's main rival for leadership of the Asian nations and to provide economic support for Indian efforts at modernization. This policy of aid to New Delhi as the alternative to Peking's totalitarian brand of development continued through the 1960s, making India the largest recipient of U.S. economic assistance during that decade. Aid was not always readily forthcoming, however, for the Johnson administration refused to rescue the Gandhi regime from a severe food crisis until the Indian government pledged to give greater attention to agricultural programs. Whatever the merit of Washington's attitude, the United States was condemned in India for callous disregard of human suffering combined with an intolerable interference in India's internal affairs.[173]

Beyond large-scale economic aid, American policy during the 1960s was largely characterized by gradual disengagement, a withdrawal of influence which came to be replaced by Soviet attention. The border war between India and China in late 1962 marked the beginning of Washington's lessened ties with Pakistan, since the United States provided military assistance to India over Pakistani opposition and in the face of Pakistani threats to India's other frontiers. American-sponsored attempts to resolve the conflicts between the two countries failed and gave rise to an abortive Pakistani attack on India in 1965. Washington maintained a neutral posture, cutting off military aid to both sides but refusing to become entangled in the negotiations which followed the end of fighting. Instead, these peace talks were brought to a successful conclusion through Soviet mediation. Perhaps because of the American preoccupation during these years with its involvement in Indochina—which neither India nor Pakistan supported—the Johnson administration did not try to re-establish its previous position of influence and renewed military aid to the two countries only on a very low level. (India's membership on the Control Commission set up in 1954 to oversee Indochinese affairs became a source of further friction with the United States during the mid-1960s and made New Delhi more than casually interested in the Vietnam war and its eventual outcome.)[174]

The advent of the Nixon regime thus found the United States without strong ties to either India or Pakistan. While the policy of disengagement was continued, its effects were primarily further to erode U.S. relations with New Delhi. The economic aid program was cut back, while the continuation of the Vietnam war and American-aided incursions into Cambodia and Laos deflated Indian hopes for a settlement to the war and for the withdrawal of great-power military presence from Southeast Asia, with its dangers of provoking a global conflagration. Beyond these divergences was Indian resentment against the resumption of American military aid to Pakistan—aid which, in India's view, could only be used against her own forces.[175]

Then in March 1971 a revolt broke out in East Pakistan over the Pakistani government's failure to abide by elections awarding power to the Awami League of Sheik Mujibur Rahman, the East Pakistani leader. West Pakistani troops were sent to crush the rebellion, and refugees from the East began to flow into India in large numbers. Sympathetic to the plight of the refugees and anxious to undercut its Pakistani rival, New Delhi started to provide increasing aid to the rebels, permitting them sanctuary on Indian territory and in some instances training and arming them. Throughout the rebellion, which continued through the remainder of 1971, the United States refused to cut off all military aid to Pakistan or to denounce its massive and brutal suppression policies. The result was a substantial outcry in Congress, where attempts were made to curtail the arms aid shipments, and especially in India, which now saw Washington as aligning itself wholeheartedly with the Pakistani government. Partly as a result of Washington's stance, and also as a reflection of the increased Soviet presence over the preceding decade, India signed a friendship treaty with Moscow in August 1971 pledging mutual assistance in case of attack and, in effect, ensuring New Delhi of full Soviet support in a clash with Pakistan, thereby helping to nullify Chinese support for her antagonist.[176]

When war came in December 1971 as the result of Pakistani air strikes and Indian incursions into East Pakistan, the Nixon administration found itself supporting a military regime that had been committing mass slaughter against its countrymen for the past nine months, against the world's most populous democracy, the largest recipient of American aid, and the country most often regarded as the counter to Chinese designs in Asia. Washington's efforts did nothing to prevent the decimation of the Pakistani army by the larger, primarily Soviet-equipped Indian forces, nor was the United States able to prevent the collapse of Pakistani rule over its eastern region and the rise of a new state (Bangladesh) closely tied to India and the Soviet Union. Moreover, American aid to Pakistan before the war and its condemnation of and warnings to India during the fighting appeared to drive New Delhi even closer to Moscow than had previously been the case.

Why did the United States follow this seemingly unrealistic and disserving policy rather than accepting the unavoidable and seeking to counter Indian overdependence on Moscow? Perhaps part of the answer lies in the administration's apparent view that India grossly violated Pakistan's most basic and "legitimate" interests—its territorial integrity and political independence—at a time when a peaceful solution of the crisis seemed possible as a result of American diplomatic initiatives.[177] Hence New Delhi was portrayed as deliberately sabotaging Washington's plan for preserving regional stability in order to achieve the partition and possibly the elimination of her long-standing rival. The moral condemnation of India in the United Nations, warnings to the Soviet Union, and the dispatch of a naval task force to Indian waters were all seen as having forced Indian restraint, preventing the exploitation of its position of South Asian predominance for further conquest and providing the basis for restoration of some form of regional balance of power.

The American brief against India, then, was that it sought to take advantage of another country's internal divisions to commit disguised aggression and win regional predominance. A similar incident (but one that received much less publicity) occurred in the Middle East in September 1970. Internal war broke out in Jordan between Palestinian guerrilla forces and the government of King Hussein. The Palestinians were supported by Syria, which dispatched tank units up to and across the Jordanian border. Presented with what he regarded as "the gravest threat to world peace since this Administration came into office," President Nixon warned Syria to withdraw its forces and avoid further intervention. These warnings were backed up by the positioning of a large portion of American forces in the Mediterranean and Central Europe for possible use. Confronted with this show of force, the Syrian regime retreated, and the Jordanian army was left to deal with the guerrillas.[178] The 1971 report justified Washington's actions as follows:

> The United States had no responsible choice but to prevent events from running away with the ability to control them. We took a firm stand against the Syrian intervention. We acted to stabilize but not to threaten, to discourage irresponsibility without accelerating the momentum of crisis.[179]

For these countries if not for the larger states which supported them, the Nixon administration was prepared to rely on unilateral measures including the threat of force. If countries refused to resist the temptation to pursue immediate individual gains, Washington would turn to coercion to remind them of their higher interest.

Conclusion

The difficulties faced by the Nixon administration in implementing its "strategy for peace" were the result of dilemmas central to the Nixon policy. Despite the administration's statement regarding mutual accommodation based on mutual respect and noninterference in decision processes, the "emerging structure of peace" (in the revealing subtitle of the 1972 foreign policy report) represented a structure essentially imposed by the United States. The United States had not assumed the responsibilities of all, but it had presumed to dictate what these responsibilities should be. It was, after all, the *American,* and specifically the administration's, conception of what constituted "legitimate national interests"—both for the United States and for other major states—that was at the heart of the Nixon plan for world order. The balances of power which were to operate regionally and globally were to have their rules and procedures and most importantly their limits determined by Washington's view of what was best for the countries involved, as well as what was best for the United States. The assumptions that there were objective national interests and that one country could successfully judge which of another country's interests are legitimate and illegitimate presumed a degree of consensus among major states that has rarely been achieved. It was, basically, the same reasoning which had underlain various attempts at collective security, most notably the hopes placed in the United Nations Security Council in 1945. The failure of these hopes and the deadlock of the Security Council were the results of what happened when great powers disagreed.

Systems of world order based on collaboration among the great powers have nearly always been based on an overriding fear of war. When that fear has become less urgent and other foreign policy goals more appealing, then the basic common interest holding the states together has eroded, and the structure of cooperation has collapsed. There was, in these Nixon years, no immediate, general crisis portending world war. The crisis which existed was rather in American foreign policy. For domestic support, if for no other reason, a fundamental adjustment of American policy was seen as necessary in the aftermath of Vietnam. And that adjustment was based in part upon the reduction of the American role abroad. For these reasons, a policy designed to persuade allies and adversaries to pursue goals and take actions which were in the American interest as well as their own may indeed have been the best strategy for the Nixon administration to follow. But no one should be especially sanguine about its results.

The continuation of discord among the major states and the difficulty of attempting to impose settlements on lesser states provided the background for the Nixon program. On the one hand, the United States was unable to persuade other countries to adhere to its conceptions of what national interests should encompass and how international politics should be conducted. On the other hand, when its efforts at persuasion failed, the administration saw itself as having no recourse but to threaten (and, in Vietnam, to implement) dire consequences involving the substantial commitment of American military force, even if that force was restricted to naval and air components.

In addition, for all its rhetoric about new departures, the administration's foreign policies were not basically different from those followed by the United States since World War II. Superpower collaboration, both bilaterally and as a guarantee of regional stability, had antecedents in Franklin Roosevelt's plans for "the four policemen" patrolling the postwar world. The notion that aggression and subversion anywhere threaten all was clearly Wilsonian, and the corollary that, if nations together cannot act, the United States alone should do so, had its postwar origins in the Truman Doctrine. Rather than retrenchment, the global extent of American concern was reemphasized by the administration, and the willingness to use force as a means of protecting or advancing those interests was repeatedly demonstrated, most prominently in Indochina, but in South Asia and the Middle East as well.

Finally, as noted at the outset, there were substantial pressures within the United States for fundamental change both in the direction and the implementation of the nation's foreign policy. It was suggested earlier that major shifts of direction in twentieth-century American foreign policy had occurred after, and largely in reaction to, the participation of the United States in war. While the Vietnam experience was hardly on the scale of the world wars, it nonetheless represented the most massive American military involvement (whether measured by troops in combat, battle deaths, or resources expended) since World War II. Given the current revulsion against the conduct of that war and the attempted refocusing of attention on domestic concerns, the pattern of war-related change seems likely to continue and to be reflected in a basic downward revision of foreign policy commitments and resources.

The Nixon policy was an attempt to accommodate to demands for retrenchment abroad without the sacrifice of some of the basic objectives the United States had pursued since 1945. The success of this policy hinged upon Washington's ability to convince other major countries—allies and adversaries alike—that it was in their own interests to advance these objectives. It was by no means clear, despite the summits at Peking and Moscow, that the administration's efforts succeeded in either the short or the long run. What was clear was that it would become increasingly difficult for the United States government to use the threat of unilateral involvement either as a means of promoting this cooperative design or as a substitute for it.

John B. Starr

China and the New Open Door

Considered from the American point of view, interesting parallels exist between the present period in Sino-American relations and the period at the turn of this century when the United States first enunciated its policy of maintaining an "open door" in China. In the early period, the United States was attempting to hold open a door which the Chinese themselves had initially attempted to bolt against Western intrusion and which rival powers in the West, having first secured their own access, had subsequently sought to close against their American competitors.[1] More recently, American policy has been directed at "reopening" China to American diplomatic and trade relations after a hiatus of more than two decades.

The similarities between the two periods are striking. In both cases Americans have tended to overemphasize the degree of isolation suffered by the Chinese prior to the opening of her doors to an American presence. In both cases, the United States was a late arrival at China's door, encouraged to call primarily by rivalry with her fellow callers. Most important, in both cases, the United States was initially confronted with a regime that perceived and related to other nations in a unique way, different from the way in which Western states have traditionally dealt with one another.

There are important differences, as well, in the circumstances surrounding the period of the "open door" policy in the years following 1898, and the present period which began with the Chinese invitation to an American Ping-Pong team to visit China in the spring of 1971. The power positions of both the United States and China have altered radically since that time. It was from a position of weakness relative to its Western rivals that the United States dispatched its Open Door Notes. China's influence in world politics was at its nadir at that time, and she found herself wholly unable to resist the incursions of Western imperialism. During World War II it was the United States that argued for China's being regarded as among the world's major powers in the postwar period.[2] It was anticipated that a China friendly to the United States should assume the role Japan had played and overplayed in the prewar period—that of the major power in the Far East. It was not anticipated, however, that the Communist-led revolution in China which had gone on for more than two decades would be successful in overthrowing the Kuomintang (Nationalist party) government with which the United States had come to associate itself so closely.

More recently, power relationships have again been altered. The postwar period has been one in which the Soviet Union—which came to be China's closest ally in the years following the successful conclusion of her revolution—and the United States—which China came to regard as its primary enemy as a result of American participation in the Korean war and American support of the Kuomintang government in its exile on Taiwan—have dominated world politics as the "superpowers" in the world arena. As Sino-Soviet relations changed gradually from those of alliance to those of conflict, China began to view international relations less as a rivalry between two hostile camps—the Soviet Union and its satellites and allies in one camp; the United States, its dependencies, and allies in the opposite camp—and more as a balance of power between several rival states in which China would play an independent role, helping to offset the independence of the two superpowers. Although China's leaders seem free of illusions as to the present strength of their nation, Sino-American relations are being conducted in the most recent period as between states of potential equality.

In many ways, this view of world politics as involving a balance of conflicting forces marks an important departure for the Chinese from earlier ways of conceiving international relations. Despite enormous differences between the structure and political philosophy of the Ch'ing dynasty regime with which the United States treated at the turn of the century and the structure and political philosophy of the current regime, until quite recently interesting and significant parallels could be drawn between the two views of China's position in the world and the positions of other nations in world politics as held by the two Chinese regimes.

We sometimes use the term *culturocentrism* to describe the Chinese view of China's position in the world in traditional times. This term is preferable to *ethnocentrism* because it was invariably the acceptance of Chinese culture and not possession of Chinese ethnicity that the Chinese used to distinguish between "insiders" and "outsiders" in their dealings with the world around them. In the wake of the Renaissance in the West, a nation-state system had grown up within which each nation reacted with other nations as potential equals. By no means every nation realized this potential, but at least no single state dominated European culture, politics, and trade on a permanent basis. On the other hand, China occupied just such a dominant position vis-à-vis other nations on her periphery and did so almost continually during the nearly two thousand years of her history.[3]

Her culturocentric view gave rise to a system of foreign relations best represented by a series of concentric circles. All the circles centered on Peking, and each represented a degree of dependency of a group of neighboring states. These states manifested their subservience to the Chinese emperor and the culture he represented by bearing gifts periodically to Peking as a form of tribute to the emperor. This tribute system cannot very well be regarded as a form of imperialism, since the value of tribute brought from abroad seldom equalled the value of the gifts with which the emissaries returned from their tribute missions. Nor was the system characteristically backed by armed force. The Chinese empire never maintained large standing armies and only seldom dispatched troops to force the hand of a reluctant tributary state. It would be difficult to make a case for regarding China historically as an aggressive power. Existing on the periphery of this system, a country such as Japan grew accustomed to the idea that cultural innovation could come from abroad. Existing at its center, the Chinese had no experience to assist them in assimilating the same lesson.

The criterion, then, on the basis of which the Chinese distinguished between "inside" and "outside," was that of culture. The etymological root of the Chinese word for culture, *wen-hua*, suggests the imposing of a pattern—the process of rendering orderly a naturally chaotic situation. As the Chinese saw it, those who accepted the pattern of Chinese culture were, for practical purposes, Chinese; those who refused were outsiders, barbarians.

One purpose of a revolution is to overthrow and replace the society's existing set of cultural patterns. The Chinese revolution was no exception. It was the very weakness which the Ch'ing rulers manifested in the face of the nibbling away at Chinese sovereignty by rival Western imperialists which led the first Chinese dissidents toward revolutionary, and away from reformist, solutions for China's problems.[4] Initially, it was Western liberal democratic patterns that the Chinese revolutionaries espoused.[5] Gradually, however, some began to see these patterns as undesirable, given the imperialistic foreign policies of Western liberal democracies with regard to China and the apparent discrediting of Western liberal principles in the debacle of World War I. Following the successful October Revolution in Russia, the cultural patterns implicit in Marxism exerted a strong appeal for these disillusioned young Chinese nationalists.[6] Marxism was not only the doctrine underlying the successful revolution in backward Russia, but it was also a doctrine the espousing of which could put the Chinese among the avant-garde of the West: it claimed to be a scientific explanation and was thus more "modern" than the principles of liberal democracy.[7] Properly interpreted, it provided the explanation for Western imperialist policies and for Chinese backwardness. Most important, it suggested that the Western nations were doomed to destruction by a movement which could be set off by revolution in the colonial and semicolonial "East."[8]

As the Chinese revolutionary cultural pattern finally emerged during the course of the decades which followed, the strong shaping influence on that pattern exerted by Mao Tse-tung became clear.[9] Mao's political philosophy, as it developed over those decades, came to be guided by two fundamental and interrelated concepts: that of the dialectic and that of a kind of pragmatism.[10] A dialectical cast of mind gives rise to a characteristic sense of how the world is ordered and how it changes. As used by Marx and his successors, the dialectic sees the world as ordered in terms of pairs of conflicting forces or "contradictions." Development or change is the product of the conflict of these forces. To one who accepts the dialectic, then, conflict and change are ubiquitous, perpetual, and normal; consensus and maintenance of the status quo are temporary aberrations from the normal state. Sharing this view of society and social development, Mao opened the article with which his *Selected Works* begins, "Who are our enemies? Who are our friends? This is a question of the first importance for the revolution." [11]

Like this crucial distinction, however, every distinction Mao makes is subject to revision. Theory—the compilation of distinctions such as these—must be put into practice. The object of theory is not merely to comprehend the world, but to change it through revolutionary practice. In the process, theory itself undergoes change; indeed, theory and practices are themselves subject to the dialectical laws of development. Although he reaches his idea of the relationship between theory and practice by a very different logic, Mao's conclusions bear a striking resemblance to those of John Dewey, the American exponent of pragmatism. Thus, as we shall see, to distinguish between the "ideologically determined" policies of the Chinese and the "pragmatic" foreign policies of the United States is to be misled: a strong pragmatic strain lies at the heart of the Chinese ideology, and there are occasions when it would appear that ideological elements contend with the purely pragmatic in determining American policies.

The dialectical way of thinking enters into the formulation of Chinese foreign policy in a number of ways. Still among the most important of the contradictions in contemporary Chinese diplomacy is that between "inside" and "outside." Although the nature of the cultural patterns have been altered radically, the new patterns are as important as the old ones in determining the way Chinese leaders perceive international affairs and the way in which they formulate answers to Mao's questions: "Who are our enemies? Who are our friends?"

Closely related to distinguishing between *people* as insiders or outsiders, there is the contradiction between domestic and foreign *issues* as well. Generally speaking, the completion of their revolution at home has occupied much of the attention of the Chinese, often to the exclusion of attention to foreign issues.

There is, in addition, the contradiction between revolution and peaceful coexistence, a contradiction which some see as having given rise to alternating periods of a more forward foreign policy and those of a more moderate policy over the course of the last two decades. Yet another relevant contradiction is that between the state and society, sometimes manifested in the view that the government and the Communist party—acting as the agent of the society—can be in contradiction with one another. More recently, during the course of the Cultural Revolution, the argument has been advanced that the party itself can become corrupted and cease to act as the agent of the people: a contradiction arises, that is, between society and the alienated party. The product of these ideas in the international realm is the tendency of the Chinese to employ a three-level concept of international relations: formal, state-to-state relations, party-to-party relations in those areas where Communist parties or national liberation movements operate actively, and people-to-people relations based on the idea that even in those countries controlled by hostile forces, "the masses" have a fundamental unity of interests with the Chinese people.

As treated in Chinese political philosophy, social change is not brought about by the mere existence of contradictory forces. Mao shares in the deterministic side of Marxism to a degree; but more than most of his predecessors in the history of the development of Marxist thought, he believes in the necessity and efficacy of human action to alter social conditions. Contradictions must be "resolved" or "handled correctly" in order to ensure that development proceeds at an appropriate pace toward desirable goals.

The need to resolve domestic contradictions determined China's position in world politics during the years immediately following

Liberation. China needed to "lean to one side," as Mao explained it in 1949—to rely on the assistance and the example of the Soviet Union.[12] During the early 1950s the international Communist movement generally operated in consonance with the policies determined by Stalin and regarded the Soviet Union as the legitimate leader of that movement. Although Stalin had consistently underestimated the capabilities of the Chinese Communist party, led by Mao and his cohorts, and had, during the course of the Chinese revolution offered much bad advice and misdirection, and although he was less than generous in his initial agreements to aid the Chinese government after its establishment, the Chinese party nevertheless regarded (and continues to regard) Stalin's rule as a legitimate one.[13]

As a result of China's policy of "leaning to one side," she came to regard international politics in terms of a conflict between two opposed camps—socialist and capitalist, "East" and "West." Moreover, the Chinese regarded the "East"—the camp of socialism—to be steadily gaining in power as compared to the West, a point of view expressed in Mao's 1957 speech in Moscow in which he spoke of the "East Wind prevailing over the West Wind." [14]

During the late 1950s China's relations with the Soviet Union began to deteriorate, and this altered relationship, perhaps more than any other factor, has influenced the subsequent course that Chinese foreign policy has followed.[15] The causes of the falling out between the two largest socialist states are many and complex. The issues that now divide them can be categorized under three rubrics: ideological differences, territorial disputes, and a clash of personalities.

In ideological terms the Chinese, who once regarded the Soviet system as a model to be emulated in their own government-building process, now argue that the Soviet leaders who succeeded Stalin have espoused a series of incorrect policies and as a result have undertaken to alter the Soviet state and Communist party in illegitimate ways.[16] The Chinese summarize these policies as constituting a "restoration of capitalism" in Soviet domestic politics and a system of "social-imperialism" in collusion with the United States in the international realm. Fearing that a similar course could befall China if she were to continue to emulate the Soviet example, Mao has argued that China should find her own path toward socialism and communism and that, although the international Communist movement needs central direction, the direction emanating from the Kremlin under its present set of leaders is illegitimate.[17]

Ideological differences such as these are thought by some to be no more than a means of obscuring the actual points of difference between two nations. My own inclination is to take seriously the ideological arguments raised by the Chinese, both because much can be learned about an individual or a group from the nature of the arguments they make in order to persuade others and, more important, because the Chinese take their own polemics very seriously indeed. Nevertheless, it would be incorrect to suggest that differences of world view alone can account for the Sino-Soviet rift.

Important unsolved issues exist between the Soviet Union and China relating to their common border, the world's longest common border save that dividing the United States and Canada.[18] On the Chinese side, questions arise with regard to territory annexed by Russia prior to the Bolshevik Revolution—territory to which the Soviet Union still lays claim. The border has never been mutually agreed upon over its full length. Indeed, specific instances of conflicting territorial claims resulted in open armed conflict between the two states in 1969. On the Soviet side is a strong ethnically based feeling against the Chinese. Whereas the Soviet Union occupies much more territory than does China, the Chinese population far outstrips that of the Soviet Union. The implicit assumption on the part of the Russians is that the pressures of China's enormous population will ultimately drive her leaders to a quest for *Lebensraum*—space to settle and resources to feed and clothe her people. In response to these threats—whether real or imagined—the Chinese and Russians presently have massive armies facing one another across their common frontier, a situation that does little to bolster Marx's idea of a "proletarian internationalism" based on the transnational common interests of working people.

Finally, it seems clear that personal psychological factors must also be taken into account when analyzing the Sino-Soviet split. Although Mao and Stalin do not seem to have been close personal associates, nevertheless Mao seems genuinely to have respected Stalin as a revolutionary leader. Mao also appears to have regarded his own revolutionary experience and his ability to draw theoretical conclusions from that experience to have been superior to that of Stalin's successors—particularly Nikita Khrushchev.[19] Khrushchev, on the other hand, appears neither to have known or understood Mao nor to have respected him sufficiently to have made an effort to understand him better.[20] Much the same can apparently be said for Khrushchev's successors to political power in the Kremlin. Thus some part of the Sino-Soviet dispute can best be understood in terms of the psychology of individual leaders in rivalry with one another for legitimacy in the eyes of the same constituents.

One crucial aspect of the conflict between the Soviet Union and China focuses on the appropriate way in which the transition occurs as between the capitalist and the socialist stage in a nation's development. The Chinese have, fairly consistently, argued for the inevitability of armed revolution as the means by which this transition is made. The Soviet Union, emphasizing the dangers of a major and irreversible confrontation with the United States, have argued for policies permitting "peaceful coexistence" with the United States and other capitalist countries. Specifically, they have emphasized the possibility of a "peaceful transition" to socialism through the electoral process. The Chinese have argued their side of this question primarily in connection with the struggle for national liberation in the colonies and former colonies in the Third World—Asia, Africa, Latin America, and the Middle East. As a result, while their identification with the Soviet Union gradually declined, their identification with the Third World increased. Gradually the salient division of the world for the Chinese ceased to be that between East and West and began to be that between North and South—the developed states vs. the underdeveloped or, as it was metaphorically put in 1965, between the world's "cities" and the "countryside" surrounding them.[21]

The period of strong identification with the Third World, characteristic of Chinese policies in the early 1960s, saw China interacting with developing nations at all three levels at which her diplomacy is conducted.[22] At the state-to-state level, aid and technical assistance programs were undertaken, particularly in Africa, and an effort made to secure widespread diplomatic recognition for the People's Republic. There was a clear element of competition with the Republic of China on Taiwan in these state-to-state efforts. At the level of party-to-party relations, efforts were made, especially with regard to some of China's neighbors in Southeast Asia, to train and support incipient national liberation movements. "Support" of these movements, however, has been clearly defined as involving training, logistic support, and technical assistance, but not the dispatching of Chinese troops. A revolution, the Chinese leaders very firmly believe, must be a domestic product; it cannot be exported.[23] At the level of people-to-people relations, the Chinese have made attempts at reaching popular elements in the Third World countries through organizations such as that of Afro-Asian writers, by encouraging visits by foreign nationals to China, and by means of undertaking foreign assistance programs with high popular appeal.[24]

In the more recent period the salient contradiction in the international realm as the Chinese see it has apparently become that between the superpowers and the smaller, less powerful states. In consequence, China's self-image appears to have shifted again. Now, while still regarding herself as a socialist state and as a developing state, she has come to see herself as a middle-range power having as yet unrealized potential for becoming a superpower. In this new identity, China sees her role as that of working together with other middle-range powers to limit the freedom with which the superpowers are able to impose their joint decisions and their conflicts on the rest of the world.[25] "Great power chauvinism" has long been an error denounced by Mao and his colleagues, and the Soviet Union and the United States are equally guilty of this erroneous stance in the Chinese view.

It is only in connection with this shift in what the Chinese regard as the salient contradictions in the world arena, and the consequent shift in their international self-image, that one can begin to understand the initial steps toward a Sino-American rapprochement taken during the last two years. During the late 1930s and the early 1940s, the possibility existed for friendly relations between the United States and a Communist regime in China. American observers, both diplomats and journalists, who had occasion to make comparisons between the Communists' administration of the territories they occupied and the Kuomintang's administration of the national government in Nanking often expressed the opinion that the Communists were both more effective in their struggle against the Japanese and less corrupt in their domestic administration than were the Kuomintang leaders.[26] Indeed, as we now know, Mao and Chou En-lai expressed an interest in making a trip to Washington to present their case to President Roosevelt in person and to seek ways in which the United States and the Communist revolutionaries could cooperate directly.[27] Unsympathetic American officials, a long-term and popularly upheld commitment to the support of Chiang Kai-shek, and a hesitancy to offer any support for an avowedly Communist movement, however tenuous may have been its actual ties to Moscow, all prevented the formation of a close relationship during the closing years of World War II. The relationship deteriorated further when the United States cooperated with the Kuomintang by transporting its troops to receive the Japanese surrender in the important industrial areas of Manchuria. The Chinese Communist party regarded this as American intervention in its conflict with the Kuomintang, for without this assistance Red Army troops and not Kuomintang forces would have occupied this strategic area. Despite American efforts at conciliating the conflict between the two parties, civil war began within a year of the victory over Japan—a war which ended three years later with a remnant force of the Kuomintang established in exile on the island of Taiwan and, with a rapidity and thoroughness that astonished Soviet and American observers as much as it did the Communists themselves, the Communists established in control of the Chinese mainland.

Although the United States decided during the course of that civil war to cease its massive support of the Kuomintang—support which showed decreasing results as the years went on—and gave indications that it would not intervene in any attempt by the new government in Peking to complete its revolution by the capture of Taiwan from Nationalist control, nevertheless, this policy was reversed when the decision was taken to intervene under United Nations auspices in the Korean conflict.[28] It was at that point that the American defense perimeter was redrawn to include Taiwan and a contingent of U.S. Navy ships assigned the task of patrolling the straits separating Taiwan from the coast of Fukien Province. The development of the hostility between the Soviet Union and the United States which we now call the "cold war," given China's strong identification with the Soviet Union during the same period, hardened the lines of Sino-American conflict.[29] Meanwhile, the postwar period marked the growth of long-term American involvement and military presence in East Asia. As her relations with China deteriorated, American policy with regard to the reform of Japanese political and economic life through the American occupation of Japan changed sharply. Thoroughgoing reform was set aside in favor of creating a strong Japan capable of long-term competition with a developing and hostile socialist China. Looked at from the Chinese point of view, United States policy in the postwar period involved the concluding of a series of treaties and agreements and the equipping and manning of a chain of bases by means of which China was encircled by forces hostile to Peking and friendly to Washington.

The Chinese shift away from a view of the world as divided between hostile camps, East and West, was not marked by an improvement in Sino-American relations. Although Chinese hostility toward the Soviet Union increased, there was no proportional decrease in hostility toward the United States. On the contrary, whereas China had regarded the United States as the leader of a camp of capitalist nations, she came to regard the United States as more importantly the leader of a group of imperialist and neocolonialist powers engaged in the exploitation and opposed to the liberation of the people of the Third World. This view of the United States was confirmed, in Chinese eyes, by American involvement in Vietnam.

Our discussion heretofore errs in the same way that many discussions of contemporary China err: we have spoken of "China" as though that vast country were a uniform entity, and of "China" and

"Mao" as essentially synonymous. Both usages are incorrect. As the Cultural Revolution showed us, although Mao's view ultimately prevailed in determining Chinese domestic and foreign policies, his was by no means the only view, nor was its ultimate predominance always clear. "China" is riven with internal contradictions—regional, organizational, generational—and the foreign policy pursued by the nation, although generally identifiable as the product of a particular set of organizations, staffed by men of a certain generation and with local roots in specific areas, has by no means always met with universal approval among members of other organizations, generations and regional groupings. We have, for example, rather extensive documentation of a major disagreement over policy in the late 1950s in which a group of the most senior officers in the People's Liberation Army argued for the maintenance of close relationships with the Soviet Union regardless of the ideological, territorial, or personal consequences involved.[30]

Thus, when the United States took the decisions that led to the escalation of the war in Vietnam, there were apparently several reactions among the Chinese leaders.[31] Some argued that the United States intended to push the war to the point where Chinese involvement was unavoidable. These men then concluded that a forward policy of opposition to the American presence in Vietnam was appropriate. The American forces should be attacked with Chinese troops and equipment. Such a policy presupposed a rapprochement and cooperation with the Soviet Union in the support of North Vietnamese and Viet Cong forces.

Another group of Chinese policy makers apparently argued for a much more defensive strategy, contending that the likelihood of American invasion of China was so great and the probable consequences so grave that all domestic programs should be suspended in favor of a nationwide defensive mobilization. A third policy alternative—the one associated with Mao because it was ultimately adopted at a time when he was returning to active control of policy making in China—assessed the danger of American attack on China as relatively low. Consequently domestic reform programs—specifically, the Great Proletarian Cultural Revolution—could go forward. No rapprochement with the Soviet Union was deemed necessary, even in the interest of cooperation in the assistance of the Vietnamese Communists, since a completely indigenous anti-American war in Vietnam supported from without with Chinese and Russian equipment and technical assistance was seen as both possible in practical terms and desirable in ideological terms. Such a course would require little, if any, Sino-Soviet cooperation; indeed, the Chinese sought to increase their influence in Hanoi at the expense of that of the Soviet Union.[32]

The Nixon administration was not the first in the postwar period to consider the possibility of improving Sino-American relations. Efforts were begun by the administration of President Kennedy and continued under that of President Johnson to ease travel restrictions on Americans wishing to visit China, and to encourage the exchange of journalists and scholars. Informal meetings between Chinese and American diplomatic representatives were conducted on an irregular basis. Both administrations, however, were too closely associated with the Vietnam effort to make their overtures appealing to the Chinese. Even more important, having chosen the course of resolving domestic problems by means of the Cultural Revolution—restoring Mao to a position of direct control over policy making and taking steps to prevent the occurrence in China of the "restoration of capitalism" which Maoists saw as having taken place in the Soviet Union—the Chinese declared a kind of moratorium on foreign affairs in the late 1960s. Chinese representatives abroad were recalled and the Foreign Ministry in Peking underwent the same kind of shakeup of personnel and procedures that occurred in organizations throughout the society.[33] It was not a time for major innovations in Chinese foreign policy.

The Chinese appear to have taken very seriously the so-called Guam Doctrine enunciated by President Nixon shortly after his inauguration. This doctrine called for a gradual withdrawal of American forces from Asia and implied an increasing role for Asian states friendly to the United States in their own national defense. This American policy initiative—however optimistic the Chinese interpretation of it may appear in retrospect given its implementation by means of the substitution of air and naval power for ground forces— set the stage for a reciprocal policy initiative by the Chinese. Thus the "open door" of the 1970s has been opened by the Chinese themselves, unlike the "open door" of the 1890s, which was forced on a powerless China by powerful Western nations.

The new foreign policy of post-Cultural Revolution China is, as it is often described to be, a pragmatic one; but China's previous policies have been equally pragmatic. It is wrong to assume that Chinese policy makers are only "pragmatic" when they choose to engage in friendly relations with the United States. It is a policy closely controlled and implemented on a day-to-day basis by the urbane, intelligent, and astoundingly energetic premier, Chou En-lai. As Chou has frequently insisted, however, it is a policy which originates with Mao. It calls for increased interaction with foreign states in direct relations and in international forums such as the United Nations. It calls for the isolation and gradual assimilation of the Kuomintang government on Taiwan. It seeks the elimination of an American presence in Asia and the prevention of an increased Soviet presence there as the American forces are withdrawn. It seeks to influence international policy through direct relations with those governments which it considers by nature fundamentally inimical to China, such as those of the United States and Japan. It seeks as well to mitigate the chances of open conflict with the Soviet Union by alleviating as much as possible the chance that the United States would cooperate with the Soviet Union in that conflict. It seeks to influence from a position of strength the conclusion of nuclear disarmament agreements to which every nation would be a party.

As a result of the Chinese, American, and Japanese policy initiatives in recent years, the international politics of East Asia look very different at the end of Nixon's first term in office than they did at the beginning of that term. Sino-American relations are very likely to improve and to become formalized as American involvement in the Vietnam conflict is finally terminated and the details of American withdrawal from Taiwan are settled. To the extent that the "Guam Doctrine" is implemented and American forces are withdrawn from Asia, it seems clear that the course of international affairs in that area will be increasingly shaped by the economic and political competition between Japan and China for influence among Asian states.

The most uncertain element in such calculations about the future of Asian politics is the degree to which there will be continuity in Chinese foreign policy after Mao ceases to be able actively to determine that policy. As was revealed by the death of Lin Piao, Mao's one-time chosen successor and "closest comrade in arms," even he favored a rapprochement with the Soviet Union rather than the United States, thus suggesting that strong differences of opinion still exist within China over what her foreign policy orientations should be.

However long China's door may remain open to Americans, it is important that both Americans and Chinese take the opportunity to reduce so much as possible the numerous and gross misconceptions of one another which are the product of the long period when both China's and America's doors were closed to one another.

Vernon V. Aspaturian

Moscow's Options in a Changing World

During the past four years there has been a dramatic transformation in the fortunes of Soviet foreign policy and a remarkable revitalization of Soviet decisiveness and self-assurance in foreign affairs. The Soviet leadership appears to have overcome much of its previous feelings of inferiority and inadequacy in facing up to the manifold issues that confronted it both as a global power and as the leader of an ecumenical revolutionary movement. Only in dealing with the Chinese do the Soviet leaders fail to exude the self-confidence they have acquired over the past four years and instead continue to betray signs of irresolution, uncertainty of purpose, and indecisiveness. There are good explanations for these distinctive Soviet postures in dealing with the West and with China, just as there was considerable warrant for the irresolution and demoralization that characterized the Soviet leadership in foreign affairs between 1961 and 1968.

The Period of Defeatism, 1961–68

Before 1968, the Soviet leadership was divided, hesitant, and confused about its direction in foreign policy. On the global level, its ambitions were blocked by the United States; within its own Communist world, it was challenged by the Chinese; and its East European empire appeared to be in the throes of dissolution as individual countries responded favorably to the seductive siren calls of the Johnson administration's "bridge-building" policy and the Erhard-

Kiesinger brand of West German *Ostpolitik*. The Soviet leadership, sitting in Moscow, seemed gripped by paralysis as Czechoslovakia under Dubček appeared to be slipping out of the Communist community. But the Czechoslovak Spring was only the latest in a succession of minor and major disasters in Soviet foreign policy since the Berlin crisis of 1961 and the Cuban missile crisis of October 1962. Although the Partial Nuclear Test-Ban Treaty of July 1963 had stabilized Soviet-American relations, the embryonic condominium it established worked clearly to the advantage of the United States, the most powerful of the dyarchs. The Soviet position in world affairs, instead of being enhanced by the Khrushchev détente, was diminished to that of a tired, wornout revolutionary power content with permanent status as "Number 2," while the United States was left free to flex its diplomatic and military muscles all over the world and to undermine the Soviet position in Eastern Europe with subtle policies of "bridge-building" and "peaceful engagement." Although the Johnson administration faithfully refrained from aggressive and overtly hostile moves against the Soviet position in Eastern Europe, its selective enticement of individual Communist states proved to be a device against which the unimaginative Soviet leaders had no defense except military intervention to arrest the growing forces of autonomy. Furthermore, China had been progressively transformed from an alienated ally into a hostile and threatening neighbor, the world Communist movement was fractured and demoralized, and the national liberation movement was deprived of its protective umbrella.

Confident of its superior power and relying on a prudent Soviet Union to refrain from any action that might endanger Soviet-American collaboration, the United States in 1965 massively escalated the war in Vietnam against Moscow's North Vietnamese ally and landed marines in the Dominican Republic to prevent the establishment of a revolutionary-minded regime. Furthermore, not only in Moscow but also in Belgrade, Cairo, and elsewhere, particularly after the Arab-Israeli war of 1967, the impression that the Johnson administration had been using the détente not to preserve international stability but to mount a cleverly conceived political offensive against Soviet and radical nationalist positions all over the world achieved widespread acceptance. The Dominican affair, the ousters of President Sukarno in Indonesia and of João Goulart in Brazil, the fall of Kwame Nkrumah in Ghana, the overthrow of Mohammed Ben Bella in Algeria, the Greek military takeover, and finally the Israeli attack upon Egypt appeared to many in Moscow as part of an overall United States design. Gamal Abdul Nasser complained openly in Cairo that the chief danger to peace and progress was the absence of any force that could deter or contain the United States, while the Italian Communist journal *Rinascita* flatly claimed that the Johnson administration was pursuing a cleverly concealed "rollback" policy:

> For the policy of the *status quo* and the attempts to divide the world into zones of influence between the two superpowers, U.S. imperialism is gradually substituting a revised and corrected reedition of the old policy of *rollback,* giving birth, within the framework of nuclear coexistence with the USSR (caused by reasons of *force majeure*), to a series of local interventions (economic, political, military) designed to modify the world equilibrium by means of setting up reactionary regimes, or by support given to them, and by liquidating the progressive forces and movements in individual countries.[1]

Only in the Middle East, where Khrushchev's successors embarked upon a bold effort to develop a Soviet sphere of interest in the eastern Mediterranean through the transformation of Egypt into a client state, did it appear that the new leaders were making headway. But this effort also culminated in a debacle of substantial magnitude as the tremendous Soviet investment in Egypt was incinerated by Israel in the lightning six-day war of June 1967. The defeat of Moscow's Arab client states was a humiliating and sobering experience, and it perhaps convinced the Soviet leaders that unless they altered their behavior, they might sink in the morass of defeatism.

The generally defeatist, hesitant, and vacillating mood of the Soviet leadership continued to manifest itself for over a year as Moscow helplessly watched developments in Czechoslovakia (and to a lesser extent in Rumania) approach a climax that could prove catastrophic for the Soviet Union. The Soviet leaders opted at this stage to adapt and adjust to the developing situation in Czechoslovakia, not only out of a sense of responsibility and prudence but also out of fear of the consequences of forcible Soviet intervention, particularly if it were to fail.

Revival of Self-Confidence

But in the meantime there had been several developments that impelled the Soviet leaders to risk a reversal of their previous pattern of behavior and to act more militantly. First of all, the gap in strategic capabilities between the Soviet Union and the United States had narrowed considerably, thus diminishing the risk of American counteraction. Second, the United States itself was gripped by domestic turmoil that caused President Johnson not to seek a second term, which meant that the United States would be temporarily governed by a lame-duck President less likely to act vigorously in countering Moscow. Third, the U.S. President was psychologically vulnerable because he was anxious to cap his political career by making a state visit to Moscow and was therefore predisposed not to react in a way that might result in the cancellation of his prospective trip. And fourth, the Chinese leadership was involved in a debilitating internal power struggle that deprived it, too, of the capacity to react effectively.

Whereas the Israeli defeat of Egypt in 1967 had had a traumatic impact in Moscow, the successful outcome of the decision to intervene in Czechoslovakia seems to have had an electrifying effect upon the Soviet leaders. Since that time, they have appeared more decisive, self-assured, and confident in the correctness of their judgments. The regime has been considerably strengthened, and although Brezhnev still has his critics and detractors, his position in the leadership has been conspicuously enhanced. The most immediate manifestation of this new self-confidence was the enunciation of the Brezhnev Doctrine wherein Moscow announced in advance that the Soviet Union would no longer tolerate any internal or external challenge to its authority and hegemony in Eastern Europe.[2]

The reassertion of Soviet self-confidence has produced dramatic results in the form of a string of successes in foreign policy since the Czechoslovak occupation, and this has continued to reinforce Soviet self-assurance. The most important practical results have been the reversal by the Brandt government of the Erhard-Kiesinger *Ospolitik* and the halting of the Western policy of "bridge-building" to Eastern Europe with the formal acceptance by the Western powers of the post-World War II East European status quo.[3] Juridically this has been expressed in the two treaties concluded by West Germany with Poland and the Soviet Union, the Quadripartite Agreement on Berlin signed on September 3, 1971, Bonn's instrument of adherence to the Treaty on the Non-Proliferation of Nuclear Weapons, and other related documents.

Although the original reach of the Brezhnev Doctrine has been contracted somewhat to exclude Yugoslavia, the Soviet sphere in Eastern Europe has been largely stabilized, with the defiance of Rumania considerably muted. The reassertion of Soviet confidence may also have been instrumental in impelling the Soviet Union to confront the Chinese militarily on the Ussuri in early 1969—a confrontation which seemingly achieved its immediate aim of frightening the Chinese, but was also instrumental in persuading the Chinese to mend their fences with the United States. Just as the China problem has been an important stimulus to the USSR to reach agreements in the West, the Soviet problem has impelled China to move toward the West as well, given favorable circumstances. To this degree, the Soviet reassertion of confidence may have set in motion patterns of realignment that will have long-range implications.

The revival of Soviet self-confidence has left its imprint not only in Central and Eastern Europe but also in other parts of the world where the Soviet Union has undertaken the commitments of a global power. The decisive nature of Soviet action in Czechoslovakia and its salutary impact (from the Soviet point of view) on West Germany, the United States and NATO, and others, aroused expectations—on the part of Moscow's non-Communist client-states—of more credible Soviet commitments, and these expectations were reciprocated by Soviet willingness to give these commitments formal juridical expression. Thus, during the past year, the Soviet Union has signed no less than three "Treaties of Peace, Friendship and Mutual Assistance" with non-Communist states: Egypt, India and Iraq, in that order. While these treaties are not formal treaties of alliance, they can only be defined as protomilitary alliances, since a common feature is that their provisions are so devised that the stronger party can, if it wishes, come to the assistance of the weaker in accordance with the articles dealing with "mutual consultations" and "appropriate effective measures" in the event of attack or threat of attack. Furthermore, each of these new Soviet treaty partners is the beneficiary of increased Soviet military and economic assistance. In short, the treaties convert all three countries into de jure client-states and de facto protectorates of the Soviet Union.[4]

The treaty with India, moreover, effectively eviscerates the legal remains of the Sino-Soviet military alliance in the event of a Sino-Indian war. Indeed, during the Indo-Pakistan war of late 1971 it was revealed that the Soviet Union engaged in "appropriate effective measures" to deter the Chinese from supplying material assistance to Pakistan, including the discreet movement of Soviet troops along the Chinese border. Conversely, the treaty formally involves India in the Soviet encirclement and containment of China, a matter which will be discussed later in another connection.

The Shifting Strategic Balance

What accounts for this resurgence of self-confidence in the Soviet leadership, and how will it affect future Soviet behavior in world affairs? The first question is easier to answer than the second, because the new horizons created for Soviet foreign policy by the factors which have brought about the recrudescence of Soviet self-assurance are many, and the Soviet leaders themselves remain sharply divided as to whether they should use the occasion to exercise self-restraint and magnanimously agree to choices that would reduce international tensions or to opt for policies designed to exploit to the maximum whatever momentary advantage exists.

In any event, the Soviet leaders appear to have become persuaded, soon after their remarkably smooth operation in Czechoslo-vakia, that the conditions and circumstances that enabled them to act decisively and successfully in that instance were not momentarily fortuitous but represented a condition of flux in the military, politi-cal, and psychological balance of power that would continue for some time. The Soviet reappraisal of power trends since 1968 seems to stress three major elements. First of all, it takes cognizance of the extraordinary growth of Soviet strategic and conventional military capabilities, which has brought the armed strength of the USSR up to rough parity with that of the United States.[5] Second, it sees a cor-responding decline of the relative strategic power of the United States resulting in part from the costs of the Vietnam war and in part from U.S. volitional restraints on further quantitative armaments ex-pansion. Third, it posits an increasing American infirmity of purpose and weakening of will and commitment brought about by domestic turbulence, by racial and generational conflict, and by the social, id-eological, and political polarization that has resulted. What in 1968 appeared to Moscow to be perhaps just a momentary upsurge of public demoralization and disillusionment with the Johnson admin-istration over Vietnam now seems to the Kremlin to have the char-acter of a continuing and more enduring condition.

Among other causes of the revival of Soviet self-confidence, one might mention the resurgence of anti-American revolutionary move-ments, forces and regimes of various hues in the Third World and elsewhere. Although the Soviet reception of such revolutionary movements is mixed because they often represent kaleidoscopic me-langes of sectarian and Peking-inspired groupings that at best may be of marginal value to Soviet policy and sometimes may even be counterproductive, the proliferation of these groups is usually ac-cepted by Soviet strategists as further evidence of the disintegration and dissolution of the fabric of bourgeois and feudal societies.

As a consequence of all these factors, there has been a remarka-ble revitalization of Soviet will and a dramatic expansion of Soviet capabilities. Before World War II, the Soviet leaders possessed the will and were gripped by a fanatic, focalized purpose, but they were bereft of capabilities; after the war they possessed both, but unfortunately for Moscow, the United States possessed even more of both essential ingredients, with the result that for more than two decades the Soviet Union was compelled to play second fiddle to the United States on the world stage. Today, there is little doubt that the Soviet Union, if it cannot boast a clear or even meaningful superiority, is at least no longer second to the United States in strategic weapons capability.[6]

If the old bipolar international system were still functioning, with just two players opposing each other in a dangerous sort of zero-sum game, this development would be cause for grave alarm in an immediate operational sense. But the international system is no longer bipolarized, and power is no longer—if it ever was in its entirety—distributed and redistributed within the context of a zero-sum game. Other powers, particularly China, have assumed a greater importance, and although they are not sufficiently powerful to challenge the two global powers, they are sufficiently influential, individually in some cases and collectively in any event, to seriously alter the balance between the two global giants and thus to function as objective and prescriptive balancing actors.

For this reason, while most members of the world community—with only the clear exception of China—are fundamentally interested in a meaningful rapprochement or détente between the United States and the Soviet Union, they share with the Chinese an opposition to any arrangement that would be tantamount to a condominium or dyarchy, with or without a division of the globe into spheres of influence. Today, at least three secondary power centers (Japan, China, Western Europe) and possibly India are too powerful to be subordinated or assimilated into a sphere of influence of the global powers. The United States and the Soviet Union individually still remain in a distinct class by themselves in terms of power magnitude—possessing together perhaps 90 percent of effective operational strategic power in the international community—and could conceivably impose solutions upon the rest of the world if they were able to act in concert and with a unified will. Such a true dyarchy, however, no longer seems possible, and any attempt by the two global powers to impose solutions on the secondary power centers, increasingly sensitive and alert to any such tendency, could be expected to meet with more intensive and extensive defiance and incur higher costs than previously.

Internal Debate on Global Strategy

These fortuitous changes in the strategic balance create both opportunities and risks for the Soviet leaders. They provide Moscow with a wider range of options, including some that would stabilize the existing situation and reduce international tensions as well as others that would expand Soviet power and influence at the risk of generating greater tensions and dangers. As in the past, these choices can be expected to divide the Soviet leadership, but whereas before 1968 the divisions reflected a condition of relative Soviet strategic inferiority, since 1968 they have revolved around options created by the growth of Soviet power and the contraction of American global commitments. The Kremlin's choices, however, are complicated by the fact that Chinese power has also grown qualitatively during this period. The Soviet Union, unlike the United States, now finds itself vulnerable to nuclear devastation from two directions, and some Soviet leaders tend to see the problem as one of how to take advantage of the new strategic balance while China is still relatively weak. For the Chinese, on the other hand, the question is how to postpone a showdown with the USSR while they are still weak. The immediate resolutions of these interlocking sets of problems have apparently been separate decisions by Moscow and Peking to reduce tensions with the United States. These decisions suggest that both Communist powers no longer see the United States as posing an immediate threat to themselves—or rather that each of them views the other as a greater threat to its own interests than the United States.

The evidence is strong that elements in both the Chinese and Soviet leaderships perceive the lessening threat from the United States as reflecting American decline, although some Soviet commentators warn that the U.S. retreat from globalism, rather than reflecting a crippling of objective potential, is volitional and represents merely a temporary phase of debilitation of will stemming from disappointment and disillusionment over the costs, both domestic and foreign, of trying to police the world. Given the immense industrial and technological capacity of the United States, according to this view, the situation could once again change very quickly if the American public should become sufficiently aroused to resume the arms race. Hence, there have been powerful voices in and around the Soviet leadership arguing that the time is ripe for a stabilization of the arms race at current levels, since it would provide Moscow with ample "sufficiency" to pursue its aims without provoking fears in America that might refuel demands for an escalation in U.S. capabilities. These voices still recall with concern the consequences of Khrushchev's irresponsible bluffing in the late 1950s which gave rise to the "missile gap" myth in the United States and the consequent spurt in American strategic capabilities.[7]

Furthermore, a détente with the United States, and with NATO generally, would defuse international tensions, stabilize the status quo in Germany to Soviet advantage, reconfirm Western recognition of Eastern Europe as a Soviet sphere of interest, and open up vast opportunities for expanding trade and commercial relations with the industrial capitalist states. The Soviet leadership is particularly eager to import advanced technology from the United States, especially in the computer realm, and is interested in importing consumer goods which its own economy is unable to deliver in sufficient quantities, as well as entire factory installations. Finally, détente with the United States and the West, in addition to protecting Russia's western flank in the event of a conflict with China, would create the conditions for a shift in economic priorities away from heavy industry and defense to consumer goods, light industry, agriculture, and public services.

The controversy over options in Soviet foreign policy thus merges with the debate over economic priorities. For decades now, the continuing postponement of priorities for the consumer sector has been officially justified in terms of Soviet foreign policy obligations and security considerations. Soviet Premier Kosygin's revelation at the Twenty-fourth Party Congress that the Soviet military establishment had been absorbing about 25 percent of all funds available for economic development over the preceding five years was tantamount to an accusation that development of the consumer sector of the economy was being frustrated by the terrible appetites of the military, whose chief spokesman at the Congress, Defense Minister Marshal A. A. Grechko, demanded an even larger share of the nation's resources as he continued to emphasize that the United States and NATO were plotting aggressive actions and spending huge sums on armaments in order to dictate to the Soviet Union from "a position of strength." [8]

As Soviet policy has tended to become increasingly oriented toward internal constituencies, various groups, institutions, and personalities have become polarized into two competing constellations: a security-productionist-ideological grouping and a consumptionist-agricultural-public services grouping, which take opposite stands with reference to the distribution of investments, resources, and expenditures on the basis of their conflicting assumptions and/or expectations concerning the likelihood of heightened international tensions or of a relaxation cum détente.[9] This issue has agitated the Soviet leadership since Stalin's death, the basic arguments remaining relatively intact as leading political personalities changed sides and exchanged arguments in accordance with their political and factional interests at any given time. Thus, Khrushchev, when he was challenging Georgi Malenkov before 1955, emerged as a leader of the security-productionist-ideological forces against Malenkov, but once he became firmly installed in power after July 1957, he switched over to the consumptionist-agricultural-public services constellation.[10]

By and large, Leonid Brezhnev and Aleksei Kosygin have attempted to steer a middle course between the two principal demand-sector coalitions. Although on balance the military and heavy industry groups appear to have increased their influence in shaping Soviet priorities and their preferences continue to be favored over those of the consumptionists, the regime has compromised the issue by simultaneously supporting both détente abroad and a high level of defense expenditures and priority for heavy industry at home in an endeavor to demonstrate that détente policies need not lead to an immediate reorientation of budgetary priorities detrimental to the interests of the military and heavy industry. However, stepped-up Soviet military commitments to Egypt, stronger political commitments to India, the growing Chinese nuclear capability, the deteriorating situation in Czechoslovakia before August 1968, and the ambivalent character of the defense debate in the United States have all had a part in reinforcing the skepticism of the military and their allies as to the desirability of détente-oriented policies. Furthermore, it is possible that the military's opposition to détente policies is also motivated by expectations of new opportunities for the expansion of Soviet influence as the strategic power balance vis-à-vis the United States becomes more favorable. At the same time, Soviet military leaders apparently perceive that the exploitation of these opportunities will involve risks, and this in turn leads them to keep on pressing for higher margins of safety and hence greater defense expenditures.

The Kremlin's Options

The revival of Soviet self-confidence, the changes in the strategic balance, America's redefinition of its global role, and China's efforts to force her way into the global club have combined to present Moscow with a variety of discrete options in the choice of grand strategy. Some of these, if elected, could plunge the world into a new era of violence, uncertainty, turbulence, and confrontation; others might provide the foundations for mutually agreed-upon adjustments and arrangements of outstanding questions, thus ushering in a long era of negotiation and reduced tensions. Whatever choices are made by the Kremlin, they will inevitably be affected by domestic Soviet interests as well as by the external environment, and all the available options involve both dangers and opportunities for the Soviet leaders. What these options are with primary reference to dealing with the United States on the global strategic level may be briefly summarized as follows:

1. Strategic superiority. This would require the retention of current economic priorities and continuous maximization of Soviet power in order to achieve a permanent, clear-cut superiority over both the

United States and China, individually and jointly. Such a policy would be based upon the assumption that the Soviet Union will be more able than was the United States to convert military muscle into diplomatic and foreign policy gains because Soviet power will be consonant with the rhythm of historical processes whereas U.S. power attempted to arrest and reverse the wheels of history and consequently was crippled by the weight of its own internal contradictions. This policy would, in effect, result in the unilateral assertion by Moscow of a role as "world gendarme" with all that that would imply: threats, intervention, imposition of solutions upon local conflicts, and continuous global surveillance.

2. *Condominium/détente based upon Soviet strategic superiority.* This policy would be similar to the first, except that it would not require the same magnitude of superiority because it would involve a limited détente relationship with the United States. As Moscow would not challenge the security or vital interests of the United States directly, the policy would be less likely to arouse the kind of fears and anxieties that might provoke the American public to support another round in the arms race. In addition, it would envisage expanded commercial contacts with the West, enabling the Soviet Union to exploit the tremendous industrial and technological resources of the capitalist world and thus to lessen the pressures for an immediate shift in internal economic and budgetary priorities; but cultural contacts would remain minimal, and there would probably be a tightening of ideological controls. Finally, this option, which presupposes further and perhaps escalating conflict with China, would permit Moscow to concentrate on the Chinese danger without at the same time forefeiting the right to make gains at the expense of its capitalist American partner at the global level—a right which would be impaired if Moscow were to accept a limited sphere of interest temporarily off limits to Soviet intrusion.

3. *Condominium/détente based upon strategic parity.* This option would more accurately resemble a condominium or dyarchy based upon an authentic détente relationship. Such a policy would involve formal agreements establishing both *quantitative* ceilings and limitations on *qualitative* development and deployment of weapons; furthermore, it

would require agreement on joint measures to keep other powers in check by enforcing the nuclear nonproliferation agreements and obtaining ceilings on the development of capabilities by other nuclear powers (France, Britain, and China). Beyond this, there would be a clear though tacit and indirect demarcation of U.S. and Soviet spheres of influence; joint action would be taken to resolve selected local conflicts; agreements would be devised to allow continuing rivalry in marginal and peripheral areas of the world involving minimal risks of direct confrontation and nuclear war. Most importantly this option—in calling for a wider orbit of cooperation and a more restricted arena of rivalry than does the preceding option—would create the conditions for a drastic shift in Soviet domestic economic and budgetary priorities and a restructuring of the distribution of social and political power in Soviet society; hence, it is vigorously opposed by the Soviet military-industrial complex embracing the military professionals, the defense industries, heavy industry, and key personalities in the party apparatus. Advocates of this policy, on the other hand, wish not only to solve internal economic problems but also to diminish the disproportionate influence of the Soviet military-industrial complex and enhance that of other social and functional institutions and groups in Soviet society. The policy would perhaps allow a wider degree of cultural, educational, and scientific exchanges, but even under this option Moscow would not formally relinquish its broad ideological goals or accept "ideological coexistence" as the basis for agreement.

4. Entente with the United States. An entente would involve radical changes in Soviet attitudes tantamount to agreement on first principles with the United States. It is doubtful that any serious sentiment exists within the inner circles of Soviet power for this option, although some progressive and democratic intellectual groups centering upon individuals like the dissident nuclear physicist Andrei Sakharov advocate what amounts to an entente relationship.[11] Thus, the "democratic movement" in Russia calls not only for administrative reforms designed to enhance efficiency, but also for drastic political and social reforms that would indeed result in the possibility of agreement on first principles with the United States.

5. *Triarchy with the United States and China.* This also is not a likely possibility as it would involve agreement with China, which poses insuperable problems for the Soviet Union. It would entail satisfying not only Chinese national demands against the USSR (on territorial boundaries, for example) but also Peking's demand for parity in the world Communist movement. If agreement could be reached with the Chinese on these two vital issues, Moscow would presumably have little use for a condominium or triarchy of any kind with the United States as Soviet policy could then be founded on Sino-Soviet reconciliation, which would in effect present Moscow with a whole new set of possible options. (As indicated earlier, Soviet options relating primarily to relations with China will be discussed later.)

The Case for Détente-cum-Parity

These, then, are the broad options that have confronted the Soviet leadership in deciding the USSR's global strategy. I have discussed at considerable length elsewhere the views and attitudes of different Soviet groups with respect to some of these options.[12] Suffice it to note here that controversy within the leadership has probably centered on the first three options, and that the debate has apparently tended more and more to narrow down to the second and third—that is, to condominium/détente based on Soviet strategic superiority vs. condominium/détente based on strategic parity. The terms of the strategic arms limitation agreement (SALT) signed in Moscow during President Nixon's recent visit suggest that those in the Soviet leadership who advocate détente based on parity have won out in the internal debate—at least for the time being. It may therefore be useful to take a detailed look at the perceptions that appear to underlie this decision.

Although certain members of the top Soviet leadership—notably Premier Kosygin, President Podgorny, D. S. Poliansky, and G. I. Voronov—can be identified as advocates of the détente-cum-parity position, its most articulate public proponents appear to be the Americanologists in the Soviet Academy of Sciences, the most conspicuous of whom are the two doyens of Soviet Americanology,

Georgi Arbatov, director of the Academy's Institute of the U.S.A.
and N. Inozemtsov, director of the Academy's Institute of World
Economy and International Affairs. The former is also a member of
the Central Auditing Commission, and the latter is a candidate
member of the party Central Committee. Thus, both are members of
the outermost rings of the inner circles of Soviet power and have access to the top decision makers.

In a succession of remarkable and audacious expositions of this
position over the past several years, Arbatov bases his arguments on
a subtle and relatively sophisticated analysis of U.S. domestic and
foreign policy. His analysis is extraordinarily nonpolemical in tone
and marked by pragmatic realism; yet it is framed within orthodox
doctrinal parameters, positing the steady growth of Soviet power on
the one hand and the bankruptcy of U.S. globalism and continued
U.S. domestic turmoil on the other.

Writing in 1970, Arbatov asserted that U.S. globalism based on
the concept of "world gendarme" had failed, but at the same time,
he gave no comfort to the advocates of Soviet superiority when he
emphasized that "no single country can govern worldwide processes." [13] In another roundabout hint that strategic superiority fueled
the arms race and created temptations to engage in actions that undermined the possibility of détente and coexistence, he recited his
version of how President Johnson—at a time when the United States
enjoyed strategic superiority—had converted the policy of "bridge-
building" into a ploy to undermine Soviet authority in the USSR's
own sphere:

> At the time it [i.e., the policy of bridge-building] was an-
> nounced, it could still be regarded by many as a kind of re-
> sponse to the challenge of peaceful coexistence hurled by the so-
> cialist states. It was no accident that, at the outset, it was
> subjected to a fire of criticism by the extreme Right in the
> U.S.A. . . . However, the "bridge-building" policy soon pre-
> sented itself . . . as a platform for extended subversive activity
> aimed at dissolving the socialist commonwealth and undermin-
> ing [its] . . . social system.[14]

In the same article, Arbatov argued that while U.S. global strategy was crumbling and the role of "world policeman" had already been renounced by President Nixon prior to his election to the White House,[15] the collapse of U.S. "globalism" as distinct from its role as a global power not only could create problems for U.S. foreign policy but would confront the Soviet Union and other countries with new, hard choices. The United States, he cautioned, would remain a powerful and formidable power for many years, although its opportunities would progressively diminish. Under these circumstances, Arbatov saw the appropriate Soviet response to be one of continuing to blunt American foreign policy and to deter Washington from residual acts of foreign intervention as the United States retrenched, but at the same time acting to prevent acute local conflicts from escalating or spreading. "The matter at issue," he wrote, "is essentially that of further limiting the freedom of action of imperialism—above all, U.S. imperialism." [16]

More than a year later, in May 1971, Arbatov emphasized the increasing impact of domestic conflict and disturbances as a factor restraining U.S. foreign policy and suggested that a new strategic balance was taking shape as a result of this in combination with the growth of Soviet power:

> The past five-year period confronted imperialism, including American imperialism, with new realities—above all a further change in the alignment of forces between the two world social and economic systems in favor of socialism. Throughout the past few years, this process has grown in two ways, so to speak. It has proceeded both through the further strengthening of the positions of the Soviet Union, the other socialist countries and the international workers' and liberation movements, and through the serious exacerbation of the internal contradictions in the imperialist camp itself.[17]

The United States was thus being forced to adjust to the new strategic equation, and Arbatov went on to pose the logical question: "How should the attempts of the imperialist bourgeoisie to adapt to the new world situation be treated?"

Arbatov's counsel was both measured and prudent. He gingerly warned against resorts to threats and force to take advantage of the situation and explicitly advocated that the Soviet Union should respond positively to any realistic adjustments the United States sought to make in order to ameliorate its difficulties, even though such a course might be attacked by unnamed quarters as "reformist" or "revisionist":

> . . . it does not at all follow from this [new strategic balance] that elements of realism in the domestic and foreign policies of the capitalist powers have no importance and should be rejected on the ground that such attempts express an endeavor to preserve imperialism, to prevent new shocks and political failures for imperialism. Needless to say, any concessions by imperialism, any steps in the direction of adapting to the existing situation, objectively express this kind of class interest of the bourgeoisie. But such steps signify forced concessions under the pressure of the forces of peace and progress and objectively can have consequences that correspond to the people's interests. . . . The peoples of socialist states are by no means indifferent to the direction in which international relations develop—in the direction of preparations for thermonuclear war or in the direction of the peaceful coexistence of states and a political detente which, of course, does not abolish the struggle between the two systems itself but moves it into channels in which this struggle does not lead to military conflict. The significance of these distinctions was emphasized by V. I. Lenin, who pointed out that one should take different attitudes toward those representatives of the bourgeois camp who "gravitate toward the military resolution of questions" and toward those who "gravitate toward pacifism, even if they are of the very worst sort and, from the standpoint of communism, cannot withstand even the slightest criticism." [18]

But perhaps the most ambitious and elaborate examination of the preconditions for, and general configuration of, a détente based on strategic parity was provided by Arbatov in November 1971. Hailing the projected visit of President Nixon to Moscow as a "positive act," he noted:

The possibility of the normalization of Soviet-American relations, just as the sphere of such normalization, is determined by the interests of the two states. If spheres of common interests exist, normalization is possible. If there are no such spheres, it will be impossible to achieve normalization. How do things stand in this case? Are there problems whose solution would be in the interests of the Soviet Union and the U.S.A. and at the same time would not be contrary to the legitimate interests of other countries? There certainly are.[19]

As the "most important" of these problems, Arbatov listed "the prevention of nuclear war," stating that everybody, including "most representatives of the ruling circles" in America, considers thermonuclear war "a 'useless' instrument of policy." This common foundation of concern, he argued, establishes the basis not only for a "normalization" of relations but for a détente as well. Alluding to previously signed U.S.–Soviet agreements designed to reduce the possibility of accidental or unauthorized employment of nuclear weapons, including the "hot line" agreement and its various refinements, Arbatov advocated further measures that would involve closer Soviet-American collaboration in order to reduce the possibility of inadvertent confrontation as a result of incremental escalation:

There is another danger that is less noticeable and therefore perhaps more serious: Even if they do not deliberately want a world thermonuclear war, states may be drawn into serious conflicts whose escalation at some point may get out of control and make war unavoidable. This danger can be prevented only if there is a radical improvement in the international situation.[20]

That the Soviet leaders already accept the wisdom of this view was demonstrated by their refusal to be dragged into a confrontation with the United States over the mining of the Haiphong harbor on the eve of President Nixon's visit to the Soviet Union. When asked at a Moscow lecture on the President's visit why the Soviet navy did not sweep the mines, V. S. Glagolev, a Soviet specialist on arms control, replied that "the sweeping of mines takes a great deal of time, and furthermore *such action on our part would greatly aggravate the situation.*" [21]

In his November 1971 article, Arbatov went on to cite the recent Soviet and Polish treaties with Bonn as examples of settlements which defused crisis situations and relaxed tensions. His general implication was that particular situations, such as that in the Middle East for example, could be defused without the necessity of a substantive or definitive settlement:

> Not to stop with what has been achieved, not to rest content with an unstable equilibrium between peace and war, but to seek a more stable foundation for strengthening peace and international security—this is an important common interest of the Soviet and American peoples, as well as of all the other peoples in the world. If this interest finds proper reflection in U.S. policy, the sphere of possible cooperation in international affairs will be expanded considerably. Within the framework of the overall normalization of the international situation, we must extinguish the hotbeds of international crises in the Near East and Southeast Asia, take new steps to improve the situation and set up a reliable security system in Europe, and create conditions precluding the possible outbreak of new crisis situations. Only in this way can really durable guarantees of peace be created.[22]

Arbatov further cited the termination or limitation of the arms race as lying within the sphere of common U.S.–Soviet interest. Emphasizing the onerous drain on economic and financial resources for both countries, he asserted that these political goals are becoming ever more attainable in our era. Then, shifting from "normalization" to more positive measures of "détente," Arbatov stressed that "expansion of commercial, economic, scientific, and technical cooperation can be an important sphere of common interest for the USSR and the U.S.A." and offered these vistas of potential cooperative endeavor:

> In conditions of détente, broad possibilities would open up for cooperation in such spheres as the development of science, the utilization of natural resources of the oceans, the struggle against pollution of the natural environment, etc.[23]

It should be noted, however, that in all of his analyses Arbatov stresses the difficult task of reaching agreement on specific points and issues and warns that "it would be unrealistic to close one's eyes to the very serious obstacles blocking improvement of Soviet-American relations." Understandably enough, he points in particular to "influential forces in the U.S.A. that oppose such an adjustment and are trying to drag the country back to the time of the 'cold war,' " but needless to say, he could also have mentioned the "influential circles" in the Soviet Union, including the Soviet military-industrial complex, that would like to resume the cold war under conditions of Soviet strategic superiority.

It should further be noted that Arbatov is careful to base his prescriptions on the line laid down by Brezhnev at the Twenty-fourth Party Congress, thus indirectly invoking the authority of the party General Secretary:

> As for the Soviet Union's position, our line was clearly set forth by L. I. Brezhnev, General Secretary of the CPSU Central Committee, at the 24th CPSU Congress: "We proceeded from the premise that the improvement of relations between the USSR and the U.S.A. is possible. Our principled line with respect to the capitalist countries, including the U.S.A., is consistently and fully to implement in practice the principles of peaceful coexistence, to develop mutually advantageous ties and—with those states that are ready to do so—to cooperate in the field of strengthening peace, making mutual relations with these states as stable as possible." [24]

The Brezhnev statement quoted by Arbatov ended with a cautionary declaration that the Soviet Union, while seeking détente with the United States, would still have "to consider whether we are dealing with a real desire to settle questions at the negotiating table or with an attempt to pursue a 'positions of strength' policy." Similarly, although the results of President Nixon's visit to Moscow would appear to confirm that a majority of the Soviet leadership has accepted détente based on strategic parity rather than on Soviet superiority, it must be remembered that there are powerful elements in the Soviet hierarchy that are undoubtedly still wedded to the goal of superiority, as expressed in the following statement by a Soviet military writer in 1969:

> . . . Vladimir Ilyich taught that one must pay the closest attention to the enemy's possibilities, study his strong and weak points, and carefully weigh the balance of forces. "Everyone will agree," V. I. Lenin wrote, "that the army that does not train itself to master all types of weapons, all means and methods of struggle that the enemy has or may have is behaving unwisely or even criminally" (vol. 41, p. 81). . . . Here special attention should be given to the words "may have." This means that it is necessary to evaluate the military, economic and scientific potential of a possible enemy on the basis of a careful study both of the existing situation and of realistic prospects. *Only with such a sober and scientific approach can one outline the correct path to the achievement of superiority over the enemy in the balance of forces.*[25]

Moscow's Two Worlds

So far we have focused our attention on Soviet–United States interaction and Moscow's strategic policy options primarily in relation to the United States. But Soviet interaction with the United States takes place in only one of the two international environments in which the Soviet Union operates, i.e., the general interstate system and the parallel world system of Communist states and parties. The network of fourteen Communist states constitutes a subsystem within each of the two international environments, and thus cuts across the two. Indeed, from the Soviet point of view, the present group of Communist states represents the vanguard of a universal system of such states which will eventually displace the existing international order made up of Communist and non-Communist states poised in varying degrees of protracted coexistence.

While this is the theory, that theory has in recent years foundered on the shoals of both logic and national interests. The world Communist movement has become transformed from an instrument of Soviet foreign policy, first, into an arena of conflict, controversy, and debate among Communist states and parties, and second, into a distinctive international environment in which the Soviet

Union and other Communist states must act and react. Instead of assuming the contours of a placid and harmonious community in accordance with the idyllic visions of "socialist internationalism," this distinctive Communist environment now functions increasingly like a microcosmic international countersystem akin to the general interstate system it has penetrated and seeks to displace. Organized into nation-states or national Communist parties that are proto- or potential Communist states, the Communist world, in faithful reproduction of the general international order, is divided along developmental, racial, and geographical lines, structured vertically rather than horizontally, and organized hierarchically rather than laterally, with the Soviet Union at the apex. Furthermore, it is polarized by great-power rivalries, spheres of influence, and constellations of client-states and parties, and it is regulated by an internal balance-of-power mechanism. Its principal mark of distinction from the existing order it seeks to replace is the ideological and sociopolitical content of its constituent states.

Curiously enough, the Soviet Union increasingly occupies essentially identical positions in both international environments, and its behavior in one environment inevitably creates perturbations and reverberations in the other, as imperatives and responsibilities generated in each tend to come into collision, forcing the Soviet leaders to establish priorities not only within environments but between them as well. The contradictory imperatives stem from the fact that in the Communist environment the challenging power is China, whereas in the general interstate system Moscow's principal rival is the United States.

Recently, the situation in both environments has become even more seriously complicated for the Soviet leaders because China has now burst out of the confines of the Communist environment and is demanding recognition and a role as a third global power in the general international system. This means that the Soviet Union is now challenged by two global powers: by the United States in one environment, and by China in two.

In dealing with the Chinese, the Soviet leaders have failed to exude the self-confidence that they have evinced in dealing with the

Americans. Indeed, they have periodically given vent to outbursts of irrationality and desperation where China has been concerned. The reasons transcend the mere fact that China shares a 4,000-mile-long frontier with the Soviet Union and that her 800 million population presses down like an oppressive incubus upon the Soviet psyche. More important, the Chinese constitute an inside threat to Soviet power and ambition because China is part of the socialist common-wealth and challenges Moscow's legitimacy and power within the world of Communist states and parties as well as in the overall inter-national system. For example, Peking cannot be credibly termed an interloper in the Kremlin's ideological garden, which is roughly con-gruent with the Soviet Union's regional sphere of influence. Hence, while Soviet leaders have had a fair amount of success in employing non-Communist states like India as means of countering the Chinese challenge, they have been less successful in achieving this purpose by using the Communist states, which frown on the notion of intra-Communist ideological and military coalitions arrayed against one another. Only Mongolia (which shares a common border with both China and the USSR and fears engulfment by the Chinese) and oc-cupied Czechoslovakia have signed military alliances which could be invoked in the event of a Sino-Soviet war; moreover, all attempts by Moscow to read China out of the world Communist movement or to transform the Warsaw Treaty Organization into a potential anti-Pe-king alliance have thus far been unsuccessful.[26] Broadly speaking, then, the Chinese challenge within the Communist camp continues to cripple Russia's consolidation of control over Eastern Europe, as well as over nonruling Communist parties elsewhere, and it has been instrumental in facilitating the erosion of the Soviet Union's ideolog-ical legitimacy and in forcing her to behave more like an imperial rather than an ecumenical power.

The Dual Threat of China

Thus, of all the states in the international system, only China today poses a direct threat to the Soviet territory and at the same time is in a position to threaten the Soviet Union with means other than nuclear weapons. The American threat to the Soviet Union has always exhibited a synthetic, abstract quality at the olympian level of strategic and global rivalry: U.S. and Soviet troops have never clashed, and neither country has territorial demands against the other. Their rivalry has mainly been one for "world leadership" as champions of contending ideological social systems. And in this contention the Soviet leaders have derived comfort and sustenance from their belief that, no matter how powerful the United States, the civilization and social order that it represents are in the long run historically obsolete, that no matter how protracted and erratic the contest, history and the dialectic will at some point catch up with the United States, and it will inevitably enter into a period of decline and social dissolution.

But the same historical and ideological convictions that sustain the Soviet leaders in their rivalry with the United States have tended to produce irresolution, ambivalence, and cognitive inadequacy in their approach to China, for the ideological prism that they employ to perceive the world provides them with little or no guidance about how to cope with those who use the identical prism but perceive a different rainbow. The Chinese subscribe to the same convictions as the Soviets, yet their prognosis for "Soviet revisionism" is remarkably similar to some of the Soviet predictions of doom for "American imperialism." Moreover, the Soviet leaders view China not as a declining power, but as an ascending one; and their awareness of the tremendous material and human potential of China, combined with their inherent faith in the inevitability of growth and development, can only create in their minds the ineluctability of Chinese paramountcy if they continue to subscribe to their own doctrinal postulates. Thus, their ideological presuppositions lend credence to their visceral fear that Peking's claim to future world hegemony may be stronger and perhaps more warranted by history than their own. Chinese efforts to move the epicenter of the international Communist movement, which the Soviets regard as the historical vehicle for the future transformation of the world, from Moscow to Peking have further stoked this fear. According to one Soviet commentator,

> The course of the "great leap" pursued the ambitious goal of taking a vanguard position among the socialist countries. This

appealed to Maoist hegemonic aspiration. . . . No matter what ultrarevolutionary phraseology was used to cover up this course, its essence remained unchanged . . . to establish hegemony in a world devastated by war. . . .

It [Peking] would like, in implementing its plans, to use the military and economic might of the socialist countries, the strength of the international working class and the possibilities of the national liberation movement, striving to turn these factors into tools of its great power hegemonism. . . . It sees the Soviet Union, the policy of the CPSU . . . as the main obstacle to the implementation of its hegemonic aspirations in the international arena.[27]

Furthermore, as a result of these historical and ideological beliefs, the Soviet leaders have seemed to assume that China's baffling, obstinate, and persistent hostility toward the USSR reflects a Chinese conviction that Soviet power will eventually be destroyed or subjugated to Chinese hegemony on the road to the final Armageddon with imperialism.[28] This assumption, in turn, has caused the Soviet leaders increasingly to regard the military and strategic components of the "balance of forces" between Moscow and Peking as critically important.

Looking at the Soviet position vis-à-vis China from another angle, one can see that Soviet advocates of détente with the United States based on strategic parity have a powerful ideological argument to support that policy, but that the same argument collapses when applied to China. The argument is that strategic parity with the United States is sufficient to achieve Soviet aims and purposes because the natural movement of world social, political, and historical processes is in tune with Soviet goals and because, given a constant military equilibrium, any alterations in the overall "correlation of forces" can only be in a direction detrimental to the U.S. position. It holds further that strategic parity is sufficient to deter any attempts by the United States to intervene in order to arrest or reverse these processes (as was possible under conditions of U.S. superiority), although on the Soviet side it may mean foregoing the option of intervention (i.e., "export of revolution") designed to force or accelerate revolutionary transformations in marginal situations. All these assumptions become implausible, however, in dealing with Peking. Seen from the perspective of the Soviet leaders, China—unlike the United States, which is viewed as a powerful capitalist industrial nation in a state of decline and on the brink of being consumed by its own developing internal contradictions—is an underdeveloped giant on the rise. Furthermore, and most critical, China's visions and purposes are also in tune with the social and revolutionary processes of history, and while the unfolding of the historical dialectic may be to the detriment of the United States, China will inevitably share some of the benefits. Hence, in its confrontation with China, Moscow cannot rely on the assumption that revolutionary forces in the world operate solely to Soviet advantage, for though the "correlation of forces" may enhance the Soviet position vis-à-vis the United States, it may simultaneously weaken Moscow's posture vis-à-vis China.

For the moment, the Soviet leaders can safely accept strategic parity with the United States by freezing weapons at current levels and still enjoy considerable superiority with respect to China. However, some Soviet leaders undoubtedly feel that such a freeze will inevitably create conditions which will allow China to improve its relative military position. This is more crucial for Moscow than for Washington, for while China is in no position to use its developing military capability directly against American targets, it can employ both conventional forces and strategic weapons against the Soviet Union. As a consequence, the Soviet leaders will probably continue to be concerned about erosion of their relative strategic power as long as it remains frozen by agreement with the United States—unless China in the future also enters into arms control agreements placing a ceiling on her military capabilities.

Options Vis-à-vis Peking

What options, then, do the Soviet leaders have in dealing with the Chinese problem? Hypothetically, there are at least three, conceptualized as follows: (1) reconciliation, (2) annihilation, and (3) pragmatic adaptation.

The avowed Soviet preference is *reconciliation,* and there is no doubt that the Soviet Union is willing to make a number of compromises and concessions to achieve it, although so far all these efforts have failed. Apparently, there are factions and influential individuals in and around the Chinese leadership who favor some sort of limited reconciliation with Moscow in preference to rapprochement with the United States, and the Soviet rulers doubtless continue to hope that the death of Mao Tse-tung may bring to the fore new Chinese leaders who would prefer to select the United States rather than the Soviet Union as the "main" or "immediate" enemy. But the Soviet leaders seem to entertain no illusion that any reconciliation would be more than limited and temporary in essence, reflecting the current calculation of some Chinese leaders that China's immediate interest would be better served by colluding with Russia against America rather than the other way around. Still, they would probably accept even a temporary reconciliation as a welcome respite.

On the Chinese side, however, Mao Tse-tung and Chou En-lai are apparently persuaded that under existing conditions, with Soviet power on the upswing and U.S. power on the decline, a Soviet embrace might be more perilous than continued hostility. Furthermore, they recognize that China's leverage with Moscow against the United States is rapidly diminishing, particularly since they believe that the United States is now retrenching and withdrawing from the Asian mainland. Finally, just as the Soviet leaders are determined never again to accept strategic inferiority vis-à-vis the United States, Mao Tse-tung is equally determined that China will never again play second fiddle to Russia in the world Communist movement, and since the Soviet Union is clearly unwilling to accept "parity" with China and China does not possess sufficient capability to assert equality with the Soviet Union in the Communist movement unilaterally, the necessary prerequisite for a reconciliation appears to be absent.

This leads to the second possible option, *annihilation*—i.e., the destruction of China's military capability, especially nuclear and strategic. This option apparently was pressed vigorously by some elements in the Soviet military shortly after the successful invasion of

Czechoslovakia and the enunciation of the Brezhnev Doctrine. Sentiments in favor of administering the Chinese a "bloody nose," as well as the notion of a "surgical strike" to arrest or destroy China's burgeoning nuclear arsenal, became quite current in Soviet circles. But cooler heads prevailed, and Soviet action in the 1969 border conflict on the Ussuri was kept at a level sufficient to provide a warning "lesson" for the Chinese. However, now that China possesses a modest nuclear arsenal and has developed intermediate-range missiles capable of reaching major urban and industrial centers in the USSR, the risks of a Soviet preventive attack have escalated, and annihilation is no longer a viable hypothetical option. The Soviet leaders must thus learn to live with and adjust to the reality of growing Chinese nuclear and missile power and must seek other means to deter the Chinese from attempting to employ that power against the Soviet Union.

This leads to the third option, *pragmatic adaptation,* which of course may cover a wide range of specific policies, depending upon conditions and circumstances. Currently, Soviet strategy toward China appears to involve four separate but interrelated links. The first is a policy of encirclement and containment involving primarily non-Communist powers, the chief of which is India. Moscow would also like to involve Japan in its encirclement strategy now that it can no longer count on the United States as a tacit partner. The second link is an effort to forge an effective, if initially selective, anti-Chinese coalition within the Communist system of states. So far only Czechoslovakia and Mongolia have been recruited, but the Soviet effort will continue.

The third link is active Soviet reinvolvement in Southeast Asia and stepped-up assistance to North Vietnam. But North Vietnam poses a problem for both Communist giants, who have successively caused concern in Hanoi as each in turn welcomed Nixon to its capital while pledging its own undying support of North Vietnam and charging the other with designs for a "sellout." In both summit episodes, the North Vietnamese have tried to complicate matters by deliberately escalating the war and compelling President Nixon to retaliate, hoping that this would create sufficient embarrassment, first in Peking and later in Moscow, either to cause them to cancel their invitations to the President or to cast a pall over the negotiations. Both Communist giants, however, apparently felt that they had their own fish to fry and gave Mr. Nixon's visits higher priority in their respective calculations than they gave to the feelings of North Vietnam. Since both Moscow and Peking welcomed the U.S. President, neither could gain any advantage over the other in Hanoi on this issue. And since North Vietnam is dependent upon the Soviet Union and China for its military supplies it is hardly in a position to threaten them, individually or collectively.

Moscow's decision virtually to ignore the mining of Haiphong harbor and other North Vietnamese ports and to extend a warm welcome to President Nixon was a signal to Hanoi that a détente with the United States and the Western powers was of more vital interest to the Soviet leaders than the specific character or degree of Hanoi's victory. As Moscow views the situation, the United States has already conceded virtual defeat in Vietnam and is merely seeking an "honorable" exit, while the North Vietnamese are only delaying the inevitable U.S. withdrawal because of the specific character of the victory they seek. As far as Moscow is concerned, this is a luxury for which Hanoi must be prepared to pay, and the Soviet Union has shown, by receiving President Nixon, that it will not allow Hanoi to complicate its larger design. The initial reassertion of Soviet interest in Vietnam after Khrushchev's ouster was clearly designed to prevent Hanoi from falling completely under Chinese influence, and it is not likely that Moscow anticipates that North Vietnam, once the war is over, will join Moscow's Chinese encirclement strategy. Instead, Hanoi will probably continue to play its two Communist allies off against one another—and perhaps even engage in its own version of "collusion" with the United States.

The fourth and final link in the Soviet leaders' current China policy is détente with the United States and the West. This détente, which encompasses the new treaties with West Germany, means in effect U.S. and West German acceptance of the East European status quo, and it also creates at the very least a foundation for defusing and managing Soviet-American conflict over the Arab-Israeli question. The détente thus serves to stabilize and secure the Soviet western flank and ipso facto strengthens the Soviet Union's strategic position in dealing with a hostile China. Détente with the West is therefore one of the main ingredients—together with the USSR's quasi-military treaty with India, its anti-Chinese alliances with Czechoslovakia and Mongolia, and continued assistance to North Vietnam in order to at least neutralize Hanoi in the Moscow-Peking conflict—in the Soviet leaders' current policy of pragmatic adaptation to China's growing power.

For the long run, Moscow no doubt hopes for an amelioration of the China situation, either through changes in the Peking leadership and the assertion of authority by new generations, or through more "responsible" Chinese behavior as a result of growth and development. But should this not occur, the Soviet leaders envisage that there will be sufficient basis for Moscow to form a common front against China with other major powers in the world, who will presumably become increasingly threatened as China's development extends her strategic reach to all corners of the globe. The Soviet leaders probably anticipate that at some future date China may become the single most powerful state in the world, but surely not sufficiently mighty to overwhelm all the others combined. This also suggests that at some future point the disparate policies which Moscow has been pursuing in the Third World, in Western Europe, with the United States, and elsewhere will be merged and unified. For the time being, the Russians will continue to operate on the dual track of global power and revolutionary power, but at some point these two may be brought into inevitable conflict as Moscow attempts to mobilize both Communist and non-Communist countries against the Chinese threat.

The Impact of De-Bipolarization

In all this it is apparent that the Soviet leaders have had to revise their strategic thinking drastically as a consequence of the new triangulation of world politics. Originally, they evidently anticipated that a change in the strategic balance between the United States and the USSR would merely alter the power relationship between the two global powers. Thus, it would greatly increase the Soviet Union's freedom of action around the world. But things did not turn out as Moscow expected, for the shift in the strategic balance altered the entire international landscape by encouraging China and the United States to move toward a rapprochement. This rapprochement can be viewed as stemming from the virtually simultaneous realization in Peking and Washington that existing Sino-American animosity strengthened Moscow's hand with both of them, and that, correspondingly, a rapprochement would diminish and even in some respects nullify Soviet gains flowing from the changing balance of power.

From the standpoint of the Soviet leaders, the conversion of the bilateral Soviet-Chinese and Soviet-American relationships, in which the USSR was either clearly the strongest party or on the way to becoming the stronger party, into a triangular relationship has served to reduce the relative leverage of the Soviet Union with respect to both China and the United States, for it has restricted the options and latitude of action that they would have enjoyed in a bipolar or a double-bipolar situation. President Nixon's visit to Peking, in short, has tended to limit whatever gains the Soviet Union made as a result of the change in the strategic balance. In fact, the Soviet leaders were fearful, at least for a time, that Washington and Peking might conspire and collaborate against Moscow, and their fears received wide and repeated articulation in the Soviet press. It should be underscored, however, that the Soviet apprehension was not that a Washington-Peking axis threatened Soviet security or interests directly, but rather that it would ultimately rob Moscow of the possible fruits of strategic parity or superiority.

The impact of the triangulation of global politics is perhaps most readily visible in the Asian context, for it was there that Moscow appears to have entertained the greatest hopes of capitalizing on its new strategic position to expand its influence and to cut China down to size. Let us, therefore, explore the Asian situation briefly.

Before the dramatic escalation in Soviet military capabilities, it seemed clearly in the Soviet interest to keep the United States involved on the Asian mainland for the short term. Indeed, the Kremlin leaders initially sought to use the United States as a tacit part of an encirclement and containment strategy for dealing with China. That strategy relied upon the continuation of China's diplomatic isolation, in which Sino-American animosity played the key role. What enabled Moscow to think in such terms, of course, was the fact that Washington's pursuit of a policy of isolating and containing China placed the Soviet and American positions in tandem—something that the Chinese leaders recognized quite well, as their repeated denunciations of Soviet-American collusion against China demonstrated.

But after the USSR had accomplished its military buildup, Moscow's interests, while not altogether clear, seemed to lie in a quick American departure from Asia. The buildup had already put the USSR in a position to take advantage of a number of situations on the Asian continent to enhance its influence, as the subsequent course of events in South Asia proved. With the United States gone from the region, the Soviet Union would plainly be the most powerful state there, and this circumstance might in itself suffice to persuade Asian states fearful of Chinese hegemonic aspirations to scramble under the protective umbrella of an Asian security system, a scheme which the Soviet leaders have advanced on a number of occasions. The American-sponsored SEATO might thus give way to a Soviet counterpart.

To Moscow, the enunciation in 1969 of the "Nixon Doctrine" and its specific application to Southeast Asia, the policy of "Vietnamization," appeared to be a major step in the desired direction, for the Soviet leaders perceived the action as a signal of U.S. intent to withdraw militarily from the Asian mainland and to allow local conflicts to become indigenized and subject to resolution without benefit of American intervention or involvement. However, the Chinese discerned similar implications, and while one of their more obvious goals has been to expel all external intruders from East Asia and they have consequently welcomed the U.S. policy of indigenization of Asian conflicts, they obviously felt that the premature withdrawal of the United States might simply redound to the advantage of the Soviet Union as long as the latter chose to assert itself as an Asian power. For this reason, they not only have endeavored to reach a measure of understanding with the United States but have shown remarkable patience regarding the American timetable of withdrawal, including the ambiguous matter of the continuing U.S. presence on Taiwan.

The Soviet leaders, then, foresee the possibility that instead of being able to translate their new prowess into political gains in Asia, they will be prevented from doing so by the Sino-American rapprochement. One Soviet commentator has expressed the matter thus:

> Outwardly, the Chinese leadership appears uncompromising in its assertion that the affairs of Asia should be settled by Asians, the affairs of Europe by Europeans, and the affairs of Africa by Africans. It may seem that Peking is really concerned over defending the national interests of the peoples and states of Asia, Europe and Africa against "the superpowers' interference." But here, too, this is only camouflage. In proclaiming the slogan, "Give Asians the opportunity to settle their own affairs and eliminate the dominance of the 'superpowers' in Asia," the PRC leadership hopes that China, as the largest power on the continent, will be able to impose its will and solutions on the Asian peoples.
>
> In this respect, the contacts between unofficial American representatives and Chinese leaders in preparing the ground for Nixon's visit to the PRC are indicative. Mao Tse-tung, in an interview with the American journalist E. Snow in December 1970, gave a positive evaluation of the "Vietnamization" policy. According to E. Snow, high-ranking officials in China said that Nixon is "withdrawing from Vietnam and Asia." They saw this as an opportunity to restore the grandeur of the Middle Kingdom and the Asian people's vassal dependence on China.[29]

The Japanese Enigma

The rising power of Japan introduces another complex element into the new triangular configuration of world politics. Japan remains an enigma for the Soviet Union as much as for the Chinese. Both Moscow and Peking respect Japan's mighty industrial and technological base and fear her military potential should the restraining influence of the United States be withdrawn or jettisoned. In immediate terms, both Peking and Moscow recognize that Japan could become the dominant power in East Asia virtually overnight should she choose to transform her tremendous industrial and technological capability into a military one. Each would like to use Japan as a counterpoise against the other, without at the same time exposing itself to manipulation by Tokyo. The Sino-American rapprochement having ruptured a vital link in Moscow's chain of encirclement around China, Japan could become an acceptable surrogate, and in a sense her cooperation would be indispensable to Moscow's design. On the other hand, a Sino-Japanese rapprochement could be disastrous for the USSR in East Asia as such a combine might conceivably force the Soviet Union out of the area, or force it to maintain massive military formations there, draining the Soviet economy and depriving Moscow of the will and energy to pursue global policies elsewhere.

Thus, the diminution of American strategic power, instead of simply creating unambiguous advantages for the Soviet Union, confronts Moscow not only with greater opportunities but greater dangers as well. The most frightening of these dangers might be a Soviet Union faced with a united Europe in the West and a Sino-Japanese coalition in the East, which could effectively and perhaps even permanently seal Soviet power within its present boundaries and create the conditions for its contraction and dissolution in its own developing contradictions. Much of this is sheer fantasy—for the Soviet leaders, no doubt, nightmarish fantasies—but Soviet commentators, particularly those who have since 1966 been vocally articulating the fantasy of a Sino-American rapprochement, are now fantasizing along these lines. One recent article put it this way:

> Recently Chou En-lai stated that the Common Market is the "first step on the road to an independent Europe." Peking warmly welcomes Britain's entry into the Common Market.

. . . This position on the part of the Chinese leaders indicates that they are eager to see a united "Europe for the Europeans" as a counterweight to the Soviet Union and as their possible partner.[30]

China, of course, has comparable fantasies concerning Japan, but fantasies based on concrete historical memories, not simply nightmares. A Soviet-Japanese rapprochement in conjunction with a Soviet-Indian partnership in the South could vitally cripple China's ambition to function on the world stage as a global power. But there are formidable barriers to a Soviet-Japanese rapprochement—some trivial, some symbolic, and others of substantial magnitude.

The first is the territorial issue arising from Japanese demands for the return by the USSR of three small islands off the coast of northern Hokkaido. These islands are of little or no strategic value to the Soviet Union, nor do they contain any important resources. Nevertheless, they have assumed great symbolic and psychological importance for Japan, and the issue continues to agitate Soviet-Japanese relations, having been responsible most recently for Japanese refusal to undertake projects involved in the development of Soviet Eastern Siberia. If the issue did not go beyond Soviet-Japanese relations, there is little doubt that Moscow would willingly relinquish the islands in return for a dramatic improvement in relations. But Tokyo's territorial demands are psychologically connected with other territorial demands against the USSR. In fact, Mao Tse-tung himself, in an interview with a group of Japanese visitors, not only agreed that Japan's claim to the islands was justified, but proceeded to associate Japan's territorial claims with those of Finland, Poland, East Germany, Czechoslovakia, Rumania, and China against Russia.[31] Thus, Moscow fears that a territorial settlement involving the return of territories to one country would establish a precedent, arouse expectations, and certainly aggravate many of the muted claims against Soviet territory. More importantly, as the Soviet-Chinese border conflict on the Ussuri over Chenpao/Damansky island demonstrated, the territorial issue is a particularly volatile one in Sino-Soviet relations, and a return of some small islands to Japan might serve to reexcite the appetites of the tigers in Peking.

The dilemma of both Communist countries in their attempt to use Japan against the other is that the chief beneficiary of such a policy might be Japan itself. Unlike the United States, Japan is a regional power, and her interests are more intimately connected with the Asian mainland. A strong United States might be a temporary interloper in Asian affairs, but a powerful Japan would be a permanent fixture, with all that that implies. What the Japanese propose to do with their tremendous capability will in large measure determine the responses of the Soviet Union and the Chinese. The tripolar world is still in embryonic form and could easily be aborted before it achieves definitive or even recognizable configuration, if Japan chooses to play a diplomatic and military role in world affairs commensurate with her potential. Should Japan "go nuclear," for example, and succeed through adroit maneuvering in developing a powerful strategic capability, it would seriously alter the overall balance of power and once again force a realignment among the major powers of the world.

The Outlook for Moscow

Confronted by all the manifold complexities of the drastically altered global distribution and alignment of power, how is the Soviet Union likely to behave? Generally speaking, Moscow will probably prefer to continue along prudent and well-worn paths, attempting to retain the main configurations of the bipolar system and refusing to recognize that a tripolar or multipolar system is already here or on the horizon. Now that the Soviet Union has achieved genuine equality with the United States in the international arena, the Russians are loath to debase their newly achieved eminence by accepting China as a global power, since this would mean according China a standing of equality not only in the general interstate system but in the world Communist movement as well.[32]

Thus, the Soviet leaders are likely to try to keep membership in the global club restricted to Moscow and Washington. At the same time, however, they have now recognized the existence of a broader nuclear club than they were previously willing to acknowledge. Such recognition was implicit in Moscow's call, issued at the Twenty-fourth CPSU Congress in April 1971, for the convocation of a conference of the five nuclear powers, including China. Peking, however, has spurned the call and awaits formal recognition as the third global (as opposed to nuclear) power, while simultaneously professing to renounce any such heady ambition.[33]

Meanwhile, Moscow can be expected to keep on refraining from imprudent adventures, but this does not mean that the Soviet leaders do not intend to employ their strategic prowess so as to score diplomatic gains commensurate with the changing strategic balance. Since the United States appears to be ready to make adjustments conforming to the new distribution of power, Moscow will doubtless proceed with the West along the path of limited détente through the negotiation of formal agreements, the postponement of some problems, and limitation of bipower confrontations to certain geographic areas where the vital interests of neither party are likely to become involved. Strategic parity may be sufficient to enable Moscow to make incremental gains in marginal areas of the world, and even marginal gains in more significant regions, particularly in the Middle East at American expense and in South and Southeast Asia at the expense of both the United States and China. Marginal gains may be anticipated in Latin America as well, particularly if more revolutionary regimes of the Allende type come to power constitutionally or extraconstitutionally.

Thus, a prudent Soviet foreign policy is not to be confused with an inert one, but it remains to be seen how successful the Soviet Union will be in converting its new military muscle into diplomatic gains. It should be remembered that the USSR, unlike the United States, is a *revisionist* rather than a *status quo* power, and as long as Soviet revisionist aspirations coincide with the objectives of local revolutionary movements, Moscow may well be able to make more gains with less power than was the United States. For a status quo power simultaneously to deter a powerful revisionary and quash or deter indigenous revolutionary movements around the globe requires clear-cut and overwhelming nuclear superiority, whereas for Moscow to deter intervention designed to quash revolutions requires only parity.

Nevertheless, Soviet adjustment to a de-bipolarized world in which the USSR may be the paramount strategic power will be difficult. The Soviet leaders will be catapulted into a strange world, for they are accustomed in both thought and action to think in terms of bipolarity and zero-sum situations. The world is no longer "we and/or they": a loss in American power is no longer an automatic gain for Moscow. The decline in American power may simply create opportunities for other powers to assert themselves and thus create more rivals and more problems for Moscow to deal with.

Alexander J. Groth

United States Policy Toward Eastern Europe, 1969–73

Before Nixon

When the Nixon administration took office in January 1969, the prospects for improved U.S.–East European relations were heavily overshadowed by recent events in Czechoslovakia. In August 1968, in the midst of the U.S. presidential campaign, the Soviet Union and four other Warsaw Pact members (East Germany, Poland, Hungary, and Bulgaria) had invaded the territory of Czechoslovakia and crushed the liberal-reformist regime of Aleksander Dubček. In the aftermath of this event came the so-called Brezhnev Doctrine, first enunciated by the CPSU general secretary in September 1968, re-serving to the USSR the right of military intervention in order to preserve "socialism" in Eastern Europe, however loosely that might be interpreted.[1] The doctrine was widely believed to signal a resurgence of Soviet toughness in dealing with the former "satellites" of Stalin's day, and was seen as particularly ominous for the regimes of Yugoslavia and Rumania, with whom Moscow had often quarreled.[2] The events connected with the Czechoslovak invasion and the Brezhnev Doctrine had a doubly chilling effect on U.S.–East European relations. Given Soviet nervousness about the loyalties of the so-called People's Democracies, it seemed that East Europe's Commu-nist leaders who wanted to stay in Moscow's good graces would be-ware of developing any overly close ties with Washington. Moreover, the domestic American reaction to the suppression of the Czechoslovak reformers rather discouraged favorable dealings with governments stained, as it were, by the blood of Czechoslovakia's patriots and freedom fighters.

Yet, the balance of trends confronting the United States at the beginning of 1969 was by no means wholly negative and discouraging.

In 1949, with the exception of Yugoslavia, whose defection Stalin was somehow unable to reverse, Soviet hegemony in Eastern Europe seemed undisputed. Each of the governments took its cue from the Kremlin in virtually all its affairs, foreign or domestic. Stalin was the master of Russia, Eastern Europe, and the international Communist movement as well.

But Stalin's death in 1953, the subsequent struggle for succession, the process of de-Stalinization, and the Sino-Soviet dispute all served to promote what might be called the institutionalization of diversity in Eastern Europe. It was followed with varying degrees of alacrity. With some differences in scope and timing, greater freedom of expression was given to artists and writers. Dialogue within the ruling parties and state institutions became more generally tolerated and sometimes encouraged. Police terror was eased if not eliminated. Satisfaction of popular wants underlay a pattern of proposed reforms: decentralization of planning, more incentives to farmers, and more state investment in consumer goods and services were all attempted. Poland, Hungary, Rumania, Albania, and Czechoslovakia all asserted varying degrees of external as well as domestic independence of Moscow.

While the once united Soviet bloc was falling into disarray, economic, social, and political developments in Western Europe bolstered the confidence of our Atlantic allies in their own ability to meet the Soviet threat—if a threat still existed. Indeed, the very fact of polycentrism worked to erode the psychology of insecurity upon which the North Atlantic Treaty Organization (NATO) was based.

Was a Soviet attack on Western Europe still likely? If not, was NATO still necessary in the 1960s? To some, the mere presence of an American nuclear umbrella began to seem adequate security. Was it any longer possible to believe that the interests, aspirations, and policies of the Eastern Europeans were identical? Could Poland, Rumania, and Albania still be regarded as mere bridgeheads for the USSR? The more such questions were raised in the West, the more "polycentric" did all of Europe seem to become. In Rumania, Nicolae Ceausescu seemed an Eastern counterpart of the West's de Gaulle. Their respective attitudes toward the Warsaw Pact and NATO were not dissimilar. The Rumanians refrained from participating in Warsaw Pact military activities from 1964 until 1967, and obliquely questioned its usefulness. The French in 1966 asked for withdrawal of NATO forces from France and saw their wish consummated in the spring of 1967.

General de Gaulle, arguing that East-West antagonisms had become irrelevant and outdated, appealed for a rapprochement between Eastern and Western Europe on the premise of common European interests. The de Gaulle position had sound historical and economic foundations. After all, the iron curtain which Stalin had thrown across Europe separated traditional trading partners from one another and severed age-old cultural links. It could well be regarded as artificial and, in the long run, untenable. Was it not time at last to remove it?

In fact, the Warsaw Pact Political Consultative Committee first proposed a nonaggression pact with NATO at a meeting in Moscow, May 24, 1958. At a subsequent meeting in Moscow on February 4, 1960, it called for an atom-free zone in Europe and cessation of nuclear testing; in March 1961 it endorsed a proposal for universal disarmament. On July 4, 1966, in Bucharest, it had proposed a military détente through the medium of a general East-West Conference on European security.[3]

Judged in terms of such events as ministerial visits, trade missions exchanged, and trade agreements concluded, East-West contacts had been rising in a substantial, one might say, secular, fashion since the 1950s.[4] In the period from 1961 to 1964, for example, there were fourteen trade agreements concluded between Bulgaria and major western states (U.S., U.K., West Germany, France, and Italy) as opposed to only one between 1957 and 1960; Hungary had concluded eight as opposed to two in the earlier period, and Rumania sixteen as compared with just two between 1957 and 1960.

Between 1958 and 1969, the dollar volume of East European trade with Western Europe actually doubled, with some states, such as Bulgaria and Rumania, recording several-fold increases in the magnitude of their Western trade. Between 1962 and 1966 the import of consumer goods from the Western world into Eastern Europe increased almost fourfold.

Despite political conflicts, West Germany in particular reestablished a traditionally strong trading position in Eastern Europe and had won diplomatic recognition from Rumania in 1967, first among the USSR's once so-called satellites.

In the last decade, the Common Market as a whole has been the most important Western trading partner of Eastern Europe, much more so than the United States. Illustratively, where only one-half of one percent of American trade in 1963 was with all the so-called Soviet bloc countries, 3 percent to 5 percent was the average among the EEC nations. Conversely, about 50 percent of the Western trade of Rumania was with the EEC; 45 percent of Bulgaria's; 39 percent of Hungary's; 26 percent of Poland's; and 21 percent of the Soviet Union itself.[5]

East European exports to the Common Market countries rose from $430 million in 1958 to $1.3 billion in 1968; imports from $415 million to $1.58 billion: this was altogether a more than threefold increase in the volume of EEC trade.[6] Nevertheless, where the total volume of trade with the Common Market countries thus reached $2.88 billion, the value of East European trade with the Soviet Union was still three times as much (over $10 billion)—a clear indication of the continuing preponderance of Eastern Europe's new (i.e., post-World War II) Eastern economic orientation.[7] American trade with Eastern Europe rose from virtually nil before 1958 (e.g., $7 million exports and $56 million imports in 1955) to slightly over $400 million in 1968.

While the planned integration of East European economies under the Soviet-led Council of Mutual Economic Assistance

(COMECON or CEMA) lagged, Western manufacturers had been busy installing automobile, tool, and textile plants in Eastern Europe. If, contrary to the aspirations of the COMECON established by Moscow in 1949, Eastern Europe was turning more and more to the West, this represented a return to a historic pattern of trade relations characteristic of this area before Soviet penetration and domination in the aftermath of World War II.

There had also been steady advancement in Western tourism to the countries of Eastern Europe. Only 6,500 Americans traveled to Bulgaria and Hungary in 1958, but seven times that number did in 1967. American visitors to Poland increased nearly threefold (from 7,800 to 21,400) and to Rumania more than tenfold (from a mere 583 persons in 1958 to 11,600 in 1967). Even more impressive penetration of Eastern Europe by Western tourism had come from West Germany, Austria, and France, in 1967 involving nearly half a million West German nationals alone.

Apart from the expansion of East-West trade and tourism, however, Europe continued to experience serious problems stemming from a quarter century of cold war divisions on the Continent. All of these problems bore directly or indirectly upon the issues of American security, upon American alliances, and the prospects of peace. Among the more important were:

1. The embittered relations between East and West Germany that related to
   a. East German claims for full recognition of the sovereignty, independence, and territorial status quo of the so-called GDR (German Democratic Republic) by West Germany and all the Western powers;
   b. the contrary claim of West Germany under the Adenauer, Erhard, and Kiesinger governments for reunification of *all* Germany, a claim in which the GDR was seen as merely a Soviet puppet regime, and referred to on West German maps as the "Soviet zone of occupation";
   c. East German, and occasionally Soviet, restrictions on the access by West Germans to the city of West Berlin and reciprocally the access of West Berliners to the West;

d. the right of the United States, Britain, and France to maintain their military and political presence in West Berlin against Soviet and East German challenges; and

e. resentment over the severance, ruthlessly enforced by the GDR, of virtually all contacts, personal, economic, and cultural, between the two Germanies.

2. The claims of Poland for West German and international recognition of the permanency of Polish western frontiers, formed in 1945 out of substantial, then German territories. Here, too, West German claims throughout the 1950s and 1960s clashed with the Polish.

3. The political conflict between West Germany and the Soviet Union: the latter supported the claims both of Poland and East Germany *and* also shared in the occupation of pre-1939 German territories of East Prussia. Soviet propaganda traditionally had concentrated since World War II on West Germany as a dangerous "revanchist," quasi-Hitlerite power, bent on destroying the post-1945 status quo—with the help of "American imperialism." The USSR thus exploited the fears of East and West Europeans alike of German military revival, unifying the East behind Moscow and seeking to divide the West against itself.

4. Increasing pressures of governments and public opinion in both Western Europe (e.g., France, Italy) and Eastern Europe (e.g., Rumania, Hungary) for greater economic, cultural, and political cooperation and interchange between the two parts of the Continent.

Whether out of economic, political or cultural motives (e.g., revival of nationalism), these pressures could be described as assertions of independence and tendencies to various self-serving forms of neutralism. In Western Europe these tendencies were expressed partly by efforts to create a third force of Common Market states against the giants of both the East (USSR) and the West (U.S.); they were also expressed by a still different phenomenon, as in Gaullist France, the dedication to going one's own way, above all else. In parts of Eastern Europe (Rumania, Yugoslavia, Hungary, Poland) there was a strong, apparent desire to eliminate or at least reduce Soviet dictation and intervention by removing its international causes and by moving from a rigidly bipolar to a loosely multipolar politics.

5. Increasing pressures for a reduction of the arms burdens, with consequent reexamination of the roles of the NATO alliance in the West and the Warsaw Pact in the East.

The Nixon Approach

In facing all these problems, the Nixon administration resisted whatever temptation the tragic events of 1968 may have furnished for the resumption of a policy of intransigence toward Communist Eastern Europe. The rhetoric of "liberating the satellites" still heard in the 1950s was not revived. The United States opted rather for a continuation of the course set by the Johnson administration to build bridges to Eastern Europe, gradually overcome the division of the Continent into East and West, and replace cold war confrontations typical of the 1940s and 1950s with a cautious movement toward cooperation and mutual security. In February 1970 President Nixon declared in his first foreign policy report to the Congress:

> It is not the intention of the United States to undermine the legitimate security interests of the Soviet Union. The time is certainly past, with the development of modern technology, when any power would seek to exploit Eastern Europe to obtain strategic advantage against the Soviet Union. It is clearly not part of our policy. Our pursuit of negotiation and detente is meant to reduce existing tensions, not to stir up new ones.
>
> By the same token, the United States views the countries of Eastern Europe as sovereign, not as parts of a monolith. And we can accept no doctrine that abridges their right to seek reciprocal improvements of relations with us or others.
>
> We are prepared to enter into negotiations with the nations of Eastern Europe, looking to a gradual normalization of relations. We will adjust ourselves to whatever pace and extent of normalization these countries are willing to sustain.[8]

Other things being equal, an improvement in the relations between the United States and Eastern Europe could be advantageous to the United States in terms of (1) loosening the ties between the USSR and its erstwhile satellites—with corresponding effects on the European and world balances of power;[9] and (2) encouraging more liberal attitudes on the part of Communist rulers toward their own people—an aspiration of historic importance to the millions of Americans of East European ancestry; (3) assuring America a generally increased political, cultural, and economic influence in the area; (4) promoting U.S. trade; and, above all, (5) relaxing world tensions that had, among other things, placed considerable burdens on the American taxpayer.

Characteristically, however, the American problem was one of balancing policy initiatives in different directions. Under some circumstances diplomatic overtures in Eastern Europe could well prove dangerous and counterproductive. The Nixon administration was hard-pressed to balance its regional and its worldwide objectives. At one end of the policy spectrum, improvement in relations with Eastern Europe could not be allowed, by arousing Soviet suspicions, to jeopardize other American interests, above all a more general détente with the Soviet Union that could lead to major nuclear disarmament and lessen the danger of global conflicts; at the other end, the structure of American alliances could not be rashly compromised against the contingency of a Soviet "change of heart," a stiffening of the Kremlin's world policy. American influence in the Mediterranean and in the Middle East was also at stake in any possible reshaping of the Western European defense and security systems, such as the Soviets demanded.

President Nixon resorted to considerable summitry in pursuit of his cautious détente in Eastern Europe. Having made a singularly successful visit to Poland in 1960 as the then vice-president during the Eisenhower administration (and as a private citizen in 1967), Nixon returned to Eastern Europe several times as President. He visited Rumania in 1969, Yugoslavia in 1970 and, above all, Moscow in May 1972, to conclude, among others, the strategic arms limitation agreements between the United States and the USSR. This trip was followed by a brief stopover in Warsaw.

The Nixon visit to Rumania set the pattern for American demonstrations of interest and influence in Eastern Europe. In an area where the United States has long enjoyed considerable popularity as a symbol of freedom, Western affluence, and opposition to Soviet domination, President Nixon received a very warm welcome from hundreds of thousands of people. His trips to Rumania, Yugoslavia, and Poland underscored American interest in the fate of these nations at a time when Moscow was rattling the saber toward all its Communist "mavericks."

In late October 1971, President Tito of Yugoslavia reciprocally visited Washington, and drew the Nixon administration's pledge of support to Yugoslavia's "independent and non-aligned position and policy." There had also been a visit by Rumania's party leader, Nicolae Ceausescu, to the United States in 1970. Ceausescu was given the "red carpet" treatment at the White House. In November 1970 Rumania signed an agreement with Pan-American World Airways for an air route linking New York and Bucharest. Trade between the two states rose from $24 million in 1968 to $75 million in 1970. In September 1972 it was announced in Washington that the United States would assist Rumania in Black Sea offshore-oil-drilling operations. Substantial trade agreements with Poland and the Soviet Union for the purchase of American machinery and technological (particularly computer) know-how were expected before the end of 1972. Not even in the case of Czechoslovakia, whose regime under Gustav Husak had turned subservient to Moscow in the aftermath of the Soviet invasion, did American relations in the 1969–73 period deteriorate over the preceding decade.

Though, admittedly, total figures of trade were still small, U.S. exports to Eastern Europe in 1969, valued at $249 million, increased to $353 million in 1970; U.S. imports at $196 million in 1969 grew to $226 million in 1970. This was actually a greater proportional expansion of U.S. trade than in any other principal trading area, such as Canada and Latin America, Western Europe, Asia, Near East, Africa, or Oceania.[10] Much of this trade continues into the 1970s on the pattern of exchanges between developed and developing nations: the United States (and EEC) supply Eastern Europe predominantly with finished goods, including capital equipment of the kind and quality not available there, in exchange for food products, mineral fuels, and raw materials; the share of finished goods in East European exports to the West has actually declined since 1958 due probably to the poor quality and service on East European manufactures.[11]

In 1969 the Nixon administration sent a Department of Commerce mission to Eastern Europe. It visited Bulgaria, Czechoslovakia, Hungary, Poland, Rumania, and Yugoslavia to explore the possibilities of trade expansion. In 1969 the U.S. Congress passed an Export Control Act which reduced restrictions on the export of more than eleven hundred U.S. commodities to Eastern Europe, including electronic equipment and variius metal products. The main stumbling blocks to further and more significant trade exchanges continued to be lack of the most-favored-nation treatment for Eastern European states (except Poland) and denial of U.S. credit facilities for these states, lacking hard-currency resources.[12]

The penetration by American tourists, businessmen, and officials of the former iron curtain continued at an impressive rate under the Nixon administration. Where 42,000 U.S. nationals had visited Bulgaria and Hungary in 1967, over 58,000 did so in 1969. American visitors to Rumania grew from 11,600 in 1967 to 16,800 in 1969. And the trend was upward in 1970 so far as available UN data discloses: 17,688 in Bulgaria as compared with 14,987 in 1969; 43,799 in Czechoslovakia as compared with 38,350; 27,926 in Poland, increasing from 24,230. In 1970, 205,929 U.S. nationals visited Yugoslavia, as compared with 163,938 in 1969.[13] Data for 1971 and 1972, covering U.S.–East European trade and tourist exchanges, were still lacking in early 1973.

In some cases, progress in U.S. ties with East Europe has been indirect. While the Nixon administration succeeded in establishing a new relationship with Communist China, China's East European ally, Albania, has continued its attitude of hostile aloofness toward the United States. Nevertheless, the Albanians not only modified their intransigence toward other countries of the Balkan region—in the 1970s establishing diplomatic relations at the ambassadorial level with Yugoslavia and Greece—but also with several West European countries, notably Switzerland, Finland, Denmark, Norway, and Sweden. Similarly, relations *among* the so-called dissident members of the Communist bloc (i.e., those displaying greatest independence of the USSR) were improving, particularly those of China and Albania with Yugoslavia and Rumania.

In some cases, American efforts for a gradual détente benefited by the action of other countries. In 1970 Chancellor Willy Brandt of West Germany launched his *Ostpolitik*, seeking a rapprochement with the East European powers. The process involved extended negotiations at all levels of new economic and political contacts between West Germany and the USSR as well as East Germany, Poland, Rumania, Czechoslovakia, Hungary, and Bulgaria. In March 1970 Chancellor Brandt journeyed to Erfurt in East Germany for talks with the premier of the GDR, Willi Stoph. It was the first meeting of top leaders of the two Germanies ever to take place. In May a similar meeting took place in Kassel, West Germany. At last the two German states, which had for so long recognized each other only by way of mutual denunciation, were engaged in peaceful dialogue. The hopes for an ultimate reunification of Germany may still have been very distant, but the possibility of mutual recognition and cooperation began to take shape.

The most dramatic concrete results of Brandt's policy came with the Soviet-West German nonaggression treaty signed on August 12, 1970. Both sides renounced the use of force and pledged to "respect without restriction the territorial integrity of all states in Europe within their present frontiers." This amounted to West German recognition of the annexation by the USSR and by Poland of large parts of prewar German territory: East Prussia, Pomerania, Silesia, and Danzig (Gdansk). The most obvious, immediate concession by the Soviets was the abandonment of a belligerent stance toward West Germany, pictured by Soviet propaganda for more than twenty years as a quasi-Hitlerite state waiting to set the torch to the structure of European and world peace. West Germany at last became a political persona grata in the East. The Soviet–West German pact was shortly followed by a treaty with Poland signed in December 1970. Backed by a precariously small majority of the West German parliament, and opposed by vociferous refugee organizations in his own country, Chancellor Brandt nevertheless undertook to recognize the Oder Neisse line as Poland's permanent frontier. Poland agreed to allow the repatriation to West Germany of some 90,000 Germans still resident in Poland, and both sides pledged themselves to eschew force and promote cooperation in their relations with one another. In early December 1970, the chancellor had traveled to Warsaw for the signing of the treaty, and knelt before the monument to the Jewish martyrs of the Warsaw Ghetto: a gesture at once symbolic of atonement and of a new spirit of goodwill toward Germany's eastern neighbors. Still, as of 1970 the *Ostpolitik* seemed to be just a beginning. The new treaties remained to be ratified, with considerable domestic opposition to them in West Germany. The attitude of the East Germans remained one of hostility and suspicion; traffic to and from West Berlin was subjected to harassment. Nevertheless, considerable expansion in political and trade contacts with the East was taking place.

One of the more impressive and promising developments in American policy toward Eastern Europe was the conclusion of a four-power agreement on September 3, 1971, governing the access to and status of West Berlin. The agreement climaxed seventeen months of negotiations among the United States, Britain, France, and the Soviet Union; it became practically effective through a subsequent pact between East and West Germany in December 1971 to implement its provisions.

The East Germans and the Russians agreed to ease traffic restrictions to and from the city. Payment of individual tolls by Westerners and West Berliners was eliminated and cargo controls simplified. Access was also assured for the West Berliners to both East Berlin and to East Germany as before 1966 and 1952, respectively. West Berlin was recognized as an entity independent of the West German Federal Republic, but at the same time the right of the West German government to maintain its official agencies there and even to represent West Berlin diplomatically was recognized. The right of the Western powers to maintain their presence in the city was likewise explicitly sanctioned. Provisions were made for improved links in telephone, telegraph, and road transportation between West Berlin and East Germany.

Thus, one historic crisis ground of Europe, the site of a Soviet blockade and American airlift in 1948, the Berlin Wall of 1961, and numerous clashes over access rights for three decades, headed for normalization. In view of the declining population and vitality of West Berlin in the 1960–70 decade, the new agreement may well have saved the beleaguered city from demise. Beyond Berlin itself, however, the ability of the two sides to come to terms was clearly a contribution and forerunner to still further détente.

In 1972 the West German parliament's ratification of the Soviet and Polish treaties increased the prospects for a liquidation of the cold war confrontation in Europe and led to the establishment of diplomatic relations between West Germany and Poland. The year also marked a turning point in the relations between East Germany and West Germany, with profound implications for United States policy. In December, after eighteen months of negotiation, the two German states signed a treaty providing for mutual recognition, respect of each other's sovereignty, and development of "normal, good neighborly relations." From the standpoint of the East Germans and the Soviets, this meant that at long last they had won for themselves West Germany's official acquiescence in an indefinite division of Germany and the legitimacy of the Communist regime in what Bonn had referred to as the "Soviet zone of occupation." According to the treaty—which recognized that the two sides still differed on the "national question"—only peaceful means consistent with "unrestricted respect of each other's territorial integrity" (Article 3) could be invoked between the parties to resolving mutual differences. Thus, in three successive steps, the Brandt government had agreed to the territorial and political changes made by the USSR, Poland, and the GDR within the frontiers of pre-1939 Germany. The way was paved for the admission of both East Germany and West Germany to the United Nations in the fall of 1973. Among the implications of this was a shift in the costs of financing the UN, with West Germany and East Germany scheduled to assume about 9 percent of the costs, while the United States was expected to cut back its contribution from 31 percent to about 25 percent. Much more significantly, the conclusion of these treaties and the apparent resolution of the Berlin problem cleared the way for wider East-West negotiations on a general European settlement. This, in turn, would enable a reduction of the U.S. military commitment to the support of NATO.

Still, there was ample room in 1972 for doubt as to whether the improvement in relations between East Germany and West Germany was quite as encouraging as the text of the Treaty of December 21, 1972, implied. The Berlin Wall remained intact. Communist policies with respect to exchanges of persons between the two states remained, both officially and unofficially, restrictive. Statements published in the East German press and comments by GDR party leader Erich Honecker indicated that a posture of wary watchfulness and hostility toward "West German imperialists" had not been abandoned. In fact, alleging "technical difficulties," the East Germans reneged on the pledge for a live telecast of the treaty-signing ceremonies, gave them a largely private character, and insisted on keeping Chancellor Brandt out of East Germany to prevent popular demonstrations. Information reaching West Germany indicated that the Communists were collecting signed pledges from citizens of the GDR promising *not* to invite West Germans to visit in East Germany, which the new treaty had at least made possible. Many observers understandably wondered whether the concessions made by the Brandt government would be reflected in terms of eased people-to-people contacts. West German opposition leader Rainer Barzel voiced his objections in these blunt words: "This treaty legitimizes an illegal system and an inhuman border equipped with automatic killing devices [and] we will not go along with it."

To most governments, however, including that of the United States, Brandt's *Ostpolitik* seemed to be a move in the right direction —toward détente. Privately, a number of governments, including the French, were not dissatisfied with an institutionalization of a divided Germany. Historic memories of German domination of the Continent were still strong, and even in the West many thought that two Germanys would be safer than one.

In November 1972 the long anticipated preparatory Conference on European Security and Cooperation finally began in Helsinki. The United States, Canada, the USSR, and thirty-one European states attended. Albania was the sole East European "holdout," refusing to sit at one table with equally damnable "Soviet and American imperialists." However, the participation of Switzerland, Spain, Yugoslavia, and East as well as West Germany, gave the conference an appearance of European reconciliation all but unprecedented in the twentieth century. Although the preparatory conference has not settled any of the fundamental conflicts of the post-World War II period, it has succeeded in defining some aspirations and directions pursued by the several powers. The United States adopted a "low-profile" posture, allowing and encouraging Europeans to assume leadership in negotiations affecting the fate of Europe. The Soviet Union seemed primarily interested in winning full international recognition of the political-geographic status quo achieved since 1945.

Both East and West seemed agreed, in principle, to seek some form of treaty guaranteeing peaceful resolution of conflicts in all parts of Europe. Particularly noteworthy in this connection were the proposals put forward by Rumania and Switzerland. The former sought an ironclad guarantee against any form of armed intervention anywhere, by one European nation against another. This proposal seemed to be aimed more against the Soviet Brezhnev Doctrine than against the Western powers, but it did not elicit a specific Soviet reaction. The Swiss proposal called for the creation of mediation and arbitration institutions in Europe to ensure the peaceful resolution of disputes among member states. An important area of conflict, identified in the preliminary Helsinki negotiations, has proved to be the issue of greater exchanges of persons and information between East and West. Although at the beginning of the conference the Soviets emphasized an interest in improving commercial, scientific, and cultural contacts between the two sides, suspicion of Western subversion and concern for the "sovereignty, laws and customs of the socialist states"—in Leonid Brezhnev's words—quickly became apparent.

Articles in the Soviet press warned of the allegedly sinister connotations of Western imperialist attempts to "build bridges" to Eastern Europe. Perhaps the most substantial agreement at Helsinki was to seek arms reduction in another forum.

Security Issues

As these talks indicate, an important concern of American policy makers in the Nixon years has been the problem of adjusting the balance of forces between NATO and the Warsaw Pact in the light of the developing détente in Europe. At the April 1969 meeting in Budapest, the East European countries reiterated their earlier proposals for the mutual elimination of these organizations. In March 1971 CPSU General Secretary Leonid Brezhnev called for a European security conference to mutually end the two antagonistic military-political pacts. Heretofore, the NATO treaty of 1949 sanctioned the maintenance of a large number of U.S. forces on the continent of Europe. The Warsaw Treaty of 1955 extended an analogous footing to Soviet troops on the territory of the countries of Eastern Europe. Nevertheless, the Warsaw Treaty, due to expire in May 1974, has been only one of the legal foundations for a substantial Soviet presence outside the frontiers of the USSR itself.[14] The Soviet Union has concluded equivalent bilateral treaties with East Germany (1964), Poland (1965), Hungary and Bulgaria (1967), and Czechoslovakia (1970). Thus, the simultaneous dismantling of the NATO and Warsaw Pact systems per se might actually leave the USSR in a much stronger position in Europe than the West.

The Nixon administration has been willing to negotiate balanced and mutual reductions of forces in Europe, but it has also exerted its efforts to maintain the NATO military shield against the contingency of failure to reach mutually satisfactory agreements.

Despite pressures for troop and weapons reductions both at home and abroad, the United States under the Nixon administration managed to keep its contribution to NATO on an even keel. In fact, in November 1971 total U.S. ground forces in Europe were slightly increased from 300,000 to 310,000. American criticism of dangerously lackadaisical and indifferent European attitudes toward NATO produced a 1971 pledge of an additional $1 billion in 1972 contributions from the so-called Eurogroup (defense ministers of Britain, West Germany, Italy, the Netherlands, Belgium, Luxembourg, Norway, Denmark, Greece, and Turkey). West Germany, which supported the largest NATO continental ground force, twelve divisions, also agreed to pay the United States an additional $400 million toward the costs of keeping the American forces in Europe.

Not all the signs in Eastern Europe and the USSR have been pointing to a smooth and indefinite expansion of the détente with the United States.[15]

Actually, despite an expansion of trade, tourism, and other friendly contacts between East and West in the last two decades, and particularly during the Nixon administration, there has been a considerable buildup in Europe of Soviet and Warsaw Pact power vis-à-vis the West. The balance of forces, and of national resources, committed to military purposes in the last decade has kindled fears in various quarters that the USSR and its allies have been shifting the European balance of power—under the guise of a détente.

In 1949, the founding year of NATO, Belgium, Canada, Denmark, France, West Germany, Greece, Italy, Luxembourg, Netherlands, Norway, Portugal, Turkey, the United Kingdom, and the United States spent an average of 5.6 percent of their gross national product on defense. Interestingly, the proportional American contribution (5.7 percent) at that time was exceeded by Britain (7.0), Turkey (6.7), Greece (6.4), and France (6.4). NATO's peak commitment occurred in 1952, with an average expenditure of 13.0 percent of GNP, the United States at 14.9 percent exceeding all other participants. Beginning with 1953, however, with the end of the Korean war and the death of Stalin, there began a marked decline. The percentage of all NATO members fell from 12.4 in 1953 to 8.2 in 1960, rose to 8.5 in 1962; fell to a fifteen-year low of just 7.0 percent in 1965; and climbed back to 8.2 percent in 1967.[16] In terms of the participation of the largest powers, the U.S. share of its peak GNP commitment to defense (heavily taxed by the Vietnam effort, in any case) was down by about one-third (14.9 to 10.0); Britain and

France each declined by about 40 percent (11.2 to 6.7 and 11.0 to 6.2); Italy by a fourth (5.1 to 3.7). Only West Germany marginally increased its commitment, from a low of 4.9 percent in 1953 to a modest 5.1 percent in 1967.

How did this situation compare with changes in Soviet and East European capabilities? As late as 1969, Premier Kosygin estimated the share of total Soviet resources devoted to defense at 25 percent; one Soviet economist put them at about 40 percent. Some Western estimates have placed defense costs more conservatively at between 10 percent and 15 percent of the Soviet GNP.[17] Both Poland and Czechoslovakia are believed to be spending between 5 percent and 6 percent of their respective GNPs on defense in the last decade.[18] Since 1967 considerable increases in East European defense budgets (particularly East Germany's 60 percent increase) have been publicized by the Communist governments.[19]

In terms of what economic resources have purchased for each side, the military advantage of the East European forces is undeniable.

According to a Yugoslav 1969 estimate, the Soviet Army, at 3,220,000, was eight times the size of the West German or British armies; more than five times as large as the French—most of it deployed in Western Russia and Eastern Europe.[20] In 1967 East Germany spent—officially—3.7 percent of its GNP ($1.7 billion) on its defense budget as compared with West Germany's 4.3 percent ($5.1 billion). Yet, somehow, with a then population of some 17 million as compared with West Germany's 58 million, GDR maintained a military force virtually equal to that of West Germany! [21]

In the estimate of a 1971 analyst, the Warsaw Pact forces marshaled 450 light bomber aircraft (400 of them Soviet) to just 50 deployed by NATO in all of Europe; 3,000 interceptor aircraft (2,000 Soviet) compared with 720 in NATO, and 750 medium-range land-based (all Soviet) missiles as opposed to none in NATO.[22] In terms of manpower, the opposing forces were more nearly equal, with about 1 million troops in NATO and 1.2 million in the Warsaw Pact European theater.

The East European contributions—of variably reliable quality

—were comprised of 62 divisions: 6 each from East Germany and Hungary; 15 each from Poland and Czechoslovakia; 10 each from Rumania and Bulgaria. The Soviet Union was believed to maintain 115 of its 140 divisions west of the Urals; 20 in East Germany; 2 in Poland; 4 in Hungary; 5 in Czechoslovakia.[23]

All in all, Warsaw Pact forces included 36 armored divisions with an estimated 22,000 tanks and a total of 4,050 aircraft—most of them Soviet. There were also some 250,000 troops of security police forces in the several East European states backing up regular ground units.[24]

Of additional significance has been the enormous buildup of Soviet naval power now challenging that of the United States for world supremacy. Three of the Soviet Union's fleets—the Baltic, the Black Sea, and the North Sea—operate in support of Warsaw Pact forces. While the navies of the East European states themselves are generally small and obsolete, the Soviet Union has created, among other elements of its formidable naval power, a fleet of some 400 submarines—about eight times the size of the Nazi U-boat fleet at the start of World War II, including about 50 vessels believed comparable to U.S. Polaris submarines.[25]

Troop concentrations and deployment also favored the East, inasmuch as the bulk of WTO manpower could be readily used for operations against the North German Plain and the heartland of Europe. A large portion of NATO strength, on the other hand, was dispersed at the periphery of potential conflict—in Portugal, Norway, Greece, Turkey, and Britain. Unlikely as an attack might be, the ability of the Soviets to deliver a quick, knockout blow in Central Europe (even with little, if any, aid from some 900,000 East European troops) could not be discounted. As Edgar Bottome notes: "A conservative estimate of the time that it would take a determined Soviet effort to break through the northern front would be less than a week." [26]

Of course, even if we were to grant that the balance of ground and air forces in Europe has steadily shifted, and is now heavily in favor of the Soviet Union and its allies, the prospects of Warsaw Pact aggression and of war remain uncertain; some argue highly unlikely.

Perhaps the threat of nuclear deterrence and virtual annihilation, particularly between the United States and the USSR, may have ended resort to war as a realistic option for either side. Perhaps, also, the continuing accumulation of superior military power by the WTO nations is not inconsistent with a desire for reducing the economic burdens of the arms race. No one could deny that there are formidable popular pressures on both sides of the NATO-WTO divide for an alternative commitment of resources.

As one observer put it:

> The cohesion of the Soviet bloc has been weakening during the period of detente, as has been that of the Atlantic Alliance. On both sides of the ideological divide, popular demands for higher standards of living have taxed the national resources and the policy-making ingenuity of governments. Increasingly, East and West Europeans have sought in political, economic, and cultural cooperation the way to the solution of this problem.[27]

Consumerism has been a powerful force of discontent in Communist societies, and it has won numerous concessions from the party planners of these states in the last decade. The Soviet Union's 1971–75 Five Year Plan has been specifically geared to substantial augmenting of consumer goods shortages for the Soviet people. The new party leadership of Poland under Edward Gierek in 1971–72 stood solemnly pledged to improve the lot of the Polish consumer, as did the leaders of East Germany (even before the resignation of Walter Ulbricht) and the Hungarians under Janos Kadar.[28]

A détente could certainly enable the East Europeans to (1) make a substantial shift in resource allocations to domestic needs, and (2) make increased purchases of goods and technological know-how from the West. There was every evidence that for vast numbers of people behind the old iron curtain, relative deprivations since World War II in terms of food, clothing, housing, appliances, and other consumables have been actually much more severe than in the West. The resulting discontent frequently translated itself into unrest, and sometimes even revolts against Communist regimes, as most recently in Poland in December 1970.

The countries of East Europe have made impressive, and in some cases well-nigh spectacular, gains in industrial production, but they have generally failed to match this performance in satisfying the bread-and-butter needs of their peoples. Poland produced almost four times as much coal in 1967 as in 1937; seven times as much steel; and twelve times as much electricity. Yet her housing shortage continued all but unabated into the 1970s; cars and appliances continued to be extremely scarce and expensive. Food, particularly meats, and clothing remained in relatively short supply, with meager choices of quality and style for the consumer. Agricultural output lagged well behind industry in all the Communist countries, even those which, like Hungary, attempted to satisfy consumer needs by easing rigid, centralized planning methods.

During the 1960s Hungary had increased her industrial output by almost 60 percent but her agricultural output by less than 15 percent. Analogously, Czechoslovakia, before the establishment of Dubček's ill-fated regime, had risen to the forefront of the world's industrial nations; yet a Czechoslovak worker needed to work almost twice as long to buy the same quantity of bread, rice, butter, ham, eggs, or apples as a worker in Belgium; he needed to work more than seven times as long as the American worker for the same amount of sugar, coffee, butter, margarine, or eggs.[29] Granted that the severe economic problems of Communist regimes, including the Soviet, owed much to causes other than the burdens of military preparedness—collectivization of agriculture, for example—all these regimes could greatly benefit by any substantial easements on their economies.

Perhaps in response to domestic needs, as well as the emerging Central European détente, the United States and its NATO allies (excluding France) opened arms reduction negotiations in January 1973 with the Soviets and other Warsaw Pact states in Vienna. Amid reports that Soviet tank forces in Eastern Europe were being rapidly and substantially augmented, the Vienna conference began somewhat inauspiciously. The USSR insisted that what was needed was simply "mutual reductions" of military forces between the two sides. The Western powers sought "balanced reductions" involving much larger withdrawals of Soviet troops as compared with the American in order to offset the Soviets' geographic-logistical advantage. The USSR sought to enlarge the conference by bringing in neutral European states, while the West attempted to limit the conference to the actual participants in the NATO-WTO confrontation. Additional disputes in February and March concerning the status of various participants, particularly Hungary and Italy, threatened to abort further negotiations. As this book went to press, no breakthroughs had been achieved in these East-West arms talks.

Between Present and Future

The United States in the 1970s was clearly prepared to work toward a gradual détente with the East European regimes, and with reasonable assurances to the USSR that its vital security interests would be respected.

The direction of American policy was summed up in the words of President Nixon in early 1972 thus:

1. Every nation in Europe has the sovereign right to conduct independent policies and therefore be our friend without being anyone else's enemy.

2. The use or threat of force by the Soviet Union in Eastern Europe can only lead to European crises. It is therefore incompatible with détente in Europe and détente in U.S.–Soviet relations.

3. We do not want to complicate the difficulties of East European nations' relations with their allies; nevertheless, there are ample opportunities for economic, technical and cultural cooperation on the basis of reciprocity. The Eastern European countries themselves can determine the pace and scope of their developing relations with the United States.[30]

Thus, the United States condemned the Brezhnev Doctrine while simultaneously arguing that it was not really necessary; American pursuit of better relations with Eastern Europe would *not* jeopardize Soviet security or unilaterally upset Soviet-East European alliances or indeed tinker with the structure of Communist regimes in the area:

> We base our ties with . . . these countries on mutual respect, independence and sovereign equality. We share the belief that this should be the basis of relations between nations regardless of divergence or similarity in social, economic, or political systems.[31]

No threats were thus posed to the legitimacy of the whole fabric of Communist institutions in Eastern Europe. No attempts to launch policies over the heads of Communist governments "to the people" were either being threatened or promised. Mutually beneficial cooperation respectful of the status quo was sought instead.

Admittedly, assurances given were not always or necessarily assurances accepted. One of the continuing East-West controversies in 1971–72 centered about the role of Radio Free Europe, a relic of cold war anticommunism, in the view of some East European governments.[32] It is clearly impossible to overlook the striving for internal security, cohesion, and political "purity" on the part of Communist leaders, both Soviet and East European. Trade and cultural contacts with the West have a political potential.[33] Its significance does not escape Warsaw Pact leaders. Western influence and example, unless carefully measured and restricted, could undermine the cohesion of Soviet alliances; the cultural and propaganda efforts of the Marxist-Leninist parties; ultimately perhaps, the special role of these parties as self-appointed guardians and watchdogs of their societies.

One factor that will continue to check the growth of autonomy in Eastern Europe derives from the vested interests of certain indigenous and unpopular rulers, who require the umbrella of Soviet power to stay in office. To be sure they require and want some measure of autonomy, too, in order to be able to respond to local pressures and adjust to changing conditions. But one of the implicit premises enabling these men to exact obedience from their populations is a popular appreciation of the Soviet presence. As Gomulka once told Polish voters, a vote against the party was a vote "to cross Poland off the map of Europe," to invite, in other words, wholesale Soviet intervention.

Without the implicit threat of Soviet intervention, a great many

Poles, East Germans, and Hungarians would undoubtedly shed their attitudes of resignation and passive acquiescence toward their rulers. If Novotny could be toppled in Czechoslovakia, what would keep Gierek or Kadar from suffering a similar fate? Too much Western influence and liberalization could be "dangerous." And would not the toleration of unorthodox practices in Eastern Europe have untoward consequences within the Soviet Union itself?[34] If the Soviet party made concessions abroad, it might be pressed to make them at home. Indeed, the general consequences of de-Stalinization in Russia were already having effects in many respects like those in Eastern Europe. Soviet writers and intellectuals from Ilya G. Ehrenburg to Yevgeni Yevtushenko, Yuri M. Daniel, and Aleksander Solzhenitsyn were already expressing views critical of various aspects of Soviet life. Here, too, the demands for more freedom and a better life were being heard.

While the progress of Brandt's *Ostpolitik* and the agreement between the United States and the USSR on Berlin in 1971, nuclear arms limitations and expansion of trade in 1972 are all encouraging, the meaning of the invasion of Czechoslovakia in 1968 cannot yet be regarded as erased. In fact, the Soviet Union was clearly ready to intervene militarily again in Poland in 1970, this time to prevent the popular revolt against Gomulka from "going too far." The USSR's interest and ability in expanding contacts with the United States and other western states could be readily exaggerated. This could be additionally inferred from the continuing and even augmented toughness of Soviet domestic policy toward all forms of diversity and dissent. After all, it has been under the leadership of Brezhnev and Kosygin that the Soviet Union has tapered off Khrushchev's de-Stalinization campaign; selectively increased measures of surveillance and repression against dissidents, and dampened efforts at any democratization of party leadership at the most recent, 1971 Twenty-fourth CPSU Congress. Yet, clearly, what the United States can and cannot accomplish in its relations with East European states is heavily contingent on the watchful tolerance of the Soviet Union.

As John C. Campbell noted in 1970, Soviet moves toward détente with the United States need not imply such a basic change of heart as is sometimes assumed:

> Their main aims then [i.e., in the 1950s] were to preserve their zone of control in Eastern Europe, to secure international status for the German Democratic Republic, and to divide and weaken the West. We may assume that these aims still obtain. . . .[35]
>
> . . . when Soviet spokesmen say that a European settlement can only be built on acceptance of the outcome of World War II and recognition of the realities, they mean primarily that all of Europe will have to accept the continued existence of Soviet power where it is today.
>
> A negotiated agreement with the United States on strategic weapons is compatible with that purpose. So is an agreement on mutual reduction of conventional forces or the establishment of a freeze on atomic weapons in certain zones. So too is the development of cooperative relations with West Germany. This is the basic Soviet concept of detente; an easing of relations with the West, for which there may be good economic, political and even strategic reasons, without any give on the fundamental requirement of holding the Soviet security zone intact.[36]

If the acceptance of polycentrism among Communist states, domestic political liberalization, "consumerism" in economics, and a leveling off or even a reduction in military spending are all related to prospects of East-West détente, then the attitude of the Soviet Union during the past four years still leaves room for skepticism about the future.

Between 1968 and 1972 American policy toward Eastern Europe succeeded in increasing mutual contacts—economic, cultural, and political. Partly through the efforts of the United States, and partly through the efforts of others, notably West Germany, and France, Britain, and Italy, a marked thaw has been felt between the cold war alliances of the NATO and Warsaw Pact states. The changes have occurred thus far without any diminution of American troop strength in Europe and even alongside modest increases in defense contributions by the European members of the North Atlantic

Treaty Organization. Some of the preconditions for an all-European security conference which might lead to even greater progress have been met—largely through the successes of Willy Brandt's *Ostpolitik,* through Franco-Soviet agreements, and through the apparent settlement of the Berlin issue and the demonstrated capacity of the United States and the Soviet Union to reach substantial agreements on arms limitations and the expansion of trade.

Nevertheless, all that has been negotiated and achieved thus far, and all future prospects of détente, are perpetually conditioned, above all, on the willingness of the USSR to act out the part of a fundamentally secure, status quo power: one interested not in new conquests but in the preservation of national security and an increase in the material and cultural well-being of its people. It is conditioned also to a high degree by an ideological indifference on the part of Communist rulers, both in the USSR and elsewhere, which would allow continuing contacts with the Western world without raising the once familiar spectre of bourgeois imperialist subversion and contamination.

The international position of the Eastern European regimes at the present time still hovers somewhere between subservience to the Soviet Union and the self-determined orientation of each of the ruling parties.

Whether and which way that position may shift are important questions for policy makers in the United States. If the trends toward external autonomy and internal reforms should continue, notwithstanding the Czechoslovak experience, eventually the prefix "Communist" might cease to be substantively descriptive of the foreign and domestic policies of Communist states. It might simply become an "honorific" term. With the adoption of genuinely free elections within the party and the open debate of issues, such as Dubček hoped to promote in Czechoslovakia, Communist parties would become broad vehicles for the expression of popular opinion. They would indeed be vehicles rather than drivers and, as such, useless to Moscow's concept of rule by "the workers' vanguard."

On the other hand, if polycentrism develops more along lines suggested by the experience of Rumania rather than that of

Czechoslovakia, the emergence of autonomous national dictatorships would characterize the future of Eastern Europe. Such regimes would retain the Communist party's monopoly of power at home but separate their external interests and policies from those of the Soviet Union. Lacking the democratic roots and traditions characteristic of Czechoslovakia, they would parlay polycentrism into dictatorships fitted out with some Communist ideological and symbolic trappings but pursuing national interests that are particularistic and centuries old.[37]

Either development, whether along Rumanian or Czechoslovak lines, would put an end to Soviet domination of Eastern Europe and present new opportunities for United States policy makers.

In the United States and Western Europe, on the other hand, more than merely good intentions condition further normalization of East-West relations. An insistence on mutuality and balance in the deescalation of conflict between East and West seems needed to prevent awkward power vacuums and any overly tempting opportunities from upsetting orderly progress toward a more unified and peaceful Europe.

Robert J. Lieber

Britain Joins Europe*

British membership in the newly enlarged Common Market enhances the importance of European unity and brings with it the possibility of expanded European strength and international impact. The implications internationally and for the United States are here considered (1) by reviewing the development of European unity, (2) by exploring the particular experience of Britain in her delayed and painful progression toward Common Market membership and a European orientation, (3) by examining the newly visible outlines of a Europe of the Nine, and (4) by analyzing the prospective relationships between America and Europe in a period of transition.

European Unity: An Overview

The European unity movement emerged from the ashes of World War II. Essentially, that war had pitted two European coalitions against each other, but by its end in 1945 the chief victorious powers stood on its periphery: America and the Soviet Union as continental superpowers, and Britain as an offshore island base with its own separate empire.

Many countries of continental Europe had suffered terribly from the war. They experienced terrible loss of life, destruction of property and productive capacity, and devastation or discrediting of their social and political institutions. In essence, they underwent a breakdown of those things that hold a society together. As a result, traditional nationalisms came out of the war badly discredited, not only in terms of the virulent fascist and quasi-fascist variants of nationalism in Germany, Italy, and Eastern Europe, but also in the case of the nationalisms of the democratic Western European countries. Ultimately, the continental Europeans emerged from the war with an appreciation that self-contained nation-states were somehow no longer sufficient. The traditional European nation-state could not provide effective security and it either brought about, or else could not withstand, the tidal waves of war that had twice devastated Europe in the space of three decades. These shared experiences created the conditions in which the ideals of European unity and the various proposals to begin implementing them could find a ready reception.

The major exception to this pattern was Britain. From the vantage point of the 1960s and 1970s, the British failure to join and indeed to lead the European unity movement in its formative stages may appear puzzling, and it is something many British later came to regret. But seen in the immediate postwar context, it is readily understandable. Unlike most other countries of Western Europe, Britain had not been defeated or occupied. She had stood alone in the darkest hours of the war. And in the end, even though Britain had suffered heavy losses in men, material, productive capacity, and resources, she emerged not only as one of the Big Three victors, but also with her substantial Empire still intact. In a sense Britain's national identity had been reaffirmed by the ordeal of World War II.

Of equal importance in explaining the British position is the "three circles" concept. The idea, as expressed by Winston Churchill, Anthony Eden, and other Conservative policy makers, and less explicitly by at least some Labour party leaders, was that Britain possessed a unique position in the world. Even though Britain was a relatively small island—(and the British Isles themselves occupy a piece of territory smaller than the state of Oregon, with a population of only 55 million)—they nonetheless conceived of their country as standing at the intersection of three geopolitical circles, in each one of which it played a key role.

The first and most important circle was the Empire and Commonwealth, containing three-quarters of a billion people, covering large areas of Africa and Asia, and including the old white dominions of Australia, New Zealand, and Canada. It held a multitude of races, ethnic groups, languages, political systems, and ways of life, and Empire and Commonwealth institutions of trade, investment, language, and education tended to funnel into or out of London. In this sense London and the British Isles themselves stood at the center of a broad world enterprise.

The second circle, or special relationship, which Britain felt privy to was that across the Atlantic with the United States. World War II collaboration with the Americans, together with the legacies of language, culture, and history, were felt to enable Britain, even though endowed with only one-fourth the population and even less than that in terms of wealth and resources, to play the role of the senior wise adviser to the brash, young, powerful United States. During the late 1940s under Labour, and throughout the 1950s under the Conservative governments of Churchill, Eden, and Harold Macmillan, Britain gave importance to this special relationship. And, despite serious setbacks such as the McMahon Act and Suez, there was a measure of substance to their idea, symbolized, for example, by bilateral agreements on nuclear weapons cooperation in 1955, 1956, 1957, 1958, 1959, and 1962, and by American legislation in 1958 which in effect gave Britain a uniquely privileged access to American nuclear technology.[1]

Finally, there was a third circle, that of Europe. Yet while she was geographically European, Britain, as Churchill observed, was *in* Europe but not *of* Europe. While Britain had always played a major role in Europe, her world role extended well beyond it. Throughout the 1940s and 1950s the British saw themselves at the hub of these three intersecting circles—a unique world position linking the Commonwealth, the special relationship with the United States, and finally the European continental relationship.

Added to these geopolitical considerations were still other factors that contributed to a British aloofness from European unity, some of them more characteristic of the man on the street than the policy maker. There was, for example, substantial insularity and suspicion of foreigners. Britons, despite their proximity to the Continent, tended to picture Europeans as unclean, devious, even immoral. But the differences also ranged beyond prejudice to significant political matters. In mid-1945, while the war was still in progress, Britain held her first general election in ten years. The result was a peaceful revolution: the Conservative party of Winston Churchill was defeated in a landslide and replaced by the Labour government of Clement Attlee. Committed as it was to a major program of peaceful democratic and socialist reform within the British Isles, Labour introduced the welfare state, the National Health Service, and nationalization of major industries such as coal and steel. At the same time, the Labour government regarded the continental European countries, and particularly the leaders of the European unity movement, with substantial distrust because of the predominance of the more conservative Christian Democrats (who also enjoyed the backing of the United States). All in all, these differences of ideology, religion, insularity, wartime experience, and Atlantic and Commonwealth orientation help to explain why it was that in this period after the war the opportunity for Britain to participate from the start in constructing a united Europe was not taken.

But if the British were aloof, the Europeans were nonetheless active. Following the end of the war, there began a series of imaginative efforts at creating European unity.[2] The first of these took place in September 1946 at Zurich, Switzerland, where a conference of European leaders gathered to discuss means of reconciling national differences. Addressing this body, Winston Churchill, then out of office but nonetheless possessing very considerable prestige and influence, called for a United States of Europe. Yet he maintained considerable vagueness about the British role; his notion, which was in fact to typify the attitudes of both Labour and Conservative political leaders toward European unity for the next fifteen years, was one which saw Britain as a friend, associate, and sponsor, but not a participant, in a united Europe. The Zurich meeting produced little in the way of concrete results; only in 1948 did the first noteworthy effort toward European cooperation come into being. It was the Organization for European Economic Cooperation (OEEC), a grouping of sixteen European nations. Its purpose was to coordinate trade, investment, and the Marshall Plan aid which the United States was in the process of distributing. Britain took part in this body, but the OEEC was basically an intergovernmental organization, since no nation gave up sovereignty to it. The next major European development, NATO, was also stimulated by and included the United States. Although NATO developed considerable military integration among the fifteen member states, it too provided no framework for European unity.

The first exclusively European grouping, and one which was begun with the hope it would be a real first step in creating a united Europe, was the Council of Europe. At the time it loomed as a very major venture, although it soon declined in significance. The Council was established in May 1949, with conservative statesmen such as Konrad Adenauer, Paul Ramadier, and Winston Churchill quite involved in its formation. Initially, there was an effort to give the Council of Europe rudimentary but real European federal authority with power over the member states in some matters. The British Labour government, however, deeply feared the loss of economic sovereignty to the nonsocialist European governments of the continental countries, and, as the most important European power, Britain was successful in her policy of weakening the whole body so that it would become little more than a forum for the discussion of European matters. This British orientation of opposition to any supernational authority and preference for intergovernmental arrangements with the retention of national veto powers persisted for another decade. Yet while the Council of Europe did not become a significant political or economic enterprise, it did endure as a meeting place of parliamentarians, and the arrangement of its Assembly, where seating and voting began to follow ideological (Christian Democrat, Liberal, Democratic Socialist) rather than national (French, German, Italian, Dutch) lines, foreshadowed a pattern which would appear in the Assemblies of the Coal and Steel Community and the European Economic Community.[3]

The next major step along the road to European unity—the European Coal and Steel Community (ECSC)—was proposed initially by French Foreign Minister Robert Schuman in May 1950. The essential idea of the Schuman Plan; which originated with Jean Monnet and enjoyed the then exceptionally influential blessings of American foreign policy makers, was to tie together the coal and steel industries of Germany and France so closely that these two countries could never again make war against each other. And this linkage was to take place under a joint high authority which would hold real economic and political power. Robert Schuman invited the other countries of Europe to join; in addition to France and Germany, Italy, Belgium, the Netherlands, and Luxembourg accepted the invitation. Ultimately these six countries were to form the Common Market. The British were invited but did not participate because they objected to handing over control of their steel and coal industries to a supranational authority. The Labour government also remained wary of the Christian Democratic founding fathers of the Coal and Steel Community—Konrad Adenauer in Germany, Robert Schuman in France, and Alcide De Gasperi in Italy. Even though prominent Democratic Socialists, such as Belgium's Paul Henri Spaak, came to play a significant role, European unity initially looked to be much more a creature of the Christian Democrats—capitalist, conservative, and Catholic.

The Coal and Steel Community treaty was signed in May 1951, and the community itself was established in July of 1952. It was governed by a nine-man high authority, whose participants were appointed by the member governments, but who were expected to act independently of their own governments in the interest of the Coal and Steel Community itself. In addition there was a parliamentary assembly resembling that of the Council of Europe. By a two-thirds vote, this body could force the high authority of the Coal and Steel Community to resign. It never actually did so; nonetheless this constituted the first European parliament with any autonomous powers. There was also a European court of justice, established to decide legal matters under the treaty, with the power to levy fines, for example against producers violating regulations of the Coal and Steel Community. In this sense, European supranationalism had at last come into rudimentary being; European cooperation was no longer merely intergovernmental in the sense of cooperation without loss of sovereignty. For the first time, states were relinquishing powers to a new authority which would exercise them above and beyond the nation-state.

Following the Schuman proposal, a number of additional, though ultimately abortive, efforts were made to promote substantial European integration. The most important of these was the European Defense Community (EDC), which would have created a European army. A major impetus for this undertaking was the American insistence on German rearmament after the outbreak of the Korean war as a counter to a possible Soviet thrust in Europe. This effort at sudden and substantial integration of such a sensitive area as defense immediately encountered severe obstacles. One critical problem was that the British remained unwilling to join. Distrust of Germany, the legacy of wartime experience, and the conception of a broader world role inherent in the three circles concept all played a part in determining the policy of the Labour government and also that of the Conservatives after their return to power under Churchill in late 1951. And because of the British unwillingness to participate, as well as painful memories of wartime hatred against the Germans and the balance of French politics, the French parliament in mid-1954 refused to ratify the Defense Community Treaty. Subsequently the rearmament of Germany proceeded within a less ambitious European body, Western European Union (WEU), and within the framework of NATO, but without the kind of integration which EDC would have involved.

Following a period in which the prospects for any real progress appeared slight, the establishment of the European Economic Community (EEC) marked a crucial rejuvenation of the European effort. This time however the procedure involved a more indirect pathway toward ultimate political integration by means of functional economic integration. In June 1955, the foreign ministers of the six member nations of the Coal and Steel Community met in Messina, Italy, to initiate the steps that would ultimately lead to creation of the EEC. In 1957 the Treaty of Rome was signed, establishing the EEC or Common Market. Its institutions were not unlike those of the ECSC. They consisted of a Commission, whose fourteen-member executive (later absorbing the ECSC high authority) would direct the operations of the Community, a Council of Ministers, which would meet several times each year to consider Commission proposals and make decisions upon them and (eventually) to do so by a system of weighted majority voting, a parliamentary Assembly (later named the European Parliament) along the lines of the ECSC body (with which it later merged), and a Court of Justice to adjudicate disputes under the treaty.

The British were invited to participate and yet again refused. The previous conception of Britain as having a wider world role to play through the Commonwealth and Atlantic relationships shaped the reluctance to integrate within a supranational European framework. The British also remained loath to participate for fear that an integrated and supranational venture would have a standing above and beyond the nation-state. As previously, the British idea of European cooperation remained intergovernmental. Britain preferred that participating countries in any European body retain full sovereignty through the unanimity principle. By contrast, the Common Market provided for ultimate majority voting, meaning that a country could be overruled. In 1956, the British government had suggested the establishment of a very loose trading arrangement to link the Six with other European countries in a Free Trade Area (FTA). Negotiations subsequently began, but the proposed FTA provided only for industrial free trade, and not for the inclusion of agriculture, the establishment of a customs union, the harmonization of national economic and social policies, nor the creation of common supranational institutions. The future Common Market members in general, and France in particular, were unwilling to accept the British notion of this broad free trade area in which barriers to trade among the countries would be eliminated, but in which no other important economic arrangements would exist. Ultimately, in November 1958, Charles de Gaulle vetoed the establishment of the Free Trade Area. In response the British then established a European Free Trade Association on a narrower basis. This loose grouping, which included Britain, Sweden, Norway, Denmark, Austria, Switzerland, and Portugal, proved moderately successful economically, but remained unimportant politically.

Britain and the Common Market

By 1960 the British had begun to reassess the policy that had prevailed since the end of World War II. And in July 1961, the Conservative prime minister, Harold Macmillan, announced to Parliament that Britain would at last seek entry into the Common Market. This change resulted from numerous factors, perhaps the most critical being the erosion of a basis for the "three circles" concept.

As already stated, Britain had regarded herself as standing at the intersection of three geopolitical circles, the first and most important of which was the Commonwealth. Yet by 1961 most of the Commonwealth countries had become independent. Commonwealth trade (though still very large) was beginning to decline in relative importance to the U.K., and it had become apparent that Britain's role as head of the Commonwealth was increasingly symbolic. To be sure, the Commonwealth countries met periodically, based their currencies on the pound sterling, and often pictured the queen on their postage stamps, yet the practical political and economic importance of the Commonwealth was declining.

Second, the special relationship with the United States had weakened dramatically. The passing of the old wartime leaders, an increasing divergence of interest (as reflected for example in the Suez crisis), and an obvious asymmetry of power all played a part. In fact the Kennedy administration began to urge that Britain join the Common Market in order to create an Atlantic partnership resting on the twin pillars of a strong America and a unified and vigorous Western Europe. (Subsequently this conception provided the basis for President Kennedy's "Declaration of Interdependence" on July 4, 1962.)

Finally, there were the Europeans who were making progress of a very dramatic sort. European unity was developing economically and politically; in general there was a sense that things in Europe had become dynamic while Britain was stagnating. Britain faced persistent economic problems and declining influence in the world; movement into Europe seemed to offer a means to redress this, to provide Britain with a new sense of purpose, economic prosperity, and a world role. Yet in their first attempt to enter the Common Market, beginning in July 1961, the British sought entry in a manner hedged with qualifications.[4] Most importantly they very stubbornly fought for safeguards to protect their agriculture, Commonwealth trade, and partners in the European Free Trade Association. And during a year-and-a-half of negotiations there developed mounting dissension within Britain, opposition by some pressure groups, and in particular, the growth of Labour antagonism.

Until 1962 the Labour and Conservative parties had, in effect, maintained similar policies toward Europe. But in September 1962 the leader of the Labour party, Hugh Gaitskell, took his party in a direction highly critical of Common Market membership. This helped to break down Macmillan's domestic consensus on the question of entry. Nonetheless, there was still a prospect of success in the negotiations, and in the absence of General de Gaulle, it remains more than likely that Britain would have negotiated Common Market membership in late 1963 or early 1964.[5] However, in mid-January 1963, General de Gaulle rendered the second of his famous "No's," stating that Britain was insufficiently European. One of the key factors in the de Gaulle veto was a view that Britain constituted an American Trojan horse, that the British still had closer affinity for the United States than they did for Europe. And this suspicion fed upon the Nassau Agreement of December 1962 between President Kennedy and Prime Minister Macmillan in which the Americans canceled the *Skybolt* program, which was to have been the heart of Britain's nuclear deterrent, but in its place agreed to provide Polaris missiles for British nuclear submarines.

The second major British effort to enter the Common Market took place under the leadership of a Labour government. In October 1964 the Labour party had returned to power under the prime ministership of Harold Wilson. In a period of eighteen months Wilson, who had been an opponent of British entry into the Common Market, shifted position. It had become increasingly clear that Britain's freedom of maneuver was severely constrained, and neither the Commonwealth nor Atlantic relationships any longer offered the kind of role for Britain that Europe might provide. By November 1966, the Labour government essentially decided to negotiate entry into the Common Market, but in the following year this effort was blocked by French opposition. De Gaulle still regarded Britain as excessively pro-American and insufficiently pro-European.

Even after de Gaulle's 1967 veto, the Labour government continued to press the British application on the table. Wilson refused to take "No" for an answer, but in the presence of de Gaulle the willingness of the other five Common Market countries to have Britain in the Common Market was insufficient. The French were legally able to veto Britain and they did so. However, in April 1969 de Gaulle resigned the French presidency, and a year later he was dead. His more flexible and pragmatic successor, President Georges Pompidou, was prepared to negotiate Britain's entry at a price. Meanwhile, the Labour government was upset in the June 1970 general election; the new British government under Prime Minister Edward Heath thereupon launched an aggressive effort to bring Britain into the Common Market. Heath had been the negotiator for Harold Macmillan in the first British attempt at Common Market membership and was a passionate and convinced European. At the same time, and for a number of reasons, the French were more willing to see Britian enter Europe. In addition to the different outlook of President Pompidou, it had become clear that the Gaullist policy of an independent France balancing off America and Russia was not viable because France lacked sufficient stature, resources, and military capacity. There was also the factor of West German political and economic influence, which was becoming more and more the central feature of the Common Market; indeed, at least tacitly, the French welcomed British entry as a counterbalance to Germany.

Serious negotiations for British entry began in late 1970 and in May 1971 an important political breakthrough occurred when Prime Minister Heath met President Pompidou in Paris. At a dramatic press conference in the Élysée Palace, ironically the scene of the de Gaulle vetoes, the French president announced, "Many people believed Britain was not and did not wish to become European and that she wished to enter the Community only to destroy it or to divert it from its goals. Many also thought France was ready to use all pretexts to put up a new veto to the entry of Britain. . . . Well, ladies and gentlemen, you see before you this evening two men who are convinced of the contrary." [6] This crucial political impetus facilitated the reaching of accord on complex technical issues and in late June 1971 the EEC negotiators concluded a successful agreement on British entry. Agreements involving Ireland, Norway, and Denmark followed soon afterward.

Britain's EEC membership had only come after ten years of effort, yet there remained difficulties within the country. Opinion polls consistently indicated that a plurality of the British public opposed EEC entry. In large measure this stemmed from concern that the Common Market's Common Agricultural Policy (C.A.P.) would lead to a 20 percent rise in food prices and a net increase in the cost of living of at least 5 percent. Any sense of creating a new Europe or of building an enterprise that would help to ensure the end of centuries of European antagonisms was of less immediate importance than a large increase in the price of butter, though objection to Europe on political grounds such as concern for parliamentary sovereignty, distrust of the Community's bureaucracy, conservatism, and lack of democratic procedures, a resentment of bigness, and a residual British insularity all contributed to this opposition. Nonetheless, the broader public's antagonism to EEC entry was not for the most part held with strong intensity, and a majority of the British people expected that Britain would enter the Common Market despite their objections.

Broadly speaking, the British pro-Europeans rested their case on the long-term political and economic opportunities in joining. In particular, they stressed the great population size and scope of the Market and the opportunities for competition, growth, and market specialization which these presented. They also hoped for an improved economic growth rate; during the period from 1958 to 1969, Britain's rate had been under 3.0 percent per year, whereas the EEC countries had enjoyed an average yearly growth of 5.4 percent. Proponents of entry also gave weight to the ultimate political aim of building a united Europe, and the (increasingly beleaguered) group of Labour supporters stressed their hope of achieving reforms and improvements in the Community—including steps toward a socialist Europe—once Britain entered.

Prime Minister Heath faced a difficult situation in obtaining parliamentary approval of membership. During the period following its June 1970 electoral defeat, the Labour party, long divided on the issue, had become increasingly anti-European as its center of gravity shifted somewhat leftward. Without formally rejecting the principle of EEC membership, the Parliamentary Labour party decided to oppose the terms which the Heath government had negotiated. Coupled with the votes of more than a score of Conservative MPs bitterly opposed to European entry, this could have led to the defeat of the European Communities legislation, the fall of the Conservative government, and the calling of new elections. However, an ardent pro-European minority within the Labour party, led by Roy Jenkins, chose to support the prime minister.[7] These Labour defections offset Conservative opposition and enabled Heath to obtain a slight parliamentary majority in approval of entry.

Within the Labour party there developed strong sentiment for pledging that a future Labour government would withdraw from the Rome Treaty altogether.[8] However, the October 1972 Labour Party Conference narrowly rejected a resolution calling for such a policy. Instead it approved resolutions urging renegotiation of certain treaty provisions. The more strongly supported of these resolutions, backed by the Labour leadership, identified as subject to renegotiation the C.A.P., Value-Added Tax (V.A.T.), financing of the EEC budget, proposals for monetary union, and the retention of certain economic and regional policies by Parliament. Although the Rome Treaty is technically unbreakable, and the outgoing president of the EEC Commission, Sicco Mansholt, specifically ruled out the possibility of renegotiation, Labour's policy called for the use of Britain's veto powers once inside the Community as a lever to effect changes within it. It also committed a future Labour government to provide for a general election or consultative referendum on any negotiated terms, or even in order to consider British withdrawal from the European Communities if renegotiations failed to succeed.[9] Despite the difficulties for the EEC (or for Britain's future place in it) implied by this position and by an even stronger resolution (though one passed by a narrower margin), the policy actually preserved a degree of freedom of maneuver for Harold Wilson and the Labour leadership. Since certain features of the EEC, for example the C.A.P., have previously elicited demands for reform from within the Community, there could well be at least some changes which would allow a Labour government to remain within the Common Market while still claiming to fulfill its party mandate.

Europe of the Nine

Despite the British Labour party's position and the rejection of EEC entry in the Norwegian referendum, Britain, Denmark, and Ireland became members of the European Communities on January 1, 1973. There was thus established a new situation in Europe—a Common Market of nine European countries in a grouping of real size, power, and influence. This Europe of the Nine possesses population and economic strength which place it on the same scale as the Soviet Union and the United States.

The world politics of the last two decades has been dominated by the two continental superpowers, countries of over 200 million in population, occupying vast continents with great resources and talented populations. But the unified Western Europe of the Nine foreshadows another continental power in the making. According to 1970 census figures, Europe of the Nine, with 253 million persons, has a larger population than either America (with 207 million) or the Soviet Union (242 million). In terms of gross national product, Europe of the Nine has a GNP very roughly 75 percent of that of the United States, and larger than that of the USSR. In addition, Europe of the Nine produces more steel than either the Americans or the Russians (139 million metric tons compared to approximately 138 million for the Russians and 132 million for the Americans). And as for computers, a critical component of modern technology, the United States had 60,000 in use in 1970, the Europe of the Nine had 21,000, and Russia had approximately 5,000. Thus in terms of population, gross national product, steel production, and computers, the three groupings—America, Russia, and Europe—are of roughly comparable magnitude. Finally, the Europe of the Nine is by far the most important trading group in the world. It accounts for about 40 percent of world trade—far more than the Americans, Russians, and Japanese put together. And its recent agreement to incorporate several non-EEC European states in a looser free trade area gives it even greater trading impact.[10]

Yet for all this, it would be misleading to regard an expanded EEC as an emerging superpower ready to take its place alongside the Americans and the Russians. There are two critical reasons why this is not the case. The first has to do with nuclear weapons. Even though the French and British possess modern aircraft, nuclear submarines, and thermonuclear weapons, they lack sufficient quality and quantity in advanced delivery systems (particularly in missile and warhead technology) and in weapons research and development. To be sure, the British do operate four nuclear submarines, each armed with sixteen Polaris missiles, and the French are in the process of building a similar submarine force on their own (as well as deploying solid-fuel ballistic missiles in silos in Southeastern France). Antisubmarine warfare (ASW) has not reached the stage where it would be reliable against even such forces as these, so despite the development of the Moscow ABM, Britain and France do possess the ability to inflict at least a measure of damage against a presumed Soviet enemy. Yet the fact is that only America and Russia are nuclear superpowers. The British and French—as well as the Chinese—lack the deterrent credibility of being able to absorb an all-out nuclear attack and then retaliate by inflicting unacceptable damage upon the attacker. Although their weapons are significant, they do not provide real strategic muscle. But there is another and ultimately more important reason why Europe is not a superpower: Europeans are not yet unified. They are not entirely unified economically, although they have made major strides, and they certainly are not unified politically. In the absence of such unification, Europe necessarily remains without the international presence which its scale and wealth would otherwise bring.

How unified is Europe? Since July 1968 there has been free trade among the original six Common Market countries, yet there remain some barriers that have not disappeared; for example, disease control measures, currency controls, quotas, and miscellaneous regulations. A customs union has also been achieved, so that a common external tariff already exists around the Six and after a transition period will encompass all nine countries. Despite the absence of complete economic integration, there have been major successes, especially in agricultural policy. In fact, agricultural policy in a united Europe today may be determined more in Brussels, the seat of the European Economic Commission which runs the Common Market, than in the individual national capitals. Where farm groups seeking changes in agricultural policy would once have gone to Paris or Rome to demonstrate, it is now as appropriate to try to influence the European Commission in Brussels. And, indeed, Common Market farmers have protested agricultural policies by driving their tractors into Brussels. On one such occasion they fought a pitched battle with the Belgian police and one person was killed. The riot occurred where it did because European farmers felt that policy really was made by the supranational commission in Brussels. Suffice it to say that there is real integration in the agricultural sphere. It is an omelet, in a sense, with the eggs not easily unscramblable. In other areas too, the EEC has made progress or at least is committed to further steps toward integration which are embodied in the Rome Treaty. Longer-term objectives, toward which there have been at least limited steps, include the free movement of persons, services, and capital. And in addition, there is the objective of harmonizing transportation policies, rules of competition, the business cycle, balance of payments, social policy, and taxation. Finally, the Paris summit meeting of October 1972 produced significant commitments to the development of further integration in crucial areas, in particular those of regional policy, foreign policy, and, by 1980, economic and monetary union.

All these intended areas of integration have been set out for the ultimate purpose of political unity. Indeed, since the time of the Schuman Plan, European economic integration has been conceived of and pursued as instrumental to noneconomic goals. Thus Walter Hallstein, former president of the European Economic Commission, has said in a widely quoted remark about the EEC, "We are not in business, we are in politics." And, in fact, those "eurocrats" who run the enterprise have not abandoned this perspective.[11]

Since the creation of the EEC, the European Commission in Brussels has gained increased political and economic power, and the question of its accountability may create pressures for a degree of overt political integration. The Commission already administers an annual budget in excess of $4 billion, and it derives revenues from duties on imports into the Common Market, from a percentage of agricultural levies, and from a levy on coal and steel production. There is a growing problem of responsiveness and accountability in dealing with this budget and in administering the EEC, and one way of providing for control would be to establish a popularly elected European parliament (for which Article 138 of the Rome Treaty provides). Had it not been for the presence of de Gaulle, such a body (rather than the present weak and indirectly chosen European parliament) might already exist. Indeed, it is conceivable that such an innovation will yet come to pass within the next decade. Among the proposals which have gained attention has been that of Jean-Jacques Servan-Schreiber, French publisher and leader of the French Radical party. He has proposed a popularly elected European parliament, and the establishment of a multinational executive elected by universal suffrage to draw up a federal constitution with real powers. Under this scheme, Europe would also have a common currency, defense, and foreign policy. Other proposals for the popular election of a European parliament have come from the EEC Commission.

There have already been efforts at a joint foreign policy, and the development of a common European position at the Helsinki Conference on Security and Cooperation in Europe has been surprisingly successful. Meanwhile, European public opinion, especially among the younger generations, is favorable toward a united Europe.[12] This is likely to provide a reservoir of support so that if the circumstances ever arise in which political leaders in each country simultaneously favor concrete measures of political integration, they may have sufficient support to make this politically feasible.

The dynamics of the EEC create possibilities for real political union. That is, questions of monetary and fiscal policies, exchange rates, taxes, customs duties, wages, and social services, as well as the spillover of integration from one economic sector to another, lead to concerns that are political at least as much as economic. And because they are political, an inherent need exists for European political control of them. Finally, the individual European countries have only a limited international impact politically, militarily, and economically. They can, however, develop a major world presence to the extent that they cooperate within the expanded European Community. Thus, provided the requisite political will exists among the members of the EEC, the circumstances exist in which European unity can in fact make real progress over the next generation.

America and Europe in a Period of Transition

In the past the United States has been deeply involved in European recovery and defense, and in the encouragement of European unity. America has in a sense played midwife at the birth of united Europe, and has done so as part of a very successful postwar policy established around the Marshall Plan, NATO, and containment. The application of these ideas in Asia may have led to some major failures, but in Europe the political, economic, and military success has been undeniable. European recovery has brought prosperity and stability to a region long in disarray. And it has done so in a situation in which those countries remain basically friendly toward the United States.

During the period from the late 1940s to the late 1960s, the United States viewed European unity as inherently desirable, believing that European unity would strengthen the Europeans as partners and allies, make them more viable, more prosperous, and stronger militarily and politically. And so the United States was willing to make economic sacrifices in the interest of European unity. The policy worked, but at the same time a profound transformation has been taking place in relations between Europe and America. Because America's postwar European policies have come to fruition, a new policy is inescapable.

For one thing, the nature and relative strength of the two sides is changing, and there has been a gradual shift of the Europeans away from a situation of very considerable dependence upon the United States toward one of enhanced autonomy (though with substantial interdependence in monetary, economic, and military matters). This change, however, has been slow in developing, and as late as 1970, public opinion polls showed that mass attitudes in France, West Germany, and Italy were such that there was a higher degree of good feeling from each one of these countries toward the Americans (and the Swiss and British) than toward each other.[13] Nonetheless, by the late 1960s, the postwar legacy had begun seriously to erode. An absorption with and admiration of the United States in terms of its education, culture, business, and politics, and even a sense that the United States was the model toward which the Europeans ought to strive, had faded.

The effects of the Vietnam war and problems of the American political system, coupled with the increasing recovery and economic prosperity of the Europeans, brought a situation in which the whole orientation toward the United States began to alter. For one thing, certain critical events encouraged a fundamental change. The Suez crisis of 1956, the abortive multilateral nuclear force, Gaullism, and especially the Vietnam war loom large here. Almost without exception, the Western Europeans were dismayed with the American entanglement in Vietnam and certainly none of the NATO allies seriously contemplated dispatching troops or major aid. The Nixon administration's international economic policies, the measures taken in August 1971, a recurrent obsession with toughness (directed more against our allies than our adversaries),[14] and the devaluation of the U.S. dollar also played a role, but there have been longer-term underlying factors as well: shifts within leadership generations and changes in public attitudes, a gradual alteration in the American balance of payments and balance of trade, some decline in perceptions of the Russian threat and the cold war, nuclear proliferation and the development of virtual Soviet nuclear parity with the United States (which called into question the credibility of the American commitment to defend Western Europe against conventional attack).

It is also necessary to appreciate that the circumstances of the last two decades were historically unique. For a time, the United States played a major role as a healthy allied superpower in relation to a prostrate Europe. From an historical perspective, the two postwar decades may come to appear as an important interlude in which the Europeans, who were momentarily laid low by the war, regained their feet militarily, economically, politically, and socially. Meanwhile the U.S. decline has been relative rather than absolute. While the United States now appears overextended in the world, the Europeans have once again become a factor to be reckoned with, and American support for a united Europe has undergone reevaluation.

It is quite clear, however, that resentments and animosities directed toward the EEC are mistaken. At a minimum, a fundamental heritage linking Western Europe and the United States still exists. Ties of economics, politics, culture, history, and—above all—of defense, mean that America and Europe will remain closely linked over the foreseeable future, even though their policies on specific issues will no doubt fluctuate—as the Vietnam example points up. Beyond more diffuse considerations, specific economic factors should keep Europe from turning "inward" or markedly against the United States. Europe of the Nine derives 18 percent of its total gross national product from exports. The comparable figure for the United States is 4.5 percent. International trade is so important to the Europeans that an enlarged Europe is likely to promote increased world trade rather than divert trade from the United States. Indeed, EEC expansion generally has not taken place by a process of excluding American imports; the common external tariff of the enlarged European Community actually requires an average lowering of the external tariffs of Britain and the other new members.[15] It will thus be easier for the United States to export its products to Britain, Denmark, and Ireland than it has been in the past. The United States has basically benefited from the EEC's prosperity. In agriculture, for instance, American exports to the European Common Market countries during the 1966–71 period actually increased faster than to the rest of the world. And in fact, total U.S. exports to the EEC tripled in the same period. Indeed, until the modest trade deficit of 1972, there had been a large and consistent balance of EEC trade in America's favor. Although EEC trade policy has been illiberal in a few areas (reverse preferences, certain nontariff barriers), these are not, apart from agriculture, of great significance. On balance, protectionist fears that the Europeans are somehow shutting the United States out of their expanded market are therefore statistically and factually incorrect.

There are other factors as well which induce even a prosperous and increasingly autonomous Europe to maintain substantial linkages with the United States. The need for highly advanced American technology may be one of the strongest such incentives. In the face of a growing technological gap, and the predictability of major technological breakthroughs in such fields as controlled thermonuclear reaction as a power source, magneto-hydrodynamic processes of power generation, superconductivity, advances in the development of marine resources, and major improvements in laser technology, European dependence upon the United States is likely to become steadily more critical.[16] Furthermore, although massive American investment in Europe, related as it is to the huge and unredeemed pool of dollars, has provoked considerable European concern, it facilitates high and indispensable levels of prosperity and employment. And even France, at the height of de Gaulle's power, found it useful to welcome investment in certain industries and regions. Finally, whatever the changes in America's world role and in perceptions of the Soviet threat, Europe remains dependent on the U.S. military presence—whether or not with some reduction in troop levels—and an American nuclear guarantee.[17] Military reliance upon the United States is explicitly acknowledged by the Europeans, and during the 1973 French legislative elections, President Pompidou paid specific attention to the necessity of the Atlantic Alliance. Although the expanded EEC theoretically enjoys the population and economic strength ultimately to hold its own vis-à-vis the USSR, these resources are not translatable into viable superpower rank and strategic credibility until such time as genuine European political unity—conceivably a generation away—and the development of a full scale nuclear deterrent—a diversion of resources that the Europeans are not likely to consider in the absence of a major international upheaval—may come into existence.

Figure 1

Degree of European Unification

		More Unified	Less Unified
Affinity with U.S.	*Closer*	Atlantic Partnership, "Twin pillars"	Dependent and Atlanticized Europe
	More Remote	Third-Force Europe	19th-century Europe, possible "Finlandization"

Because Europe does not yet possess the kind of international superpower rank of the United States and the USSR, the recently recurrent theme of a rapidly developing movement toward five-power politics, for example as espoused by the Nixon administration, is quite premature. While it is true that the bipolar confrontation between the United States and the USSR has lessened, that alliances have weakened, and that additional major participants have entered or reentered the international arena, it is not yet the case that Europe stands in a position of comparable magnitude to the Americans and Russians. Indeed, the Chinese and Japanese are also likely to share second-rank status: the former not yet possessing the developed industrial base, the latter lacking nuclear weapons and the requisite political orientation and maneuverability. Thus, while there have been changes in world power configurations, the notion of a fluid five-power world politics, operating perhaps along the lines of the nineteenth-century European balance of power, is no more than hyperbole.

The future of the expanded European Community involves highly divergent possibilities. Its course of development depends upon the way in which two fundamental questions are resolved: What will be the degree of European unification? And what will be the extent of European affinity with the United States? All projections and prescriptions are necessarily based on assumptions or preferences (either made explicit or else assumed) regarding the outcome of these two questions.

If only two possible answers to each question are assumed—that Europe will become either more or less unified, and that it will become either closer or more remote from the United States—there are four conceivable outcomes (see figure 1). But the range of outcomes jumps to nine when the matrix is expanded to include a third realistic possibility—that of the "same" degree of extent (i.e., maintenance of existing patterns) along each dimension (see figure 2). Indeed, even this framework rests on certain additional assumptions about the course Europe will take during the next one to two decades: (1)

Figure 2

Degree of European Unification

		More Unified	Same	Less Unified
	Closer	1. Atlantic Partnership, "Twin pillars"	2. Postwar Pattern	3. Dependent and Atlanticized Europe
Affinity with U.S.	*Same*	4. Enhanced Status within Western Alliance	5. Contemporary Europe	6. Divisive Europe
	More Remote	7. Third-Force Europe	8. Gaullist Europe	9. 19th-century Europe, possible "Finland-ization"

that there will be no imperial conquest or domination of Europe by an outside power, nor a shift to pro-Soviet alliance or indigenous Communist government; (2) that Soviet-American superpower competition will continue, albeit in a less ideological, more muted form, and along more traditional lines of power and self interest; (3) that unification would bring with it at least the remote possibility of a credible European nuclear force; and (4) that Eastern Europe will not yet experience truly fundamental change in its foreign policy orientation and constraints, even though some internal changes may occur.[18]

What then is the nature of these possibilities? The concept of Atlantic Partnership (possibility 1), enunciated with special vigor under the Kennedy administration, foresees a unified Western Europe in close cooperation and interdependence with the United States. The next notion, the Postwar Pattern (2) or what Buchan calls "Atlanticized Europe," implies Atlantic cooperation in which Europe is no more unified than at present and therefore is not an equal partner with America. Dependent and Atlanticized Europe (3) also postulates a very close Atlantic linkage, but one in which European unity has regressed and the individual states are therefore more highly dependent upon the United States. Possibility 4, Enhanced Status within Western Alliance, assumes a greater degree of European unity than at present, but no marked upgrading or downgrading of the Atlantic tie. The Europeans remain within NATO, whether or not it is modified, but their view of unity gives them a more powerful and independent role vis-à-vis the Americans. Contemporary Europe (5), or what Buchan terms "Evolutionary Europe," constitutes essentially a continuation of the present picture with Europe experiencing no fundamental increase or decrease in either its own unification or in its affinity with the United States. Yet another possibility, Divisive Europe, (6) brings intra-European divisions based on a breakdown in unification. While the persistence of the Atlantic tie at the existing level may forestall either excessive dependence upon the United States or domination by the USSR, the situation implies a lessened European international presence and possible economic difficulties caused by problems of trade and a worsened technological gap. Third-Force Europe (7), Buchan's "Independent Federal Europe," means unification and assertive independence from both the United States and the USSR, probably coupled with a more vigorous European world role. Gaullist Europe (8) is similar, but based upon retention of much greater national independence without fundamental integration. Finally, 19th-century Europe (9), Buchan's "Fragmented Europe," involves a decay in European cooperation and a relapse to intra-European national rivalries, perhaps more characteristic of the nineteenth century and interwar Europe. However, its remoteness from the United States, probably involving a total American troop withdrawal and the collapse of NATO, makes probable the onset of "Finlandization," or a degree of Soviet hegemony.

Of the more comprehensive range of possibilities outlined in figure 2, some are much more likely to occur than others during the next one to two decades. A "surprise-free" prediction would tend to assume no drastic changes in either degree of unification or affinity for the United States. To the extent that change does occur, it is less likely to be along both dimensions (unification and affinity) than along one or the other, thus lessening the likelihood of the purer types, Atlantic Partnership (possibility 1), Dependent and Atlanticized Europe (3), Third-Force Europe (7), and Fragmented Europe (9). In addition, some directions of change are more probable than others. As far as degree of unification is concerned, a sharp decline is rather less likely than a continuation of present trends or a marked advance in integration. This would tend to diminish further the likelihood of possibilities 3 and 9, as well as that of 6. In regard to the Atlantic relationship, the drift of the last decade is unlikely to be redirected to closer European-American relations. On the other hand, the progressive decline in affinity may be somewhat constrained because of the previously cited elements of reliance upon American nuclear deterrence, technology, trading relationships, investment patterns, and more diffuse historic ties. This would tend to decrease still further the likelihood of Atlantic Partnership (1), Dependent and

Atlanticized Europe (3), Third-Force Europe (7) and Finlandization (9), and would also lessen the chances for a return to the Postwar Pattern (2) and Gaullist Europe (8).

Following this deductive logic to its inexorable conclusion leads to a hierarchy of possibilities (figure 3) based on the frequency with

Figure 3

A Hierarchy of Possibilities

Most Likely:	Contemporary Europe (5)
Possible:	Enhanced Status within Western Alliance (4)
Conceivable:	Gaullist Europe (8) Postwar Pattern (2) Divisive Europe (6)
Less Likely:	Third-Force Europe (7) Atlantic Partnership (1)
Least Likely:	Dependent and Atlanticized Europe (3) Finlandization (9)

which obstacles have been raised against each possibility.[19] The most likely outcome becomes some continuation or extrapolation of the present pattern, Contemporary Europe (5). Following that, there is the possibility of an Enhanced Western Alliance Role (4). Next, in the "conceivable" category come Gaullist Europe (8), Divisive Europe (6), and a reversion toward the Postwar Pattern (2). Less likely are Third-Force Europe (7) and Atlantic Partnership (1). Least likely are Dependent and Atlanticized Europe (3) and Finlandization (9).

To say the least, these conclusions are problematic, based as they are upon assumptions that may be altered by logic and by events. Nevertheless, the likely trend remains a slowly integrating Europe, moving (with occasional reverses) in the direction of increased economic integration along the pattern of the previous decade, and beginning to undertake small initial steps in the direction of political unity as well. The relationship with the United States will not be entirely intimate, and American choices of trade protectionism, total troop withdrawal, or a collapse of monetary cooperation would produce major upheavals in European-American relations. Over the long run, though, a stable and rather independent Western Europe, in a region characterized by some progress and vitality, should be something to be welcomed by the United States in an otherwise very imperfect world.

Shahrough Akhavi

The Middle East Crisis

The Middle East is a place today where local rivalries are intense,
where the vital interests of the United States and the Soviet Union
are both involved. . . . In this region in particular, it is imperative
that the two major powers conduct themselves so as to strengthen
the forces of peace rather than to strengthen the forces of war.

> —Richard M. Nixon, Address to the United Nations
> General Assembly, October 23, 1970.

Vietnam is our most anguishing problem. It is not, however, the
most dangerous. That grim distinction must go to the situation in
the Middle East with its vastly greater potential for drawing Soviet
policy and our own into a collision that could prove uncontrolla-
ble.

> —Richard M. Nixon, "U.S. Foreign Policy for the
> 1970's: Building for Peace," a Report to the Congress
> by the President of the United States, February 25,
> 1971.

Today, when the citizen picks up his daily newspaper, he is likely to
read about some new round or escalation of conflict in the Middle
East. Whether it is an Israeli armored incursion into the south of
Lebanon or guerrilla attacks in Europe or Israel, the Middle East
continues to represent a crisis area of the world second to none in its
potential danger. President Nixon's remarks have probably been
shared by at least the last two, if not more, of his predecessors. And
one wagers that Soviet leaders in private express the same misgivings. Why are the politics of this zone so intractable? Why do the

Arabs not sue for peace in exchange for presumably good prospects for the future development of their societies? Why can the Israelis not get it through their heads that they have to solve the problem of the Palestinians, rather than simply calling them "the refugees" and ignoring them? Why does the United Nations not solve the problem?

More importantly, what can the United States do about the Middle East crisis? The very posing of this last question begs a host of others: How did the American connection come about in the first place? What are the American interests to which the President has alluded? What openings does America have to Israeli and Arab opinion and policy makers on the basis of which to help buttress the cause of peace? What are the instruments of American policy, and how are they influenced?

Clearly it is not enough to try to answer the basic question about why neither the Arabs nor the Israelis have bit the bullet and arranged a permanent state of peace between them by making the obvious responses: (1) the Arabs have not sat down to talk peace directly because they fear future Israeli economic and political colonialism in the zone;[1] (2) the Israelis have not agreed to a maximal plan for repatriation and/or compensation to those Palestinians who left their homeland in 1947–48 because they are afraid of subsequent Arab subversion of their state.[2] What is needed, instead, is an analysis of the historical roots of the problem, roots that are inescapably embedded, in turn, in the colonialist phenomenon and imperialism. It is to these considerations that I shall now turn.

The Eastern Question

Those persons who feel that the Middle East problem ought to be susceptible to an internationally organized solution based on some United Nations formula may be forgiven for forgetting the extraordinarily long history of this problem. It is not too much to say that the Middle East crisis as we know it today is an emanation of the old Eastern Question with which European chancelleries had grappled since the failure of the second siege of Vienna by the Ottoman Empire in 1683. From that time to the collapse of the empire in World

War I, the "sick man of Europe" stayed just healthy enough to cause
no end of problems for the European great powers. While it would
not be appropriate at this juncture to survey a history of European-
Ottoman relations throughout this long period of Ottoman decline,
it must be said that Europeans never succeeded in solving their Eastern Question among themselves.[3] The extent of their failure can be
seen in the perennial phenomenon of crisis today in the Middle East.
It is nothing short of ironical that with all the power and might at
their disposal the European actors in the international system were
unable to impose a regulatory system or regime upon the area whose
operational expression would be a mechanism to advance European
interests.

To an individual versed in the history of the area, however, the
failure of twentieth-century attempts by the great powers, whether
through or outside the United Nations, was predictable. The reason
is to be found in the dynamics of the area's subordination to the
West, a phenomenon that has led Leonard Binder to call the Middle
East "a subordinate international system." [4] These dynamics have
the peculiar quality of paradox: namely, for all the technological,
military, and economic resources and power available to it, the West
has been typically impotent in its attempts to order the zone's events
according to prescribed patterns. The paradox of Middle East subordination as an international system and great-power impotence will
interweave as a theme throughout this essay.

It is interesting to note that at one time the Middle East was not
the subordinate international system that it is today. While not necessarily agreeing with the organic theories of the state—i.e., the moment the state stops to "grow," it begins to decay and collapse internally—this much is undeniable: the Ottoman Empire began its long
illness, as it were, with the death of the tenth in a line of truly extraordinary sultans (ruling collectively from 1312 to 1566) under
whose aegis the state expanded its frontiers tremendously. For a century after the death of the tenth, Sulayman the Magnificent (ruled
1520–66), the European-Ottoman confrontation remained at an
even standoff. However, precipitous decline set in during the eight-

eenth century and continued right up to the end of the empire in 1922.[5]

Western contact with this Muslim world actually began centuries before Emperors Francis I of France and Sulayman signed commercial accords in the 1500s. The Crusader Knights of the eleventh and twelfth centuries preceded, enabling the Christian powers of Europe to establish a toehold in the Levant and especially the Holy Places. But in the case of the Crusades, as well as in the later agreements with Francis I, the Muslims maintained the upper hand. The Knights managed to hold onto Jerusalem for but a brief period of time before relinquishing effective control to Saladin (Salah al-Din) and his successors. And it is no exaggeration to say that the ambassadors from the court of France were met in Istanbul under Sulayman's reign with the condescension befitting the status of that country as a second-rate power at that time. It was only upon repeated entreaties for trade and concessions by these envoys in the name of their sovereign that the sultan magnanimously "capitulated" to their propositions to permit trade on Ottoman territory. Note that the concept "capitulation," therefore, with all its latter-day connotations of economic and political prerogatives for the Western powers, originally signified patronizing acquiescence to appeals humbly submitted from below by unworthy Europeans.

Be that as it may, it is clear that the European great powers, having undergone such major transformations as the Renaissance, Enlightenment, French Revolution, and a rapid series of scientific-technological breakthroughs, easily pulled ahead of the Islamic world in ideas and achievements. Ottoman endeavors to emulate these Western advances, above all in the area of military development, soon led to the importation of Western personnel and thought. Thus we see the reforming sultans, Selim III and Mahmud II (ruled consecutively from 1789 to 1839), embarking on a series of administrative, juridical, educational, and social reforms that actually were entrained as part of the original impetus to *military* modernization. Out of the original desire to confront the West and surpass it through military capability, entirely new areas of human endeavor became susceptible to well-intentioned attempts at social engineering. Though the motivation of all this was to recapture the glory of the past, the ultimate result in the Ottoman Empire was to jettison the old ways without bringing about an organic and internally coherent set of solutions that were fully integrated with the social and political realities of the Ottoman Imperium. It is in this light that we should interpret the "Tanzimat" period of reforms from 1839 to 1876, as well as the "Nizam-e Cedid" of the earlier sultans, Selim III and Mahmud II.[6]

To cut a long story short, the Ottoman reformers ultimately failed to develop a system that could confront the West and defeat it after the fashion of the past. Throughout the nineteenth and early twentieth centuries the attempts, though in themselves very sophisticated, were not enthusiastically backed by the Ottoman elites on a consistent enough level to achieve the desired successes. Thus the peoples of the Ottoman Empire, and in particular, of course, the politically aware segments, grew simultaneously to resent and admire the Western superiority. Out of this emanated the peculiar love/hate relationship that the peoples of the area today still direct at the West: admiring it for its material capabilities, cultural advances, etc.; and resenting it for precisely the same reasons.

Also released in the Ottoman Empire was a growing tide of nationalist feeling and aspirations that brings us closer to the heart of the problem today. The Ottoman state, much as Tsarist Russia and Imperial Austria, consisted of a polyglot empire of diverse nationalities, and it, like them, was beset by currents of nationalist fervor throughout the nineteenth century. For the *Sublime Porte* (as the Ottoman government was known), the Arab revolt of 1916 was merely the last of a series of nationalist revolts throughout the empire that had begun with the Greeks in 1821. But in many ways it is the Arab revolt that continues to be the most fascinating of these rebellions because it constitutes one of the sources of the present-day Middle East crisis. The other is Zionism, the political movement of Jewish nationalism that had its public debut with the World Zionist Congress that met in 1897 in the Swiss city of Basle. Out of the collision between these two movements has come, as I. F. Stone said in his arresting article in the *New York Review of Books* in August 1967, the "tragedy in which Arabs and Israelis today find themselves." And by this tragedy Stone meant an ineluctable conflict between parties, both sides of which are in the right to some extent. These two movements, however, on their own, would have remained inert, very like two chemical elements that fail to react with one another in the absence of a catalyst. In this case the catalyst was Western imperialism and the crucible was the historical territory of Palestine.

It goes without saying that neither Arab nationalism nor, still more, Zionism would have gotten anywhere without recourse to Western imperialism. The chief partners in the Western coalition were originally Britain and France. Today the imperialist phenomenon is embodied in the roles played by the United States, which has inherited the traditional role of the Western powers, and the Soviet Union. The latter, incidentally, both under the tsars and the commissars, has played a historically imperialist role in this area, but has, nevertheless, remained imperceptible to the Arabs until very recently. One of the interesting consequences of the 1967 war is the growing perception in the minds of the Arabs about the imperialist role of the Soviet Union.

Evolution of the Eastern Question

In the beginning the Zionists petitioned Great Britain for support of their idea of founding a national home in Palestine.[7] For their part, the Arabs in 1915 contacted British representatives and officials with the idea of rebellion against the Ottoman Empire, then a belligerent state hostile to the United Kingdom in the war.[8] The British followed up these Arab suggestions with some alacrity, whereas the response to the prior Zionist appeals had been one of temporizing and delaying. Clearly the resources of the Arabs at this stage of the game were more potent than those available to the Zionists. Apart from their sheer numbers, the Arabs had a trump card that the British wanted played for their side, the ability to strike a crippling blow at a state with whom they were at war. In the days of 1915 and 1916, Winston Churchill, who was at that time First Lord of the Admiralty, had an ambitious scheme that the way to defeat Germany was to begin a front in Southeastern Europe, the continent's "soft underbelly." If the Arabs could open a breach in this region, then the Western coalition could carry on from there and sweep north to victory in Central Europe.

The Arabs revolted in the wake of promises made to Sharif Hussein, an Arab serving as the Ottoman governor of that part of present-day Saudi Arabia that contains the two Islamic holy cities of Mecca and Medina. In the course of communications between this Sharif Hussein and His Majesty's Government, known as the Hussein-McMahon correspondence, the Arabs agreed to rise up against Istanbul in return for the promise of a unified Arab kingdom under Hussein's rule. Much ink has subsequently been spilled over whether the British in fact did mean this country to be unified, whether the existing territory of Palestine was to be part of the coastal strip specifically excluded by McMahon from the projected Arab state, and so on. What is not questioned at all, however, is that independence and the foundation of a sovereign Arab state in the area of the Fertile Crescent were part of the bargain. While Hussein did not agree with some of the exclusions of McMahon in the correspondence, he nevertheless decided to declare war against the Ottoman Empire based on the existing promises made to him, with the hopes later on of pushing through his other demands.[9]

These details are important because subsequently, as a result of British, French, and Russian policies of secret covenants secretly arrived at, the West utterly discredited itself in the eyes of the Arabs over the Eastern Question. Through the covert Sykes-Picot Treaty (May 1916) and the Treaty of London (March 1915), Britain, France, and Russia partitioned the Ottoman Empire among themselves, with a view to the postwar political disposition of the area. When the Arabs carried out their part of the bargain in 1916, they were, of course, ignorant of the contents of the antecedent secret treaties, or indeed of their existence. In point of fact, the British promises to the Arabs and these earlier secret treaties worked directly at cross purposes with one another. Then on November 2, 1917, the Balfour Declaration was issued by the British government. This document promised British support for the Zionist objective to the extent that it stated as follows:

> His Majesty's Government view with favor the establishment in Palestine of a national home for the Jewish people, and will use their best endeavors to facilitate the achievement of this object, it being clearly understood that nothing shall be done which may prejudice the civil and religious rights of existing non-Jewish communities in Palestine or the life and political status enjoyed by Jews in any other country.[10]

With the Balfour Declaration, yet another inconsistent chapter in the story of great-power involvement was written upon the heels of the Hussein-McMahon agreements and the secret treaties already alluded to above. Even the internal language and meaning of the Balfour Declaration itself were contradictory: on the one hand, promising a national home to the Jewish people; and on the other, apparently denying, by implication, the political articulation of Zionist objectives—that is, denying a sovereign territorial state of Israel.

Enter the United States

Alfred Thayer Mahan's theories of naval strategy serve as the initial forum for the use of the term *Middle East.* Earlier terms, such as Near East or the Nearer East or simply The East, all signify that the area lay in a certain location relative to how outsiders viewed the international system. Surely there exists no better symptom of the area's subordination to other parts of the international system. The area was "middle" with regard to the naval strategies and commercial routes evolved by Westerners. The irony of all this resides in the ultimate acceptance and appropriation of the term Middle East by the people of the area itself. Today the Arabs still refer to the territory that they occupy as "al-Sharq al-Awsat" which means the Middle East, or the Middle-most East, really.

The United States role in the Middle East originated in the activity of Christian missionaries. American political presence in the region, however, did not begin until the end of World War II, although, three prior instances of indirect American involvement may be cited: (1) Iran was used as a transit route for the sending of Lend-Lease supplies to the Soviet Union from 1941 until 1945; (2) Aramco, the Arabian-American Oil Company, was established in Saudi Arabia in 1938; (3) America influenced Arab nationalist movements in the early 1920s through its democratic ideals.

To begin with the last instance, Woodrow Wilson's administration dealt with the Middle East through the contact of American delegates to the Versailles Peace Conference with Arab, Armenian, and Egyptian nationalists who also were there. Meanwhile, Zionist activity in America had already begun and powerful spokesmen for the Jewish cause existed: Supreme Court Justices Louis Brandeis and Felix Frankfurter, among others. At Versailles, Wilson's Fourteen Points served as the touchstone of efforts by nationalist movements and smaller states generally, to evolve a settlement based on self-determination, a peace without annexations, and an end to the colonialist policies of the great powers prior to the war. No more eloquent shibboleth to embody the Wilsonian ideas existed than "open covenants openly arrived at." The revolutionary Bolsheviks had already dramatically denounced the secret treaties that the tsarist government had contracted with the "imperialist bourgeois governments." Thus, when the Armenians, the Arabs, and the Egyptians—who sent a separate delegation to the Versailles Conference to plead an end to the British protectorate over Egypt—argued their causes on the Wilsonian principles, the rebuff they received at the hands of Georges Clemenceau and David Lloyd George appeared conclusive proof that colonialism was retrenching in the region.

Wilson's sympathies lay with the small states in general, but these feelings seemed directed more to the Central European states, such as Czechoslovakia and Yogoslavia. And there self-determination seemed to be meeting with incredibly difficult problems anyway. The translation of the demands for self-determination into reality in Central Europe was enormously difficult. Who had time for the Arabs in this setting? Nevertheless, Wilson did reserve enough residual attention to the Middle East that he supported the creation of a special tripartite commission to inquire into the wishes of the population of Syria and Palestine regarding their future political systems. The French, who were none too happy about the Fourteen Points in general, succeeded in persuading the British not to cooperate with Wilson's commission. Consequently, although it constituted a high-powered group, the King-Crane Commission, named after its two leading men, represented a unilaterally instigated board of inquiry with advisory powers only.[11] The commission's determinations were that the people of Palestine were opposed to Zionist objectives, and the Syrians violently against the proposed French mandate over Syria. Instead, the Syrians preferred an American protectorate above any other dependency relationship, if they had to have one at all. Only if this scheme were to abort, and as a poor second, would they choose a British mandate.

However, the work of the King-Crane Commission, which the Zionists had set out to block in the first instance, had no practical impact. From that time until the establishment in 1938 of Aramco, America played a negligible role in the Middle East. This interwar era was a period of isolationism, and the Middle East was not the only area where American attention lagged. After that date, however, the politics of international oil made it imperative for the United States to take an active role in the Middle East. The oil companies were the first American interest group that sought to caution against ignoring the Arab point of view on the Palestine question. It was natural that they took this position in view of their need for political stability and friendship on the part of the conservative shaykhs and rulers of oil-rich lands. The extent of the investments by American concerns in the Middle East needs little commentary here. It became in the interest of the U.S. government to back these conservative regimes in order to protect the investments of their own nationals. And it became increasingly clear that European recovery in the post-World War II period was to be intricately linked to Middle East oil above the oil of any other world region. Finally, the American balance of payments depends on Middle East oil to a large extent. American corporations play a middleman role for the oil that Europe consumes out of this region. Eventually, sectors of the American bureaucracy, the military establishment, and particularly State Department hands specializing in the Middle East formed the firm nucleus of a latent "pro-Arab" lobby within the United States. These diplomats, ambassadors, and chargés, stationed in the zone, later joined by senior military officials, gradually came to see greater risks to American security from an exaggeratedly pro-Israel stance than from a cautious, nonaligned one.

All of this leads to a compelling point: the transformation of the American image of the Middle East rested on newly formed perceived threats to the security of the United States. This stemmed from anxiety lest its leading rival, the USSR, might be able to make inroads in the area, thus simultaneously jeopardizing the security of Europe by disrupting the "lifeline" of oil and blocking the zone's communications network. Theretofore, oil and communications in the Middle East had been a Western monopoly.

The Cold War: Early Conflicts with the USSR

Having traced in broadest outlines the historical development of Middle East international politics, my task in the remainder of this essay is to focus specifically on American policy and behavior since World War II. What has happened since the late 1930s to alter the American image? Briefly put, two factors coalesced: European economic hardships after the Second World War and a probing, even adventurous Soviet policy in the peripheral areas where the spheres-of-influence agreements of the war period had not delineated any clear-cut guidelines. At any rate, in the Middle East the Soviets seemed, from 1945 until 1950 (and even up to 1955) to be behaving much as though their 1940 secret protocol with the Nazis concerning Turkey and Iran were still operative. This protocol, it will be recalled, asserted that "the Soviet Union declares that its territorial aspirations center south of the national territory of the Soviet Union in the direction of the Indian Ocean." [12]

U.S. involvement in the Middle East in the first five years after 1945 can be summarized by a list of four countries: Iran, Turkey, Greece, Palestine-Israel. As a result of commitments rendered—some of them less serious than others, it turns out in retrospect—to these non-Arab states, the United States laid the foundations for later involvement in the Arab zone for which, to put it mildly, it was not prepared. Revelations by the then ambassador to Iran, George V. Allen, some twenty years or so afterward to William B. Quandt of the Rand Corporation, show that American interest and involvement in that country's problems with the Soviet Union in 1946 were minimal. There, it was largely a result of accidents and fortuitous circumstances that the Soviets suffered two defeats (rebuffs on the oil concession demand and on the Azerbaijan issue) at the Iranians' hands without Washington ever committing itself to more than isolated mild statements of support for Iran's sovereignty and independence. Secretary of State Dean Acheson's remark, quoted by the *New York Times* on December 11, 1946, that America did not want to get involved in an internal Iranian affair (Soviet evacuation of Azerbaijan Province) demonstrates the casualness with which Washington apparently viewed things. Quandt also bemusedly reports that the liberation of Azerbaijan Province by the central Iranian government appears to have been facilitated tremendously by spurious reports that American troops were leading the military columns on the road to Tabriz, Azerbaijan's capital. Apparently, the rumor grew out of the presence of three American journalists in an army jeep flying an American flag.[13]

In the case of Turkey, Soviet behavior seemed provocative. Inasmuch as Greece lay to the west of Turkey and possibly subject to pressure from the east by a resurgent USSR, the American government adopted a harder line on Turkey than it did on Iran. Essentially, the Soviets were demanding three different things: (1) the "return" of Turkey's three Eastern provinces to the Soviet Union; (2) Soviet partnership with the Turks in administering the Bosphorus and Dardanelles straits (that is, a unilateral change in the international regime of the Turkish straits); (3) Soviet military bases in Turkey. In fact, Greece's geopolitics may have prompted President Truman to seek to ensure that the Soviets would not be able to entrench in Turkey. Stalin had earlier arrived at his well-known "percentages" agreement with Churchill in October 1944, whereby Greece was to be under 90 percent British influence. It may well be that pressure on Turkey presaged, for the American administration, an effort to undo the percentages deal. Even though Stalin himself appeared to be honoring the deal and was actively discouraging the Greek Communists from continuing their rebellion, the Western powers were not sure how the late dictator was going to behave. If Iran and Turkey were precedents, then it augured badly for Greece. By this time British and American hopes for friendly relations with their erstwhile Soviet ally were turning sour.

It would seem that Stalin was a firm advocate of the spheres-of-influence policy, whereby it was commonly agreed among the leaders of the great powers that zones of the world would be distributed among them by common consent. In his relations with Hitler, this orientation clearly emerged. Stalin's statement to Anthony Eden that he regarded declarations (such as the Atlantic Charter, the Four Freedoms) as "algebra" and agreements (such as the percentages agreements, presumably) as "practical arithmetic" comes into mind. The late *vozhd* explained helpfully to Eden: "While I do not mean to decry algebra, I prefer practical arithmetic." [14] But certain parts of the world existed where the spheres policy was inoperative, either because no agreements had been reached or else tacit and inarticulated understandings were given which upon later examination turned out to have been *mis*understandings. Iran seemed one such area; Turkey another. Korea, too, fits into this mold. Secretary of State Acheson, whose reluctance to involve the United States in Iran has already been noted, could say with aplomb in a press conference in January 1950 that the Koreans would have to fend for themselves, subject to the assistance of the United Nations. And later, in May of the same year, he publicly declared Korea to be militarily indefensible, and what is more, he held, the Congress of the United States knew that this was the case.[15] Obviously, Stalin could not resist testing to see if American determinations on such areas as Korea and Iran were really as weak as they seemed.

On the other hand, Greece had been explicitly ruled out of bounds of Soviet ambitions. So too Italy and France. In France, for example, Stalin ordered the French Communist party to desist from making revolution and in a letter to Tito in 1948 he conceded almost wistfully that France would not "go Communist." The reason we do not have a People's Democracy in France is that the Red Army was unable to reach French frontiers, he noted. And the reason for that, in turn, was that France was denied him in the Allies' strategy for liberating various European regions from German occupation.

Oddly enough, Stalin adopted a "correct" position on the Palestine Question as far as the West was concerned. The Soviets recognized the state of Israel, albeit within the frontiers established by the UN partition plan of November 1947. Also, Western observers seldom recall that prior to the famous arms deal between Czechoslovakia and Egypt in September 1955 there was an earlier Czech arms deal with the Zionists in Palestine. Just prior to the 1948 hostilities, a shipment of Czech arms arrived in that territory, and it is largely conceded that the Czech arms played a significant, although one cannot say decisive, role in the victory of the Zionists over the Arab armies that poured into the state of Israel in 1948.

Stalin's Israel policy rested on the expectation that the Zionists, who are socialists, after all, would look more to the USSR for political and economic guidance. He could not ignore the fact that Jews had played a tremendously vital role for socialism in the Bund (the Jewish labor movement in Europe at the turn of the century). Although the Zionists were closer to European social democracy than to radical Marxism-Leninism, there is no denying the Bolsheviks' optimism regarding their tie with the new state of Israel. Recognition also helped along the process of British decolonialization and opened a breach in the Middle East that permitted the establishment of a possible Soviet foothold. Finally, Jews played disproportionately leading roles in the tiny Middle Eastern Communist parties that were completely ineffective in generating any kind of support from the Arab majority populations of territories in the Middle East.[16]

For tactical and strategic reasons, therefore, it made sense for Stalin to pursue a pro-Israel policy even at the risk of antagonizing native Arab populations. We must not forget that in the late Stalinist period such nationalist leaders of the Third World as Gandhi were regarded as British espionage agents by Stalin and the Soviet media. Furthermore, the Free Officers who seized power in Egypt on July 23, 1952, were simply regarded in the Soviet media as fascist putschists who glorified militarism. Nevertheless, it soon became clear to the Soviet leadership that the Israeli connection was counterproductive. The parting of the ways began with the "Doctors' Plot," an apparent concoction on the part of Stalin in an endeavor to crush his internal enemies. Some of these latter had already been implicated in the curious "Leningrad affair" whereby leading party functionaries of the Communist party were supposed to have united against Stalin's internal policies of ideological and social retrenchment in the late 1940s and early 1950s. Stalin evidently saw enemies everywhere. The great purges of the 1930s (the *Yezhovshchina*) still served as a reminder of what might befall Soviet society. The fact that many of the physicians arrested in the Doctors' Plot were Jews served to lend credence to charges of a new round in the periodic anti-Semitic campaigns. The signs were ominous enough to provoke precisely the fears of the *Yezhovshchina*, combined with a furious pogrom that could be used as a façade behind which to liquidate all internal enemies, real or imagined.

The Zionists, meanwhile, were turning to the West for economic and political support. Clearly the natural constituency for voluntary fund-raising institutions, such as the United Jewish Appeal, lay in the West rather than the USSR or the People's Democracies. The Soviets, for their part, had begun gradually to take a second look at the Third World and concluded that perhaps it constituted what they called a "peace zone" which might be exploited for their own interests. When Egypt declared its neutrality in the United Nations over the Korean question, the foundations already existed in the Middle East for a more active Soviet policy. It took Stalin's death, however, to bring about a reorientation.

A major point stands out from this discussion of the early cold war years. American involvement in the zone seems to have been ad hoc responses to challenges posed by outside forces upon the Middle East. As such, the American involvement lacked coherence, systematization, or consistency. Yet, in some respects this period was the most successful for the United States. Reacting to what it felt to be Soviet challenges, Washington seems to have won on all fronts in the contest for political support in the Middle East. Ironically, it was when the Americans began more systematically to develop a policy in the 1950s that Western influence began to dissipate. Here is the paradox of Middle East subordination and Western impotence once again.

American Policy in the 1950s: The Arab Question

Prior to 1950, Britain and France had been responsible for guaranteeing the Western channels of communication to and within the Middle East and defending the oil interests. This was only natural in view of the preeminent position of those two states in the area since World War I. Britain held League of Nations mandates over Palestine, Iraq, and Transjordan, plus the protectorate over Egypt (officially ended in 1922, but British presence in Egypt was terminated only in June 1956). British treaties with the Trucial States on Saudi Arabia's perimeter, and French mandates over Syria and Lebanon (1920–46) had served to establish this Anglo-French hegemony. Just prior to the outbreak of the Korean war, the United States joined these two powers in a declaration of intent called the Tripartite Declaration of May 1950.

The declaration, the second American pronouncement after the Truman Doctrine (March 1946), further established the lines of American policy for the entire Middle East. The Truman Doctrine pertained mainly to Greece and Turkey and amounted to a commitment "to support free peoples who are resisting attempted subjugation by armed minorities or by outside pressures" so that they could "work out their own destinies in their own ways." [17] Under its umbrella, Greece and Turkey gradually become incorporated into the NATO pact. Four years after the Truman Doctrine's issue, the Tripartite Declaration arrayed the United States alongside the colonial powers, Britain and France, in an arrangement to maintain the security of the Middle East. The operative parts of the declaration set forth: (1) American (and British and French) opposition to arms races in the area; (2) American insistence that any arms aid to a given state in the zone not be used in aggression against other states there; (3) American commitment to promote peace and stability in the area by its military assistance policies. By so defining its position, the United States asserted its determination to join in preventing any violation of sovereignty by the enforcement of an arms boycott, if necessary, or even intervention against the offending party.[18] Essentially, the declaration led to America adopting a policeman's role for the Middle East.

Because the British had already established the Middle East Supply Center during World War II, and also had at that time founded the Middle East Defense Command, Western efforts at organizing the defense of the Middle East appeared much facilitated in the early 1950s. By joining in the Tripartite Declaration, however, the United States made an irrevocable commitment on the side of Western imperialism. Subsequent attempts to get the Arab states formally to join Western-sponsored defense alliance systems were to backfire and cause the erosion of Western influence. The Arab states could not fail to have noted President Truman's very personal decision to push for immediate recognition of strong backing for the state and cause of Israel over and beyond the advice of his secretary of state, the joint chiefs of staff, and a number of other officials in the American foreign policy bureaucracy.[19] Coming on top of this the Tripartite Declaration seemed to favor continued American underwriting of Israeli military superiority. For this reason, of course, the Arab states showed pronounced hostility to the declaration. When Western spokesmen sought to convince Arab elites of the Soviet threat, these latter laughingly pointed to the map and the long distances from Moscow to Arab capitals. Instead, as they rightly pointed out, it was *Western* troops that were in Egypt and other Arab lands. Consequently, the Western-backed Middle East Defense Organization (MEDO) proposed in 1951 fell on deaf Egyptian and Syrian ears. Iraq and Jordan, by contrast, appear to have been interested.

Britain had already run afoul of Egyptian hostility to its actions in the area in 1944. In that year the British encouraged the Fertile

Crescent plan of Nuri al-Sa'id, the strong man and frequent prime minister of Iraq. This plan would have brought Jordan, Lebanon, and Syria under Iraqi tutelage in some federative manner. It would have greatly eased British attempts to secure the region against external pressure. Egypt, however, which has traditionally been Iraq's rival in regional politics dating to ancient, pre-Islamic times, was outraged over this blatant favoring of Iraq. Egyptian opposition effectively put an end to the Fertile Crescent scheme. In response, the British pushed the idea of an Arab League, which officially came into existence in 1945. They hoped that they could use the vehicle of the league to foster their objectives of regional defense. However, once again Egyptian opposition appeared too great.

We see, therefore, that two major issues were involved in Arab rancor against the West, including, of course, the United States: (1) its role in the creation of Israel; (2) its seeming support for British policies that followed the classic divide-and-rule principle. In the latter case, the British were dividing the Iraqis from the Egyptians and trying to bring the rest of the Arab world down on the side of Iraq.

This is how matters stood up to January 1955. We have already seen that by that time the Soviets had decided upon a fresh approach toward the underdeveloped countries. The festering dispute between the Arabs and Israel made the Middle East an extremely dangerous part of the world. The 1948 war had only settled one thing: Israel was a viable state and could not easily be defeated. Neither Arab governments nor Arab opinion were in a mood to negotiate a peace settlement, however, given their deeply held view that the creation of Israel was morally wrong and a grave injury to the Arab sense of justice. Hence, the armistice lines created in 1949 between Israel and each of Egypt, Jordan, Lebanon, and Syria were notoriously weak. This was particularly true of the Egyptian-Israel frontier. Prime Minister David Ben-Gurion adopted the policy of massive application of force by Israel against the Arabs. This policy set the stage for the dramatic Israeli incursion into Gaza of February 1955, the climax of a series of border incidents in the area. The incident resulted in a couple of dozen Egyptian deaths and the destruction of the Egyptian Gaza Police Headquarters.

In that same month, the Americans, together with the British, had finally induced Iraq to join a military alliance with Turkey, then part of NATO. This bilateral defense alliance was to form the foundation of the Baghdad Pact, an alliance that was also to include Iran and Pakistan (which joined in October 1955). The Gaza incursion, the Iraqi-Turkish treaty, and Nasser's trip to the Bandung Conference of unaligned countries (April 1955) came rapidly in succession. It is against the backdrop of these events that American policy in the Arab Middle East must be viewed.

Egypt had been seeking in vain to purchase arms from the United States with which it could confront Israel. The price asked by the Americans seemed to have been Egyptian agreement to participation in the Western security system for the area. Due to this misguided effort, climaxed by Secretary of State John Foster Dulles' visit to Cairo in 1953, Egyptian suspicion of U.S. motives continued to grow. Apparently, the Chinese had meanwhile agreed to serve as go between for Cairo and Moscow concerning a possible arms sale with the socialist bloc when Nasser attended the Bandung Conference.[20] It is known that Egyptian desires to purchase up-to-date weapons in large quantities were extremely strong after the Gaza incident. Notwithstanding, Egyptian policy makers far from trusted the Soviet Union. They much preferred purchasing from the West.[21] Nevertheless, buying from the Soviets in the end served two worthwhile purposes: (1) it broke the Western monopoly on arms supplies into the zone, and with it the *cordon sanitaire* imposed in a de facto manner by the terms of the Tripartite Declaration around the Arab states; and (2) it demonstrated the sovereignty of Egypt in the face of that country's erstwhile colonial masters.

Needless to say, the impact of the "Czech" arms deal with Egypt—announced in late September 1955—was most pronounced on Great Britain. British exasperation with Egypt over the question of Sudanese independence, the Palestine problem, and Arab nationalism (with the threat the latter posed to Britain's two client states, Jordan and Iraq) mounted apace after the arms deal. Combined with this seemed to be a very personal antipathy on the part of the British prime minister, Eden, to Nasser. Eden's memoirs, written after his resignation over the Suez debacle in 1956, reveal that he had regarded Nasser as an upstart dictator with Hitlerian appetites. Appeasement of this "dictator" was out of the question.

Interestingly, Western investments in Egypt had received encouragement from the military regime.[22] When the question arose as to the construction of a huge dam to provide water and electricity for one-third again of the country's area, the prospects of Western financing appeared very good. However, the excessively moralistic approach toward Nasser by Dulles and Eden, who were basically responsible for formulating a Western policy for the Middle East, hindered the negotiations. Most observers feel that Dulles suddenly appeared to waver and raised certain conditions that would have to be met before the American share to the IMF loan could go through. It would appear that the Americans used the High Dam financing project as a prod to convince the Egyptians to be more accommodating on the question of Middle East defense and anticommunism. When it became clear that Washington was having second thoughts, the British, too, withdrew their commitment to providing a share of the IMF loan. These twin defections from the IMF effort proved too much, and the question of Western financing fell by the wayside. The dam issue proved yet another problem that unsettled Western-Arab relations.

Nasser's nationalization of the Suez Canal in July 1956 constituted a severe jolt to British policies. Part of the Egyptian justification for the nationalization was that the country needed the revenue to build the Aswan Dam. However, it is fairly certain that Nasser had earlier made up his mind to nationalize the Canal and merely bided his time for the right moment to make his move. The Suez Canal, built in 1869, was one of the chief reasons that the British established their presence in the country in the first place. France, too, had considerable investments in the waterway. Nationalization meant displacing the French and British, a considerable loss in both money invested and prestige and influence built up over the years. The French had an additional ax to grind against Nasser for his military and sanctuary support of the Algerian revolutionary movement, beginning in 1954.

Clearly this is not the juncture to examine in detail the Suez affair. But the basic point to note is that by summer 1956 Egypt's propaganda campaign on behalf of Arab nationalism was in high gear. The position of the Jordanian monarch became so precarious that he was compelled to dismiss the British commander of his Arab Legion in March 1956 and replace him with an Arab. Meanwhile, Iraq was the target of vitriolic attacks in the Egyptian media. In the face of this adversity, the British and French governments conspired to overthrow Nasser and substitute in his place a more compliant figure. In this endeavor, the two governments recruited the assistance of the Israel government. The ultimate invasion-attack of October 1956 came without a shred of consultation with the United States.

Apparently as a result of poor coordination, the British bombardment in the Port Said area failed in its objective to produce a rout. While the Israelis succeeded in achieving their maximum objectives, the bungling of their allies undid these victories. The American government's electrifying condemnation of these operations placed the final nail in the coffin of the Suez adventure. The Soviets have regarded the defeat of the Anglo-French-Israeli attack as a function of their warnings and threats. However, such an interpretation is entirely misleading inasmuch as Nikolai Bulganin's saber-rattling *pronunciamentos* came only after the American policy had been articulated.

In this spectacular fashion did Western influence in the Middle East diminish almost to the vanishing point. The United States, however, emerged with a refurbished image in the minds of Arab nationalists. Once again, according to the paradox of subordination, a great power became most potent in the zone when it did the least! In this case, the United States did not participate in the show of force that resulted in the Suez war. On the contrary, it *opposed* this show of force. Thus, for a fleeting moment (November–December 1956), the United States seemed to have abandoned the bluster and tough talking of a Dulles seeking to thrust Egypt into a Western defense pact for a Dulles (under Eisenhower's orders!) who was insisting that force did not pay.

American prestige, seldom higher in the Arab world in these two months, rapidly dissipated, however, with the promulgation of the Eisenhower Doctrine in January 1957. This doctrine became incorporated into a joint resolution of both houses of Congress in March 1957. In tone, it sounded much like the Truman Doctrine of a decade earlier. It asserted that the independence and integrity of the states in the Middle East was a vital American interest and indispensable to international peace. The Congress gave the President authorization to enter into economic and/or military aid programs with any state in the area asking for it. Finally, it committed the American administration to use armed force to help any nation of the area ward off "armed aggression from any country controlled by international communism." [23] Following the lines of the classic containment policies of the late 1940s, the Eisenhower Doctrine was seen to fill a serious need: to define more explicitly American reactions to revolutionary threats to the peace of the Middle East.

Nevertheless, the Arab nationalist movement did not see things in the same terms as the American President and Congress. The spokesman of the movement, Nasser, interpreted the new doctrine as yet another colonialist ploy to fetter his and other Arab countries. The clause evoking the threat of international communism seemed disingenuous because Arab regimes were having little difficulty dealing with indigenous Communist movements. Nasser's riposte was to take the offensive and exert great pressure on Iraq, Syria, Jordan, and Saudi Arabia to defect from, or steer clear of, Western wooing. Among the tensions in 1957 was the summer "war scare" between Turkey and Syria. While local issues were involved between those two states, Turkey seemed to be acting as a proxy for the West in an attempt to isolate Syria due to increasing Communist strength there. Another tense moment came in the Jordanian crisis of April, in which the Eisenhower Doctrine was actually invoked on behalf of King Hussein. It was maintained that his kingdom actually was the target of international Communist aggression. The American Sixth Fleet was accordingly placed on the alert, and American assistance to Jordan began. This aid has not stopped yet, it should be noted, and the American administration as recently as 1970 once again ordered Sixth Fleet vessels to cruise off the eastern Mediterranean coast in response to a crisis between Jordan and Syria.

In 1958 the United States was entirely on the defensive in its Arab policy. In May civil war broke out in Lebanon. The Eisenhower Doctrine could not be invoked by any stretch of the imagination, yet American marines landed on the beaches in a comical operation that cartoonists had a field day satirizing. While no hostilities occurred between Lebanese and Americans, the general feeling in Lebanon to the American effort was negative. In July, much more serious events occurred: a revolution in Iraq, toppling the monarchy and installing a vehemently nationalist republican regime. Derivative of the events in Iraq was another crisis in Jordan, resulting in the dispatch of British paratroopers to that land. Iraq withdrew from the Baghdad Pact, and with it left the only Arab state that had participated. The alliance was changed in name to the Central Treaty Organization (CENTO), but its effectiveness in the endeavor to contain the USSR was moot to say the least.

Despite these reversals, it is fair to say that the United States was the dominant power in the area during the mid- and late 1950s. The USSR had only entered the Middle East in 1955. It was in no position to contest the Eisenhower Doctrine except through verbal polemics. Its role in the Suez war was equivocal to the Arabs, something which the Egyptians in particular never forgot.[24] During the decade of the 1950s the outlines of several levels of conflict in the Middle East became articulated. It is especially difficult to disentangle the conflicting demands and goals represented by each of these levels due to their mutual cross-cutting and interpenetration.

Briefly, the following levels of conflict need to be analyzed: (1) superpower competition in the zone for tactical and/or strategic advantage in the larger global context; (2) inter-Arab conflict, which in itself is riven with crisscrossing cleavages of an ideological, social, and power-political nature (incidentally, it is due to these countervailing currents in the inter-Arab conflict that one might speak of an Egyptian-Jordanian axis at certain periods, from March 1956 to April 1957, or June 1967 to September 1970; and then, on the other hand, venomous relations between these two states at other times, for example, April 1957 to June 1961, and further, September 1962 to June 1967); (3) Egyptian-Israel conflict; (4) Arab-Israel conflict; (5) Palestine guerrillas and the conflict with Israel as well as with certain Arab governments.

The present-day manifestations of the five levels of conflict are arms races and escalation of these races. It is simply too complicated a subject to be discussed satisfactorily in the course of one short essay.[25] We would do well to note, however, that the demand for arms provides its own internal dynamic of reinforcing a client relationship on the part of the respective regional states relative to the superpowers while simultaneously forcing increasing and more intense commitment by the superpowers to positions staked out by the local forces. In this way, the maddening paradox of Middle East subordination enters in. According to this pattern it is the superpowers, not their clients, that are the tail being wagged by the Middle Eastern dog. And in the Middle East, what reinforces this "tail-ism," as Lenin called it, is that the street serves as a forum for "the continuation of politics by other means," to paraphrase Clausewitz.

The American Policy Environment and the Levels of Conflict

The institutions of America's Middle East policy have been ably summarized by William Quandt in his 1970 Rand Corporation study on the domestic influences on this foreign policy. According to him the relevant organs are: (1) the President and his White House staff (for present purposes, this means President Nixon and Henry Kissinger, national security adviser. Two other White House staffers have traditionally included an adviser on Jewish affairs and an assistant to the national security adviser on the Near East, North Africa, and South Asia); (2) the State Department, numerous officials and organs of which take part in formulation and execution, including the secretary of state, undersecretaries of state, assistant secretaries of state, deputy assistant secretaries of state, ambassadors to the countries of the area and to the United Nations, the Intelligence and Research Division; (3) the Defense Department, including the secretary, the joint chiefs of staff, the International Security Affairs branch; (4) the CIA; (5) the armed services and foreign affairs committees of both houses of Congress; (6) organized interest groups, notably a variety of pro-Zionist lobbies, the oil companies, and cultural and religious groups (e.g., the American Friends Service Committee); (7) the press; and (8) public opinion.[26]

While pro-Arab lobby groups exist (such as the American Friends of the Middle East), it is obvious that the American Jewish community, well informed in matters of politics generally and organized to mobilize opinion, plays a visible role in America's Middle East policy. However, this influence may very well have been exaggerated in the minds of the public in terms of shaping policy content from day to day, or from month to month. Recently, Nahum Goldmann, the controversial Israeli public figure, has asserted in a speech that the halcyon days of President Truman are a thing of the past. Now it is no longer possible for any Jew in America to call the White House and speak with the President. This hyperbolic statement serves to show that Israel and the Zionists have traditionally enjoyed the sympathy and ear of American administrations that the Arabs have lacked.

The United States has typically relied on economic and military assistance and trade programs with the countries of the Middle East. Of lesser importance have been technical assistance projects (Point IV, for example) and sociocultural exchanges. It will be argued that it is in this last area that the United States can do the most in the short and medium runs to promote its interests in the zone.

Examining the levels of conflict in the area, what might be American policy in the next five or ten years? Washington has demonstrated by the Nixon-Brezhnev summit of May 1972 that it is possible for the superpowers to act together on the Middle East. Perhaps "act" in this case is the wrong word, for apparently the superpowers have decided to restrain their competition in the area by agreeing not to elevate the arms race spiral another notch. Here the superpowers have simply discovered that it is in their mutual interest not to keep feeding their clients with hardware in the absence of promising developments toward eventual leveling off of their conflict. Clearly the Soviets could not go on forever sending the latest radar equipment, airplanes, and defensive missiles to Egypt and still have enough to go around for their own economic plans at home and in their relations with other Communist states. The United States prefers the existing situation because of Vietnam and because it fears a conflict that would involve itself against the Soviet Union. In retrospect, the Soviet Union appears to have lost the gamble it took with Nixon in May 1972 in view of President Anwar Sadat's expulsion of the USSR advisers and technicians.

It is hard to see how the nongovernmental institutions (the lobbies, the press, public opinion) were mainly responsible for this American policy decision in Moscow. Rather, it seems that it emanated from the White House and the State Department in light of national interest and security considerations. The United States has also joined the Soviet Union in four-power negotiations designed to induce both Arabs and Israel to get on with the implementation of the November 22, 1967, UN Security Council resolution. This decision, taken by the Nixon administration over vigorous Israeli objection, seems clearly to have been motivated by the felt need to take a more active role in finding a solution to the dispute.

As far as American policy aimed at inter-Arab conflict is concerned, the United States has seldom sought to make inroads in the united front of "revolutionary" Arab states against its policies and positions. Perhaps the recent (July 1972) resumption of relations with the Sudan and Yemen (San'a) is an exception to this. And from 1959 until 1963, following a policy of live and let live with Egypt seemed to offer possibilities. The United States, by its support for Jordan and Saudi Arabia and Libya (before September 1969), has at least implicitly taken sides in the inter-Arab conflict. Its choices have been dictated by international oil, but more is involved than these companies' investments. The U.S. government obtains tax revenues from these companies' business in the area. Furthermore, Western security depends on European consumption of Middle East oil. Finally, a question of geopolitics is involved, in which the United States feels it necessary to prevent the growth of a vacuum in the zone which the Soviet Union might be tempted to fill. Geopolitics largely explains U.S. support for King Hussein, for instance. The United States sometimes suffers attack by its clients in the Middle East due to its close affiliation with Israel, as in June 1967 or the fire that burned al-Aqsa mosque in Jerusalem in 1969. This restricts the scope for maneuver at the U.S.'s disposal. But continued rivalry among the states in the area causes some of them (Morocco, Jordan, Saudi Arabia) to require American support against their "revolutionary" competitors. It is in this light that one must interpret the $450 million military aid program to Saudi Arabia in 1964–65. How does one explain this program but as a counter to Egyptian policies in Yemen, which included the bombing of certain Saudi towns on the frontiers and the threat of ideological-military subversion across frontiers?

The formulation of policy relative to the Egyptian-Israel conflict is very much derivative of the policy formulation process toward the larger Arab-Israel confrontation. After the failures of the mid-1950s, the best that the United States could do was to maintain as low a profile as possible. The PL-480 program of wheat shipments to Egypt beginning in 1959 introduced a new pattern of relations. Egypt's feud with the USSR in this period helped set the stage for this. Due to the diversity of institutions and individuals involved in formulating American policy toward the Middle East, cross pressures developed (mainly between the Kennedy administration and Congress) that impaired coordination. Mutually competitive positions on the part of the United States and Egypt over the Yemen war, the Congo, and elsewhere threatened the continuation of the food shipments. Congress brought pressure to bear on the White House that renewal of PL-480 with Egypt was contingent upon the latter's moderation toward America and Israel. Thus, by the time of the June 1967 war, the United States relations with Egypt had seriously deteriorated. To a large extent, this had much to do with the preoccupation of the Johnson administration with the Vietnam war, thus leaving little time and energies to the Middle East.

Since the 1967 war, the position of the United States has been that Israeli evacuation from the occupied territories must be made within the framework of a final peace settlement (i.e., Israel should not be compelled to retreat without a quid pro quo, as in 1956). This reflects a change in American policy. In the meanwhile, the two administrations since 1967 have committed themselves to maintaining a strong military posture for Israel to contain possible Arab belligerance. President Johnson's speech of June 19, 1967, seemed to go even beyond the previous attitude (if not policy) of America by placing the brunt of responsibility for the war on the Arabs. Above all, the United States has sought to avoid becoming involved in a Middle East war, given the lessons of Vietnam. Apparently, top officials of the Defense Department, including the joint chiefs of staff and the secretary of defense, shared this view with the State Department and the White House. The swift victory by Israel in this sense was welcomed by the policy formulators, although the State Department hands generally felt that America had seriously compromised itself in Arab eyes by its actions or inactions.

American policy toward the Arab-Israel conflict has necessarily contained contradictions. One reason is that among the various Arab states, Syria, Jordan, and Egypt (those in the "front line") have adopted varying degrees of hostility toward Israel. The Syrian regime under the extreme left wing of the Ba'th (since 1966) has never recognized the 1967 UN resolution. Jordan has been a client state of the United States in the region and gets its F-4 Phantom jets from the same source as Israel. As for Egypt, no doubt the best chance for peace in the area lies in an agreement between Egypt and Israel as the strongest and most important parties to the dispute. The possibility, however, that Egypt could singly come to terms with Israel and induce such diverse regimes as those of Syria, Iraq, and the Palestinian community generally to agree is slim, given the prevailing mood and positions of the rivals.

Nevertheless, the United States has sought to promote precisely this kind of Egyptian-Israeli "détente" through the "Rogers' Plan," a project to open the Suez Canal in a limited settlement arrangement. Not to be discounted in American calculations to influence

Egypt is the relative weight and importance of the Egyptian middle sectors (which tend to be less radical), whereas these groups are practically negligible political factors in Syria or Iraq, for example. It seems clear that United States policy in the Arab-Israel conflict has been multifaceted: protect the oil investments and "lifeline" to Europe; promote gradual social change in the area rather than sponsor radical development; maintain the integrity of the communications and transport routes in the zone (i.e., keep them open); defend Israel as a "bastion of democracy"; and prevent the buildup of Soviet influence in the Middle East. Up to now, it has been most successful in the first, third, and fourth areas. Radical developments in Libya, Yemen, and South Yemen in the mid- and late 1960s demonstrate that the second objective has been more than difficult to achieve for the United States. And if the two treaties of friendship with Egypt and Iraq by the USSR are an indication, containing Soviet influence has not succeeded. There have been most recently some compensations to the United States, none of which were of its doing, however. These are the federation between Libya and Egypt (announced August 1972) and Sadat's expulsion of Soviet advisers and instructors (July 1972). As mentioned, resumption of relations with the Sudan and Yemen in summer 1972 have also helped the American position.

As far as the Palestine commandos are concerned, this is a level of conflict that the United States can do little about. In the 1970 crisis, the United States helped King Hussein when Syrian tanks entered Jordan during the civil war in Jordan between the commandos and the government. Under the Kennedy administration the United States did try to sponsor moves to solve the problem of the Palestine refugees. The basic ingredient of the plan—named the Johnson Plan, after Joseph E. Johnson, president of the Carnegie Endowment for International Peace (this is not to be confused with the Johnston plan of the mid-1950s for utilizing the waters of the Jordan River)—was Israeli compensation and/or repatriation of the Palestinian refugees to a maximum extent consistent with the maintenance of the territorial integrity and sovereignty of the existing state of Israel.

This plan never received the support of Israel, and Zionist interest organizations mobilized against it in the United States.[27]

Since that time, 1961, the area has been the growth of militant Palestine military and political organizations. This is not the place to review the details of the myriad institutions and their political and military arms. The important point is to note their relative success in recruiting cadres and in establishing little enclaves in existing refugee camps in Jordan (until 1970–71), Lebanon, and Syria. With their own chains of command, funding procedures, civic programs, and educational projects, together with their limited successes in harassing Israel through military operations, the various guerrilla movements have become the focus of Arab opinion.

The commandos have presented a problem for U.S. policy because their quarrel is both with Israel and with America's other client states—especially Jordan, but also Lebanon.

Briefly, the Arab summit conference of January 1964 brought into existence a body called the Palestine Liberation Organization (PLO), with headquarters in Egyptian territory. This PLO was to constitute the infrastructure for the state-to-be of Palestine. Subsequently, institutional arms of the PLO were created on the political and military sides respectively: the Palestine National Council (PNC) and the Palestine Liberation Army (PLA). The executive branch of this political system-in-exile in Egypt was known as the Executive Committee (EC). The first director of the PLO, appointed by the Arab governments sitting in their regional organization, the Arab League, was Ahmad Shuqayri. The latter, of Palestinian origin, had previously been a diplomat and an ambassador for the Saudi Arabian government to the United Nations. That he was hardly a revolutionary can be seen from his obviously patrician background and the scorn and contempt that the Soviets and Marxist-Leninists generally had for him. Shuqayri's singular claim to notoriety lay in the bombast of his language and chilling verbal imagery regarding Israel's future fate at the hands of the Arab revolution. Malcolm Kerr, in *The Arab Cold War*, says of him that "he enjoyed the reputation of an opportunist and a charlatan." [28] Shuqayri was replaced following the June war by a less vocal individual, after a postmortem appraisal showed that Arab propaganda and public relations had been counterproductive in its impact on world opinion.

The bewildering array of guerrilla organizations—not part of the PLA, though adjunct to it—has perhaps confused even the Arabs themselves. By far the largest of these has been *al-Fath*, which is an acronym with the letters in reverse (HTF), standing for the Arabic words: Movement for the Liberation of Palestine. The leader of this group is Yasir 'Arafat, a nonideological activist who nonetheless shares with all other guerrilla groups, from Marxist to anarchist, the goal of creating in the current frontiers of Israel a territorial state governed by a Palestinian Arab majority. This state, which would be binational, would contain a Jewish population that could grow and flourish, subject to the condition that the Arab population would always constitute the numerical majority. Controversy exists in the programs of these diverse commando groups over whether only Jews who were in Palestine prior to 1917, 1948, or some other date would be allowed to stay. All this would mean an end to Zionism, including the integral factor of unrestricted immigration.

The second guerrilla group, much smaller in numbers than *al-Fath* but as renowned, if not more so, is the Marxist-Leninist Popular Front for the Liberation of Palestine, led by George Habash. Ironically, the guerrillas' "man in Moscow" has tended to be 'Arafat, the non-Marxist. Habash's affinity with the Chinese communism model of revolution helps explain this anomaly. Moscow is under increasing pressure to recognize the guerrillas. So far, however, the closest it has come to this is the use of terms in *Pravda* such as "patriots" in reference to the guerrillas. This word implies that their ties to the territory of their fatherland (Palestine) are legitimate and morally valid. This was the extent of the USSR's commitment to the commandos until early 1972.

With respect to this level of conflict, which is perhaps the most deadly in the long run, one must note the complete and total mutual exclusiveness of goals. Yehoshafat Harkabi, a leading Israeli defense scholar, has called this "politicide," a term he has coined to designate a struggle in which both sides adamantly claim the same territory.[29] This is to be contrasted to the irredentist phenomenon, where an intermediary solution is at least possible because competition exists for slices of territory, rather than the entire area.

Syria, Libya, and Iraq support the military solution stance of the guerrillas. Egypt and Jordan do not. In this way the levels of conflict interpenetrate one another and thus complicate finding a coherent American policy for the area as a whole. Because the commandos are the heroes of the moment to many Arabs, the Egyptians cannot afford to fall too far out of step with the more militant posture of the guerrillas. This is reflected in the debate between Israel and Egypt over the implementation of the UN resolution of 1967. Both sides have accepted it. In February 1971 the Egyptian president publicly stated his willingness to make peace with Israel, albeit in somewhat ambiguous terms. (He used the word "agreement" rather than "treaty.") The two differ on frontiers and Jerusalem, but commitment to the implementation of the resolution exists. The chief problem is one of procedure and timing. Who makes the first move? The typical metaphor is that of two scorpions in a bottle, both of whom are exhausted and fed up with confrontation and conflict but neither trusting the other to make good on their tacit agreement in principle that the removal of their stingers by the doctors gathered around the bottle would be the best solution. To extend the metaphor, those doctors are none other than the actors in the bipolar and United Nations international systems. And the problem is so much more complicated because these esteemed doctors all have their own particular surgical modus operandi.

The Nixon Administration

Do the four years of the Nixon administration represent a period of continuity or change in American policy toward the zone? Two diametrically opposed currents have emerged in this period that indicate a break in continuity. The administration came into office with the intent of applying an "evenhanded" policy in the Middle East. To the extent that this implied a departure from strong support of Israel by Democratic administrations, the Israel government began to have doubts and misgivings. When Secretary of State William Rogers proposed in early 1970 a cease-fire plan, Tel Aviv's doubts and misgivings evolved into fears of abandonment. The year 1971 proved to be the worst period in American-Israel relations, with Premier Golda Meir accusing Rogers and the State Department generally of having allowed American policy positions to erode into support of Egypt.[30]

In late 1971 and early 1972, however, the Nixon administration reached a new decision on the supplying of arms to Israel that proved a significant break from the past: Washington contracted to provide Israel with warplanes over a two to three year period of time.[31] This seemed to imply that the former pattern of limiting sales to a year-to-year basis (with its concomitant aspect of providing a check to an overly recalcitrant Israel) was henceforth to be discarded. In fact, the Arabs, who initially were intrigued about Washington's evenhanded policy, have ended by regarding the current administration as one of the most pro-Israel governments ever. For their part, Israel's leadership has come to look favorably on American policy after three years of anxiety.

U.S. disagreement with Israel on the question of peace in the Middle East can be summarized as follows: In the first place, no American administration has approved the territorial gains sought by Israel, with the possible exception of the Golan Heights. Even there, the American view seems to be that some form of internationalization is necessary. President Johnson had this in mind when he asserted that a political settlement in the zone should not "bear the weight of conquest." Second, the United States has differed with Israel over the interpretation of Dr. Gunnar Jarring's role as the United Nations representative appointed in connection with the Security Council Resolution No. 242 of November 22, 1967. Israel feels his function is limited to arranging for contact between and/or among the parties to the conflict. The United States, however, feels that Jarring has the right to put detailed questions to both parties. Thus, Assistant Secretary of State for the Near East Joseph Sisco told the CBS television show "Face the Nation" (February 14, 1971): "We feel [Jarring] has a very broad mandate and he is acting strictly in accord with that mandate." Jarring's famous memorandum of February 8, 1971, to which Sadat responded by agreeing to peace with Israel, infuriated the Meir government.

In the third place, the United States feels that Israel deliberately delayed answering President Sadat's offer in February 1971 to open the Suez Canal in return for an Israel withdrawal into Sinai. The United States seemed particularly hopeful about movement in the talks over the Canal after the May 1971 crisis in Egypt and Sadat's triumph over his "antiparty" opposition. Secretary of State Rogers visited the Middle East at this time and expressed guarded optimism. The Israelis later accused Rogers in particular of having reneged on an understanding he had allegedly reached with Tel Aviv that any Canal settlement must not be accompanied by any Egyptian deadlines for ultimate withdrawal of Israel forces from Sinai. From July to December 1971, Washington held up the shipment of Phantom F-4s contracted for by Israel in order to prod Israel to accept negotiations over opening the Canal. Israel refused as long as the Egyptians insisted that such a solution must be only part of a larger settlement of the territorial and refugee question. In all this, Israel has consistently refused to make any advance commitments over what the future frontiers would be as a precondition to negotiating.

American differences with the Arabs, and in particular with Egypt, can be summed up in this way: A final peace settlement must include an Israeli presence in Sharm al-Shaykh (albeit under Egyptian sovereignty). The United States also criticized Egypt for violating the standstill cease-fire in the Suez Canal zone proposed by Rogers in early 1970 and finally accepted by President Nasser in August 1970. Immediately after the cease-fire, the Soviets and Egyptians emplaced SAM missiles throughout the Canal area. They claimed that the missiles were already in the zone and thus emplacing them was not in violation of the cease-fire. Israel blamed Rogers for imprecision in working out the modalities of the cease-fire; moreover, it accused Cairo and Moscow of outright deception.

Fourth, Washington has quarreled with Sadat's deadlines. In February 1971, when the six months established as a deadline by

Nasser when he accepted the Rogers Plan the previous August had expired, President Sadat (after Nasser's death in September) merely extended it by a month. He did this to prod the United States to commit itself to exploring the paths to peace in the arena of four-power talks among the U.S., U.K., USSR, and France. These talks, incidentally, were yet a further issue that antagonized Israel: she wanted no role for the Soviet Union in arranging a peace settlement. The Americans were more worried than angered at the penchant for establishing deadlines. Among other things, it tended to box the Egyptians in and placed them in a difficult position once the period had come to an end.

While 1971 was the "year of decision" for Egypt, it proved to be a year of decisions for the United States as well. In the end, as we have seen, the United States entered 1972—a presidential election year—with firmer support for Israel than any time in the previous three years. Apart from the longer-term sales of Phantoms to Israel, there were the following signs of disenchantment with evenhanded-ness: (1) agreement in January to help Israel develop its own defense industry;[32] (2) a Senate vote in November 1971 approving $500 million in credits for Israel's defense needs. This resolution was tacked on as a rider to the Military Aid Procurement Bill of 1971 by Senator Henry Jackson (Dem.-Wash.);[33] (3) the impact of international terrorism, symbolized by the names Zurich, Lod, Munich, Khartoum, and by the bomb-through-the-mails phenomenon most recently.

The impact of recent Palestinian guerrilla activity has been to harden American policy against the Arab states. The United States has been strongly pressing for international conventions and agreements against the highjacking of airliners and harboring of international terrorists. In the 1972 presidential election atmosphere, the most promising movement since 1967 on the conflict—that is, the opening of the Suez Canal—suffered a check. It will be virtually impossible for the United States to undertake any more initiatives in the cause of peace in the area as long as the commandos are able to divert attention in such spectacular fashion from negotiations to their avowed objective of a "military solution." And here, since its ouster from Egypt in July 1972, we are witnessing the evolution of Soviet policy in the zone as well. Banking its fortunes basically on the militant Iraqis and Syrians, the Kremlin is presently engaged in deepening its commitment to the commandos. From verbal acknowledgments of the legitimacy of the grievances of the Palestinians, the USSR has moved to sending, in an open way, military shipments to them through Syria.[34]

Choices and Options for the Future

The United States' basic resources for influencing Middle East politics are military, economic, and cultural aid and exchange programs. The carrying out of these programs depends upon the institutions of policy making mentioned above. Essentially, this policy is the captive of previous positions adopted. Hence, no administration could seriously contemplate reneging on President Truman's original commitment to support the existence of Israel. The organized interest groups play their role somewhat obliquely, setting, as Quandt says, certain limits beyond which the government may not go rather than actually contributing to policy content directly.

The options open to the United States—and they are numerous, at least in theory—will all be constrained by this single inescapable fact: diminished capability to sustain a vigorous and active policy in the wake of the Vietnam war. First, the United States could reach an understanding with the Soviet Union to limit their rivalry in the region. This has, in fact, occurred as part of the summit conference of May 1972. However, the United States will perhaps be tempted to take advantage of the most recent Soviet reversals in the area: (1) the defeat of 'Ali Sabri and the Egyptian left in May 1971; (2) the crushing of the Communist movement in the Sudan in July 1971—an enormous loss for the USSR that has not been sufficiently appreciated in the West; (3) the expulsion of the Soviet advisers and instructors from Egypt in July 1972; (4) the "organic unity" between Libya and Egypt in August 1972; (5) resumption of diplomatic ties, in July 1972, between the United States and two "radical" Arab states, the Sudan and Yemen. Notwithstanding the temptations to the United States, the missing ingredient that would enable Washington to move in boldly at this juncture is money. No American administration is going to be able to get the kind of foreign aid program that could sustain such a policy. Perhaps the major consolation to the United States here is that the Soviet Union itself is experiencing the problems of diminished capacity in light of domestic and socialist commonwealth demands upon Moscow's funds.

Second, the United States might choose to increase its commitments to Israel, as in the form of even longer-range contracts to supply advanced military hardware than agreed upon in 1971. The obvious advantage of such a scheme from the point of view of American global strategy is that it would hamper Israeli bids to manufacture weapons of this caliber at home, and especially nuclear weapons. The disadvantages would appear to be too great, however, in view of the impact that highly visible move would have on Arab elites and societies.

Third, the United States could continue the current state of policy formulation and execution. Although chaotic and segmented, lacking coherence and coordination, it has not proved disastrous by any means. The United States could, after all, pursue the critical objectives of American policy in the zone while maintaining a relatively low profile as at present.

In the fourth place, some kind of resuscitated PL-480 scheme, directing assistance to Egypt and the Sudan, could have significant albeit not earth-shattering consequences. This policy would be a tactical one, preliminary to a more substantive position geared to defusing the Arab-Israel conflict. Again, the current mood of the American public, plus the Congress, which defeated foreign aid for the first time in history last year, would be obstacles to this. Given the relatively modest amount of funding these programs require, however, such an approach is not out of the question. It is true that this would require strong leadership by the President and a certain willingness to ride out Zionist objections, a promising task if, along with such programs, the United States could institute modest technical assistance programs. Here, ironically, the Americans could learn much from Israeli programs in tropical Africa and in such Asian states as

Burma. These programs are well known to have fairly high payoffs with relatively low outlays.

But the one area where the United States has been truly derelict has been in the field of cultural policy. The Arab world has suffered immense psychological distress in its relations with the West. With little cost to itself, the American government could easily launch a cultural exchange program and a public relations effort in which Arab contributions to civilization and human history might be stressed. Secretary of State Rogers asserted in Bahrayn in July 1972 that "America still has friends in the Middle East." This is true, and nowhere is it more evident than among the cultural elites in some of these countries. This is not to say that American international politics enjoy the firm support of the cultural elites. It is of note, though, that American society, literature, the arts continue to fascinate many in the Arab world. If the Soviet Union could have translated some of its political, economic, and military influence in the zone into cultural penetration, it would have been much harder for President Sadat to make his decisions of July 1972. In fact, culturally the Middle East's natural orientation is still toward the West, mainly to France but also to the Anglo-Saxon societies. Why the Americans have failed to utilize this approach is a mystery. Even the smallest effort here is bound to be productive when preexisting endeavors were nil.

The success of American foreign policy depends, in the last analysis, upon detaching some of the "revolutionary" Arab states from the positions adopted by the radical groups in the area that are committed to a military solution. This is another way of saying that the commandos' influence among the populations of the Arab states will be the greater the less the West is able to convince the Arab masses that it basically cares about the Arab world. However, any big-power policy planner will have to remember the paradox of the Middle East as a subordinate international system. He will have to know that the greater are the efforts by outside forces to influence events in the area, the larger and more disproportionate will seem the energies wasted in trying to bring this about.

After the 1967 war, the Soviet Union seemed to be experiencing a shift toward congruence between its power and its ability to call the shots in the zone. Successive treaties of friendship with Egypt and Iraq appeared to promise much, based as they were on years of economic and military assistance and the reconstruction of the Egyptian military machine in toto. However, Sadat's stunning announcements demanding the withdrawal of Soviet instructors and advisers on July 18, 1972, coming in the wake of the disastrous events in 1971, demonstrated anew the peculiar patterns of Middle East subordination. As we know, the rosy vision of a series of radical Arab states allied with Moscow—requested by Kosygin in his visits to Syria and Egypt in May 1966—has given way to grim reminders on the pages of *Pravda* and *Izvestia* that the Arabs should realize that Soviet assistance to the Arabs has been "priceless." [35] It would take a very naive observer, however, to assume that the Western star is on the rise and will continue its ascent for the next five to ten years. Experience in the politics of the Middle East should lead one to be more cautious.

Donald Rothchild

Engagement Versus Disengagement in Africa: The Choices for America

Up to now America's policy toward Africa could be characterized as one of "benign neglect." The United States has certainly given extensive symbolic support to African objectives of self-determination and modernization; substantive support for these goals has been less forthcoming, however. Unlike its relationships with the Latin American and South Asian countries, America's policy toward Africa is distinctly low-keyed and cautious in nature. In the African case, at least, the sin of omission seems preferred to that of commission. Such a posture, concludes a prominent African theoretician, means that "the United States had done fewer bad things in Africa than she had done in Asia and Latin America. But she has also done fewer good things in Africa than elsewhere." [1]

Nevertheless, there are increasing signs that this passive outlook cannot be maintained for an indefinite period. Domestic political pressures are mounting, particularly from black American leadership, for a more positive identification with African needs and aspirations, and the conflict over continuing relations with the white-dominated regimes of southern Africa is becoming acute. American opinion leaders in all walks of life are beginning to recognize that governmental acceptance of the status quo works to the benefit of regimes currently in power—irrespective of the goals of these rulers. Thus economic, social, and diplomatic contacts with Africa mean American involvement in that continent's affairs, no matter how low a profile American leaders consciously adopt. As David D. Newsom, the assistant secretary of state for African affairs, sums up the matter: "The question is not, *Why should we get involved?* We are involved." [2]

This inevitable involvement, with the necessity for choice that it implies, is most poignant with respect to the southern African question. The interconnectedness of capitalism, culture, social activities, and race cause American leaders, already preoccupied internationally with deescalation in Vietnam, alliance conflicts, and a possible trade war, to hesitate over championing revolutionary change in Africa. But America cannot remain quietly on the sidelines. Its deep embarrassment over racial inequality at home precludes indifference to white dominance systems abroad. Such internal contradictions compel a constant reappraisal of priorities at this juncture.

As such contradictions make "benign neglect" a less and less tenable approach toward Africa, policy makers may find themselves compelled to choose between various combinations of engagement and disengagement in Africa north and south of the Zambezi. In view of the enormity of the issues at hand, it behooves us to examine both the factors influencing these decisions and the options availing. Insight into these questions can be provided at the outset by looking first at American doctrine and then at specific dilemmas on self-determination, the use of force, aid, trade, and investment. Then we will be at a vantage point from which to examine such courses of action as engagement and disengagement in terms of American foreign policy interests.

The Status Quo Orientation

If the concept of a status quo power has tended to lose its meaning in Asia, where the United States and the Soviet Union both seek to stabilize the area, it retains considerable import under present-day African circumstances. The inherited economic ties of colonial times remain largely intact, and political structures and cultural patterns have changed much less than anticipated. In this context, the United States, despite an oft-proclaimed "revolutionary" tradition, has acted to buttress this inherited order. Its diplomatic and economic contacts with postcolonial Africa have been supportive in the main of long-standing Euro-African linkages. In this sense, the United States has emerged as a key force for stability, not transformation. The United States inclines toward a status quo outlook as a consequence of its interests in Africa and of the capabilities at its disposal in the 1970s. Its interests in Africa are somewhat marginal—the need for diplomatic support, strategic advantage (i.e., tracking stations and port facilities), access to raw materials and agricultural products, and opportunities for trade and investment. Although these interests are gaining importance rapidly, they are a long way from arriving at an equivalent status to that of Western Europe, Latin America, or Asia. In the opinion of key policy makers, Africa's position is little changed from that described by a leading academician and economic adviser in 1958:

> The absolute figures on our trade with Africa and our investments in Africa look fairly impressive but are relatively not very important. The commodities we get from Africa are of course very useful and even indispensable for some purposes, but it would be possible for the American economy today to get along without them. Our total spending on African commodities is less than one-eighth of one per cent of our gross national expenditures, and Africa buys an even smaller percentage of our gross national output.
>
> The loss of the American imports from Africa would undoubtedly cause hardship to some industries, raise costs somewhat to others, and might cause heart-break to girls who would have to get engaged without receiving a diamond ring—but one can scarcely claim that Africa is economically vital to us at present. We could get along without African commodities and African markets with an imperceptible ripple in our standard of living.[3]

Perhaps this evaluation would be revised in the 1970s to take account of Africa's contribution of petroleum products to Western consumers, but American policy makers seem to have altered this overall conclusion little with the passage of time. Africa's dependence upon infusions of Western capital, manpower, and enterprise leaves these policy planners free to accord this continent a substantially lower priority than prevails elsewhere.

In addition, it is becoming increasingly apparent that American capabilities are more circumscribed than once recognized. With respect to fiscal capabilities, evidence of increasing performance difficulties is made manifest by a look at the 1973 federal budget. Although outlays were set at a massive $246.3 billion, several factors made this less favorable for social and humanitarian (including African) interests than might otherwise be expected. After taking account of a number of long-standing commitments (some $83.4 billion of total expenditures were allotted to defense requirements), the budget revealed a planned deficit of $20.8 billion, a calculation considered on the conservative side in light of the last three years' record. Africa, which was no congressman's constituency and not included in major cold war confrontations, was in a poor position to further its interests in competition with domestic and other foreign claimants. This became evident a month after President Nixon sent the budget to Congress, for the House and Senate conferees agreed to cut overall foreign military, economic, and humanitarian aid to $3.2 billion, less than one-tenth of this amount being allocated for technical assistance and capital projects on the African continent. Declining fiscal capabilities were thus reflected in total expenditures committed abroad (although the declines were by no means equal from area to area) and meant that the United States, in comparison with other powers, would become a less active agency of change than had heretofore been assumed.

These budgetary constraints upon policy making are directly related to shifting psychological and political capabilities. Thus the fact of fiscal imbalance gains political impact (and often a disproportionate one) as it is affected by attitudinal responses. Certainly leaders are highly sensitive to the implications of resource limitations. Senator Edmund Muskie, when referring to America's responsibilities toward Africa's development, independence, and racial justice, went on to warn that we must have no "illusion about the limits of our influence and resources." [4] And Governor Nelson Rockefeller, warning in part against overspending abroad, called for a realistic perspective on budgetary matters.

In a sense, it's time to balance our hopes and our aspirations with the realities of life. We must face the fact that government, just like a family, can't spend way beyond its income for very long without weakening its credit and without undermining its strength.

We are a generous people by nature. We want to help those in need at home and abroad. It's part of our whole Judeo-Christian heritage and it's a wonderful quality. But we can't do it all at once. And we, as a people, are close to being dangerously overcommitted.[5]

It is this sense of being overburdened which is crucial. The fact of budgetary deficits becomes translated into a feeling on the part of leaders of having gone beyond the point strictly warranted by state capabilities. Such psychological strain, whether soundly based or not, reduces national capabilities, causing policy makers to shun weighty commitments and to prefer stability to revolutionary change. This inclination to shrink from entanglement is particularly evident in the wake of an unpopular involvement in Vietnam; as Senator Muskie asserts, ". . . even if we end our military involvement in Indo-China . . . many Americans will be reluctant to assume any involvement elsewhere in the world." [6]

Diminished diplomatic capability is also evident as superpower hegemony has declined vis-à-vis Africa. The Soviet-American detente has lessened the urgency of superpower concerns in this area, and this reduced involvement has allowed Africa a greater diplomatic manoeuvrability on the world scene. In this sense, Chinese backing for the Tanzam railroad and African endorsement of the Chinese Communist position on representation at the United Nations are more indications of African *raison d'état* than a basic change of alignment policies to meet new ideological preferences. The decline in Western diplomatic hegemony was no doubt occasioned in large part by Africa's quest for an independent and authentic voice on international affairs; nevertheless, the West's decline of influence was surely hastened by America's disinclination to become involved in matters far from its shores as well as by a perceptible slippage in that country's capabilities.

All these restrictions upon positive action have led the United States to adopt a low-keyed approach toward Africa. As a consequence, the emphasis upon stability and gradual change can be seen as a consistent theme in American policy from Eisenhower days to the present. In the late 1950s, as self-government became imminent for many African countries, American spokesmen, anxious to avoid possible unrest following decolonization, encouraged African lands to retain close links with their former European rulers. By their emphasis upon orderly transition and minimal change, State Department spokesmen seemed to qualify their approval of African self-determination itself. As a former United States assistant secretary of state put the matter in 1959,

> We support African political aspirations when they are moderate, nonviolent, and constructive and take into account their obligations to and interdependence with the world community. We also support the principle of continued African ties with Western Europe. We see no reason why there should be a conflict between these two concepts.[7]

As the trauma of independence came and went in the early 1960s American policy makers began increasingly to accept the new world of African states and to deal with them directly rather than through European capitals. There were setbacks in this regard, such as early American contacts with Sekou Touré's Guinea, but in time America emerged as less and less deferential to its European partners. The waning of American deference made autonomous policy indispensable. If the Kennedy, Johnson, and Nixon administrations varied noticeably in preferred alignment styles, they nonetheless agreed upon overall objectives: the ensuring of continental African stability, irrespective of cold war vicissitudes. Thus Kennedy made conscious efforts to court the more radically inclined Sekou Touré and Julius Nyerere, while the Johnson administration seemed to move steadily toward the center, favoring such reformist leaders as Mobutu Sese Seko and Jomo Kenyatta. But these different administration initiatives could be interpreted as variances on a status quo theme: the first a hegemonial response to cold war competition and the second a less grandiose return to great power diplomacy.

During the 1970s, another aspect of American conservatism

came to the fore regarding Africa. By this time, America was to emerge as a leading world proponent of evolutionary change in Southern Africa. It officially opposed general sanctions against South Africa and stressed the necessity of nonviolent solutions. Quite symbolically, the United States was to cast its first veto in the Security Council in March 1970 over a resolution condemning Britain for failure to overthrow by force the illegal, white-minority regime in Rhodesia. While voicing strong opposition to racial injustice in Southern Africa, the United States rejects revolutionary deeds, and prefers "communication" to forcible "liberation." President Nixon's first annual foreign affairs message to Congress in February 1970 sets out American doctrine on this issue as follows:

> Though we abhor the racial policies of the white regimes, we cannot agree that progressive change in southern Africa is furthered by force. The history of the area shows all too starkly that violence and the counter-violence it inevitably provokes will only make more difficult the task of those on both sides working for progress on the racial question.[8]

Nixon's third report to Congress reemphasized his opposition to violent change even more explicitly: "My Administration will not condone recourse to violence, either as a means of enforcing submission of a majority to a minority or as a formula for effecting needed social change." [9] Such an outlook makes America anything but a revolutionary power in today's African context, all references to the "spirit of '76" notwithstanding. The American emphasis is upon orderly change and reform within existing structures, not radical transformation. As a result, the United States stands out prominently as a status quo power in a rapidly changing African context.

The Dilemmas of Conservatism

America's status quo orientation toward Africa gives rise to a series of dilemmas. Although these dilemmas of self-determination, national violence, trade, investment, and aid are interrelated, they will be dealt with on an individual basis for the sake of comprehensiveness.

THE DILEMMA OF SELF-DETERMINATION In principle the United States supports—even champions—political self-determination. From the time President Woodrow Wilson transformed World War I by the publication of his Fourteen Points, American statesmen have elevated national self-determination to the status of doctrine. It both explains and justifies American backing for the Congo (now Zaire), Yugoslavia, South Vietnam, Formosa, Israel, and so forth, and provides a consistent moral underpinning for a variety of initiatives. The right of national self-determination is vital to the American world view, being as indispensable to American doctrine as class struggle is to the Communist interpretation of international events.

As Africa's independence neared, American policy makers, despite qualms over possible Soviet inroads, nonetheless hove closely to established doctrine on self-determination. "We only seek to leave people's destinies in their own hands," declared Adlai E. Stevenson in 1960.[10] It was an expression of sentiment typical of the times. Even when cautioning most strongly against the incompatibility of national independence with communist control, these spokesmen were firm in their commitment to African self-rule.

Such views retain considerable emotional appeal among present-day American leaders and their public at home. Former Vice-President Hubert Humphrey described self-determination as the path of the future during a trip to Zambia in 1968; three years later Secretary of State William P. Rogers, on a stopover in Zaire, affirmed that his country would identify with African objectives of self-determination. America has been faithful to the Wilsonian world-view. But such commitment was not without grave contradictions. As the goal of self-determination came into conflict with those of orderly change, containment of communism, and respect for domestic jurisdiction, policy makers seemed uncertain as to their priorities. The Wilsonian commitment became troublesome at this point, for it provided critics at home and abroad with the grounds for attack. Senator John F. Kennedy, for example, appealed to "the moral principles of self-determination" in 1958 when calling for an end to American neutralism on the Algerian controversy.[11] And African leaders have accused the Western powers of buttressing white minority regimes in Southern Africa through their economic investments. Despite all the successes of the liberation movements in Angola and Mozambique, argued Zambian President Kenneth Kaunda in 1971, "NATO powers are still supporting the fledgling Portuguese government." [12] In the eyes of such African leaders, the West is indifferent to racial injustice and prepared to stand aside while the majority population is denied the right of self-determination. No one is to be permitted the luxury of noninvolvement on the Southern African question. And the United States, which proclaimed self-determination as a universal right, is especially exposed, being caught in a dilemma largely of its own making.

In fact, the application of moral principles of self-determination is more complicated than sometimes recognized. At least two major questions are pertinent. First, what units are to be legitimate candidates for statehood? Wilson's secretary of state, Robert Lansing, had serious misgivings at the time of the peace negotiations on precisely this point:

> When the President talks of "self-determination" what unit has he in mind? Does he mean a race, a territorial area, or a community? Without a definite unit which is practical, application of this principle is dangerous to peace and stability.[13]

Although the units for statehood are reasonably evident in Southern Africa, they are sometimes less so in the multiethnic states north of the Zambezi. The integrity of Zaire, Nigeria, and the Sudan have all been threatened by the forces of ethnic separatism, and other instances of secession by subnational groupings may occur at any time. Thus, the United States lives constantly with the possibility of having to determine when revolutionary elements have a justified claim to statehood, and when not. Here the values of stability, orderly change, and respect for domestic jurisdiction possess more equal claims to support as against the doctrine of political self-determination. Following the bitter outcry against United States intervention in the Congolese conflict, American policy makers appear to have retreated to a position of low visibility on the question of ethnic separatism. But is this low-keyed approach necessarily unconscionable? No rule can be set out in advance. Certainly it is important to note that African leaders have shown a greater ability to manage conflict when freed of great-power intervention. Since great-power involvement brings an escalation of conflict in its wake, perhaps their restraint, even if something of a recoiling from principle, could be justified in terms of lowering the scale of conflict, thereby making it easier for African diplomacy to take effect.

A second question is related to the above discussion. What conditions must be present for self-determination to be an operative norm? Are standards of majoritarianism, democracy, or nationalism applicable, and how are statesmen to measure their vigor? Certainly opinions differ markedly on how to evaluate these tests of legitimacy and what to do to ameliorate tensions. While State Department officials were speaking in 1968 of federal type solutions for Nigeria, Senator Eugene McCarthy, more convinced that the conditions for genuine self-determination were present, was arguing that America should give positive support for a temporary division of Nigeria "until the United Nations or any organization of African states—not the Biafrans and the Nigerians themselves—work out a settlement." [14] What objective basis was there for either a status quo or interventionist approach? Was majoritarianism of the whole or the part to be regarded as decisive? What type of democracy—direct or indirect—was to be a test of legitimacy? Why was genuineness of nationalism grounds for validating secession in Nigeria, when not in the Sudan? Objective criteria for action were obviously lacking. American statesmen paid homage to the principle of self-determination but largely ignored it when intra-African disputes flared up.

In most circumstances, then, the doctrine of political self-determination is something less than useful as a guide to decision makers. It helps to set broad lines of policy on Southern Africa, because the interests of the black majority are so blatantly overridden by white minority governments. But in situations of African self-rule, the principle seems imprecise and unhelpful. Indeed the problem of decision making defies simple and consistent formulas. On the one hand, a status quo orientation can prove to be insensitive (i.e., Bangladesh);

on the other hand, an interventionist orientation can be divisive, even dangerous to public order. Thus there is no easy way out of the dilemma of self-determination. Each case must be dealt with individually, necessitating great pragmatism on the part of a doctrinally bound country.

THE DILEMMA OF NATIONAL VIOLENCE   When discussing the subject of violence, it is necessary first to define the sense in which it is used. Certainly American policy makers are not directly concerned with personal assault, gang warfare, youth-wing intimidation, or tribal skirmishing. They become involved only as violence is internationalized—through coup d'etats, revolutions, insurgencies, genocide, and wars. In these latter cases, violence, which is by no means an African phenomenon alone, is explained primarily by the fragility of institutions in the newly independent countries and by a lack of governmental legitimacy, particularly in Southern Africa. Where governments rule irrespective of the wishes of the governed, violence can be seen as a logical response to uncontrolled power. Since, in the Southern African context, the majority African community has lost faith in the efficacy of normal channels, they have turned in their despair to the main alternative availing—revolution and insurgency. But this decision must be regarded as the last resort of the oppressed, not the characteristic of a people who love life and value peaceful creativity.

America's dilemmas on national violence stem directly from its status quo orientation. It accepts the validity of the insurgents' case against white minority domination while rejecting their solution to the problem. Certainly violence cannot be lightly advocated, but in this instance, the United States, somewhat uncharacteristically, becomes the apostle of peace without offering any detailed program for moving toward a just society. In this vein, the argument put forward by Secretary of State William P. Rogers to the effect that "resort to force and violence is in no one's interest," seems to beg the fundamental issue at hand.[15]

Unable to disentangle the various strands implicit in the problem of national violence, American policy makers have drifted toward a kind of negative neutralism. Assistant Secretary of State Newsom has denied both that the United States has chosen sides in the Southern African conflict and that it would necessarily intervene on the side of the white regimes in the event of a violent confrontation.[16] Even so, through its ongoing investment and trading activities, it is supportive of the Southern African regimes' economic capacity to suppress challenges from within or without. Moreover, despite arms embargoes against South Africa and Portuguese assurances against using NATO equipment outside Europe, it is evident that some American-trained personnel and U.S. military supplies are being employed at present by the white minority governments of the area. Portuguese officers have received military training in the various NATO countries and, in addition to the technical knowledge they have acquired about the manufacture of advanced military equipment, have received destroyer escorts on loan and Boeing 707 jetliners. Similarly, in 1969, some $3 million in military supplies were reportedly sold to South Africa (largely consisting of spare parts for C-130 transports purchased before the arms embargo came into effect), and in the following year, there were indications emanating from the State Department to the effect that the government was prepared to approve the sale of small civilian planes (suitable for reconnaissance purposes) to South Africa.[17] Such a negative neutrality undercuts the forcefulness of American pronouncements on violence. The United States seems consistent not on the use of force in international affairs but in the preservation of the status quo, even if it means bending a little to the advantage of established regimes.

The tendency on the part of American policy makers to "tilt" in favor of established Southern African regimes has its counterpart in the Middle African states as well. The United States remained largely on the sidelines throughout the Nigerian and Sudanese civil wars, quietly maintaining links with governmental authorities at the center while bitter combat ensued at the periphery. A more startling insight into this noninvolvement psychology came to light in 1972 when more than one hundred thousand leading members of the majority Hutu people of Burundi were killed by the dominant Tutsi regime—without major protest from world powers. "For a variety of different reasons," notes Stanley Meisler,

> all institutions that might have protested—church groups, governments, international organizations—made individual decisions to look the other way. Each decision seemed logical and right to those who made it. But the net result was that the Burundi government escaped any punishment or even condemnation for the horror it inflicted on so many of its people.[18]

In keeping with its noninvolvement psychology, the Nixon administration was quick to join other Western and African governments in playing down the issue. The U.S. Embassy in Bujumbura, concerned for the safety of American residents in Burundi and convinced that protests would be ineffective, attempted to keep stories about the massacres from publication in overseas newspapers. American officials expressed private disapproval of the killings, but no formal action on their part was forthcoming. As a consequence, American support for the established government in Burundi led to an embarrassing silence in the face of considerable suffering.

THE DILEMMA OF TRADE For much of the nineteenth and early twentieth centuries, barriers to African trade were a persistent problem for American businessmen. The colonial powers carved out spheres of influence for themselves and, in doing so, placed extensive restrictions upon American commercial activity in the area. Only where British and French control was weakest (South Africa, the Belgian Congo, Liberia, and Ethiopia) did American commercial enterprise reach significant proportions.

Such exclusions declined noticeably with the approach of independence. African self-rule carried with it a broadening of economic opportunities for American business and commerical interests. Thus American imports rose dramatically from an estimated $100 million a year prior to World War II to $590 million in 1956, and American exports climbed from $100 million to $630 million in the same period.[19] By 1970, these totals had doubled again; American imports from Africa rose to $1,110 million and exports to $1,575 million. If the American market had now emerged as a vitally important outlet for many African minerals and commodities (uranium, iron ore, chrome, diamonds, copper, rubber, coffee, cocoa), only a small fraction of total United States exports required the African market. The dependency resulting from economic linkages therefore tends to be unidirectional.

Although the internal conditions of American economic life (a declining raw materials base, a growing balance of payments deficits, and increasing worldwide product competition) appear to press policy makers to continue present, advantageous trade policies with Africa, external factors (the impact of fluctuating world commodity prices upon African development and the bolstering of white minority regimes) seem to pull them in a somewhat different direction. Thus something of a contradiction exists between American laissez faire practices and the goal of African development. Whereas the modus operandi of free trade gave the American industrialist assurance of necessary minerals and commodities at relatively low prices, except perhaps under extraordinary circumstances, the advantage was purchased dearly. Great fluctuations in world prices for these items of trade left Third World countries poor and unable to set meaningful plans for future economic modernization. In some cases where their economies have become overloaded, the political repercussions have been severe; legitimate governments have fallen and have been replaced by military regimes which rely upon their coercive capacities for survival. Such a process represents a setback for American policy which is reformist in orientation.

In addition, the contradiction between the claims of laissez faire and racial justice is apparent. In the Southern African context, trade is anything but neutral. When conducted under present conditions, it involves the United States on the side of the status quo. In 1970 United States exports to South Africa and Namibia were $563 million (17 percent of her total imports); United States imports from that country were $288 million (13 percent of total exports, not including gold). A roughly similar pattern prevailed in Angola where United States exports in 1970 came to $38 million (10 percent) and imports to $68 million (17 percent); moreover in Mozambique,

American exports during that year amounted to $22 million (9 percent) and imports to $18 million (10 percent).[20] Clearly American trade was important to the maintenance of the Southern African system. It meant that the Southern African and Western economies were to remain interconnected, thereby stimulating enterprise and giving hope of future de facto acceptability.

Nothing in recent American–Southern African experience illustrates the intertwining of the economic and political spheres more graphically than does the 1971 congressional action permitting the importation of Rhodesian chrome. This legislation, enacted in defiance of a United Nations embargo, gave a psychological boost to the Smith regime just at a point when Rhodesian morale was at low ebb. From an American standpoint, such an initiative was hardly justifiable in economic or strategic terms. The United States had some 5.3 million tons of chromium ore in its stockpile, and additional sources of this precious metal (albeit at higher prices) were available from the Soviet Union. Despite evident reasons for caution, the Senate, on an amendment to the Military Procurement Authorization Bill proposed by Senator Harry Byrd, voted to remove the President's authority to ban the importation of strategic or critical materials from non-Communist countries at a time when no prohibitions existed against the importation of such materials from Communist lands. The amendment, subsequently signed into law by President Nixon, was quickly put into effect, and in March 1972 some 25,000 tons of Rhodesian ore were unloaded in Louisiana.

For American spokesmen, the nation's change of position on the chrome question was to be explained by the weighty loads of world leadership. In Lusaka, George Bush, the permanent representative of the United States to the United Nations, defended the American reversal of policy by declaring that his country had to bear an "onerous burden" to defend itself and its Western and other allies.[21] Such an explanation could hardly be expected to convince his Zambian listeners. Only a month before the Bush visit an editorial in the *Times of Zambia* had cautioned against placing unequivocal faith in American motives and pronouncements.[22] The United States had clearly put itself on the defensive by its trade policies, and any gains from sanction-busting would be more than offset by the costs in African goodwill.

Yet the lesson of Rhodesian chrome was to some extent sanguine. If American trade policies could be altered to the benefit of the rebel government in Rhodesia, it could also be manipulated to the advantage of African nationalism. Once it is recognized that profoundly conflictive circumstances make claims to economic neutrality rather specious, then it becomes possible to make what are essentially political decisions about commitments and objectives. An American trade policy which shifted purchases of coffee from Angola (where it is grown for the most part on large European plantations) to Kenya or Colombia might have the desired effect of weakening a colonial structure. In a similar way, South Africa's sugar quota, which amounts to a direct American subsidy of over $8 million per annum, could be reallocated to other, less prosperous countries in Africa such as Uganda or Swaziland. Thus trade policies could be employed in a more imaginative manner to further America's long-term foreign policy objectives. Once American policy makers recognize the inescapability of their involvement, they will be in a better position to use their power in a creative manner—and, oftentimes, at a minimal economic cost.

THE DILEMMA OF INVESTMENT   American policy contradictions with regard to investment in Africa run parallel to those discussed above on trade. Again significant American investment is largely a post-World War II phenomenon. It has risen rapidly from $104 million in 1943 to $298 million in 1950, and to $834 million in 1959.[23] By 1970, it totaled some $3 billion, roughly divided into two-thirds north and one-third south of the Zambezi. Compared to the $12 billion invested in Latin America this total seems inconsiderable. Yet the American investor presence is important in a few specified instances: Libya ($775 million), South Africa ($755 million), Liberia ($172 million), and Angola ($150 million). Comparatively speaking, investments in Southern Africa have given the highest rates of return; in South Africa, for example, some 275 American firms earned an estimated 15 percent net return on book value. It is such levels of profitability, combined with relative safety of investment and ease of repatriation, which cause many business executives to pay scant heed to the political and social circumstances under which they carry on their enterprises.

Moreover, as with trade, investment involves the United States on the side of the status quo. This may well be desirable in much of black Africa, but the political complications from such an approach in Southern Africa are manifold. The $55 million investment in Rhodesia's chrome mining industry certainly contributed in a substantial way to the American decision to remove this mineral from the embargoed list. And by its ability to provide access to capital and consumer markets, tax revenues, employment opportunities, technical skills, and international respectability, American private investment lends vitally needed support to these politically isolated regimes. The $150 million investment in Angola's oil industry and the massive investment in South Africa's manufacturing, mining, and oil drilling enterprises contribute mightily to the survival of such political structures. This contribution to the Southern African system is well understood by African observers who are bitterly critical of the West's "business as usual" attitude. A comment from the *Nationalist* of Tanzania will suffice on this point.

> But while the American imperialists continue to do this [exploit South Africa's wealth], they should refrain from any talk of "friendship" with the African people. For, in the final analysis, it is not only insincere on their part but also criminal to continue soliciting for the goodwill and friendship of the Africans while at the same time they continue to hob-nob with the enemies of Africa.[24]

Some opinion formers, anxious to reduce the political costs of private business involvement in Southern Africa, have called for a reappraisal of priorities. They seek to escape present dilemmas by reducing investments or by withdrawing entirely from the area. Since investment creates vested interests in the status quo, they advocate various forms of disengagement to escape from the entanglements of overseas enterprise. Particularly significant in this regard was a 1971 policy panel of the United Nations Association, including among its members a substantial number from the business community, which recommended that American firms place no new investments in South Africa; it also called upon American companies to withdraw their investments if they found the adoption of fair labor practices to be economically unfeasible.[25] In addition, the panel called upon the government of the United States to discontinue underwriting trade with South Africa and to assist American companies in that country "to adopt more progressive labor practices and to become a more effective force for change."[26]

To some extent the United States has recognized the need for disengagement in Southern Africa. By letting it be known that in 1970 the Export-Import Bank would no longer grant loan guarantees for trade with Namibia, the United States has in fact acted to discourage new investment in that territory. Moreover, the refusal of the Export-Import Bank to authorize a $150 million advance to the General Electric Company to finance electrical current conversion equipment for the controversial Cabora Bassa dam project in Mozambique was interpreted as having political implications.[27] But whether the United States will move from the discouragement of new business in certain circumstances to a policy of withdrawal, partial or total, remains to be seen. Because of the interconnected nature of the world capitalist economy, a far-reaching program of withdrawal might prove difficult to effect. Nevertheless, government control of business life is becoming an increasingly accepted phenomenon, and new measures leading to disengagement (including the withdrawal of tax privileges for American companies operating in South Africa) seem a realizable objective at this juncture.

THE DILEMMA OF AID   A status quo orientation on the part of the United States gives rise to contradictions between aid objectives and outcomes. American aid policies seek such goals as economic self-reliance, military security (Ethiopia), and regional planning; in practice, however, aid seems sometimes to obstruct these very aims, creating dependence instead of independence, hostility rather than goodwill. What the donor sees as humanitarianism, the recipient interprets as interference; and the more generous the allocation of resources, the more profound the depth of suspicion. Why does the United States give aid? Why is she stingy—or generous? Is she motivated by a desire to help Africa—or to exploit her resources and to enlist her support in the crusade against communism? Such questions are recurrent in Africa today. And only occasionally does any observer on the African scene comment on what one editorialist described as the case of "you can't win" whatever your motives and actions:

> We accuse America of being unsympathetic to the poorer nations of the world when Congress reduces that country's budget for foreign aid. Yet when America's finances are forthcoming, it is immediately accused of neo-colonialist design aimed at dominating and perhaps "Americanising" other people's economies.[28]

In fact, the United States has extended its low-profile approach to the field of economic (and military) aid. The decline in the likelihood of a great power confrontation has been matched by a reduced urgency over external assistance. Thus while the United Nations continues to spend some $400 million annually in Africa ($250 million in direct aid and $150 million through the United States specialized agencies), it no longer displays an intense desire to put a *cordon sanitaire* around the continent. At present Soviet aid is not viewed as threatening American interests, and a more relaxed stance toward the outward-looking Chinese thrust seems also to be in the offing. "We are no longer lured to respond to appeals from African countries by the fact or threat of Communist aid," states Newsom.[29] In this sense the massive part played by the Chinese in the construction of the Tanzam railroad may well mark a watershed in United States policy, for American officials, after getting several chances to act as the prime mover in this important enterprise, chose to pass up the opportunity, alleging that it lacked fiscal viability.

Where the Nixon administration encountered taunts and harassment from small African powers, it reacted with firmness—at times reducing its economic and technical assistance as well as its contacts generally. The case of General Idi Amin's Uganda is instructive in this regard. American economic relations with Uganda were never extensive, and at their high point in 1971, involved an input into the Uganda economy of roughly $100 million annually (mainly comprising coffee purchases, tourism, economic assistance, and direct investments). Initially the Amin coup of January 1971 had little impact upon this low-keyed American-Ugandan relationship. The coup seemed to herald a political and economic turning to the "right" in Uganda's foreign relations, and the internal difficulties of the new regime (even the ominous disappearance of two Americans) hardly seemed to warrant major diplomatic attention in the eyes of the administration in Washington.

Such a lack of concern with Ugandan affairs began to change during the second year following the coup, as President Amin expressed hostility toward American policies and as the internal security situation in Uganda worsened. Although fulsome in his praise for American contributions to African economic development, Amin strongly criticized American bombing of North Vietnam in May 1972. By July, the attack shifted from American policy in Asia to that in Africa. Now Amin accused the United States Central Intelligence Agency of fomenting confusion and tribal divisions in Uganda.[30] A week later Amin warned the outgoing United States ambassador to Uganda, Dr. Clyde Ferguson, to inform his government that "if it wants the good relations existing between the two countries, the United States should not send Israelis to Uganda under disguise." [31]

Despite both the disappearance of the two Americans in 1971 and subsequent reports of lawlessness in the rural areas, it was not until August 1972 that the State Department acted formally and openly to discourage American travel in Uganda. The question of movement around the country came to a head when an American diplomat and his wife were roughed up by Uganda troops at a remote Uganda-Rwanda border outpost; as a consequence, U.S. authorities advised American diplomats and tourists to travel in Uganda only by airplane. Then, in October 1972, the last of some

117 Peace Corps volunteers were flown out of Entebbe; in explaining the termination of Peace Corps activities in Uganda during the current period, American officials stated that security in that country had deteriorated in recent weeks to a point where volunteers could not effectively carry out their program.[32] In acting to reduce the American presence in Uganda as well as the movement of its nationals within the country, American officials seemed more nervous over the implications of the security situation than did a number of other Western embassies in Uganda. Certainly, such actions are an insight into their state of mind at a time of surface calm and general low visibility.

As the Amin regime became more overtly anti-Western in its policy statements, the Nixon administration moved to reduce further its silhouette upon the local scene. With respect to the Amin regime's "economic war" against Ugandan Asian interests, the Nixon policy makers shunned expressions of moral indignation, even though it did admit some 1,000 stateless Asians into the United States.[33] Indeed it was Amin's bluntly worded anti-Jewish statements of September 1972, not the much-publicized Asian expulsions from Uganda, which were the immediate cause of American aid reductions. Amin's determinations to forge close links with the Arab world led him to expand his previous anti-Israeli policy into an international assault upon Jewish interests. In a message to the Secretary-General of the United Nations of September 1972, Amin not only urged the removal of all Israelis from the Middle East but wrote sympathetically of Hitler's "final solution" as well. Amin declared: "Germany is the right place where when Hitler was the prime minister and supreme commander, he burned over 6,000,000 Jews." [34] Coming on top of the economic war against the Ugandan Asians, the deteriorating internal security situation, and the impending American election, the American (and West European) reaction to this gratuitous remark was expectedly sharp. State Department press officer Charles W. Bray 3d said that "any such description of the holocaust is deeply shocking and incomprehensible in any context, but particularly when it comes from a national leader." [35] More pointedly, perhaps, Bray went on to indicate that the United States would hold up a projected $3 million loan to Uganda as a sign of its displeasure over the Amin statement.

Several months later the loan freeze remained in effect; however, the explanations for the denial of funds to Uganda were now extended to include the harassment and arrest of U.S. citizens and the expressed attitudes of Ugandan leaders on matters of deep concern to the American people.[36] On various occasions, moreover, State Department spokesman Bray asserted that the United States did not intend to undertake any new technical assistance programs in Uganda if an American company (International Television Sales), taken over by governmental authorities along with other foreign interests, was not paid prompt and effective compensation.[37] Then, in February 1973, the United States quietly withdrew its ambassador from Uganda in an apparent reaction to Amin's charges of American aggression against the Vietnamese people; in this instance, the Nixon administration did not make public its displeasure with the statement of a head of government (as in the cases of Sweden and India) but simply reduced its contacts with Uganda authorities. Clearly, American policy makers, in retreat generally from global commitments, were reacting to Uganda pressures by continually reducing an already low profile on that country's scene.

As the political urgency of aid declined, American policy makers tended increasingly to channel scarce resources toward a limited number of "selected" countries. States closely connected to the Western capitalist economy (Zaire, Uganda (pre-1972), Kenya, Liberia, Nigeria, Ghana) and states closely identified with Western strategic interests (Morocco, Tunisia, Ethiopia) received the most generous aid allocations under this policy. The sole country included on the selected list for development aid which does not meet the above criteria is Tanzania. Thus, despite demands that selection involves a choice among African leaders, some preference, likely based on current national interest values and objectives, would seem to be apparent.[38]

Moreover, the policy on selected aid recipients has been reinforced by the Johnson and Nixon administrations' emphasis upon directing United States assistance to interterritorial projects. As recently as June 1972, for example, the U.S. Agency for International

Development announced an increase in its aid to the East African Community in the forthcoming year from $1.4 million to $1.6 million.[39] Such a regional approach has appeal to American officials in that it maximizes the impact of limited disbursements on the African scene. At the same time it can by no means be said to be a departure from the inclination to limit the number of regionally directed aid recipients (fifteen in all) or to promote status quo objectives. By involving a limited number of states in long-term projects, the United States in effect encourages an outward-looking orientation which links the African states to the world economy. To some extent these general policies on channeling aid are in line with a growing preference for reformist over radical regimes. The Soviet-American détente appears to have lessened the need to court militant, socialist-oriented governments, thereby making it possible for the Johnson and Nixon administrations to follow their natural inclination on support for the more friendly and responsive African regimes. However, such aid for friends creates suspicions and even enemies, and can therefore be seen as creating almost as many foreign policy dilemmas as it solves.[40]

Toward a Redefinition of Policy

If a status quo orientation toward the African nations lands the United States in a series of contradictions, it seems logical to ask what line of policy will enable the United States to avoid a self-defeating, and possibly dangerous, entanglement. After all, the present course of American trade and investment activities could result in the creation of such vested interests in Southern Africa as to require extensive military commitments to maintain the status quo; economic relations would spill over into military alliances, most likely leading to further unintended consequences. Surely Vietnam points to the prudence of drawing back from such entanglements at an early stage.

To speak of policy in this regard is to assume some capacity for national choice. The alternative is to view American-African relations in a deterministic manner, regarding it as a necessary historical phase, i.e., the highest stage of capitalism or neocolonialism. In that event, references to the possibility of disengagement can be dismissed as obscurantist reformism. Man would be restrained by environmental conditions beyond his control and hence incapable of restructuring his relationship to the world about him. But such a deterministic outlook seems unwarranted in the case of a powerful world actor. By the fact that the United States undeniably has the ability for diplomatic and economic manoeuvre, it is in a position to make a significant impact upon world affairs. It cannot then avoid the responsibility of choice. Government's freedom of action may well be cramped by interest-group pressures (particularly those of the multinational corporations or racial and religious groups), but in a showdown, the primacy of the political arm seems apparent. It is government which decides on the construction of a road from Botswana to Zambia (unpopular to South Africa) or permits the purchase of Rhodesian chrome (unpopular to black Africa). Interest-group pressures may play a very significant part in these decisions, but ultimate responsibility for choices must rest with public officials. And if they have this responsibility, they have some capacity at least to make decisions on the nature of engagement or disengagement.

The need for a reexamination of American priorities on Africa is largely a consequence of the inability of old policies to achieve desired outcomes. This is particularly the case in such areas as economic development and racial justice where objectives remain unrealized. The resultant unacceptability of the present situation leads to a strongly stated call for change. But how deep-rooted is this appeal for greater American involvement? Rhetoric notwithstanding, there are ample indications that it is more symbolic than substantive. Neither the American nor the African publics seem psychologically prepared for full American engagement, with all its social, cultural, political, and economic implications.

Evidences of mutual withdrawal are manifest. On the one hand, the American public, "ceaselessly obsessed with the desire to possess the new goods created by the modern age," is largely inward-looking in orientation.[41] Its primary concerns, as reflected in the annual debate on foreign aid appropriations, are not over external affairs but over such domestic concerns as employment, inflation, housing, industrial growth, and pollution. The more national resources are stretched by external and internal demands, the more likely seems a struggle over the distribution process. Indicative of intense feelings over allocative priorities was a complaint, reportedly voiced by Senator J. W. Fulbright, following the Senate Foreign Relations Committee's approval of funds to assist the resettlement in Israel of Jewish refugees from the Soviet Union. Senator Fulbright is said to have remarked: "Here we are proposing to give another $85 million to Israel when I am having trouble getting $8 million for a road in Arkansas because funds are short." [42] Financial backing for preventive medicine or education in Africa is pitted against similar domestic claims, all at a time of increasing disenchantment with the results of such overseas activities. Thus the dream of a Marshall Plan for Africa, as envisaged by Kenya's Tom Mboya in 1967, comes smack up against donor fatigue, born of external miscalculation and internal burden.[43]

On the other hand, Africans evince little enthusiasm for a massive infusion of American manpower and capital into their continent. They have repeatedly voiced profound suspicions of the present role of American corporate managers, diplomats, peace corpsmen, CIA officials, and so forth. At heart, they feel endangered by American power, a force beyond their control which may come to interfere with their self-development and deflect them from a course of genuine emancipation. American power, it is contended, threatens Africa's integrity and may lead, if unimpeded, to strategic, economic, cultural, and diplomatic "aggression" against their lands. For one not atypical writer, the United States is interested in "a programme to vassalise Africa under the guise of granting it aids of some sort." [44] Foreign aid, he claims, opens the door to dollar diplomacy and the loss of independence. Consequently he urges reduced dependence upon American private enterprise: "A breakaway from capitalism would signify a break in the traditional colonial economic relations that prolong Africa's backwardness and general dependence." [45] Thus self-reliance, not interdependence with international capitalism, is seen as the road to genuine fulfillment. Freedom comes through reducing contacts, not maintaining inherited capitalistic linkages.

The two urges for limited American involvement, strikingly different in inspiration but somewhat similar in outcome, make a low profile stance more credible than is sometimes accepted—by liberals and conservatives alike. Here a distinction between neglect and low visibility seems essential. Under existing circumstances, neglect is the arrogance of power; but low visibility, where compassion merges with anonymity, is precisely the opposite. The desirability of greatly enhanced aid appropriations is unquestionable. In the face of great deprivation, a wealthy country cannot justify spending a mere 1.5 percent of its federal budget on foreign assistance. But greater economic support is not tantamount to a return of an outmoded *Pax Americana*. Clearly any idea of returning to a hegemonic and paternalistic leadership role seems as delusory as it is self-defeating. By adjusting to this fact, Americans go partway at least toward resolving the contradictions in their approach to policy making.

Once the ambition of international hegemony is eschewed, the problem of setting priorities becomes more manageable. Great, comprehensive views on African politics become less necessary, and statesmen can turn their attention to the specifics of each case of engagement and disengagement. They would then be dealing with concrete circumstances, not sweeping conceptualizations. On such questions as investments, trade subsidies, loan and aid recipients, and recognition of governments, choices could be made selectively and on the basis of enlightened self-interest. The onerous entanglement with illiberalism can be pushed aside, allowing national leaders to reverse long-standing policies which have proved burdensome symbolically in the present, and quite possibly materially in the future. Thus an enlightened view of *raison d'état* would seem to call for a termination of the current laissez faire policy toward Africa. Increased direction and control would inevitably entail a careful definition of national priorities on engagement and disengagement, enabling the United States to see its way clear to a policy both more realistic and ethical.

Geoffrey Wandesforde-Smith

Environmental Quality and American Foreign Policy

Until recently it would have seemed peculiar, at the least, for a respectable student of American foreign policy to concern himself with the probability that the future of the world was jeopardized by environmental deterioration. From time to time the press might report that a prophet of doom had led his followers to some remote canyon or mountain top to await Armageddon, perhaps in the form of a cataclysmic flood or pestilence, but this was widely interpreted as the behavior of a lunatic fringe[1]—hardly something that foreign policy planners should take into account. While the prospect of a nuclear holocaust triggered by a war among the superpowers has persisted since 1945, even this dreadful scenario for the end of the world has lost its sting. It has been some time since Americans were eager to build miniature survival centers in the form of fallout shelters in the basement or back yard. On the one hand, there is a slender but growing hope that the nuclear juggernaut can be contained by agreements such as those reached between America and the Soviet Union at the May 1972 Moscow summit. On the other hand, the United States and other world powers have prefaced their diplomacy for so long upon the need to avert a nuclear catastrophe, by maintaining the balance of terror demanded by deterrence theory, that world politics in the postnuclear age is necessarily surrounded by uncertainties. If, indeed, the security and interests of nations are less and less likely to be threatened by nuclear war, perhaps the end of the world can be delayed indefinitely. Perhaps the conduct of international relations can go forward in an atmosphere free of an end-of-the-world mentality, and American foreign policy can be adjusted accordingly.

An accumulating literature and set of events appear to deny these attractive possibilities. In place of a fear that man will almost instantaneously disappear in the white heat and radioactive dust of a nuclear bomb burst there is developing a fear that he will more gradually, but no less surely, extinguish his light and likes by exhausting his life-support systems. Among scholars and statesmen, the end of the world has again become the subject of considerable industry, and there is an increasing fascination with alternative strategies for saving the planet from ecological destruction. At the root of this activity is the perception that within a specifiable period of time pollution of the land, air, and waters of the earth by an increasing population and more advanced technology will render existing ways of life, and ultimately life itself, unsupportable. How much time remains to man if present trends are not altered is a variable quantity depending upon which prognosis is preferred. One study places the deadline within the next one hundred years, even allowing for optimistic assumptions about resource availability and advances in pollution-control techniques.[2]

This recent concern with ecological catastrophe on a global scale has been depicted in various ways. In the words of Professor Richard Falk of Princeton University, the earth has become an endangered planet.[3] Professor Lynton Caldwell invokes a similar analogy to the plight of endangered wildlife species in arguing that the time has come for the United States and other nations to act in defense of the earth.[4] Lord Ritchie-Calder refers to the earth as the old homestead that mankind has mortgaged only to find that nature is liable to foreclose.[5] Former ambassador George Kennan writes of the world as a potential wasteland.[6] And pursuing the notion that, contrary to established patterns of thought, there are limits to economic and demographic growth, economist Kenneth Boulding has likened the planet to a spaceship that can sustain life only if the inhabitants recognize the constraints imposed by living within a closed system.[7] Harold and Margaret Sprout have written a new textbook on international relations in support of their contention that the future of world politics can be understood as the politics of the planet earth, a politics that revolves around efforts "to cope with the diverse, cumulatively enormous, and still proliferating human capabilities to alter the conditions of subsistence upon this planet." [8]

The international community has been stirred to action by these and many other warnings from the academic and scientific fraternities. Since the General Assembly acted unanimously in December 1968 on a resolution introduced by Sweden to hold a United Nations Conference on the Human Environment,[9] high hopes have been placed on the outcome of a two-week meeting involving representatives from 114 nations and about 500 nongovernmental organizations. The meeting held in Stockholm, Sweden, from June 5 to June 16, 1972, was widely hailed as an opportunity to take action. Under the leadership of a self-made Canadian millionaire named Maurice Strong, a man practically unknown outside Canada at the time of his appointment as conference secretary-general,[10] an ambitious agenda was developed for the Stockholm meeting by a preparatory committee of twenty-seven nations.[11] The conference yielded several accomplishments, including a Declaration on the Human Environment, an Action Plan for the worldwide monitoring and evaluation of environmental conditions, and an agreement to establish a new organizational structure in the United Nations to deal with environmental affairs.

It is still difficult to say precisely what the UN conference will do to modify national policies. The Soviet Union and most of the countries in the East European bloc stayed away to protest the exclusion of East Germany, which was not eligible to attend because it is not a member of the UN or any of its specialized agencies. Although the Soviet response to the conference recommendations is unclear, the other major Communist power, the People's Republic of China, made it plain that it sees no clear and present danger in environmental deterioration. The chairman of the People's Republic delegation was prepared to recognize the environmental issue only as a function of "the development of capitalism into imperialism and particularly the policies of plunder, aggression and war frenziedly pursued by the superpowers." [12] His argument that the history of mankind has proved "that the pace of development of production, science and technology always surpasses by far the rate of population growth," and that man has "inexhaustible possibilities" for exploiting and using natural resources, leaves no doubt that China will change its policies slowly, if at all, in the short run. And in light of Soviet and Chinese actions, Hans Landsberg was correct in sobering the expectations of those who had anticipated much more than action of symbolic significance from such a large and divided assembly as that in Stockholm. [13]

Symbolic action nevertheless has its uses in politics. To the formal recognition and degree of legitimacy accorded to concern for the future of the world environment by the Stockholm conference there must be added the actions taken by many national governments. And in the United States at least symbolic expressions of concern have been accompanied by statutory changes. The National Environmental Policy Act of 1969 contains a section which states in part that "all agencies of the Federal Government shall . . . recognize the worldwide and long-range character of environmental problems and, where consistent with the foreign policy of the United States, lend appropriate support to initiatives, resolutions and programs designed to maximize international cooperation in anticipating and preventing a decline in the quality of mankind's world environment." [14] The second annual report of the President's Council on Environmental Quality reproduces with approval excerpts from President Nixon's report to the Congress on U.S. foreign policy for the 1970s. The report to the Congress notes the existence of environmental problems in which every country has a deep national interest, but which are not subject to simple or satisfactory resolution by national action. Commenting on the relevance for foreign policy of these problems, the President's report argues that:

> [T]here has come into being a new dimension in the foreign policy of the United States, not as a matter of choice and deliberate action on our part but as a reflection of the demanding realities of the world in which we live. Foreign policy has, of

course, always aimed at serving the nation's security and well-being. What is new is the fact that we now face an increasing range of problems which are central to our national well-being, but which are, by definition, global problems, or problems which can only be dealt with effectively on a global scale.[15]

From this premise the report goes on to speak of a new concept of the national interest that is implied by these demanding realities of environmental decay:

> [A] narrow calculation of national interests is inadequate. For viewed from that perspective, the nations of the world do sometimes have conflicting interests of a real and substantial nature. Of greater import, however, is our shared and transcendent interest in the livability of our common home, the earth. To [those problems that must be dealt with on a global scale], and the opportunities they present, that interest must be our guide and the guide of others. The nurturing of that interest has now become a prime task of American leadership.[16]

Both the obligations imposed on federal agencies by the National Environmental Policy Act and the President's 1970 foreign policy report raise intriguing questions. Much of the literature proclaiming the existence of worldwide environmental problems, as well as much of the rhetoric surrounding the UN conference, has suggested that international relations are on the verge of a significant transformation. If any doubt remained that the process, variously referred to as economic development, industrialization, or modernization, that began in England in the eighteenth century with the Industrial Revolution, had made the nations and peoples of the world increasingly and ultimately interdependent, the perception of international pollution problems served to make clear the limitations of a world order based upon national sovereignty. Policy statements by the Congress and the President seem to accept this view. They commit the United States both at home and abroad to the pursuit of a shared and transcendent world interest in protecting the livability of the planet and the quality of the human environment. However, it is less clear how this world interest is to be determined and by whom, how it is to relate to older conceptions of the national interest, and how existing foreign policy must be modified to meet the demands of a transformed international system.

In an attempt to throw some light on these questions, it should be noted first that the available data about man's impact upon environmental conditions throughout the world provide ambiguous signals for policy planners. The data certainly indicate that in the long run an expanding human population can continue to place demands upon the biosphere only at the risk of eventual breakdown. The accelerating rates of resource use, technological advance, and economic production and consumption needed to sustain ever larger populations at the living standards now associated with and anticipated in advanced industrialized societies are likely to be especially damaging.[17] Beyond this there is room for considerable disagreement and speculation.

Some arguments about the effects of pollution on the atmosphere, for example, suggest that accumulations of carbon dioxide from the burning of fossil fuels, such as coal and oil, might cause the planet to warm up and thereby trigger a melting of the polar ice caps. One result of this, of course, would be the submergence of some coastal cities due to an increase in sea level. Other arguments hold that the particulate matter emitted into the atmosphere by industrial processes, power generating facilities, and internal combustion engines could prevent some sunlight from reaching the earth. One result of this could be a reduction of global temperature sufficient to initiate a new ice age, and a net lowering of sea level.[18] In other cases the existence of limits is much clearer. The buildup of chlorinated hydrocarbons, such as DDT, in land-based species and marine life cannot be allowed to continue unchecked, given evidence about their concentration in successively higher levels of the food chain and their adverse effects on reproduction. It is equally clear that marine and terrestrial ecosystems cannot be indefinitely subjected to the stresses man imposes upon them by using them as if they were infinite sinks for the disposal of heavy metals, oil, radioactive wastes, and nutrients such as phosphorous.[19]

In the case of all environmental problems, much more information is needed to assess the full impact of man's activity and to develop more reliable estimates of the probability of man's reaching or exceeding what Fairfield Osborn described as the limits of the earth.[20] Information deficiencies are sufficiently large to warrant caution in assuming that foreign policy to deal with environmental issues must be predicated on an imminent disaster. But they also caution against the assumption that identification of the world's shared and transcendent interest in the continuing livability of the human environment, and the relating of this to national interests, can be postponed until all the facts are known.

In the absence of any scientific, objective, or even generally acceptable definition of the future policy implications of global environmental problems, we may ask whether considerations that have influenced foreign policy formation in the United States in the past are likely to be influential in policy changes made to accommodate what Richard Falk calls the ecological imperative. Perhaps the most important lesson to be learned from the past is that the United States, in common with many other nations, has been reluctant to forgo its freedom of action in international politics unless such a loss could be clearly compensated for by proportionate concrete benefits. In recent years, however, freedom of action has been more and more difficult to maintain and the United States has found it less easy to ensure that anticipated benefits flow from foreign policy actions. The use of force as the ultimate means of preserving national interests has lost credibility, and attention has shifted to the development of supranational institutions as mechanisms for advancing foreign policy goals.

To the chagrin of some, including the foreign policy planners close to President Nixon, participation in international organizations has not yielded the support for American policies that seems warranted. In the United Nations, for example, the Soviet Union, the People's Republic of China, many underdeveloped countries, and even nations that in the past have been allies of the United States have shown more interest in condemning America for its policy in Vietnam than in affirming America's vital national interest in prosecuting the war. Disagreements with Russia and China are to be expected, and there is an established tradition of bilateral negotiation among superpowers that can be and is being employed to cope with these. It is the apparent failure of multilateral arrangements to produce more favorable relations with the less powerful and uncommitted nations that is most frustrating. Since the foreign policy of the Nixon administration depends so much for its success on the ability of the United States to determine for other countries, as well as for itself, what constitute legitimate national interests, the importance of international organizations has been underplayed in practice if not in rhetoric. This is evident in administration programs for dealing with international problems of environmental quality, and in analyzing the possible consequences of the Nixon strategy it is important to understand the nature of the non-American perceptions of the world interest in environmental protection.

Consider first the implications of environmental problems for American foreign policy in general. To some degree the growing interest in these problems by many national governments stems from the realization that not all pollution originates within national boundaries. In some cases it may represent actual but not necessarily malicious invasion of one state's sovereign territory by another that is emitting noxious substances into the air and water. Thus, the dumping of air pollutants generated in Britain on the mountains of Norway, and the pollution of the Canadian section of the Great Lakes by emissions originating in the United States, underscore the need for international cooperation. No nation can afford to be indifferent to resource pollution and waste regardless of whether it occurs locally or in another country. Moreover, action taken unilaterally to protect one nation from the external costs and damages imposed upon it by another may be perceived as a hostile act and lead to serious conflict. To avoid this possibility arrangements for pollution control and resource conservation must be mutually agreed upon by the nations concerned. In this sense environmental problems argue for affirmation of a political principle that the Nixon administration believes should be central to American foreign policy, namely, that cooperation is preferable to confrontation.

This leaves open, however, questions about the terms and conditions under which cooperation can proceed. A recent National Academy of Sciences report states that America cannot tolerate the pollution or attrition, by those nations that control them, of resources upon which the United States is dependent. Such a situation would adversely affect the American economy, even though the United States is not heavily dependent upon resource imports, and would, in the words of the report, "critically disrupt any viable system of international economic relations." [21] It is tempting to interpret this strong language as a plea for the United States to maintain indefinitely its position as a principal consumer of the world's resources. In other words, no action is to be tolerated that threatens American access to supplies of oil, minerals and other resources in which the United States is presently or potentially deficient. Definitions of the world interest in environmental protection are therefore acceptable to the United States only as long as they do not jeopardize American economic interests in world trade and in a highly consumptive pattern of domestic living. Yet these are precisely the interests to which many foreign countries object. In their view the world interest in environmental protection demands that the United States consume resources at a level more nearly proportional than it is now to the United States' share of world population. Moreover, some American commentators have argued that the world interest in survival demands that the United States should deliberately foster a lower level of domestic economic development, and that this, coupled with a much more generous program of foreign aid, should be the keystone of future foreign policy. [22] At the least these views portend considerable difficulty for the United States in persuading other nations, and some internal constituencies, that efforts at international environmental cooperation can go forward in the absence of a far-reaching reassessment of America's overall policy objectives, both foreign and domestic. [23]

Consider, secondly, some of the possible consequences of world environmental problems for East-West relations. The Soviet Union takes the position that a basic cause of irresponsible use of the environment is to be found in the rapacious exploitation of resources by capitalist economies. Only socialist societies are held to be capable of solving environmental problems, which Soviet spokesmen define almost exclusively in terms of resource pollution. This firm line has to be modified in light of evidence that environmental degradation has not been confined to capitalist countries. The pollution of Lake Baykal is one of the best-known problems in the Soviet Union but, as Philip Pryde has recently shown,[24] it is only one among many. Indeed, pollution is enough of a problem in the USSR for Soviet academicians to plead for international scientific cooperation to help with its solution. The proposal of one member of the Soviet Academy of Sciences goes so far as to suggest that the Soviet Union and the United States finance a massive effort to alleviate environmental and other problems in the underdeveloped countries by contributing 20 percent of their national income over a fifteen-year period.[25]

The Soviet view that capitalist nations are more to blame for pollution than socialist states is not one that the U.S. government accepts. The implication of official American statements is that all nations must cooperate, and, in terms of official rhetoric at least, the United States is more committed to the development of new international institutions for facilitating cooperation than is the USSR. In practice the Soviet and American positions are unlikely to create serious conflict. While the ideological basis for Soviet initiatives has deemphasized the creation of new international institutions that might infringe upon efforts by individual countries to combat pollution, it has permitted the encouragement of international efforts at scientific cooperation aimed at advancing environmental research and monitoring. The United States has been willing to work with the Soviets at this level, partly to avoid the question of whether it and other advanced Western countries should pay reparations to underdeveloped countries for the damage wrought by resource extraction, and partly to steer international discussion of environmental issues away from other sensitive and controversial subjects, such as the degree of ecological disruption created in Vietnam by a war that the Soviet Union and other nations regard as unjustified imperialist aggression. As long as agreements to cooperate are restricted to matters of scientific and technological development, bilateral arrangements like the one signed at the May 1972 Moscow summit are likely to improve

Soviet-American relationships on environmental questions.[26] And this may in some small measure assist in the easing of East-West tensions.

The larger question raised by the pattern of Soviet-American cooperation on the scientific aspects of environmental problems is whether this kind of activity is sufficient to make a significant contribution to the solution of those problems. In the past, international cooperation has proceeded almost exclusively within the framework of the scientific community because a concern with the science of wildlife management, or ecosystem analysis, or pollution of the oceans by oil, has made it possible to treat environmental problems as though they were apolitical. The assumption has been that scientists could work together under the auspices of nongovernmental bodies, such as the International Council of Scientific Unions and the International Union for the Conservation of Nature and Natural Resources, in a way that would not be possible for national representatives instructed to act as government spokesmen. It would be foolish to deny the achievements that have been made by following this approach.[27] Nevertheless, conditions in the world may now be such that a more overtly political strategy is required. A consideration of the implications of environmental problems for American policy vis-à-vis the underdeveloped countries supports this observation.

Like other foreign aid programs, the American effort at development assistance is based upon the recognition that the countries of the world are differentially wealthy in economic terms. Recognizing an obligation to share their relatively abundant economic resources, the developed nations have contributed financial and other forms of aid to their less developed neighbors in the hope of reducing the inequalities that exist. They have not been successful. The developed countries account for some 30 percent of the world's population but consume the vast majority of the world's resources. The United States alone, with less than 6 percent of the world's population, accounts for roughly 30 percent of total world consumption of raw materials such as steel, tin, fertilizers, and resources used to produce energy. Together with the USSR, Japan, Canada, Australia, and the

European states, America consumes about 90 percent of all the energy and steel produced in the world. It is doubtful, to say the least, that the United States can do much to redress these inequalities by contributing $1.8 billion out of a gross national product, in 1967, of $790 billion, in nonmilitary assistance to foreign countries.[28]

The implicit assumption of American foreign aid programs for many years has been that the money should be used to help underdeveloped countries to develop along the same lines as the United States itself. This has usually meant the fostering of the processes of industrialization and modernization that have made possible the progress in economic development characteristic of what are generally referred to as advanced societies. But as several observers have realized, this approach seems less and less attractive to the developed countries. The price of economic progress has been increasing environmental deterioration. Pollution is already a serious problem in many developing countries and a substantial increase in their industrial capacity, and therefore their capacity to pollute, would have adverse consequences for developed countries as well as the underdeveloped states themselves. In some developed countries moves are being made to reflect the total costs of economic processes in the prices of the resulting products. In the United States, for example, people are becoming more willing to pay a higher price for a product, or perhaps reduce or forgo its consumption, in order to prevent or repair the environmental damage attributable to production. In the underdeveloped countries people may be less willing to make such tradeoffs voluntarily, or to see the environmental quality costs of development built into loans and grants for development assistance. For the government of an underdeveloped country pollution may be an acceptable price to pay if it permits the housing, feeding, and employment of a rapidly increasing population that has for too long enjoyed a high living standard only vicariously through exposure to movies, television programs, and *Time* magazine.

Thus, the perceptions of the developed and underdeveloped countries about the relationship between environmental quality and development are in some respects fundamentally opposed. Professor Lynton Caldwell may be correct in supposing that a new definition of the meaning of development that would be mutually acceptable to both developed and underdeveloped countries could go some way toward avoiding serious conflict.[29] On the other hand, differences in perception are so deeply rooted in the philosophy and social structure of developed and underdeveloped nations that events may not wait until Caldwell's revised concept of development can take hold and modify behavior with respect to the environment. The report of the Study of Critical Environmental Problems conducted at the Massachusetts Institute of Technology may have come closer to finding a practical solution to conflict avoidance when it stated:

> There is little reason to believe that the developing countries can be diverted from their preoccupations with the first-order effects of technology to a concern about the side-effects upon the environment. Currently, and in the foreseeable future, the advanced industrial societies will have to carry the load of remedial action against pollution. When they need or desire the cooperation of the [less developed countries], they will be able to obtain it, if they can do so at all, only by paying for it. The payment may have to cover considerably more than the costs of research or of the management of antipollution measures. It may involve the incorporation of a new component into programs of aid to the [less developed countries], in the form of compensation for extra costs or competitive disadvantages injected into the development programs of the [less developed countries] by antipollution measures.[30]

Present American foreign policy is a long way from incorporating these ideas. In recent years attention has been focused on the adverse ecological effects of developmental projects made possible by American and other foreign aid programs[31] and an attempt has been made to incorporate environmental considerations into decisions made by the Agency for International Development, as well as international agencies such as the UN Development Program, the International Bank for Reconstruction and Development, the International Development Association, and the World Bank group. However, it is not now American policy to make a substantial increase in foreign aid to developing countries. On the contrary, pressure has been exerted in the United States to reduce the foreign aid appropriations.

Even if this pressure proves to be short-lived, it underscores a phenomenon that promises to exert greater influence upon American foreign policy in the future, both with respect to relations with developing countries and in foreign affairs generally. Harold and Margaret Sprout refer to it as the dilemma of rising demands and insufficient disposable resources.[32] They point out that the resources available to the rulers of any given nation are rarely if ever adequate to fulfill all the purposes that they envisage. Allocations of resources have just as rarely satisfied all those who felt they had a claim. Although this statesman's dilemma is not new, it is acquiring new urgency, according to the Sprouts, because of changes in world conditions and changes taking place within individual nations. In the case of the United States, their contention is clearly supported. There is considerable debate about alternative plans for resource allocation in the aftermath of the Vietnam war.[33] At the risk of oversimplification, there are those who favor continued large expenditures for defense and foreign affairs and those who favor a much greater emphasis in government spending on a variety of domestic programs. However, very few participants in this debate appear to have reckoned with the resource allocation problem posed by the recommendations of the MIT study for improving international environmental quality. Expectations about domestic spending, as well as military and foreign spending, are going to have to undergo extensive revision if the only way to guarantee the future of the world is to buy the acquiescence of developing nation governments in pollution control and environmental protection measures. The alternatives of forcing their compliance, or of installing and perpetuating puppet regimes that will prolong the poverty and misery of underdeveloped peoples so that the flow of resources to developed nations is not interrupted, are perhaps only a little more unattractive to contemplate because they are closer to past practices.

The idea of buying the cooperation of developing countries in environmental programs is not without precedent. In September 1961, at Arusha in what was then Tanganyika, the International

Union for the Conservation of Nature and Natural Resources (IUCN) convened a scientific symposium on the future of conservation in the newly independent African nations. No doubt concerned that these new countries would display even less regard for African wildlife than had been exhibited by the colonial powers, the symposium organizers sought to impress upon Africa's new leaders the worldwide significance of their natural heritage. Although they were not insensitive to the economic advantages to be gained from wildlife management programs that would attract tourists and generate revenue, the response of the Africans was to say, in effect, that if non-African countries wanted to see African wildlife preserved they would have to be prepared to subsidize the endeavor. In late 1961 a series of articles by Sir Julian Huxley appeared in a London newspaper on the dangers threatening African wildlife. The IUCN responded to the interest created by the articles by launching the World Wildlife Fund under the patronage of Prince Bernhard of the Netherlands. By 1968 the fund had made grants of almost $3 million, one of the first going to a project to help save the white rhinoceros in Uganda.[34]

Although the money needed to implement what is now known as the Arusha Declaration came from private rather than governmental sources, the principle established by the African states could be more liberally interpreted, to extend beyond wildlife, and more widely applied. Several African states intended to place such a proposal on the agenda of the United Nations conference in Stockholm. The cool reception they received indicates that for the developed countries an extension of the Arusha Declaration would represent too radical a departure from existing policy.

Viewed in the context of the preceding discussion of the difficulties underlying any attempt to make substantial changes in American foreign policy in order to accommodate environmental concerns, it is not surprising that the policies actually pursued can appear to some to be grossly inadequate. If the United States is serious about subsuming its national interests in a shared and transcendent world interest in environmental protection, and if that world interest calls, as some have argued, for a major redistribution of the world's wealth, the American government would be pushing much harder than is

now the case for strong international institutions with the authority
and money to effect redistribution. By the same token, it would be
seeking much more than bilateral agreements with the Soviet Union
and other countries for scientific research and environmental monitoring. It would be seeking instead a set of political arrangements
and understandings to guarantee, for example, the setting and enforcement of international pollution-control standards and the creation of political stability between the developed and developing
countries. In fact, the interests of the United States and those of other
nations are sufficiently different that talk of a shared and transcendent world interest as the basis for American foreign policy has little
meaning, unless it refers to an interest that the United States itself
defines and enforces. From this perspective, and in the short-run,
present policies make a good deal of sense. The nation clearly must
protect the interests that it now has in securing raw materials from
abroad and in exporting a variety of products to other countries.
Foreign policy and patterns of international trade cannot be
changed radically overnight without causing disruption at home and
overseas. Nevertheless, some changes appear to be desirable and it is
reasonable to ask whether those aspects of present policy designed to
facilitate change hold much promise.

Bilateral agreements offer one approach, one that the Nixon administration has pursued vigorously. To date the agreements reached
have fallen into two categories. One involves scientific information
exchange and cooperation in research. Recent agreements in this
category with Canada, the Soviet Union, and Japan are likely to be
followed by agreements with Mexico, Spain, France, Germany, Poland, Yugoslavia, and India.[35] This activity is in line with a long tradition, noted earlier, of international scientific cooperation on environmental matters, a tradition Nicholson has discussed at length.[36] A
second type of bilateral agreement involves what might be called
neighborhood renewal. The boundary river systems the United
States shares with Canada and Mexico have each been the subject of
an International Joint Commission for many years. An agreement
was reached in April 1972 with Canada, in part through the auspices of the commission, for improving water quality in the Great

Lakes–St. Lawrence River water system. In June 1972 President Nixon and President Echeverria of Mexico issued a joint communiqué announcing that the United States will take several measures to reduce the salinity of water in the Colorado River, which the Mexican government claimed several years ago was damaging agriculture in the Mexicali Valley.

These bilateral agreements have been stressed by the Nixon administration as major and significant steps toward dealing with international environmental issues. Individually each of them is undoubtedly worthwhile, and the agreements with Canada and Mexico help to protect the administration from the criticism that it cannot presume to recommend policy to the rest of the world unless it can deal with problems involving its neighbors. However, given the large number of countries in the world and the need to do more than promote the exchange of scientific information, bilateral agreements of the kind recently pursued offer a cumbersome and limited means for international environmental problem solving. Policy initiatives involving international institutions afford additional possibilities for inducing change, but in the words of Richard Gardner, "U.S. support for multilateral institutions is in doubt or disarray all along the line." [37] Gardner had in mind particularly what he regards as the delinquency of the Nixon administration in supporting international development assistance programs, although his comments were also directed to recent policy toward the United Nations.

> We complain that the UN behaves irresponsibly. How can we expect the institution to behave responsibly if we do not behave responsibly toward it? At a time of planetary emergency, we are rapidly becoming a global dropout. Our leadership is currently fascinated by the politics of the balance of power, but I suggest the time has come to devote more attention to the politics of world order. [38]

The Nixon administration has not entirely neglected international and regional institutions. With U.S. leadership, the North Atlantic Treaty Organization (NATO) established a Committee on the Challenges to Modern Society in 1969. The committee has held conferences and developed agreements on a wide variety of subjects, including elimination of the intentional discharge of oil and oily wastes into the oceans. Other organizations with functions that are not primarily environmental have taken steps to consider environmental matters with the encouragement of the United States. They include the Organization for Economic Cooperation and Development, the Economic Commission for Europe, and the Intergovernmental Maritime Consultative Organization. These last two organizations are part of the UN system, and it is this system that is most likely to provide a global context for international environmental cooperation.[39] Transnational organizations of more limited scope both functionally and geographically, such as NATO, can perform valuable roles that extend the activities of member governments. However, only the United Nations has a large enough membership to take action on a global scale, something that is probably desirable in the long-run even though few problems yet require such action in the form of standard setting and regulation.

Considerable American involvement has already occurred in a wide range of environmental activities organized through the specialized agencies and nongovernmental organizations that, together with the several branches of the United Nations itself, make up the UN system. Indeed, the complexity of the system has yielded so many projects, programs, and plans, and so many interinstitutional relationships, that a mechanism for rationalizing them was given high priority on the agenda of the Conference on the Human Environment. The Nixon administration took the position that the Economic and Social Council (ECOSOC) would provide the most appropriate organizational framework for future United Nations operations on environmental matters. The council is responsible under the UN charter for encouraging international cooperation on economic, social, cultural, educational, health, and related matters. It conducts much of its business through six commissions and is provided with staff services through the Department of Economic and Social Affairs of the United Nations Secretariat. The official U.S. proposal at Stockholm would have created a new ECOSOC Commission of twenty-seven members to provide, among other things, policy guidance to a small UN environment unit, headed by an administrator, appointed by the UN secretary-general, and charged with broad responsibilities for coordinating environmental activities in the UN system.

Various alternative organizational arrangements were considered prior to the Stockholm conference in addition to that advocated by the Nixon administration. From a series of meetings sponsored by the American Society of International Law, the Carnegie Endowment for International Peace, the International Institute for Environmental Affairs, the Aspen Institute for Humanistic Studies, and the Institute on Man and Science, a consensus emerged in favor of two main bodies.[40] One would be a small, dynamic, and high-level policy planning, coordination, and review unit. In many respects it would be similar to the Council on Environmental Quality created in the Executive Office of the President by the National Environmental Policy Act, since the proposed UN unit would presumably work very closely with the secretary-general and would have the job of maintaining an overview of all UN activities. The environmental unit would be made accountable to a second body, an intergovernmental advisory group of limited membership elected by the General Assembly. This two-part proposal was tantamount to institutionalizing on a permanent basis the arrangements made for preparation of the Stockholm conference. The advisory group would be the equivalent of the twenty-seven-nation Preparatory Committee that provided political oversight of the work done by Conference Secretary-General Maurice Strong. The environmental unit would represent an enlargement of Strong's staff.

In a recent National Academy of Sciences report, both the administration proposal and the alternative generally preferred by the scientific community were analyzed. The report argued, in effect, that the administration scheme was too conservative because it placed emphasis upon ECOSOC, an organization that "has long been regarded by the developing countries as a rich man's club, dominated by the industrialized states." [41] The membership of ECOSOC was doubled by the Twenty-sixth General Assembly and the validity of this objection somewhat reduced. What the Stockholm conference eventually produced was a compromise scheme that differed only slightly from the administration's proposal. The new organizational structure recommended by the conference would consist of a fifty-four-nation Governing Council for Environmental Programs reporting through ECOSOC to the General Assembly, an environmental secretariat whose executive director would be elected directly by the General Assembly, an Environment Fund to cover operational costs for the new bodies as well as new monitoring and data assessment programs, and an Environmental Coordination Board, to function under the chairmanship of the executive director. Whether the role of ECOSOC in these arrangements will prove to be one that exacerbates rather than eases latent conflicts between developed and developing countries remains to be seen. The National Academy report stressed with reference to its own recommendations that substance was more important than form and that the arrangements established must above all "be capable of growth and evolution."

Of course, the ability of any new institutional arrangement to perform as intended by its designers is a function of the political environment in which it is placed, an environment that can only be partially modified by the leadership and good intentions of the people who populate the new unit. There are three features of the UN system especially worth noting in this respect. One is the difficulty that agencies of the United Nations often have in attracting senior representatives of member governments. Both the General Assembly and ECOSOC, for example, tend to attract "second- and third-string diplomats reading instructions from capitals" [42] when they are dealing with specialized and complex subjects. The proposed Governing Council for Environmental Programs is conceived as a body composed of environment ministers and senior environmental decision makers. Being subject to the final authority of the General Assembly and to review in a fashion yet to be clearly specified by ECOSOC, the Governing Council may be unable to attain the status and visibility of the European Economic Community and the OECD, wherein ministers frequently meet as a supreme decision-making body capable of taking budgetary and other decisions without being subject to review by a superior organization.

Second, notice must be taken of the heavy reliance of the UN system as a whole upon American financing. Establishment of a new UN unit for the environment has been linked to the creation of a world environment fund that the new unit would administer. The money, perhaps as much as $100 million, would be used to generate data on especially critical problems, to support research and training programs that would strengthen the capacity of developing countries to cope with the environmental impact of economic development, and to help in the preservation of natural reserves.[43] However, expectations that the world environment fund would give the new environmental unit any substantial degree of power and influence over all UN members must be tempered by the realization that the United States would contribute the bulk of the money, and that the $100 million would be expended over a five-year period.

A third important feature of the UN system is its highly decentralized way of operating. The autonomy of the specialized agencies is especially significant. The World Health Organization, the Food and Agriculture Organization, the United Nations Educational, Scientific, and Cultural Organization, the International Labor Organization, the International Atomic Energy Agency, and many others, have separate funding, their own sources of staff and expert advice, and, most importantly, their own political constituencies in national governments and nongovernmental organizations. When to this is added the organs of the United Nations itself, the departments and offices of the Secretariat, and the nongovernmental organizations, all linked to each other and to the specialized agencies by a variegated administrative machinery much of which is ad hoc, the prospects of a modest new environmental unit modifying the behavior of the system cannot be rated highly.[44]

There is in fact a danger that the advocates of new institutional arrangements in the United Nations to deal with environmental affairs have oversold their case and created unwarranted expectations, in much the same way that advocates of a Council on Environmental Quality in this country have tended to overestimate its capacity to change the behavior and policy outputs of the federal bureaucracy. Proposals for change in the UN system do not vest the new environmental units suggested with any authority to veto the actions of member states or any of the projects and programs with potentially adverse environmental consequences that they pursue unilaterally or through an international organization. Whatever success a new environmental unit enjoys is going to be in large part a function of the willingness of the other institutional actors in its environment to incorporate ecological concerns into their decision making on a voluntary basis.

This observation leads back to reconsideration of an earlier point about the dilemma of rising demands and insufficient disposable resources. To the extent that American policy displays a resolution of this dilemma that favors international action to solve environmental problems, it does so largely as the result of pressures that have been exerted by a relatively small group of scientists and government officials. The population at large and its elected representatives have not yet carefully contemplated the consequences of environmental politics on a global scale and it is not at all clear that they would support more radical and far-reaching policies. The scientific community has assumed to its credit that when the people of the United States do understand the facts and their implications, they will support the substantial changes in foreign policy that many scientists believe are consistent with these facts. While such an outcome may ultimately be desirable, it is *not* the likely consequence of present American foreign policy. For the foreseeable future, the United States is likely to be more concerned with assuring a supply of resources over the disposal of which statesmen can argue their dilemma in ways we and they can recognize as being consistent with past experience. And it remains to be seen whether such a policy will be able to accommodate the tensions and conflicts that are sure to arise in a world where economic wealth and environmental quality are grossly maldistributed.

Stanley Hoffmann

Weighing the Balance of Power

I

"The end of the bipolar postwar world" has been acknowledged by the latest presidential State of the World message. Although it is elliptic in describing the new design for a lasting and stable "structure of peace," there is little doubt that the blueprint for the future is inspired by the past. It is the model of the balance of power which moderated, if not the aspirations at least the accomplishments, of rulers in the eighteenth and nineteenth centuries. It restrained violence (without curtailing wars). It provided enough flexibility to ensure a century of global peace after the Congress of Vienna, despite drastic changes in the relative strengths and fortunes of the main actors.

If, in the quest for international stability, this model is in favor again, it is not only because of the preferences of that student of nineteenth-century diplomacy, Henry Kissinger. It is also because the Yalta system is coming to an end. For many years, the world has ceased to resemble the confrontation of Athens and Sparta. Nuclear weapons have muted the rivalry. The universal drive for independence has made each rival's hegemony over, or interventions outside, his camp costly and delicate (on the Communist side, it has led to the Sino-Soviet break). The very heterogeneity of a world filled with stubborn crises which do not let themselves be absorbed by the East-West conflict has made the cold war irrelevant for some areas and has dampened it in others, given the superpowers' reluctance to allow themselves to be dragged into partly alien causes and to let confrontations by proxies turn into direct clashes.

In such circumstances, the balance-of-power model is tempting. As long as the world remains a contest of actors without any supranational force, the ambitions of troublemakers have to be contained by the power of the other states; but equilibrium would be assured in a more shifting, subtle, and supple way than in the recent past of fixed blocs. In a world of several main actors, the need for a superpower to be not merely the architect but chief mason of global containment would fade away. Restraining a troublemaker would be either the joint affair of several major states, or even of merely some of them, on whom the United States could rely, just as Britain could often rely on the continental powers stalemating one another. The small nations would find security, not in submission to a leader or in a neutralist shelter, but in the balance of power itself, which would allow them to pursue more actively their interests within its less constraining limits.

Thus, mobility would return to the scene. A new age of diplomacy (and perhaps of its traditional concomitant, international law) would begin. Muted bipolarity has subjected the United States to maximum exertions and minimum results, or at least maximum constraints. The new system would provide two remedies for frustration: the political corrective of self-restraint, and the psychological compensation of openly pursuing one's national interest without having either to subordinate it to the solidarity, or to wrap it in the priorities, of one's camp. The United States would again be able to choose when, where, and whether to intervene at all. Therefore it could concentrate on the long-range, instead of rushing from the pressing to the urgent.

The President's reports and statements point to a pentagonal system in which the United States, the Soviet Union, China, Japan, and Western Europe would be the main actors. This vision raises three sets of questions. Is the United States, as a society and as a state, willing and able to pursue such a policy? Does the world of the last third of the twentieth century lend itself to a system based on the model of European cabinet diplomacy? If the answer to these questions should be no, what ought to be the alternative? I have dealt elsewhere with the first question.[1] This article addresses itself to the second question and only inferentially to the third. Since it is a critical exercise, two preliminary caveats are in order. First, this essay does not state that the new policy is a simple resurrection of the European balance of power. It examines the features of the present world that do not lend themselves to any direct transposition. It also asks whether recent U.S. tactics contribute to the advent of that moderate structure called for by its leaders. Second, it does not deny that the ends of international moderation and American self-restraint are highly desirable. It wonders whether they are likely to be delivered through the means of the balance. Indeed, are these ends themselves entirely compatible?

II

To use Raymond Aron's terms, the balance of power is a model of "strategic-diplomatic behavior." The essence of international relations is seen as a contest of states on a chessboard on which the players try to maximize their power at each other's expense, and on which the possibility of war makes military potential and might the chief criteria of power. This view still fits much of the "game of nations," for it follows from the logic of a decentralized milieu, whatever the specific nature of the units or the social and economic systems they embody.

For such a game to be played according to the rules of the balance, various conditions had in the past to be met. First, there had to be a number of major actors superior to two—it usually was around five or six—of comparable if not equal power. Today's distribution of power among the top actors is quite different. Only two states are actual world powers, involved in most of the globe, indispensable for all important settlements. China is still mainly a regional power, more concerned with breaking out of encirclement than with active involvement outside. While Chinese leaders assert that China will never want to become a superpower, there is no way of predicting that this will indeed be the case. Even if both dogma and growing power should push Peking toward a global role, given its internal problems the transition will be long, and China is bound to remain in the meantime a potential superpower, i.e., a major player presently limited in scope but exerting considerable attraction globally.

As for the other two "poles," they do not exist at all. Both Japan and Western Europe are military dependents of the United States. Neither, despite huge economic power, behaves on the strategic-diplomatic chessboard as if it intended to play a world role under the American nuclear umbrella. Japan, so far, does not have even a clear regional policy. Western Europe, so far, is a promise, not a real political entity. The current *relance* of her integration was made possible by a kind of tacit agreement to reverse the Gaullist order of priorities and to put the economic, monetary, and institutional tasks of enlarged community building ahead of the painful and divisive ones of foreign policy and defense coordination. In the traditional arena of world politics, pentagonal polycentrism does not yet exist. It would have to be created. Can it be?

A second condition for the functioning of the balance-of-power system in the past was the presence of a central balancing mechanism: the ability of several of the main actors to coalesce in order to deter or to blunt the expansion of one or more powers. This corresponds to two fundamental realities. One was the inability of any one power to annihilate any other, the other was the usefulness of force. Aggressively, force was a productive instrument of expansion; preventively or repressively, the call to arms against a troublemaker served as the moment of truth. The invention of nuclear weapons and their present distribution have thoroughly transformed the situation. The resort to nuclear weapons can obviously not be a balancing technique. Indeed, the central mechanism's purpose is the *avoidance* of nuclear conflict, the adjournment sine die of the moment of nuclear truth.

The central mechanism of deterrence is likely to remain for a long time bipolar. Only the United States and the Soviet Union have the capacity to annihilate each other—a capacity distinct from that which France, Britain, and China possess, of severely wounding a superpower but suffering either total or unbearable destruction in return. Only the superpowers can deter each other, not merely from nuclear but also from large-scale conventional war, and from the nuclear blackmail of third parties. Their advance over other nuclear powers remains enormous, quantitatively and qualitatively. It is doubtful that Peking could find the indispensable shortcuts to catch up with Moscow and Washington. Nor is a nuclear Japan likely to outstrip the Americans and the Russians; political and psychological inhibitions in the Japanese polity are likely to delay, for a while at least, a decision to join the nuclear race, and to limit the scope of an eventual nuclear effort. Western Europe continues to have an internal problem not unlike that of squaring a vicious circle. Mr. Heath may prudently prod Mr. Pompidou toward nuclear cooperation. But Britain's special nuclear relationship to Washington, plus Gaullist doctrine, are obstacles even to that modest proposal. A genuine "West European" deterrent would require a central political and military process of decision, of which there are no traces: nor is there a willingness by Bonn to consecrate the Franco-British nuclear duopoly or a willingness by London and Paris to include Bonn. This problem, unresolved within NATO, risks being insoluble here too.

A pentagon of nuclear powers is not desirable, and could be dangerous. It is not necessary: the deterrence of nuclear war is not a matter of coalitions. What deters Moscow, or Peking, from nuclear war is the certainty of destruction. To add the potential nuclear strength of a Japanese or of a West European strategic force to that of the United States may theoretically complicate an aggressor's calculations, but it does not change the picture. One might, of course, object with the familiar argument according to which nuclear parity between the superpowers vitiates the U.S. guarantee: would the United States risk its own destruction for the protection of Paris or Tokyo? Granted that coalitions are not important, is not the deterrence of nuclear war, nuclear blackmail, and large-scale conventional attack likely only if the most tempting targets develop their own deterrents? To this, there are three replies.

First, there is never much point in desiring the improbable. For a long time, if not forever, the inferiority of Japan's and Western Europe's nuclear forces would be such that deterrence could not be assured by them alone. At the nuclear level, the United States could not expect to play the role of nonengaged holder of the balance which theorists have described as Britain's in the past centuries. Only the two superpowers would have the capacity—if not the will —to declare that certain positions are vital to their interests, and protected by their missiles. Other *forces de frappe,* even if invulnerable, would not have a credible protective power outside of their territories.

Second, the Chinese would feel threatened by a nuclear Japan, capable of dwarfing China's costly efforts, and the Soviets would react vigorously to any formula that put a West German finger near or on the trigger of a West European integrated *force de frappe.* For the United States actually to support the nuclear development of Western Europe and Japan, in the hope of being ultimately relieved of its role as nuclear guarantor, and in the conviction that the present central balance makes any Soviet or Chinese retaliation impossible would sacrifice, if not nuclear peace, at least the chances of moderation and détente to a distant and dubious pentagonal nuclear "balance."

Third, a world of five major nuclear powers would be of questionable stability and probably foster further proliferation. Maybe five strategic forces of comparable levels could be "stable": each would-be aggressor would be deterred, not by a coalition, or by a third party's guarantee of the victim, but by that potential victim's own force. However, we are talking about five very uneven forces. The balance of uncertainty which up to now has leaned toward deterrence and restraint could begin oscillating furiously. Even if it should never settle on the side of nuclear war, it would promote an arms race *à cinq.* It is impossible to devise a "moderate" international system under these circumstances. Moreover, the very argument which stresses the dubious nature of nuclear guarantees to others would incite more states to follow the examples of Western Europe and Japan. In such a world some would have a second-strike capacity against each other, but a first-strike capacity against others.

In this area, then, the desire for moderation and the dream of self-restraint are hardly compatible. If the United States, in order to prevent proliferation to nations which are currently its allies, acts so as to keep its nuclear guarantee credible, the tensions of overinvolvement will persist, and the world will not be pentagonal. If the pursuit of a more narrowly defined national interest, if doubts about the long-run credibility of nuclear guarantees, and if the desire for "burden sharing" should lead the United States to encourage nuclear proliferation, the result would be neither very safe nor conducive to the world of the balance of power with its central multipolar mechanism. For even if global peace should remain assured by the central mechanism of bipolar deterrence, the globe would probably fragment into a series of uncertain regional nuclear balances.

What of a return to a conventional balancing mechanism comparable to that of the past? It has been asserted that the very unusability of nuclear weapons restores the conditions of traditional war. But the picture is likely to be the same. Against a nuclear power, conventional forces are simply not a sufficiently credible deterrent. Deterrence of nuclear attack, or of nuclear escalation by a "conventional" aggressor, depends on either the possession of nuclear forces, or on protection by a credible nuclear guarantor. Even if conventional war provides moments of partial truth, ultimate truth is either nuclear war or its effective, i.e., nuclear, deterrence. For Japan and Western Europe to concentrate on conventional forces alone would mean consecrating a division among the "great powers." They are unlikely to want to do so. But if they should, there would still be a qualitative difference in status and influence between the three nuclear powers and the other two.

Moreover, from the viewpoint of a conventional balance, a pentagonal world would not resemble the great-powers system of the past. All its members sought a world role. It is difficult to imagine either a West European entity or a conventionally rearmed Japan seeking one. Each one could become an important part of a regional balance of power—no more. This, of course, is not an argument against a conventional effort in Western Europe, which faces the

Russian armies. Any such effort would have a considerable deterrent value. But this is a different problem from that of a central, world-wide balancing mechanism.

Under the nuclear stalemate, the logic of fragmentation operates here too. Would, even at this level, the United States be able to "play Britain," i.e., to contribute to a regional balance merely through its nuclear guarantee? In the West European case, nothing short of a disintegration of the Soviet Union—or the most drastic and unlikely mutual and balanced force reductions—is likely to make purely West European conventional forces comparable to Soviet and East European armies in the near future. Even if one believes that somewhat lower conventional forces in Western Europe *plus* the U.S. nuclear guarantee equal a credible deterrent, the plausibility of the guarantee will continue to depend on at least some U.S. presence, in the form of troops or tactical nuclear forces.

In the case of Japan, there is a difference, obviously. The main issue is not the deterrence of an invasion; a strong Japan could theoretically replace the United States as a balancer of Chinese or Soviet conventional designs in East Asia. But third parties—especially our former Asian outposts—may not want to be protected from one or another Communist plague by what they might consider the Japanese cholera. As long as there are strong defense ties between Japan and the United States, a Japanese conventional rearmament would lead to complications for us. If we should loosen those ties in order to avoid these strains and to let an East Asian balance operate without us, we would encourage nuclear proliferation, and a loss of influence. On the conventional front, in Western Europe, the desirable is not likely; in East Asia, the likely is not desirable.

On this front, in the coming international system, three phenomena will manifest themselves. First, only the two superpowers are likely to remain, for a long time, capable of sending forces and supplies to distant parts of the globe. The world conceived as a single theater of military calculations and operations is likely to remain bipolar.

Second, as long as the fear of a nuclear disaster obliges the superpowers to avoid military provocation and direct armed clashes, and as long as China, Western Europe, and Japan remain endowed only with modest conventional means, and largely neutralized militarily by their very connection to the central nuclear balance of deterrence, other states, equipped or protected by a superpower and in pursuit of objectives vital to them, will be able to provoke their own "moment of truth" and to build themselves up as regional centers of military power, as Israel has done in the Middle East, or North Vietnam in Southeast Asia. A coalition of states with great power but limited stakes is not enough to stop a local player with limited power but huge stakes. For the superpowers and for such local players, conventional force used outside their borders still has considerable productivity (although, paradoxically, the superpowers can use such force only in small doses or in limited spheres). For the other "poles" of the pentagon, however, the greatest utility of conventional force is likely to be negative: its contribution to deterrence.

Third, the fragmentation which results both from the impact of nuclear weapons on world politics and from the regional nature of two, if not three, of the points of the pentagon, suggests that a future conventional balance of power will have to be regionalized some more. A strong Japan and a strong Western Europe are unlikely to ensure a sufficient balance in the Middle East or in South Asia, or even in Southeast Asia and the Western Pacific.

Nuclear weapons have not abolished war, they have displaced it. The central mechanism of the past was aimed at the problem of large military interventions by a main actor. Now, whether they succeed depends less on a global mechanism than on a local one. No amount of coalition building would have saved Czechoslovakia. No adversary coalition could have prevented the United States from moving into the Vietnam quagmire. Moreover, due to the fear of escalation, much of international politics on the diplomatic-strategic chessboard becomes a game of influence—less violent but more intense. There is an art of knowing how to deploy force rather than to use it, how to exploit internal circumstances in order to dislodge a rival. The traditional balancing mechanism may perhaps still function where the stakes are influence, not conquest; for military strength in an area can deter or restrict the subtle access which influence requires. A strong Western Europe associated with the United States would be guaranteed against "finlandization," for instance. However, there are complications even here. A coalition aimed at stopping a great power may actually goad it into "leaping" over the coalition, and leaning on local parties determined to preserve their own freedom of maneuver (a United States–Chinese coalition in Asia is not sure to stop Soviet influence). Also, if much depends on the internal circumstances in the area, neither military buildups nor coalitions may compensate for local weakness. Anyhow, moderation at a global or even at regional levels is compatible with occasional setbacks.

The traditional mechanism is too gross for the modern variety of the old game. Also, its logic is a logic of arms races, nuclear or conventional. A game of influence partly played out with weapons supplies, in a world in which many statesmen continue to see in force the only effective way of reaching vital goals, risks leading to multiple wars. In past centuries, global moderation was compatible with such explosions; in a nuclear world, are they certain to be as limited as, and more localized than, before? Does the need for moderation not point both toward the preservation of the superpowers' nuclear stalemate and toward more arms-control agreements to prevent unilateral breakthroughs and competitive escalations into the absurd; toward both a multiplication of regional balances of power and regional arms-control systems?

III

A third requirement for an effective balance of power used to be the existence of a common language and code of behavior among the major actors. This did not mean identical regimes, or the complete insulation of foreign policy from domestic politics, or a code of cooperation. But the existence of a diplomatic *Internationale* reduced misperceptions, if not miscalculations. In the nineteenth century, it provided for congresses and conferences that proved the existence of a European Concert, however dissonant.

Today, summits too are fragmentary. To be sure, the imperative of avoiding destruction, and the need to meet internal demands in-ject into the major powers such a dose of "pragmatism" that the purely ideological ingredient of their diplomacy, or of their rhetoric, or both, has spectacularly declined. But we are still very far from a common language. Even a tacit code prescribing how to handle con-flicts, how to avoid or resolve crises, how to climb down from high horses and how to save one another's face remains problematic for several reasons.

First, there is one important residue of ideology: the Sino-Soviet conflict, based largely on conflicts of interest but deepened and em-bittered by mutual charges of heresy. The United States can enjoy friendlier relations with either Communist state than Moscow can have with Peking, and our détente with one may help to improve our relations with the other. But this does not suffice to bring about a moderate balance of power. To manipulate that animosity so as to benefit from it while avoiding getting entangled in it may require diplomatic skills far in excess of ours. Moreover, however much their mutual hatred softens their tone toward us, each one is likely to try to manipulate us against the other, and neither can reduce his hostil-ity toward us too much—especially in so far as support of third par-ties against us is concerned—out of fear of opening the field to his rival.

Next, however much we may congratulate ourselves on having kept great-power conflicts under control and on negotiating with Moscow and Peking without ideological blinders, neither capital subscribes to a code of general self-restraint. An effective balance of power requires either agreements on spheres of influence and divid-ing lines, or hands-off arrangements neutralizing or interna-tionalizing certain areas. Today, some spheres of influence are being respected: the Soviets' in Eastern Europe, ours in Latin America. Black Africa appears to be, in effect, neutralized. But Moscow and Peking both apply to the world a conceptual framework that dictates the exploitation of capitalist weaknesses and contradictions. Regimes in which the state not only controls but molds the society are better at granting priority to foreign affairs than regimes in which the im-pulses of the society actually control the state's freedom of action.

The heterogeneity of many nations split along ethnic, class or ideological lines, which would make it impossible even for an angelic diplomacy dedicated to the principle of nonintervention to carry out its intentions, offers irresistible opportunities for diplomacies tied to a strategic (which does not mean necessarily warlike) vision of politics and to a dynamic reading of history. Khrushchev's proclamation of the "non-inevitability of war" was a landmark, but the less likely the use of overt force, the more subtly can influence be sought.

Those who, for years, feared a monolithic Soviet design for world subjugation were wrong, but so today are those who see in the Soviet Union merely a traditional power, or one interested mainly in the conservation of its sphere of influence. Prudence, yes, the simple preservation of the status quo, no. The very delicacy of the status quo in the one area where Moscow most assuredly tries to perpetuate it— Eastern Europe—the Soviet Union's inability, for domestic and external reasons, to separate security from domination there, the fact that the West cannot easily accept an equation which enslaves half of Europe, all this is likely to oblige the Soviet Union to keep trying to weaken the West in Europe, or at least to prevent it from strengthening itself. In the Middle East, in South Asia, on the world's oceans, the Soviets, without encouraging violence where it would backfire, and while supporting it where it works, behave as if any retreat, voluntary or not, of the United States and its allies, or any weak spot constitutes an invitation. This is not the code of behavior we would like Moscow to observe. But multipolarity is not Moscow's game, or interest.

Such tactics, if skillfully used, do not destroy moderation. But they test self-restraint. Of course, Moscow should be constrained to adjust its behavior to *our* code (and so could Peking if necessary), should we encourage other powers to fill the vacuum and to strengthen the weak spots. But we are caught between our own desire for détente and the fear that it would be compromised if we built up those of our allies whom our adversaries most suspect. Our rivals' game is to improve their relations with us in so far as we tend toward disengagement without substitution—in which case, our self-restraint could benefit them.

Two requirements for a new balance of power—relaxed relations with ex-enemies, and greater power for ex-dependents—are in conflict. Such will be America's dilemma as long as our interest in "flexible alignments" is matched by our rivals' search for clients; as long as their revolutionary ideology (not to be ignored just because their vision is, literally, millennial, and their tactics flexible), as well as their great-power fears or drives, result in a demand for security tantamount to a claim for either permanent domination where it already exists, or regional hegemony to exclude any rival. Whether or not Western Europe and Japan become major actors, Eastern Europe and East or Southeast Asia will remain potential sources of instability.

Multiple asymmetries are at work, therefore, insofar as a common code is concerned. There is the asymmetry between the ideologies of the Communists, and our conceptions, which envisage order as a self-perpetuating status quo, as a web of procedures and norms rather than as the ever-changing outcome of social struggles. There is an asymmetry between the active policies of the superpowers and the still nebulous ones of Western Europe and Japan—not so much poles of power as stakes in the contest between the United States, the Soviet Union and China. There is an asymmetry between the untenable global involvement of the United States, and a Soviet (and, potentially, Chinese) strategy that has to do little more than move into the crumbling positions on our front lines, or jump across into the rotting ones in the rear. Order and moderation used to be organic attributes of the international system, corresponding to domestic conditions within the main states, as well as to the horizontal ties between their diplomatic corps and codes. Tomorrow, order and moderation will be more complex and mechanical, corresponding to the necessities of survival and to the price of opportunity.

A fourth condition for an effective balance-of-power system had to do with the international hierarchy. While the world was a much wider field in days of slow communications, the international system was simple: there were few actors, and the writ of the main ones covered the whole field. In Europe, the small powers had no other recourse but to entrust their independence to the balancing mechanism. Outside Europe, the great powers carved up the world. Today, the planet has shrunk, the superpowers are omnipresent, but there are more than 130 states. The small—thanks to the nuclear stalemate, or by standing on a greater power's shoulders—have acquired greater maneuverability and often have intractable concerns. Any orderly international system needs a hierarchy. But the relations of the top to the bottom, and the size of the top, vary. In the future world order, these relations will have to be more democratic, and the oligarchy will have to be bigger.

Consequently, and given the asymmetries described above, for the United States to worry almost exclusively about the central balance among the major actors, as if improved relations among them were a panacea, is an error. There are three ways of making such a mistake. One is benign neglect; we have practiced it in the Middle East for a couple of years after Israel's victory in the six-day war, and again in the Indian subcontinent, during the months that followed Yahya Khan's decision to suppress East Bengal. This provides one's rivals with splendid opportunities for implantation.

So could the second kind of error: reacting to a local challenge in one's traditional sphere of interest in an axiomatically "tough" way—for instance, cutting off aid to and exerting pressures on Latin American regimes intent on expanding control over their nation's resources.

Third, it is a mistake to treat issues in which third parties are embroiled as if these countries were merely pawns in a global balancing game, instead of dealing with the issues' intrinsic merits and the nations' own interests. For it is most difficult to bring a theoretical balance no longer sanctioned by the moment of truth to bear on the local situation. To be sure, some important disputes among third parties, while autonomous in their origins, have become so much a part of the great-powers' contest that the balancing game makes sense, either in the direction of escalation or in that of a settlement once the risks become too high. Such have been the Middle Eastern dynamics since 1970—when first the Soviets, then the United States, displayed increasing commitments to their respective clients, but also maneuvered so as to defuse the powder keg a bit. Yet this has not been the norm.

In the India-Pakistan war of December 1971, the United States, China, and Pakistan did not "balance" India and Russia. Neither America nor China were ready to commit forces, and a verbal "tilting" toward Pakistan, aimed at safeguarding our rapprochement with Peking and at warning Moscow, merely underlined Moscow's successful exploitation of India's desire to dismantle Pakistan and strengthened unnecessarily the bonds between Moscow and Delhi. The traditional balance-of-power mechanism, while enforcing self-restraint upon ambitions, depended on the opposite of self-restraint —the readiness of the great powers to use force. If the risks are too high or the stakes too low, the balance cannot operate.

Vietnam yields a similar lesson. We have not dared escalate the war to the point of actually cutting off all Soviet and Chinese supplies to Hanoi. As a result, our attempt to coax Moscow into "restraining" Hanoi, i.e., to make of Vietnam a great-power issue, was doomed. Indeed, Vietnam, turned by us first into a test of misconstrued Chinese dogmas, now into a test of Soviet assumed intentions, shows that too much emphasis on the central balance and too little on local circumstances can be, if not globally, at least regionally destabilizing and destructive.

The proliferation of nations, like the impact of nuclear weapons, suggests a fragmentation of the traditional scene. The balance-of-power system assumes that peace is ultimately indivisible—although perhaps not every minute, as pure bipolarity does; more tolerant of minor shifts, it still sees any expansion by a great power as a threat to others. Our analysis suggests a greater divisibility of peace, and the more evanescent character of influence, as long as the central nuclear equilibrium lasts. What will have to be balanced, so to speak, are that equilibrium and the regional balances. Each one of these will have its own features, its own connection with (or perhaps, as in black Africa today—but for how long?—disconnection from) the central balance. Thus, in the traditional arena, the *model* of the balance of power provides no real prescription, however wise the *idea* of balance remains. Five powers are not the answer. What matters is, first and still, the Big Two, in pursuit of universal influence, and in possession of global military means; second, if not all of the others, at least many more than China, Western Europe, and Japan.

IV

Not only have the conditions of the old game drastically changed, but there are other games as well. The model of interstate competition under the threat of force accounts only for some of what goes on in world politics. Two distinctions which provided its bases are being eroded. One is the distinction between domestic politics and foreign policy. The latter is often the direct expression of domestic forces or the by-product of bureaucratic constellations (some of which involve transnational alliances of services or agencies) or the victim of equally transnational waves or contagions—constructive or destructive—carried by the new media. These waves both prove and promote the erosion of the distinction between public activities of states and private activities of citizens across borders.

In the nineteenth-century balance, the latter provided an underpinning for interstate moderation, but they were not the constant or primary object of states' concerns (whenever they became their concern, the system deteriorated). Today, state policies are often impaired or inspired by transnational forces that range from corporations to scientists. Partly because of the importance of economic and scientific factors in a world driven by the quest for material progress, partly because of the relative decline of the traditional arena due to nuclear weapons, transnational relations raise increasingly important issues for states, and provide many new chessboards on which states pursue their interests, compete for advantages, yet are not the only actors.[2]

The model of the balance of power is doubly irrelevant to these new games. First, the logic of behavior is not the same. Although there is a competition of players for influence (as in all politics), and there is no power above them (as in all international politics), the stakes are not those of traditional diplomacy, and there are other restraints than those which on the other chessboard the "state of war" itself creates or destroys. Here, the threat of violence (however muted or diffuse) is of no utility or rationality. In the strategic-diplomatic arena, the central assumption of the contest is that ultimately my gain is your loss. My interest consists of either preventing or eliminating your gain or, should the costs prove too high, of "splitting the difference," or extracting a concession in return for my acceptance of your gain. It is not always a zero-sum game: at times, both sides can increase their power. But the perspective is still that of the final test of strength, which requires a constant calculation of force. Two powers cannot be number one simultaneously. Unless one is a seventeenth-century mercantilist lost in the twentieth, one can see that this is not an appropriate description of rational behavior on most of the economic and technological chessboards. The rules of interdependence, which condition the competition there, are not those of strategic interaction, which structure it here. The logic of the world economy, of world science and technology, is, for better (growth and welfare) or worse (population explosion, pollution, and depletion) a logic of integration. The logic of traditional international state politics is that of separateness. One may, as the Communist states still partly do, refuse to play games of interdependence; but if one plays them, their logic becomes compelling.

Here, quite often, your loss risks becoming mine: there is a worldwide transmission of depression, unemployment, or inflation. Even when there is a test of wills—between, say, oil-producing countries and big oil companies—there is a joint incentive, often not merely to compromise but to "upgrade the common interest." A competition in fields where solidarity prevails because of the very nature of the factors in operation consists simply of the manipulation of interdependence. Even on the traditional chessboard, as we have seen, the old rules of strategic-diplomatic warfare are modified by nuclear interdependence, and tests of strength without the ultimate sanction of war become tests of will, at least among the major powers. Why apply the balancing model to new chessboards, when it falters on the old?

Second, not only does the balance of power not provide an answer, it addresses itself to the wrong problem. A world in which the autonomy of states is curtailed by transnational trends, drives, and forces which operate unevenly, unpredictably, and carry political flags and tags, a world whose states' policies reflect internal wants and bargains, is permanently threatened by "statist" reactions against global integration and outside intrusion—precisely because, however sievelike, the state remains the final unit of decision, and the more like a sieve it becomes, the more it may try to plug the holes. Hence a curse of immoderation and instability, but in an original way.

It is not the use of force which is the daily peril, it is, literally, chaos. It is not war that brings the moment of truth, it is economic or monetary or environmental disaster. It is not the failure of the balance to work and curtail excessive ambitions, or the rigidity of the balance when it splits the world into rival, frozen coalitions, it is anomie. It is not the neglect or deterioration of familiar rules. It is the failure to clarify and to understand the new rules which govern the relations between different chessboards, the transfer of power from one to the other—these have only recently become major arenas of world politics: scholars are in the dark and statesmen experiment in ignorance or by analogy. Also to be feared is the inadequacy or breakdown of those rules, not of balance but of cooperation, that were devised in the past (for instance, the law of the seas), and the absence of rules of cooperation in a variety of disruptive cases in which no state can be successful in isolation—from the environment to short-term capital movements.

To apply irrelevant concepts is dangerous for general and for historical reasons. To proclaim "the primacy of the national interest" gives a free hand to domestic forces damaged or frustrated by the way these chessboards function, and encourages an epidemic of protectionist or aggressive measures. To use the logic of separateness in fields of integration invites disintegration here and discord on the traditional chessboard. Of the five "economic blocs" among which the balancing game is supposed to go on, two—those of our strategic-diplomatic rivals—are not fully integrated into the world economy. To treat Western Europe and Japan as rivals to be contained, just as we count on them to play a growing role in balancing our adversaries on that traditional chessboard, assumes that they will draw on it no consequence from our behavior on the economic chessboards, even while we use on the latter the advantages we have on, and the strong-arm tactics appropriate to, the former. This can only be self-defeating, for while each political function of a state—defense, welfare, economic growth, etc.—has some autonomy and logic, and each corresponding international chessboard has its rules, these functions all connect again at the one level that integrates them all, i.e., a state's foreign policy.

Historically, what requires a new policy is not the passing of the bipolar era but the end of a unipolar one. The rules of trade and finance prescribed at Bretton Woods and by GATT were those the United States wanted; they established a dollar-exchange standard and tended toward a liberal system of trade, which other nations accepted in return for security or aid. The United States tolerated exceptions to these rules in return for immediate military advantages (American bases in Japan) or for expected political benefits (a would-be "Atlanticist" Europe, growing out of the Common Market). It is this system which collapsed with the monetary crisis of 1971 and the acrimonious trade quarrels between the United States and its allies. The problem is to avoid a fragmentation of the world economy, which would breed chaos as surely as, in the strategic-diplomatic arena, fragmentation is likely to contribute to moderation.

A single world system must still be the goal. Of course, in the new monetary order, there should be a modicum of decentralization. A West European monetary union, with its own rules governing the relations of currencies within the EEC, would be a part of such an order; a stronger and more coherent EEC would be better able than its members in the past to bargain with the United States for world rules of commerce, investment, and money less geared to American specifications. But this is quite different from a breakup into independent economic blocs with fluctuating relations based on nothing but bargaining strength. The aggressive pursuit by the United States of national interests narrowly defined will inevitably be seen as a naked attempt at retrieving the dominating position we lost.

The United States, which is the lynchpin of the non-Communist world's transnational system, risks playing Samson in the temple. The flexibility which the world economy needs is not that of shifting alignments and reversible alliances. Even in cases where the United States has legitimate grievances, the solutions cannot be found in the functional equivalent of the strategic-diplomatic game of chicken: reprisals and protectionist threats. Given the stakes, the building of a moderate international system and the goal of a "world community" (utopian on the other chessboard) will have to be made increasingly close. Moderation is a negative goal: organizing the coexistence of hugely different players. It has, in the past, been compatible with a variety of woes—wars, assaults on the quality of life, arms races, internal massacres, a vast amount of domestic and internal inequality.

But it is difficult to conceive of a future international system remaining moderate if there is so much inequality between its members and turmoil in some of them as to incite permanent fishing in troubled waters, or recurrent violent exports of discontent. While, especially in the traditional arena, sovereignty would continue to manifest itself through unilateral moves or concerted diplomacy (although rather more for restraint than for self-assertion), there is a growing need for pooled sovereignty, shared powers, and effective international institutions in all the new realms. Of course, a precondition is the maintenance of the central political-military balance. But American policy has tended in the past, and tends more than ever, to concentrate far too much of its energy on the precondition. There are two kinds of essential tasks: those which, if neglected or bungled, could lead to the ultimate disaster; those which the very success in postponing the "moment of truth," and the realities of a materially interdependent planet push onto the daily agenda. In a world full of active self-fulfilling memories—states which behave as if, despite nuclear weapons and the increasing costs of conquest, military might were still the yardstick of achievements, and by behaving in this way keep the past present—there ought to be equally active self-fulfilling prophecies: states moving on the conviction, so frequently asserted in words only, that on the seas of interdependence we are all in the same boat, and should worry more about common benefits than about national gains.

Community building raises formidable questions of its own. Should it be primarily the duty of the developed nations, as some advocate paternalistically? Can an international system as diverse as this one function effectively without the active participation of all its members, even if one grants both the wisdom of "decoupling" the great powers' contest from the internal tribulations of the developing countries, and the risks of paralysis, corruption, or waste present in more "democratic" world institutions? Can community building proceed in such a way as not to seem a neocolonial device through which the rich and strong perpetuate their hold on the poor? Is it compatible with economic spheres of influence? If such questions are recognized as imperative, then an economically and financially more cohesive Western Europe and a dynamic Japan would appear, not as "poles" to be contained or pushed back when they become too strong, but as contributors.

Yesterday's dialectic was that of a central balance between a handful of powers and imperialism, which pushed back the limits of the diplomatic world. Tomorrow's dialectic will have to be that of a complex balance, both global and regional, allowing for a fragmentation of the strategic-diplomatic contest under the nuclear stalemate, and an emergent community in which competition will, of course, persist, but where mankind ought, perhaps, slowly to learn to substitute games against (or with) nature for the games between what Erik Erikson has called "pseudospecies."

V

Faced with a world of unprecedented complexity, it is normal that U.S. policy makers should seek a familiar thread. But they display a basic ambivalence. They aspire to a world in which the United States could share with others the burdens of being a great power. But they understand that self-restraint would be safe only if the game were played according to rules advantageous to us, and they realize that our favorite models and concepts may not at all be those of our would-be partners. And so they fall back on another conceptual habit, derived from the more recent past: that of explaining that we must still be the leaders and teachers of others, even if the goal is now defined as the balance, and the lesson called collective moderation. Between the desire for national self-restraint, and the ambition of shaping a system in which our influence endures, there is a tug of war.

If we define, as the President does in his moments of exuberance or in his fighting moods provoked by Vietnam, our main goal as the preservation of as much influence as possible, even limited disengagement will be hard to pursue. For it increases the chance that one or the other of our main rivals will move into the void, especially in those parts of the world where our clients are weak and have depended on our military presence or on huge injections of aid. Our extrication from Vietnam has been slowed down by this fear of a loss of influence, magnified by the belief that a victory for Hanoi would encourage anti-American forces everywhere: as if we were still in the mythical world of bipolar battle to the death. Should voids be filled by one of the new centers whose emergence we call for and should these decide to play their own game, we could find ourselves as deprived of influence as if we had been evicted by our rivals (against whom it would be more easy for us to react).

Our very concern for better relations with our chief rivals argues against disengagement in Europe and East Asia: for they may well prefer a U.S. presence in their respective neighborhoods (and the strains it creates in Washington and with our allies) to the might or magnetism of their immediate neighbors. At home, within or outside the Executive, many fear that any further disengagement would open the floodgates to "neoisolationists" or protectionists. Influence remains an incentive for worldwide commitment, a goad to presidential rhetoric about indivisible peace and domino-shaped credibility. In Western Europe, it argues for having the Europeans contribute to the costs of American troops, rather than for a West European defense organization. This "burden-sharing" formula pleases the Treasury, reassures the military, and seems a better way of deflecting Senator Mike Mansfield.

If, on the contrary, we define our goal as devolution—the build-ing of new centers of power in Western Europe and Japan—we are faced with a triple problem. One is their own long habit of depend-ence, their concentration on their internal problems or economic growth, which have insulated them from world responsibilities. De Gaulle's failure to create his "European Europe" resulted even more from the resistance of his neighbors to his global concerns than from their dislike of his style. Since last July, we have often appeared to kick our allies into rebellion deliberately. But that method of inject-ing pride conflicts with our ambition of having these new centers tied to us, playing our kind of game. Up to now, Western Europe and Japan have been far more eager to develop their power where it an-noys or hurts us—in the trade and monetary fields—than in the mili-tary realm.

Second, our policy of détente encourages the West Europeans (some of whom preceded us) and the Japanese (who didn't dare) to seek their own entente with their Communist neighbors; the goal of reconciliation interferes with that of a more dynamic diplomatic-strategic entity. The result, so far, is a postponement of the defense issue.

A third obstacle is the hostility of many of our smaller allies to a reduction of American power. South Korea, the Philippines, or Tai-wan clearly prefer our economic and military presence to Japan's—a distant protector is better than a close one. Even within the Europe of the Nine, some of the smaller powers may like America's military presence better than a European defense community dominated by the Bonn-London-Paris triangle. All three factors lead, incidentally, to one conclusion: if devolution is our goal, and especially if we want it safe, with partners rather than disaffected ex-allies, its forms and timetable should be negotiated between us and them, not between us and our chief rivals, as, in Western Europe, the linkage between the issue of American troops and mutual and balanced force reductions dangerously leads to, and as, in Asia, the moment and manner of Mr. Nixon's China trip inevitably suggest.

In our ambivalence, we have attempted to get the best of all possible worlds. On the traditional chessboard of world politics, this attempt has been given a name: the Nixon Doctrine. To preserve our influence, we maintain our commitments. But we expect our allies to do more for their own defense, and to count primarily on themselves if their fight is against subversion. A limited recipe for devolution and self-restraint, it raises two questions. One, will our allies continue to accept our definition of their job, i.e., will they play, in the new game, the role we assign to them? Our reinterpretation of our commitments provides them with a choice. They may read our doctrine not as a redistribution of strength but as a retreat from the contest, feel quite unqualified to take up the assignment, and define their national interest in a more neutralist direction.

Two, granted that they'll need tools for the job, will it be our tools—as in Vietnamization—or theirs? Will we, for instance, encourage them to develop their own defense industries? We have been most reluctant to do so. Our balance-of-payments problem has been one of the reasons for not encouraging too much local competition for our arms producers. So has our belief that we could have better control if we were the providers. This may be quite wrong. For dependence on a nation whose policy is not always clear, and whose supply of the tools may fluctuate according to domestic whims or sudden external shifts, creates the kind of insecurity that may breed accommodation with our chief rivals instead of "balance."

On the chessboards of interdependence, we have devalued the dollar, and the President's State of the World message speaks of the need for a new international monetary system that will "remove the disproportionate burden of responsibility for the system from this country's shoulders." However, our current policies seem aimed at preserving or increasing our advantages, as if to compensate for limited disinvolvement elsewhere. We have not taken steps to restore even partial convertibility. The world is still submitted to a dollar standard, and it is not clear that we are willing to subject the dollar to the constraints imposed on ordinary currencies. We seek a commercial surplus that would allow us to develop our exports of capital as well as goods. Allusions to the link between our role as providers of security, our demands for trade concessions, and the dollar's dominant position (which serves our investments abroad) reveal the depth of our ambivalence about the emergence of other power blocs. Should we succeed, because of Japan's and West Germany's continuing need for American protection, or because of the penetration of the British economy by the United States, we would actually make it more difficult to extend the Nixon Doctrine to Western Europe and Japan. Japan, utterly dependent on exports to advanced countries, would face a crisis; Western Europe, whose integration barely begins to expand from trade and agriculture to currencies, would in effect become just a free trade area, and cease to be an entity.

Should they resist our attempt to get the best of all possible worlds, we might actually get the worst. American tactics could consolidate the EEC. A separate West European trade and monetary bloc could challenge the United States and destroy the chances of a single orderly world system for currencies and trade. But at the same time, the emergence of any West European diplomatic-strategic entity may be prevented by continuing divisions among EEC countries, the hostility of their public opinion to military and world responsibility, the desire of most leaders for a détente, and perhaps, if confidence in the United States declines, for some accommodation with Russia in anticipation of American force withdrawals. The United States would only have the choice between a military presence made even more unpopular at home by the EEC's economic separatism, and a disengagement that would spell a major loss of influence.

Japan has greater freedom of maneuver than Europe. She is under no threat of subjugation, however diffuse, and is part of a four-power game. American shock tactics and humiliation could breed two equally bad alternatives. One would be a rapprochement with China but in an anti-American context (by contrast with Willy Brandt's *Ostpolitik*). Japan would move toward neutralism and pay the price China would demand for reconciliation. However, this price would be high in security terms, and the switch would not provide an answer to Japan's commercial needs. The other possibility is a gradual rapprochement with Russia, and an increasing militarization—conventional or nuclear—due to the fear of Chinese hostility and to a declining faith in the credibility of America's guarantee. Such a policy might help "contain" China, but in a highly unstable way, to Russia's benefit, and, again, with a considerable loss of influence for the United States.

The worst is never sure. But to avoid it, we must face two problems: of tactics and of goals. Tactics are particularly important in periods of transition from one system and policy to the next. There are two kinds of pitfalls. Sometimes one lets the past linger on too long, as in Vietnam. Vietnamization, aimed at facilitating military retreat, has also made the necessary political concessions more difficult. The stated fear of a disastrous impact of such concessions on America's other Asian allies sounds a bit hollow, given the shock to them of the way in which we undertook our rapprochement with Peking. The other pitfall consists of acting as if a desired future were already here in order to produce it. We have, especially in Asia, moved as if the era of horizontal great-power diplomacy had arrived; and our weaker allies are disconcerted. We have, both in Europe and in Asia, behaved as if our principal allies were already part friends, part rivals; and they are resentful.

Never have consultation, clarity, candor, and coordination (as distinct from mere ex post facto information) been more important. Henry Kissinger, ten years ago, complained that the Kennedy administration, in its overtures to Russia, failed to consult and to reassure the West Germans sufficiently. The same could now be said about the China visits and the Japanese. To be sure, the present policy aims at having the three major competing powers establish together (or rather, at having each Communist power establish with the United States) the framework within which all others would have to operate. We are trying to teach our allies to swim in the proper lanes—this may be a reaction against their past tendency to leave most of the swimming to us. But they may sink, or refuse to swim at all, or insist on choosing their own lanes.

Is this merely a contradiction between high-handed "great-power tactics" (partially explained by our concentrated policy process) and the goal of a less exposed role in world affairs? Does it not rather reflect our hope to preserve our past eminence, although at bargain prices? Does it not show that our brave talk about "breakthroughs" conceals far more continuity than change? What we seem to want bears a strong resemblance to Bismarck's system. We desire, at the same time, improved relations with the Soviet Union and with China, the continuation (in perhaps modified form) of our alliances with Western Europe and Japan, an improvement of our economic position as compared with that of our main allies-competitors. Bismarck was able to have tolerable relations with France, and defensive alliances with Austria, Russia, and Italy. But the purpose of his alliances was limited to preventing France from building a coalition for revanche against Germany. They did not impose on Berlin the burden of protecting its allies against French aggression. They existed in a world of relative equality among the main powers, and considerable disconnection between *Grosspolitik* and the economic chessboards. They occurred in a century of secret diplomacy, when alliances were known to be passing affairs, and their terms could be kept in the dark without creating panics. Moreover, even Germany soon had to choose between the Russian and the Austrian connections—a choice that marked the end of the grand Bismarckian attempt at being both master and part of the balance.

Our current equivalent amounts not to a multipolar system, but to a tripolar one, with a comparably decisive but actually far heavier role for the United States. It is the United States that, in effect, protects the weakest of the three (China) from a Soviet strike; it is the United States that tries to hold the balance between Russia and China; it is the United States that attempts to contain each of these with the help of two subordinate alliances; it is the United States that guarantees its chief allies' security; it is the United States that tries to retain preponderance in the arena of interdependence. Such a vast design may be wishful thinking. Having proclaimed the primacy of the "free world" interest for twenty-five years, the United States can hardly make its new emphasis on the national interest the sole criterion of policy, and its way of using the power it enjoys on some chessboards in order to preserve or gain influence on others appear compatible with lasting alliances.

Our policy actually entails far less self-restraint than it promises and much less multipolarity than it pretends. World moderation will have to be pursued through other means. Neither in the strategic-diplomatic realm nor in all the others does a "pentagonal" world make sense: there are no likely or desirable five centers of comparable power in the former; and while there may well be in the latter, the issues and needs there have little to do with a balancing of poles. As for self-restraint, given the nature of our chief rivals, the responsibilities of nuclear might and the constraining need of a nuclear umbrella over Western Europe and Japan, there will be serious limits to its scope in the traditional arena. But our tactics of influence and instruments of policy are not doomed to remain as blunt and massive as in the past. Our goal should certainly be to build up autonomous strength in the main areas of the great-power contest.

But this does not mean worrying only about the "Big Five," nor does it necessarily mean a militarization of Western Europe and Japan. Western Europe's future offers possibilities of a conventional defense organization, which it is in our interest to encourage even by reorganizing NATO's structure. Soviet opposition could hardly be effective if these moves were linked to gradual American withdrawals in a context of increasing East-West exchanges. The failure of such an organization to emerge and to grow could breed a transatlantic conflict about American troops in Europe. But even if these should leave, and if West European military cooperation remained imperfect, economic prosperity and political self-confidence would be the keys to West European strength.

In East Asia, we have nothing to gain by encouraging Japanese rearmament, conventional or nuclear, which could revive fears of Japanese domination. But the only chance of preventing it may be to provide Japan with real productivity for the power she has—economic power. Elsewhere as well, strength need not be defined too strictly in military terms, however important military might remains as an insurance against trouble. But when no autonomous strength can be found, we should disconnect ourselves entirely—as we should have done from Vietnam or Yahya Khan's Pakistan: then, our rivals' increase in influence has a greater chance of being fleeting. In all the other arenas of world politics, self-restraint may well be a necessity, and would assuredly be a virtue. Here, we must accept, rather than resent, the shift of power that has benefited our allies, and find ways of building a community against anarchy. But here as in the traditional sphere, self-restraint, contrary to the hopes of some, will consist of a variety of involvements, not a promise of disentanglement.

Above all, let us not confuse a set of worthy goals—the establishment of a moderate international system, new relations with our adversaries, the adjustment of our alliances to the new conditions of diplomacy and economics—with a technique—a balance of five powers—that turns out to correspond neither to the world's complex needs nor to our own ambivalent desires. A "structure of peace" cannot be brought about by restoring a bygone world. Rediscovering the "habits of moderation and compromise" requires a huge effort of imagination and innovation.

Appendices: The 1973 Vietnam Cease-Fire Agreements

Appendix A: Geneva and Paris

ALAN M. JONES, JR.
Geneva and Paris: The Cease-Fire Agreements

On January 27, 1973, agreements were signed in Paris to end the Vietnam war, the longest conflict in which the United States had ever been engaged. The agreement itself, consisting of twenty-three articles and nine chapters, was supplemented by four protocols spelling out procedures for the implementation of the cease-fire, return of prisoners, deactivation of mines, and functioning of an International Commission of Control and Supervision. Both the agreement and each of the protocols took two forms: one signed by the four parties participating in the Paris conference (the United States, the Democratic Republic of Vietnam, the Republic of Vietnam, and the Provisional Revolutionary Government of the Republic of South Vietnam); the other (with a different concluding article) signed only by the United States and North Vietnam and constituting, in effect, a separate guarantee by these governments of the four-party versions of the documents. Both forms of the agreement and protocols are reprinted below. Also appended is a description of their provisions which Dr. Henry Kissinger, the principal American negotiator at the Paris talks, gave to the press. Dr. Kissinger's summary provides an excellent and authoritative guide to the meaning of these important texts.

In providing for the implementation of the cease-fire and for the political future of Indochina, the Paris agreements drew heavily on the 1954 Geneva accords which ended the first Indochina war between the French and the Viet Minh under Ho Chi Minh. Despite these similarities, however, important differences exist between the two settlements, particularly in the following areas: (1) the form of the agreement, (2) the terms of the agreement, and (3) the context of the agreement.

It is important to emphasize that there were two types of agreements reached at Geneva in 1954. The first, signed by and binding the French and Viet Minh governments, provided the means by which a cessation of hostilities was to be effected between their forces. As such, it affected directly only the countries actually engaged in the conflict. In addition, a "final declaration" was released in the name of the nine governments participating in the conference, including the other Indochinese states and the great powers. The statement, which went beyond the immediate military situation to prescribe for future political arrangements in Indochina, was not signed by any government and was, in effect, a joint communiqué of the type commonly released at the close of international meetings. As such, it constituted a declaration of intent for national policies in the area but did not obligate governments under international law to enforce its provisions.

By contrast, only one type of agreement was reached at the January 1973 Paris conference: a series of documents signed by the foreign ministers of all the participating governments and formally obligating those governments to carry out all aspects of the cease-fire agreement and its protocols. Since the principal agreement contained provisions for the political as well as the military future of Vietnam, the effective settlement was a much more comprehensive one than that of Geneva. Also, because the binding agreement encompassed both the political and military spheres, the Paris accords made for a much stronger settlement than Geneva had done. As at Geneva, however, the formal undertakings were limited to those countries directly involved in the fighting. The other Indochinese states were left to make their own cease-fires (although the United States and North Vietnam pledged to respect their sovereignty). The other world powers besides the United States had not participated in any phase of the Paris conference (unlike Geneva) and held a separate meeting in late February 1973 (also in Paris) to decide upon the nature and form of an international guarantee of the Paris accords. The Final Declaration of this later conference (signed by and obligating the governments of the major states, as well as other interested parties) is also reprinted below. Taken together, the provisions of the binding agreements concluded at Paris went as far as diplomacy could go to ensure an effective settlement.

The contents of the Geneva and Paris agreements also reveal substantial differences, although in many instances these differences are concealed by the use of identical terminology. The separation between North and South Vietnam is again referred to as the Provisional Military Demarcation Line, and it is restated that this line does not constitute a formal international boundary. The Joint Commission of the Geneva accords has become the Joint Military Commission, in each case composed of ranking officers from the opposing forces working to ensure the enforcement of the cease-fire. Only the personnel have changed. To observe the implementation of the cease-fire provisions, the International Commission for Supervision and Control agreed to at Geneva has been reconstituted as the International Commission of Control and Supervision. Here even the personnel remain largely similar. Poland and Canada have served on both, while India has been replaced by Hungary and Indonesia. As in the Geneva cease-fire agreement, the Paris text requires the removal of foreign military forces, bans the establishment of new foreign military bases, and provides that new military equipment may be introduced only if it specifically replaces previous weapons of the same type and number which have become inoperable. In addition, both agreements contain similar provisions to ensure the return of all prisoners of war and the deactivation of mines and other automatic devices of war.

There are thus many similarities between the two agreements. But these same terms illustrate some important contrasts. The dividing line established by the Geneva conference around the 17th parallel was designed to separate and provide a neutral buffer between the "military regroupment zones" into which the French and Viet Minh forces were to withdraw during the year following the establishment of a cease-fire. No such redeployment of military forces is provided in the Paris agreements. Except for U.S. forces, which would be withdrawn within sixty days, the latter constitutes an in-place cease-fire, with any future changes (particularly the removal of North Vietnamese forces) left subject to negotiation among the Vietnamese parties themselves. Since the 17th parallel has no special significance for the implementation of the cease-fire, the contents of the Paris accord make it an effective, although not formal, boundary between North and South Vietnam. Moreover, it is a boundary that each side pledges to respect "pending reunification." And whereas the Geneva final declaration called for elections two years later (in July 1956) to resolve political problems "on the basis of respect for the principles of independence, unity, and territorial integrity," the Paris agreement fails to suggest, even indirectly, the form or timing of reunification. Instead, the phrasing indicates that reunification would be a long-term process of negotiation between the Northern and Southern governments. For the foreseeable future, then, there will be two Vietnams, and these Vietnams will be separated at the 17th parallel.

The supervisory commission created at Geneva found itself hamstrung by the insistence on unanimous decisions on all but the most minor questions and by its dependence on the observed military forces for equipment and access to different areas. By contrast, the new version of the control commission, while preserving voting unanimity, is required to investigate the complaints of any party and to report the views of each of its members. Instead of the fourteen teams in Saigon and the countryside provided at Geneva, there are forty-nine, reflecting a far larger force. And these expanded observation teams are to provide their own equipment, communications, and transportation, thus making them independent of the facilities of the inspected groups. Nonetheless, this commission is in no sense an enforcement agency. It would "police" the cease-fire only in terms of reporting possible violations. What action might be taken if violation occurred is left for the governments involved to decide.

The vagueness of the Paris agreements concerning the method and timing of reunification is complemented by ambiguity regarding the political future of South Vietnam. Geneva had provided that this issue, like that of reunification, would be resolved through the July

1956 elections, to be held after extensive consultations between the Northern and Southern authorities and under the supervision of the international commission. The Paris accords, on the other hand, affirm the aim of free, internationally regulated elections, but postpone them for an indefinite period during which a National Council of National Reconciliation and Concord would deliberate over the methods and timing of elections as well as which governmental institutions would be affected by them. Since the National Council is to be made up of the South Vietnamese parties and can act solely on the basis of unanimity, a plan for elections which seemed likely to jeopardize the position of any party would be doomed from the outset. And since these parties have just concluded a long and bitter civil war, the prospect of agreement on any subject seems remote. Hence as in the cease-fire and reunification provisions, the articles relating to the political completion of South Vietnam have the effect of legitimizing the status quo.

This is perhaps the most important of the differences between the Geneva and Paris agreements: the former prescribed basic change; the latter did not. The cease-fire articles signed at Geneva were essentially a plan for the division of Vietnam into two parts, in terms of population resettlement and political administration as well as the stationing of military forces. The unsigned final declaration of the Geneva conference proclaimed the hope that the partition it had established could be erased and provided a means for its removal. The Paris agreements, by contrast, recognized the military and political situation as it existed within South Vietnam and between the North and South Vietnamese regimes. Whatever changes occurred in Vietnam would be extensions of these existing situations, not fundamental revisions of them.

Change at Geneva was necessitated by general awareness that the status quo in Vietnam had become untenable. After the French loss at Dien Bien Phu, Paris no longer felt itself able to undertake military action in Indochina, although it still hoped to exert substantial political influence there, especially in South Vietnam. The Viet Minh sought control of all Vietnam, but its victory had been primarily in the North, control of the South being fragmented among various groups. The United States, as the principal supporter of military action against the Viet Minh, underscored its determination to limit Communist gains with the threat of direct intervention. All these circumstances combined to produce the effective bifurcation of Vietnam as the settlement most in keeping with reality both in Indochina and among the most powerful states. Each party gained some but not all of its objectives: the Viet Minh won control of the industrial, administrative, and cultural center of Vietnam; France won the chance for a renewed role in Indochina; and Washington won time to create an anti-Communist bulwark in Southeast Asia.

In contrast to the clear-cut Communist military victory in the North which overshadowed the Geneva conference, the Paris talks took place in an atmosphere of military stalemate. All sides had been drained by the agonizingly long conflict, but none was prepared to yield its basic positions. North Vietnam had shown its ability to conduct major offensives despite years of American bombing. South Vietnam had demonstrated its capacity to blunt these offensives without the presence of large numbers of American ground forces. Washington, especially in the December 1972 bombings, had emphasized its willingness to risk domestic and international disfavor by the massive use of air power against the North. Each government was, if anything, stronger than it had been before, able to rally support for its actions even though the war itself had long since been condemned. The battlefield made clear that each was able to carry on, regardless of cost, into the indefinite future. In this context, no agreement could award victory to either side, although both would claim it. Instead, the result of diplomacy would reflect the ambivalent outcome of war. Here more than at Geneva, each side had to settle for partial success: Hanoi won the right to retain the territory it had gained in the South as a base for the Provisional Revolutionary Government it sponsored, Saigon still controlled much of the territory and most of the population of the South and won the right to its continued existence without having to share power with its adversaries, and Washington won extrication from a costly and unpopular war without the surrender of its main objectives or position in the area.

Appendix B: The 1973 Vietnam Agreements: A Summary Statement by Henry A. Kissinger

Excerpts from a statement describing the Paris accords made by Dr. Henry Kissinger at a news conference, January 24, 1973. Reprinted from *Department of State Bulletin* 68, no. 1755 (12 February 1973): 155–60.

OPENING STATEMENT

Ladies and gentlemen:

The President last evening presented the outlines of the agreement, and by common agreement between us and the North Vietnamese we have today released the text. And I'm here to explain—to go over briefly—what these texts contain and how we got there, what we have tried to achieve in recent months and where we expect to go from here.

Let me begin by going through the agreement, which you have read.

The agreement, as you know, is in nine chapters. The first affirms the independence, sovereignty, unity and territorial integrity as recognized by the 1954 Geneva agreements on Vietnam—agreements which established two zones, divided by a military demarcation line.

Chapter II deals with a cease-fire. The cease-fire will go into effect at 7 o'clock Washington time on Saturday night. The principal provisions of Chapter II deal with permitted acts during the cease-fire and with what the obligations of the various parties are with respect to the cease-fire.

WITHDRAWAL OF FORCES

Chapter II also deals with the withdrawal of American and all other foreign forces from Vietnam within a period of 60 days and it specifies the forces that have to be withdrawn. These are, in effect, all military personnel and all civilian personnel dealing with combat operations. We are permitted to retain economic advisers and civilian technicians serving in certain of the military branches.

Chapter II further deals with the provisions for resupply and for the introduction of outside forces. There is a flat prohibition against the introduction of any military forces into South Vietnam from outside of South Vietnam, which is to say that whatever forces may be in South Vietnam from outside South Vietnam —specfically North Vietnamese forces—cannot receive reinforcement, replacements, or any other form of augmentation by any means whatsoever.

With respect to military equipment, both sides are permitted to replace all existing military equipment on a one-to-one basis under international supervision and control.

RETURN OF PRISONERS

There will be established, as I will explain when I discuss the protocols, for each side three legitimate points of entry through which all replacement equipment has to move. These legitimate points of entry will be under international supervision.

Chapter III deals with the return of captured military personnel and foreign civilians as well as with the question of civilian detainees within South Vietnam. This, as you know, throughout the negotiations, presented enormous difficulties for us. We insisted throughout that the question of American prisoners of war and of American civilians captured throughout Indochina should be separated from the issue of Vietnamese civilian personnel detained, partly because of the enormous difficulty of classifying the Vietnamese civilian personnel by categories of who was detained for reasons of the civil war and who was detained for criminal activities.

And secondly, because it was foreseeable that negotiations about the release of civilian detainees would be complex and difficult and because we did not want to have the issue of American personnel mixed up with the issues of civilian personnel in South Vietnam, this turned out to be one of the thorniest issues that was settled at some point and kept reappearing throughout the negotiations.

It was one of the difficulties we had during the December negotiations.

As you can see from the agree-

ment, the return of American military personnel and captured civilians is separated in terms of obligation and in terms of the time frame from the return of Vietnamese civilian personnel. The return of American personnel and the accounting of missing-in-action is unconditional and will take place within the same time frame as the American withdrawal.

3 MONTHS TO NEGOTIATE

The issue of Vietnamese civilian personnel will be negotiated between the two Vietnamese parties over a period of three months and, as the agreement says, they will do their utmost to resolve this question within a three-month period.

So I repeat: the issue is separated both in terms of obligation and in terms of the relevant time frame from the return of American prisoners, which is unconditional.

We expect that American prisoners will be released at intervals of two weeks or 15 days in roughly equal installments.

We have been told that no American prisoners are held in Cambodia. American prisoners held in Laos and North Vietnam will be returned to us in Hanoi. They will be received by American medical evacuation teams and flown on American airplanes from Hanoi to places of our own choice, probably Vientiane.

There will be international supervision of both this provision and of the provision for the missing-in-action and all American prisoners will, of course, be released within 60 days of the signing of the agreement. The signing will take place on January 27 in two installments, the significance of which I will explain to you when I have gone through the provisions of the agreement and the associated protocols.

Chapter IV of the agreement deals with the right of the South Vietnamese people to self-determination.

Its first provision contains a joint statement by the United States and North Vietnam in which those two countries jointly recognize the South Vietnamese people's right to self-determination, in which those two countries jointly affirm that the South Vietnamese people shall decide for themselves the political system that they shall choose and jointly affirm that no foreign country shall impose any political solutions on South Vietnamese people.

The other principal provisions of the agreement are that in implementing the South Vietnamese people's right to self-determination, the two South Vietnamese parties will decide—will agree—among each other on free elections for offices to be decided by the two parties at a time to be decided by the two parties.

WILL NOT IMPOSE SOLUTIONS

These elections will be supervised and organized first by an institution which has the title of National Council for National Reconciliation and Concord, whose members will be equally appointed by the two sides, which will operate on the principle of unanimity and which will come into being after negotiations between the two parties, who are obligated by this agreement to do their utmost to bring this institution into being within 90 days.

Leaving aside the technical jargon, the significance of this part of the agreement is that the United States has consistently maintained that we would not impose any political solutions on the people of South Vietnam.

The United States has consistently maintained that we would not impose a coalition government or a disguised coalition government on the people of South Vietnam.

If you examine the provisions of this chapter you will see, first, that the existing government in Saigon can remain in office; secondly, that the political future of South Vietnam depends on agreement between the South Vietnamese parties and not on an agreement that the United States has imposed on these parties; thirdly, that the nature of this political evolution, the timing of this political evolution, is left to the South Vietnamese parties and that the organ that is created to see to it that the elections that are organized will be conducted properly is one in which each of the South Vietnamese parties has a veto.

The other significant provision of this agreement is the requirement that the South Vietnamese parties will bring about a reduction of the armed forces and that the forces being reduced will be demobilized.

THE ISSUE OF THE
DEMILITARIZED ZONE

The next chapter deals with the reunification of Vietnam and the relationship between North and South Vietnam.

In the many negotiations that I've conducted over recent weeks, not the least arduous was the negotiation conducted with the ladies and gentlemen of the press who constantly raised issues with respect to sovereignty, the existence of South Vietnam as a political entity, and other matters of this kind.

I will return to this issue at the end when I sum up the agreement. But it is obvious that there is no dispute in the agreement between the parties that there is an entity called South Vietnam and that the future unity of Vietnam as it comes about, will be decided by negotiations between North and South Vietnam: that it will not be achieved by military force; indeed, that the use of military force with respect to bringing about unification, or any other form of coercion, is impermissible according to the terms of this agreement.

Secondly, there are specific provisions in this chapter with respect to the demilitarized zone (DMZ). There is a repetition of the agreement of 1954, which makes the demarcation line along the 17th parallel provisional, which means pending reunification.

There is a specific provision that both North and South Vietnam shall respect the demilitarized zone on either side of the provisional military demarcation line.

And there is another provision that indicates that among the subjects that can be negotiated will be modalities of civilian movement across the demarcation line, which makes it clear that military movement across the demilitarized zone is in all circumstances prohibited.

ISSUE OF THE DMZ

Now this may be an appropriate point to explain what our position has been with respect to the DMZ.

There has been a great deal of discussion about the issue of sovereignty and about the issue of legitimacy, which is to say which government is in control of South Vietnam, and finally about why we laid such great stress on the issue of the demilitarized zone.

We had to place stress on the issue of the demilitarized zone because the provisions of the agreement with respect to infiltration, with respect to replacement, with respect to any of the military provisions, would have made no sense whatever if there was not some demarcation line that defined where South Vietnam began.

If we had accepted the proposition, that would have, in effect,

eroded the demilitarized zone, then the provisions of the agreement with respect to restrictions about the introduction of men and material into South Vietnam would have been unilateral restrictions applying only to the United States and only to our allies. Therefore, if there was to be any meaning to the separation of military and political issues—if there was to be any permanence to the military provisions that had been negotiated—then it was essential that there was a definition of where the obligations of this agreement began.

And as you can see from the text of the agreement, the principles that we defended were essentially achieved.

Chapter VI deals with the international machinery and we will discuss that when I talk about the associated protocols of the agreement.

LAOS AND CAMBODIA

Chapter VII deals with Laos and Cambodia. Now the problem of Laos and Cambodia has two parts: one part concerns those obligations which can be undertaken by the parties signing the agreement—that is to say, the three Vietnamese parties and the United States—those measures that we can take which affect the situation in Laos and Cambodia; a second part of the situation in Laos has to concern the nature of the civil conflict that is taking place within Laos and Cambodia and the solution of which, of course, must involve as well the two Laotian parties and the innumerable Cambodian factions.

Let me talk about the provisions of the agreement with respect to Laos and Cambodia and our firm expectations as to the future in Laos and Cambodia.

The provisions of the agreement with respect to Laos and Cambodia reaffirm, as an obligation to all the parties, the provisions of the 1954 agreement on Cambodia and of the 1962 agreement on Laos, which affirm the neutrality and right to self-determination of those two countries. They are therefore consistent with our basic position with respect also to South Vietnam.

USE OF BASES PROHIBITED

In terms of the immediate conflict, the provisions of the agreement specifically prohibit the use of Laos and Cambodia for military and any other operations against any of the signatories of the Paris agreement or against any other country. In other words, there is a flat prohibition against the use of base areas in Laos and Cambodia. There is a flat prohibition against the use of Laos and Cambodia for infiltration into Vietnam or for that matter into any other country.

Finally, there is a requirement that all foreign troops be withdrawn from Laos and Cambodia, and it is clearly understood that North Vietnamese troops are considered foreign with respect to Laos and Cambodia.

Now as to the conflict within these countries, which could not be formally settled in an agreement which is not signed by the parties of that conflict, let me make this plain without elaborating: It is our firm expectation that within a short period of time there will be a formal cease-fire in Laos, which in turn will lead to a withdrawal of all foreign forces from Laos and, of course, to the end of the use of Laos as a corridor of infiltration.

CHANGE BY FORCE BARRED

The situation in Cambodia, as those of you who have studied it will know, is somewhat more complex because there are several parties headquartered in different countries. Therefore we can say about Cambodia that it is our expectation that a de facto cease-fire will come into being over a period of time relevant to the execution of this agreement.

Our side will take the appropriate measures to indicate that it will not attempt to change the situation by force.

We have reason to believe that our position is clearly understood by all concerned parties, and I will not go beyond this in my statement.

RELATIONSHIP OF THE UNITED STATES TO NORTH VIETNAM

Chapter VIII deals with the relationship between the United States and the Democratic Republic of Vietnam.

As I have said in my briefings on October 26 and on December 16 and as the President affirmed on many occasions—the last time in his speech last evening—the United States is seeking a peace that heals.

We have had many armistices in Indochina. We want a peace that will last. And therefore it is our firm intention in our relationship to the Democratic Republic of Vietnam to move from hostility to normalization and from normalization to conciliation and cooperation.

And we believe that under conditions of peace, we can contribute throughout Indochina to a realization of the humane aspirations of all the people of Indochina, and we will, in that spirit, perform our traditional role of helping people realize these aspirations in peace.

Chapter IX of the agreement is the usual implementing provision. So much for the agreement.

PROTOCOLS DISCUSSED

Now let me say a word about the protocol.

There are four protocols, or implementing instruments, to the agreement on the return of American prisoners, on the implementation and institution of an international control commission, on the regulations with respect to the cease-fire and the implementation and institution of a joint military commission among the concerned parties, and the protocol about the deactivation and removal of mines.

I have given you the relevant provisions of the protocol concerning the return of prisoners. They will be returned at periodic intervals in Hanoi to American authorities and not to American private groups. They will be picked up by American airplanes except for prisoners held in the southern part of South Vietnam, which will be released at designated points in the South, again to American authorities.

We will receive on Saturday—the day of signing of the agreement—a list of all American prisoners held throughout Indochina and those parties, it is to say all parties, have an obligation to assist each other in obtaining information about the prisoners, missing in action, and about the location of graves of American personnel throughout Indochina.

The international commission has the right to visit the last place of detention of the prisoners as well as the place from which they are released.

SIZE OF COMMISSION

Now, to the international control commission.

You will remember that one of the reasons for the impasse in December was the difficulty of agreeing with the North Vietnamese about the size of the international commission, its function, or the location of its teams.

On this occasion, there is no point in reviewing all the differences. It is,

however, useful to point out that at that time the proposal of the North Vietnamese was that the international control commission have a membership of 250, no organized logistics or communication, dependent entirely for its authority to move on the party it was supposed to be investigating; and that over half of its personnel were supposed to be located in Saigon, which is not the place where most of the infiltration that we were concerned with was likely to take place.

We have distributed to you an outline of the basic structure of this commission.

Briefly stated, its total number is 1,160, drawn from Canada, Hungary, Indonesia, and Poland.

SEVEN REGIONAL TEAMS

It has a headquarters in Saigon. It has seven regional teams, 26 teams based in localities throughout Vietnam which were chosen either because forces were in contact there or because we estimated that these were the areas where the violations of the cease-fire were most probable.

There are 12 teams at border-crossing points. There are seven teams that are set aside for points of entry, which have yet to be chosen, for the replacement of military equipment. That is for Article 7 of the agreement. There will be three on each side, and there will be no legitimate point of entry into South Vietnam other than those three points.

The other border and coastal teams are there simply to make certain that no other entry occurs, and any other entry is by definition illegal. There has to be no other demonstration except the fact that it occurred. This leaves one team free for use in particular at the discretion of the commission; and, of course, the seven teams that are being used for the return of prisoners can be used at the discretion of the commission after the prisoners are returned.

ONE TEAM AT DMZ

There is one reinforced team located at the demilitarized zone, and its responsibility extends along the entire demilitarized zone. It is, in fact, a team and a half. It is 50 percent larger than a normal border team. And it represents one of the many compromises that were made between our insistence on two teams, their insistence on one team, and by a brilliant stroke we settled on a team and a half.

With respect to the operation of the international commission, it is supposed to operate on the principle of unanimity, which is to say that its reports—if they are commission reports—have to have the approval of all four members.

However, each member is permitted to submit its own opinion so that as a practical matter any member of the commission can make a finding of a violation and submit a report in the first instance to the parties.

The international commission will report for the time being to the four parties to the agreement.

INSTITUTIONS PLANNED

We expect an international conference will take place—we expect at the foreign ministers' level—within a month of signing the agreement. That international conference will establish a relationship between the international commission and itself or any other international body that is mutually agreed upon, so that the international commission is not only reporting to the parties that it is investigating.

For the time being, until the international conference has met, there was no other practical group to which the international commission could report. In addition to this international group there are two other institutions that are supposed to supervise the cease-fire.

There is, first of all, an institution called the four-party joint military commission, which is composed of ourselves and the three Vietnamese parties, which is located in the same places as the international commission, charged with roughly the same functions, but as a practical matter, it is supposed to conduct the preliminary investigations. Its disagreements are automatically referred to the international commission and moreover any party can request the international commission to conduct an investigation regardless of what the four-party commission does and regardless of whether the four-party commission has completed its investigation or not.

After the United States has completed its withdrawal the four-party military commission will be transformed into a two-party commission composed of the two South Vietnamese parties.

The total number of supervisory personnel, therefore, will be in the neighborhood of 4,500 during the period that the four-party commission is in existence and in the neighborhood of about 3,000 after the four-party commission ceases operating and the two-party commission comes into being.

REMOVAL OF MINES

Finally, there is a protocol concerning the removal and deactivation of mines which is self-explanatory and simply explains—discusses—the relationship between our efforts and the efforts of the D.R.V. concerning the removal and deactivation of mines, which is one of the obligations we have undertaken in the agreement.

Appendix C: Texts of the January 1973 Vietnam Cease-Fire Agreement and Protocols

THE CEASE-FIRE AGREEMENT
Agreement on Ending the War and Restoring Peace in Vietnam

The parties participating in the Paris conference on Vietnam,

With a view to ending the war and restoring peace in Vietnam on the basis of respect for the Vietnamese people's fundamental national rights and the South Vietnamese people's right to self-determination, and to contributing to the consolidation of peace in Asia and the world,

Have agreed on the following provisions and undertake to respect and to implement them:

Chapter I
The Vietnamese People's Fundamental National Rights

ARTICLE I

The United States and all other countries respect the independence, sovereignty, unity and territorial integrity of Vietnam as recognized by the 1954 Geneva Agreements on Vietnam.

Chapter II
Cessation of Hostilities, Withdrawal of Troops

ARTICLE 2

A cease-fire shall be observed throughout South Vietnam as of 2400 hours G.M.T., on January 27, 1973.

At the same hour, the United States will stop all its military activities against the territory of the Democratic Republic of Vietnam by ground, air and naval forces, wherever they may be based, and end the mining of the territorial waters, ports, harbors and waterways of the Democratic Republic of Vietnam. The United States will remove, permanently deactivate or destroy all the mines in the territorial waters, ports, harbors and waterways of North Vietnam as soon as this agreement goes into effect.

The complete cessation of hostilities mentioned in this article shall be durable and without limit of time.

ARTICLE 3

The parties undertake to maintain the cease-fire and to insure a lasting and stable peace.

As soon as the cease-fire goes into effect:

(a) The United States forces and those of the other foreign countries allied with the United States and the Republic of Vietnam shall remain in place pending the implementation of the plan of troop withdrawal. The Four-Party Joint Military Commission described in Article 16 shall determine the modalities.

(b) The armed forces of the two South Vietnamese parties shall remain in place. The Two-Party Joint Military Commission described in Article 17 shall determine the areas controlled by each party and the modalities of stationing.

(c) The regular forces of all services and arms and the irregular forces of the parties in South Vietnam shall stop all offensive activities against each other and shall strictly abide by the following stipulations:

¶All acts of force on the ground, in the air and on the sea shall be prohibited.

¶All hostile acts, terrorism and reprisals by both sides will be banned.

ARTICLE 4

The United States will not continue its military involvement or intervene in the internal affairs of South Vietnam.

ARTICLE 5

Within 60 days of the signing of this agreement, there will be a total withdrawal from South Vietnam of troops, military advisers and military personnel, including technical military personnel and military personnel associated with the pacification program, armaments, munitions and war material of the United States and those of the other foreign countries mentioned in Article 3 (a). Advisers from the above-mentioned countries to all paramilitary organizations and the police force will also be withdrawn within the same period of time.

ARTICLE 6

The dismantlement of all military bases in South Vietnam of the United States and of the other foreign countries mentioned in Article 3 (a) shall be completed within 60 days of the signing of this agreement.

ARTICLE 7

From the enforcement of the cease-fire to the formation of the government provided for in Articles 9 (b) and 14 of this agreement, the two South Vietnamese parties shall not accept the introduction of troops, military advisers and military personnel, including technical military personnel, armaments, munitions and war material into South Vietnam.

The two South Vietnamese parties shall be permitted to make periodic replacement of armaments, munitions and war material which have been destroyed, damaged, worn out or used up after the cease-fire, on the basis of piece-for-piece, of the same characteristics and properties, under the supervision of the Joint Military Commission of the two South Vietnamese parties and of the International Commission of Control and Supervision.

Chapter III

The Return of Captured Military Personnel and Foreign Civilians, and Captured and Detained Vietnamese Civilian Personnel

ARTICLE 8

(a) The return of captured military personnel and foreign civilians of the parties shall be carried out simultaneously with and completed not later than the same day as the troop withdrawal mentioned in Article 5. The parties shall exchange complete lists of the above-mentioned captured military personnel and foreign civilians on the day of the signing of this agreement.

(b) The parties shall help each other to get information about those military personnel and foreign civilians of the parties missing in action, to determine the location and take care of the graves of the dead so as to facilitate the exhumation and repatriation of the remains, and to take any such other measures as may be required to get information about those still considered missing in action.

(c) The question of the return of Vietnamese civilian personnel captured and detained in South Vietnam will be resolved by the two South Vietnamese parties on the basis of the principles of Artice 21 (b) of the Agreement on the Cessation of Hostilities in Vietnam of July 20, 1954. The two South Vietnamese parties will do so in a spirit of national reconciliation and concord, with a view to ending hatred and enmity, in order to ease suffering and to reunite families. The two South Vietnamese parties will do their utmost to resolve this question within 90 days after the cease-fire comes into effect.

Chapter IV

The Exercise of the South Vietnamese People's Right to Self-Determination

ARTICLE 9

The Government of the United States of America and the Government of the Democratic Republic of Vietnam undertake to respect the following principles for the exercise of the South Vietnamese people's right to self-determination:

(a) The South Vietnamese people's right to self-determination is sacred, inalienable and shall be respected by all countries.

(b) The South Vietnamese people shall decide themselves the political future of South Vietnam through genuinely free and democratic general elections under international supervision.

(c) Foreign countries shall not impose any political tendency or personality on the South Vietnamese people.

ARTICLE 10

The two South Vietnamese parties undertake to respect the cease-fire and maintain peace in South Vietnam, settle all matters of contention through negotiations and avoid all armed conflict.

ARTICLE 11

Immediately after the cease-fire, the two South Vietnamese parties will:

¶Achieve national reconciliation and concord, end hatred and enmity, prohibit all acts of reprisal and discrimination against individuals or organizations that have collaborated with one side or the other.

¶Insure the democratic liberties of the people: personal freedom, freedom of speech, freedom of the press, freedom of meeting, freedom of organization, freedom of political activities, freedom of belief, freedom of movement, freedom of residence, freedom of work, right to property ownership and right to free enterprise.

ARTICLE 12

(a) Immediately after the cease-fire, the two South Vietnamese parties shall hold consultations in a spirit of national reconciliation and concord, mutual respect and mutual nonelimination to set up a National Council of National Reconciliation and Concord of three equal segments. The council shall operate on the principle of unanimity. After the National Council of National Reconciliation and Concord has assumed its functions, the two South Vietnamese parties will consult about the formation of councils at lower levels. The two South Vietnamese parties shall sign an agreement on the internal matters of South Vietnam as soon as possible and do their utmost to accomplish this within 90 days after the cease-fire comes into effect, in keeping with the South Vietnamese people's aspirations for peace, independence and democracy.

(b) The National Council of National Reconciliation and Concord shall have the task of promoting the two South Vietnamese parties' implementation of this agreement, achievement of national reconciliation and concord and insurance of democratic liberties. The National Council of National Reconciliation and Concord will organize the free and democratic general elections provided for in Article 9 (b) and decide the procedures and modalities of these general elections. The institutions for which the general elections are to be held will be agreed upon through consultations between the two South Vietnamese parties. The National Council of National Reconciliation and Concord will also decide the procedures and modalities of such local elections as the two South Vietnamese parties agree upon.

ARTICLE 13

The question of Vietnamese armed forces in South Vietnam shall be settled by the two South Vietnamese parties in a spirit of national reconciliation and concord, equality and mutual respect, without foreign interference, in accordance with the postwar situation. Among the questions to be discussed by the two South Vietnamese parties are steps to reduce their military effectives and to demobilize the troops being reduced. The two South Vietnamese parties will accomplish this as soon as possible.

ARTICLE 14

South Vietnam will pursue a foreign policy of peace and independence. It will be prepared to establish relations with all countries irrespective of their political and social systems on the basis of mutual respect for independence and sovereignty and accept economic and technical aid from any country with no political conditions attached. The acceptance of military aid by South Vietnam in the future shall come under the authority of the government set up after the general elections in South Vietnam provided for in Article 9 (b).

Chapter V
The Reunification of Vietnam and the Relationship Between North and South Vietnam

ARTICLE 15

The reunification of Vietnam shall be carried out step by step through peaceful means on the basis of discussions and agreements between North and South Vietnam, without coercion or annexation by either party, and without foreign interference. The time for reunification will be agreed upon by North and South Vietnam.

Pending reunification:

(a) The military demarcation line between the two zones at the 17th parallel is only provisional and not a political or territorial boundary, as provided for in paragraph 6 of the Final Declaration of the 1954 Geneva Conference.

(b) North and South Vietnam shall respect the demilitarized zone on either side of the provisional military demarcation line.

(c) North and South Vietnam shall promptly start negotiations with a view to re-establishing normal relations in various fields. Among the questions to be negotiated are the modalities of civilian movement across the provisional military demarcation line.

(d) North and South Vietnam shall not join any military alliance or military bloc and shall not allow foreign powers to maintain military bases, troops, military advisers and military personnel on their respective territories, as stipulated in the 1954 Geneva Agreements on Vietnam.

Chapter VI
The Joint Military Commissions, The International Commission of Control and Supervision, The International Conference

ARTICLE 16

(a) The parties participating in the Paris conference on Vietnam shall immediately designate representatives to form a Four-Party Joint Military Commission with the task of insuring joint action by the parties in implementing the following provisions of this agreement:

¶The first paragraph of Article 2, regarding the enforcement of the cease-fire throughout South Vietnam.

¶Article 3 (a), regarding the cease-fire by U.S. forces and those of the other foreign countries referred to in that article.

¶Article 3 (c), regarding the cease-fire between all parties in South Vietnam.

¶Article 5, regarding the withdrawal from South Vietnam of U.S. troops and those of the other foreign countries mentioned in Article 3 (a).

¶Article 6, regarding the dismantlement of military bases in South Vietnam of the United States and those of the other foreign countries mentioned in Article 3 (a).

¶Article 8 (a), regarding the return of captured military personnel and foreign civilians of the parties.

¶Article 8 (b), regarding the mutual assistance of the parties in getting information about those military personnel and foreign civilians of the parties missing in action.

(b) The Four-Party Joint Military Commission shall operate in accordance with the principle of consultations and unanimity. Disagreements shall be referred to the International Commission of Control and Supervision.

(c) The Four-Party Joint Military Commission shall begin operating immediately after the signing of this agreement and end its activities in 60 days, after the completion of the withdrawal of U.S. troops and those of the other foreign countries mentioned in Article 3 (a) and the completion of the return of captured military personnel and foreign civilians of the parties.

(d) The four parties shall agree immediately on the organization, the working procedure, means of activity and expenditures of the Four-Party Joint Military Commission.

ARTICLE 17

(a) The two South Vietnamese parties shall immediately designate representatives to form a Two-Party Joint Military Commission with the task of insuring joint action by the two South Vietnamese parties in implementing the following provisions of this agreement:

¶The first paragraph of Article 2, regarding the enforcement of the cease-fire throughout South Vietnam, when the Four-Party Joint Military Commission has ended its activities.

¶Article 3 (b), regarding the cease-fire between the two South Vietnamese parties.

¶Article 3 (c), regarding the cease-fire between all parties in South Vietnam, when the Four-Party Joint Military Commission has ended its activities.

¶Article 7, regarding the prohibition of the introduction of troops into South Vietnam and all other provisions of this article.

¶Article 8 (c), regarding the question of the return of Vietnamese civilian personnel captured and detained in South Vietnam;

¶Article 13, regarding the reduction of the military effectives of the two South Vietnamese parties and the demobilization of the troops being reduced.

(b) Disagreements shall be referred to the International Commission of Control and Supervision.

(c) After the signing of this agreement, the Two-Party Joint Military Commission shall agree immediately on the measures and organization aimed at enforcing the cease-fire and preserving peace in South Vietnam.

ARTICLE 18

(a) After the signing of this Agreement, an International Commission of Control and Supervision shall be established immediately.

(b) Until the international conference provided for in Article 19 makes definitive arrangements, the International Commission of Control and Supervision will report to the four parties on matters concerning the control and supervision of the implementation of the following provisions of this agreement:

¶The first paragraph of Article 2, regarding the enforcement of the cease-fire throughout South Vietnam.

¶Article 3 (a), regarding the cease-fire by U.S. forces and those of the other foreign countries referred to in that article.

¶Article 3 (c), regarding the cease-fire between all the parties in South Vietnam.

¶Article 5, regarding the withdrawal from South Vietnam of U.S. troops and those of the other foreign countries mentioned in Article 3 (a).

¶Article 6, regarding the dismantlement of military bases in South Vietnam of the United States and those of the other foreign countries mentioned in Article 3 (a).

¶Article 8 (a), regarding the return of captured military personnel and foreign civilians of the parties.

The International Commission of Control and Supervision shall form control teams for carrying out its tasks. The four parties shall agree immediately on the location and operation of these teams. The parties will facilitate their operation.

(c) Until the international conference makes definitive arrangements, the International Commission of Control and Supervision will report to the two South Vietnamese parties on matters concerning the control and supervision of the implementation of the following provisions of this agreement:

¶The first paragraph of Article 2, regarding the enforcement of the cease-fire throughout South Vietnam, when the Four-Party Joint Military Commission has ended its activities.

¶Article 3 (b), regarding the cease-fire between the two South Vietnamese parties.

¶Article 3 (c), regarding the cease-fire between all parties in South Vietnam, when the Four-Party Joint Military Commission has ended its activities.

¶Article 7, regarding the prohibition of the introduction of troops into South Vietnam and all other provisions of this article.

¶Article 8 (c), regarding the question of the return of Vietnamese civilian personnel captured and detained in South Vietnam.

¶Article 9 (b), regarding the free and democratic general elections in South Vietnam.

¶Article 13, regarding the reduction of the military effectives of the two South Vietnamese parties and the demobilization of the troops being reduced.

The International Commission of Control and Supervision shall form control teams for carrying out its tasks. The two South Vietnamese parties shall agree immediately on the location and operation of these teams. The two South Vietnamese parties will facilitate their operation.

(d) The International Commission of Control and Supervision shall be composed of representatives of four countries: Canada, Hungary, Indonesia and Poland. The chairmanship of this commission will rotate among the members for specific periods to be determined by the commission.

(e) The International Commission of Control and Supervision shall carry out its tasks in accordance with the principle of respect for the sovereignty of South Vietnam.

(f) The International Commission of Control and Supervision shall operate in accordance with the principle of consultations and unanimity.

(g) The International Commission of Control and Supervision shall begin operating when a cease-fire comes into force in Vietnam. As regards the provision in Article 18 (b) concerning the four parties, the International Commission of Control and Supervision shall end its activities when the commission's tasks of control and supervision regarding these provisions have been fulfilled. As regards the provisions in Article 18 (c) concerning the two South Vietnamese parties, the International Commission of Control and Supervision shall end its activities on the request of the government formed after the general elections in South Vietnam provided for in Article 9 (b).

(h) The four parties shall agree immediately on the organization, means of activity and expenditures of the International Commission of Control and Supervision. The relationship between the international commission and the international conference will be agreed upon by the International Commission and the International Conference.

ARTICLE 19

The parties agree on the convening of an international conference within 30 days of the signing of this agreement to acknowledge the signed agreements; to guarantee the ending of the war, the maintenance of peace in Vietnam, the respect of the Vietnamese people's fundamental national rights and the South Vietnamese people's right to self-determination; and to contribute to and guarantee peace in Indochina.

The United States and the Democratic Republic of Vietnam, on behalf of the parties participating in the Paris conference on Vietnam, will propose to the following parties that they participate in this international conference: the People's Republic of China, the Republic of France, the Union of Soviet Socialist Republics, the United Kingdom, the four countries of the International Commission of Control and Supervision, and the Secretary General of the United Nations, together with the parties participating in the Paris conference on Vietnam.

Chapter VII
Regarding Cambodia and Laos

ARTICLE 20

(a) The parties participating in the Paris conference on Vietnam shall strictly respect the 1954 Geneva Agreements on Cambodia and the 1962 Geneva Agreements on Laos, which recognized the Cambodian and the Lao peoples' fundamental national rights, i. e., the independence, sovereignty, unity and territorial integrity of these countries. The parties shall respect the neutrality of Cambodia and Laos.

The parties participating in the Paris conference on Vietnam undertake to refrain from using the territory of Cambodia and the territory of Laos to encroach on the sovereignty and security of one another and of other countries.

(b) Foreign countries shall put an end to all military activities in Cambodia and Laos, totally withdraw from and refrain from reintroducing into these two countries troops, military advisers and military personnel, armaments, munitions and war material.

(c) The internal affairs of Cambodia and Laos shall be settled by the people of each of these countries without foreign interference.

(d) The problems existing between the Indochinese countries shall be settled by the Indochinese parties on the basis of respect for each other's independence, sovereignty and territorial integrity, and noninterference in each other's internal affairs.

Chapter VIII
The Relationship Between the United States and the Democratic Republic of Vietnam

ARTICLE 21

The United States anticipates that this agreement will usher in an era of reconciliation with the Democratic Republic of Vietnam as with all the peoples of Indochina. In pursuance of its traditional policy, the United States will contribute to healing the wounds of war and to postwar reconstruction of the Democratic Republic of Vietnam and throughout Indochina.

ARTICLE 22

The ending of the war, the restoration of peace in Vietnam and the strict implementation of this agreement will create conditions for establishing a new, equal and mutually beneficial relationship between the United States and the Democratic Republic of Vietnam on the basis of respect for each other's independence and sovereignty and noninterference in each other's internal affairs. At the same time this will insure stable peace in Vietnam and contribute to the preservation of lasting peace in Indochina and Southeast Asia.

Chapter IX
Other Provisions

ARTICLE 23

This agreement shall enter into force upon signature by plenipotentiary representatives of the parties participating in the Paris Conference on Vietnam. All the parties concerned shall strictly implement this agreement and its protocols.

Done in Paris this 27th day of January, 1973, in Vietnamese and English. The Vietnamese and English texts are official and equally authentic.

*For the Government of the
United States of America*
WILLIAM P. ROGERS
Secretary of State

*For the Government of the
Republic of Vietnam*
TRAN VAN LAM
Minister for Foreign Affairs

*For the Government of the
Democratic Republic of Vietnam*
NGUYEN DUY TRINH
Minister for Foreign Affairs

*For the Provisional Revolutionary
Government of the Republic of
South Vietnam*
NGUYEN THI BINH
Minister for Foreign Affairs

Two-Party Version
Agreement on Ending the War and Restoring Peace in Vietnam

The Government of the United States of America, with the concurrence of the Government of the Republic of Vietnam,

The Government of the Democratic Republic of Vietnam, with the concurrence of the Provisional Revolutionary Government of the Republic of South Vietnam,

With a view to ending the war and restoring peace in Vietnam on the basis of respect for the Vietnamese people's fundamental national rights and the South Vietnamese people's right to self-determination, and to contributing to the consolidation of peace in Asia and the world,

Have agreed on the following provisions and undertake to respect and to implement them:

[Text of agreement Chapters I–VIII same as above]

Chapter IX
Other Provisions

ARTICLE 23

The Paris agreement on Ending the War and Restoring Peace in Vietnam shall enter into force upon signature of this document by the Secretary of State of the Government of the United States of America and the Minister for Foreign Affairs of the Government of the Democratic Republic of Vietnam, and upon signature of a document in the same terms by the Secretary of State of the Government of the United States of America, the Minister for Foreign Affairs of the Government of the Republic of Vietnam, the Minister for Foreign Affairs of the Government of the Democratic Republic of Vietnam and the Minister for Foreign Affairs of the Provisional Revolutionary Government of the Republic of South Vietnam. The agreement and the protocols to it shall be strictly implemented by all the parties concerned.

Done in Paris this 27th day of January, 1973, in Vietnamese and English. The Vietnamese and English texts are official and equally authentic.

For the Government of the United States of America
WILLIAM P. ROGERS
Secretary of State

For the Government of the Democratic Republic of Vietnam
NGUYEN DUY TRINH
Minister for Foreign Affairs

PROTOCOL ON THE PRISONERS
Protocol to the Agreement on Ending the War and Restoring Peace in Vietnam Concerning the Return of Captured Military Personnel and Foreign Civilians and Captured and Detained Vietnamese Civilian Personnel

The parties participating in the Paris conference on Vietnam.

In implementation of Article 8 of the Agreement on Ending the War and Restoring Peace in Vietnam signed on this date providing for the return of captured military personnel and foreign civilians, and captured and detained Vietnamese civilian personnel.

Have agreed as follows:

The Return of Captured Military Personnel and Foreign Civilians

ARTICLE I

The parties signatory to the agreement shall return the captured military personnel of the parties mentioned in Article 8 (a) of the agreement as follows:

¶All captured military personnel of the United States and those of the other foreign countries mentioned in Article 3 (a) of the agreement shall be returned to United States authorities.

¶All captured Vietnamese military personnel, whether belonging to regular or irregular armed forces, shall be returned to the two South Vietnamese parties; they shall be returned to that South Vietnamese party under whose command they served.

ARTICLE 2

All captured civilians who are nationals of the United States or of any other foreign countries mentioned in Article 3 (a) of the agreement shall be returned to United States authorities. All other captured foreign civilians shall be returned to the authorities of their country of nationality by any one of the parties willing and able to do so.

ARTICLE 3

The parties shall today exchange complete lists of captured persons mentioned in Articles 1 and 2 of this protocol.

ARTICLE 4

(a) The return of all captured persons mentioned in Articles 1 and 2 of this protocol shall be completed within 60 days of the signing of the agreement at a rate no slower than the rate of withdrawal from South Vietnam of United States forces and those of the other foreign countries mentioned in Article 5 of the agreement.

(b) Persons who are seriously ill, wounded or maimed, old persons and women shall be returned first.

The remainder shall be returned either by returning all from one detention place after another or in order of their dates of capture, beginning with those who have been held the longest.

ARTICLE 5

The return and reception of the persons mentioned in Articles 1 and 2 of this protocol shall be carried out at places convenient to the concerned parties. Places of return shall be agreed upon by the Four-Party Joint Military Commission. The parties shall insure the safety of personnel engaged in the return and reception of those persons.

ARTICLE 6

Each party shall return all captured persons mentioned in Articles 1 and 2 of this protocol without delay and shall facilitate their return and reception. The detaining parties shall not deny or delay their return for any reason, including the fact that captured persons may, on any grounds, have been prosecuted or sentenced.

The Return of Captured and Detained Vietnamese Civilian Personnel

ARTICLE 7

(a) The question of the return of Vietnamese civilian personnel captured and detained in South Vietnam will be resolved by the two South Vietnamese parties on the basis of the principles of Article 21 (b) of the agreement on the Cessation of Hostilities in Vietnam of July 20, 1954, which reads as follows:

"The term 'civilian internees' is understood to mean all persons who, having in any way contributed to the political and armed struggle between the two parties, have been arrested for that reason and have been kept in detention by either party during the period of hostilities."

(b) The two South Vietnamese parties will do so in a spirit of national reconciliation and concord with a view to ending hatred and enmity in order to ease suffering and to reunite families. The two South Vietnamese parties will do their utmost to resolve this question within 90 days after the cease-fire comes into effect.

(c) Within 15 days after the cease-fire comes into effect, the two South Vietnamese parties shall exchange lists of the Vietnamese civilian personnel captured and detained by each party and lists of the places at which they are held.

Treatment of Captured Persons During Detention

ARTICLE 8

(a) All captured military personnel of the parties and captured foreign civilians of the parties shall be treated humanely at all times, and in accordance with international practice.

They shall be protected against all violence to life and person, in particular against murder in any form, mutilation, torture and cruel treatment, and outrages upon personal dignity. These persons shall not be forced to join the armed forces of the detaining party.

They shall be given adequate food, clothing, shelter and the medical attention required for their state of health. They shall be allowed to exchange postcards and letters with their families and receive parcels.

(b) All Vietnamese civilian personnel captured and detained in South Vietnam shall be treated humanely at all times, and in accordance with international practice.

They shall be protected against all violence to life and person, in particular against murder in any form, mutilation, torture and cruel treatment and outrages against personal dignity. The detaining parties shall not deny or delay their return for any reason including the fact that captured persons may, on any grounds, have been prosecuted or sentenced. These persons shall not be forced to join the armed forces of the detaining party.

They shall be given adequate food, clothing, shelter and the medical attention required for their state of health. They shall be allowed to exchange postcards and letters with their families and receive parcels.

ARTICLE 9

(a) To contribute to improving the living conditions of the captured military personnel of the parties and foreign civilians of the parties, the parties shall, within 15 days after the cease-fire comes into effect, agree upon the designation of two or more national Red Cross societies to visit all places where captured military personnel and foreign civilians are held.

(b) To contribute to improving the living conditions of the captured and detained Vietnamese civilian personnel, the two South Vietnamese parties shall, within 15 days after the cease-fire comes into effect, agree upon the designation of two or more national Red Cross societies to visit all places where the captured and detained Vietnamese civilian personnel are held.

With Regard to Dead and Missing Persons

ARTICLE 10

(a) The Four-Party Joint Military Commission shall insure joint action

by the parties in implementing Article 8 (b) of the agreement. When the Four-Party Joint Military Commission has ended its activities, a Four-Party Joint Military Team shall be maintained to carry on this task.

(b) With regard to Vietnamese civilian personnel dead or missing in South Vietnam, the two South Vietnamese parties shall help each other to obtain information about missing persons, determine the location and take care of the graves of the dead, in a spirit of national reconciliation and concord, in keeping with the people's aspirations.

Other Provisions

ARTICLE 11

(a) The Four-Party and Two-Party Joint Military Commissions will have the responsibility of determining immediately the modalities of implementing the provisions of this protocol consistent with their respective responsibilities under Articles 16 (a) and 17 (a) of the agreement. In case the Joint Military Commissions, when carrying out their tasks, cannot reach agreement on a matter pertaining to the return of captured personnel they shall refer to the international commission for its assistance.

(b) The Four-Party Joint Military Commission shall form, in addition to the teams established by the protocol concerning the cease-fire in South Vietnam and the Joint Military Commissions, a subcommission on captured persons and, as required, joint military teams on captured persons to assist the commission in its tasks.

(c) From the time the cease-fire comes into force to the time when the Two-Party Joint Military Commission becomes operational, the two South Vietnamese parties' delegations to the Four-Party Joint Military Commission shall form a provisional subcommission and provisional joint military teams to carry out its tasks concerning captured and detained Vietnamese civilian personnel.

(d) The Four-Party Joint Military Commission shall send joint military teams to observe the return of the persons mentioned in Articles 1 and 2 of this protocol at each place in Vietnam where such persons are being returned, and at the last detention places from which these persons will be taken to the places of return. The Two-Party Joint Military Commission shall send joint military teams to observe the return of Vietnamese civilian personnel captured and detained at each place in South Vietnam where such persons are being returned, and at the last detention places from which these persons will be taken to the places of return.

ARTICLE 12

In implementation of Articles 18 (b) and 18 (c) of the agreement, the International Commission of Control and Supervision shall have the responsibility to control and supervise the observance of Articles 1 through 7 of this protocol through observation of the return of captured military personnel, foreign civilians and captured and detained Vietnamese civilian personnel at each place in Vietnam where these persons are being returned, and at the last detention places from which these persons will be taken to the places of return, the examination of lists and the investigation of violations of the provisions of the abovementioned articles.

ARTICLE 13

Within five days after signature of this protocol, each party shall publish the text of the protocol and communicate it to all the captured persons covered by the protocol and being detained by that party.

ARTICLE 14

This protocol shall come into force upon signature by plenipotentiary representatives of all the parties participating in the Paris conference on Vietnam. It shall be strictly implemented by all the parties concerned.

Done in Paris this 27th day of January, 1973, in Vietnamese and English. The Vietnamese and English texts are official and equally authentic.

For the Government of the
United States of America
WILLIAM P. ROGERS
Secretary of State

For the Government of the
Republic of Vietnam
TRAN VAN LAM
Minister for Foreign Affairs

For the Government of the
Democratic Republic of Vietnam
NGUYEN DUY TRINH
Minister for Foreign Affairs

For the Provisional
Revolutionary Government of
the Republic of South Vietnam
NGUYEN THI BINH
Minister for Foreign Affairs

Two-Party Version
Protocol to the Agreement on Ending the War and Restoring Peace in Vietnam Concerning the Return of Captured Military Personnel and Foreign Civilians and Captured and Detained Vietnamese Civilian Personnel

The Government of the United States of America, with the concurrence of the Government of the Republic of Vietnam,

The Government of the Democratic Republic of Vietnam, with the concurrence of the Provisional Revolutionary Government of the Republic of South Vietnam,

In implementation of Article 8 of the Agreement on Ending the War and Restoring Peace in Vietnam signed on this date providing for the return of captured military personnel and foreign civilians, and captured and detained Vietnamese civilian personnel,

Have agreed as follows:

[Text of protocol Articles 1-13 same as above]

ARTICLE 14

The protocol to the Paris Agreement on Ending the War and Restoring Peace in Vietnam concerning the Return of Captured Military Personnel and Foreign Civilians and Captured and Detained Vietnamese Civilian Personnel shall enter into force upon signature of this document by the Secretary of State of the Government of the United States of America and the Minister for Foreign Affairs of the Government of the Democratic Republic of Vietnam, and upon signature of a document in the same terms by the Secretary of State of the Government of the United States of America, the Minister for Foreign Affairs of the Government of the Republic of Vietnam, the Minister for Foreign Affairs of the Government of the Democratic Republic of Vietnam and the Minister for Foreign Affairs of the Provisional Revolutionary Government of the Republic of South Vietnam. The protocol shall be strictly implemented by all the parties concerned.

Done in Paris this 27th day of January, 1973, in Vietnamese and English. The Vietnamese and English texts are official and equally authentic.

For the Government of the United States of America
WILLIAM P. ROGERS
Secretary of State

For the Government of the Democratic Republic of Vietnam
NGUYEN DUY TRINH
Minister for Foreign Affairs

PROTOCOL ON CONTROL COMMISSION
Protocol to the Agreement on Ending the War and Restoring Peace in Vietnam Concerning the International Commission of Control and Supervision

The parties participating in the Paris conference on Vietnam,

In implementation of Article 18 of the Agreement on Ending the War and Restoring Peace in Vietnam signed on this date providing for the formation of the International Commission of Control and Supervision,

Have agreed as follows:

ARTICLE I

The implementation of the agreement is the responsibility of the parties signatory to the agreement.

The functions of the international commission are to control and supervise the implementation of the provisions mentioned in Article 18 of the agreement. In carrying out these functions, the international commission shall:

(a) Follow the implementation of the above-mentioned provisions of the agreement through communication with the parties and on-the-spot observation at the places where this is required.

(b) Investigate violations of the

provisions which fall under the control and supervision of the commission.

(c) When necessary, cooperate with the Joint Military Commissions in deterring and detecting violations of the above-mentioned provisions.

ARTICLE 2

The international commission shall investigate violations of the provisions described in Article 18 of the agreement on the request of the Four-Party Joint Military Commission, or of the Two-Party Joint Military Commission or of any party, or, with respect to Article 9 (b) of the agreement on general elections, of the National Council of National Reconciliation and Concord, or in any case where the international commission has other adequate grounds for considering that there has been a violation of those provisions. It is understood that, in carrying out this task, the international commission shall function with the concerned parties' assistance and cooperation as required.

ARTICLE 3

(a) When the international commission finds that there is a serious violation in the implementation of the agreement or a threat to peace against which the commission can find no appropriate measure, the commission shall report this to the four parties to the agreement so that they can hold consultations to find a solution.

(b) In accordance with Article 18 (f) of the agreement, the international commission's reports shall be made with the unanimous agreement of the representatives of all the four members. In case no unanimity is reached, the commission shall forward the different views to the four parties in accordance with Article 18 (b) of the agreement, or to the

two South Vietnamese parties in accordance with Article 18 (c) of the agreement, but these shall not be considered as reports of the commission.

ARTICLE 4

(a) The headquarters of the international commission shall be at Saigon.

(b) There shall be seven regional teams located in the regions shown on the annexed map [not reprinted] and based at the following places:

REGIONS	PLACES
I	Hue
II	Danang
III	Pleiku
IV	Phan Thiet
V	Bien Hoa
VI	My Tho
VII	Can Tho

The international commission shall designate three teams for the region of Saigon-Gia Dinh.

(c) There shall be 26 teams operating in the areas shown on the annexed map and based at the following places in South Vietnam:

Region I
Quang Tri
Phu Bai

Region II
Hoi An
Tam Ky
Chu Lai

Region III
Kontum
Hau Bon
Phu Cat
Tuy An
Ninh Hoa
Ban Me Thuot

Region IV
Da Lat

Bao Loc
Phan Rang

Region V
An Loc
Xuan Loc
Ben Cat
Cu Chi
Tan An

Region VI
Moc Hoa
Giong Trom

Region VII
Tri Ton
Vinh Long
Vi Thanh
Khanh Hung
Quan Long

(d) There shall be 12 teams located as shown on the annexed map and based at the following places: Gio Linh (to cover the area south of the provisional military demarcation line)

Lao Bao	Vung Tau
Ben Het	Xa Mat
Duc Co	Bien Hoa Airfield
Chu Lai	Hong Ngu
Qui Nhon	Can Tho
Nha Trang	

(e) There shall be seven teams, six of which shall be available for assignment to the points of entry which are not listed in paragraph (d) above and which the two South Vietnamese parties choose as points for legitimate entry to South Vietnam for replacement of armaments, munitions and war material permitted by Article 7 of the agreement. Any team or teams not needed for the above-mentioned assignment shall be available for other tasks, in keeping with the commission's responsibility for control and supervision.

(f) There shall be seven teams to control and supervise the return of captured and detained personnel of the parties.

ARTICLE 5

(a) To carry out its task concerning the return of the captured military personnel and foreign civilians of the parties as stipulated by Article 8 (a) of the agreement, the international commission shall, during the time of such return, send one control and supervision team to each place in Vietnam where the captured persons are being returned, and to the last detention places from which these persons will be taken to the places of return.

(b) To carry out its tasks concerning the return of the Vietnamese civilian personnel captured and detained in South Vietnam mentioned in Article 8 (c) of the agreement, the international commission shall, during the time of such return, send one control and supervision team to each place in South Vietnam where the above-mentioned captured and detained persons are being returned, and to the last detention places from which these persons shall be taken to the places of return.

ARTICLE 6

To carry out its tasks regarding Article 9 (b) of the agreement on the free and democratic general elections in South Vietnam, the international commission shall organize additional teams when necessary. The international commission shall discuss this question in advance with the National Council of National Reconciliation and Concord. If additional teams are necessary for this purpose, they shall be formed 30 days before the general elections.

ARTICLE 7

The international commission shall continually keep under review its size, and shall reduce the number of its teams, its representatives or other personnel, or both, when those teams, representatives or personnel have accomplished the tasks assigned to them and are not required for other tasks. At the same time, the expenditures of the international commission shall be reduced correspondingly.

ARTICLE 8

Each member of the international commission shall make available at all times the following numbers of qualified personnel:

(a) One senior representative and 26 others for the headquarters staff.

(b) Five for each of the seven regional teams.

(c) Two for each of the other international control teams, except for the teams at Gio Linh and Vung Tau, each of which shall have three.

(d) One hundred sixteen for the purpose of providing support to the commission headquarters and its teams.

ARTICLE 9

(a) The international commission, and each of its teams, shall act as a single body comprising representatives of all four members.

(b) Each member has the responsibility to insure the presence of its representatives at all levels of the international commission. In case a representative is absent, the member concerned shall immediately designate a replacement.

ARTICLE 10

(a) The parties shall afford full cooperation, assistance and protection to the international commission.

(b) The parties shall at all times maintain regular and continuous liaison with the international commission. During the existence of the Four-Party Joint Military Commission, the delegations of the parties to that commission shall also perform liaison functions with the international commission. After the Four-Party Joint Military Commission has ended its activities, such liaison shall be maintained through the Two-Party Joint Military Commission, liaison missions or other adequate means.

(c) The international commission and the Joint Military Commissions shall closely cooperate with and assist each other in carrying out their respective functions.

(d) Wherever a team is stationed or operating, the concerned party shall designate a liaison officer to the team to cooperate with and assist it in carrying out without hindrance its task of control and supervision. When a team is carrying out an investigation, a liaison officer from each concerned party shall have the

opportunity to accompany it, provided the investigation is not thereby delayed.

(e) Each party shall give the international commission reasonable advance notice of all proposed actions concerning those provisions of the agreement that are to be controlled and supervised by the international commission.

(f) The international commission, including its teams, is allowed such movement for observation as is reasonably required for the proper exercise of its functions as stipulated in the agreement. In carrying out these functions, the international commission, including its teams, shall enjoy all necessary assistance and cooperation from the parties concerned.

ARTICLE 11

In supervising the holding of the free and democratic general elections described in Articles 9 (b) and 12 (b) of the agreement in accordance with modalities to be agreed upon between the National Council of National Reconciliation and Concord and the international commission, the latter shall receive full cooperation and assistance from the national council.

ARTICLE 12

The international commission and its personnel who have the nationality of a member state shall, while carrying out their tasks, enjoy privileges and immunities equivalent to those accorded diplomatic missions and diplomatic agents.

ARTICLE 13

The international commission may use the means of communication and transport necessary to perform its functions. Each South Vietnamese party shall make available for rent to the international commission appropriate office and accommodation facilities and shall assist it in obtaining such facilities. The international commission may receive from the parties, on mutually agreeable terms, the necessary means of communication and transport and may purchase from any source necessary equipment and services not obtained from the parties. The international commission shall possess these means.

ARTICLE 14

The expenses for the activities of the international commission shall be borne by the parties and the members of the international commission in accordance with the provisions of this article:

(a) Each member country of the international commission shall pay the salaries and allowances of its personnel.

(b) All other expenses incurred by the international commission shall be met from a fund to which each of the four parties shall contribute twenty-three per cent (23%) and to which each member of the international commission shall contribute two per cent (2%).

(c) Within 30 days of the date of entry into force of this protocol, each of the four parties shall provide the international commission with an initial sum equivalent to four million, five hundred thousand (4,500,000) French francs in convertible currency, which sum shall be credited against the amounts due from that party under the first budget.

(d) The international commission shall prepare its own budgets. After the international commission approves a budget, it shall transmit it to all parties signatory to the agreement for their approval. Only after the budgets have been approved by the four parties to the agreement shall they be obliged to make their contributions. However, in case the

parties to the agreement do not agree on a new budget, the international commission shall temporarily base its expenditures on the previous budget, except for the extraordinary, one-time expenditures for installation or for the acquisition of equipment, and the parties shall continue to make their contributions on that basis until a new budget is approved.

ARTICLE 15

(a) The headquarters shall be operational and in place within 24 hours after the cease-fire.

(b) The regional teams shall be operational and in place, and three teams for supervision and control of the return of the captured and detained personnel shall be operational and ready for dispatch within 48 hours after the cease-fire.

(c) Other teams shall be operational and in place within 15 to 30 days after the cease-fire.

ARTICLE 16

Meetings shall be convened at the call of the chairman. The international commission shall adopt other working procedures appropriate for the effective discharge of its functions and consistent with respect for the sovereignty of South Vietnam.

ARTICLE 17

The members of the international commission may accept the obligations of this protocol by sending notes of acceptance to the four parties signatory to the agreement. Should a member of the international commission decide to withdraw from the international commission, it may do so by giving three months' notice by means of notes to the four parties to the agreement, in which case those four parties shall consult among themselves for the purpose of agreeing upon a replacement member.

ARTICLE 18

This protocol shall enter into force upon signature by plenipotentiary representatives of all the parties participating in the Paris conference on Vietnam. It shall be strictly implemented by all the parties concerned.

Done in Paris this 27th day of January, 1973, in Vietnamese and English. The Vietnamese and English texts are official and equally authentic.

For the Government of the
United States of America
WILLIAM P. ROGERS
Secretary of State

For the Government of the
Republic of Vietnam
TRAN VAN LAM
Minister for Foreign Affairs

For the Government of the
Democratic Republic of Vietnam
NGUYEN DUY TRINH
Minister for Foreign Affairs

For the Provisional
Revolutionary Government of
the Republic of South Vietnam
NGUYEN THI BINH
Minister for Foreign Affairs

Two-Party Version
Protocol to the Agreement on Ending the War and Restoring Peace in Vietnam Concerning the International Commission of Control and Supervision

The Government of the United States of America, with the concurrence of the Government of the Republic of Vietnam,

The Government of the Democratic Republic of Vietnam, with the concurrence of the Provisional Revolutionary Government of the Republic of South Vietnam,

In implementation of Article 18 of the Agreement on Ending the War and Restoring Peace in Vietnam signed on this date providing for the formation of the International Commission of Control and Supervision,

Have agreed as follows:

[Text of protocol Articles 1–17 same as above]

ARTICLE 18

The Protocol to the Paris Agreement on Ending the War and Restoring Peace in Vietnam concerning the International Commission of Control and Supervision shall enter into force upon signature of this document by the Secretary of State of the Government of the United States of America and the Minister for Foreign Affairs of the Government of the Democratic Republic of Vietnam, and upon signature of a document in the same terms by the Secretary of State of the Government of the United States of America, the Minister for Foreign Affairs of the Government of the Republic of Vietnam, the Minister for Foreign Affairs of the Government of the Democratic Republic of Vietnam and the Minister for Foreign Affairs of the Provisional Revolutionary Government of the Republic of South Vietnam. The protocol shall be strictly implemented by all the parties concerned.

Done in Paris this 27th day of January, 1973, in Vietnamese and English. The Vietnamese and English texts are official and equally authentic.

For the Government of the
United States of America
WILLIAM P. ROGERS
Secretary of State

For the Government of the
Democratic Republic of Vietnam
NGUYEN DUY TRINH
Minister for Foreign Affairs

PROTOCOL ON THE CEASE-FIRE
Protocol to the Agreement on Ending the War and Restoring Peace in Vietnam Concerning the Cease-Fire in South Vietnam and the Joint Military Commissions

The parties participating in the Paris conference on Vietnam.

In implementation of the first paragraph of Article 2, Article 3, Article 5, Article 6, Article 16 and Article 17 of the Agreement on Ending the War and Restoring Peace in Vietnam signed on this date which provide for the cease-fire in South Vietnam and the establishment of a Four-Party Joint Military Commission and a Two-Party Joint Military Commission,

Have agreed as follows:

Cease-Fire in South Vietnam

ARTICLE I

The high commands of the parties in South Vietnam shall issue prompt and timely orders to all regular and irregular armed forces and the armed police under their command to completely end hostilities throughout South Vietnam, at the exact time stipulated in Article 2 of the Agreement and insure that these armed forces and armed police comply with these orders and respect the cease-fire.

ARTICLE 2

(a) As soon as the cease-fire comes into force and until regulations are issued by the Joint Military Commissions, all ground, river, sea and air combat forces of the parties in South Vietnam shall remain in place; that is, in order to insure a stable cease-fire, there shall be no major redeployments or movements that would extend each party's area of control or would result in contact between opposing armed forces and clashes which might take place.

(b) All regular and irregular armed forces and the armed police of the parties in South Vietnam shall observe the prohibition of the following acts:

(1) Armed patrol into areas controlled by opposing armed forces and flights by bomber and fighter aircraft of all types, except for unarmed flights for proficiency training and maintenance.

(2) Armed attacks against any person, either military or civilian, by any means whatsoever, including the use of small arms, mortars, artillery, bombing and strafing by airplanes and any other type of weapon or explosive device;

(3) All combat operations on the ground, on rivers, on the sea and in the air;

(4) All hostile acts, terrorism or reprisals; and

(5) All acts endangering lives or public or private property.

ARTICLE 3

(a) The above-mentioned prohibitions shall not hamper or restrict:

(1) Civilian supply, freedom of movement, freedom to work and freedom of the people to engage in trade, and civilian communication and transportation between and among all areas in South Vietnam.

(2) The use by each party in areas under its control of military support elements, such as engineer and transportation units, in repair and construction of public facilities and the transportation and supplying of the population.

(3) Normal military proficiency conducted by the parties in the areas under their respective control with due regard for public safety.

(b) The Joint Military Commissions shall immediately agree on corridors, routes and other regulations governing the movement of military transport aircraft, military transport vehicles and military transport vessels of all types of one party going through areas under the control of other parties.

ARTICLE 4

In order to avert conflict and insure normal conditions for those armed forces which are in direct contact, and pending regulation by the Joint Military Commissions, the commanders of the opposing armed forces at those places of direct contact shall meet as soon as the cease-fire comes into force with a view to reaching an agreement on temporary measures to avert conflict and to insure supply and medical care for these armed forces.

ARTICLE 5

(a) Within 15 days after the cease-fire comes into effect, each party shall do its utmost to complete the removal or deactivation of all demolition objects, minefields, traps, obstacles or other dangerous objects placed previously, so as not to hamper the population's movement and work, in the first place on waterways, roads and railroads in South Vietnam. Those mines which cannot be removed or deactivated within that time shall be clearly marked and must be removed or deactivated as soon as possible.

(b) Emplacement of mines is prohibited, except as a defensive measure around the edges of military installations in places where they do not hamper the population's movement and work, and movement on waterways, roads and railroads. Mines and other obstacles already in place at the edges of military installations may remain in place if they are in place where they do not hamper the population's movement and work, and movement on waterways, roads and railroads.

ARTICLE 6

Civilian police and civilian security personnel of the parties in South Vietnam, who are responsible for the maintenance of law and order, shall strictly respect the prohibitions set forth in Article 2 of this protocol. As required by their responsibilities, normally they shall be authorized to carry pistols, but when required by unusual circumstances, they shall be allowed to carry other small individual arms.

ARTICLE 7

(a) The entry into South Vietnam of replacement armaments, munitions and war material permitted under Article 7 of the agreement shall take place under the supervision and control of the Two-Party Joint Military Commission and of the International Commission of Control and Supervision and through such points of entry only as are designated by the two South Vietnamese parties. The two South Vietnamese parties shall agree on these points of entry within 15 days after the entry into force of the cease-fire. The two South Vietnamese parties may select as many as six points of entry which are not included in the list of places where teams of the International Commission of Control and Supervision are to be based contained in Article 4 (d) of the protocol concerning the international commission. At the same time, the two South Vietnamese parties may also select points of entry from the list of places set forth in Article 4 (d) of that protocol.

(b) Each of the designated points of entry shall be available only for that South Vietnamese party which is in control of that point. The two

South Vietnamese parties shall have an equal number of points of entry.

ARTICLE 8

(a) In implementation of Article 5 of the agreement, the United States and the other foreign countries referred to in Article 5 of the agreement shall take with them all their armaments, munitions and war material. Transfers of such items which would leave them in South Vietnam shall not be made subsequent to the entry into force of the agreement except for transfers of communications, transport and other non-combat material to the Four-Party Joint Military Commission or the International Commission of Control and Supervision.

(b) Within five days after the entry into force of the cease-fire, the United States shall inform the Four-Party Joint Military Commission and the International Commission of Control and Supervision of the general plans for timing of complete troop withdrawals which shall take place in four phases of 15 days each. It is anticipated that the numbers of troops withdrawn in each phase are not likely to be widely different, although it is not feasible to insure equal numbers. The approximate numbers to be withdrawn in each phase shall be given to the Four-Party Joint Military Commission and the International Commission of Control and Supervision sufficiently in advance of actual withdrawals so that they can properly carry out their tasks in relation thereto.

ARTICLE 9

(a) In implementation of Article 6 of the agreement, the United States and the other foreign countries referred to in that article shall dismantle and remove from South Vietnam or destroy all military bases in South Vietnam of the United States and of the other foreign countries referred to in that article, including weapons, mines and other military equipment at these bases, for the purpose of making them unusable for military purposes.

(b) The United States shall supply the Four-Party Joint Military Commission and the International Commission of Control and Supervision with necessary information on plans for base dismantlement so that those commissions can properly carry out their tasks in relation thereto.

The Joint Military Commissions

ARTICLE 10

(a) The implementation of the agreement is the responsibility of the parties signatory to the agreement.

The Four-Party Joint Military Commission has the task of insuring joint action by the parties in implementing the agreement by serving as a channel of communication among the parties, by drawing up plans and fixing the modalities to carry out, coordinate, follow and inspect the implementation of the provisions mentioned in Article 16 of the agreement, and by negotiating and settling all matters concerning the implementation of those provisions.

(b) The concrete tasks of the Four-Party Joint Military Commission are:

(1) To coordinate, follow and inspect the implementation of the above-mentioned provisions of the agreement by the four parties.

(2) To deter and detect violations, to deal with cases of violation, and to settle conflicts and matters of contention between the parties relating to the above-mentioned provisions.

(3) To dispatch without delay one or more joint teams, as required by

specific cases, to any part of South Vietnam, to investigate alleged violations of the agreement and to assist the parties in finding measures to prevent recurrence of similar cases.

(4) To engage in observation at the places where this is necessary in the exercise of its functions.

(5) To perform such additional tasks as it may, by unanimous decision, determine.

ARTICLE II

(a) There shall be a Central Joint Military Commission located in Saigon. Each party shall designate immediately a military delegation of 59 persons to represent it on the central commission. The senior officer designated by each party shall be a general officer, or equivalent.

(b) There shall be seven Regional Joint Military Commissions located in the regions shown on the annexed map [not reprinted] and based at the following places:

REGIONS	PLACES
I	Hue
II	Danang
III	Pleiku
IV	Phan Thiet
V	Bien Hoa
VI	My Tho
VII	Can Tho

Each party shall designate a military delegation of 16 persons to represent it on each regional commission. The senior officer designated by each party shall be an officer from the rank of lieutenant colonel to colonel, or equivalent.

(c) There shall be a joint military team operating in each of the areas shown on the annexed map and based at each of the following places in South Vietnam:

Region I
Quang Tri
Phu Bai

Region II
Hoi An
Tam Ky
Chu Lai

Region III
Kontum
Hau Bon
Phu Cat
Tuy An
Ninh Hoa
Ban Me Thuot

Region IV
Da Lat
Bao Loc
Phan Rang

Region V
An Loc

Xuan Loc
Ben Cat
Cu Chi
Tan An

Region VI
Moc Hoa
Giong Trom

Region VII
Tri Ton
Vinh Long
Vi Thanh
Khanh Hung
Quan Long

Each party shall provide four qualified persons for each joint military team. The senior person designated by each party shall be an officer from the rank of major to lieutenant colonel, or equivalent.

(d) The Regional Joint Military Commissions shall assist the Central Joint Military Commission in performing its tasks and shall supervise the operations of the joint military teams. The region of Saigon-Gia Dinh is placed under the responsibility of the central commission, which shall designate joint military teams to operate in this region.

(e) Each party shall be authorized to provide support and guard personnel for its delegations to the Central Joint Military Commission and Regional Joint Military Commissions, and for its members of the joint military teams. The total number of support and guard personnel for each party shall not exceed 550.

(f) The Central Joint Military Commission may establish such joint subcommissions, joint staffs and joint military teams as circumstances may require. The central commission shall determine the numbers of personnel required for any additional subcommissions, staff or teams it establishes, provided that each party shall designate one-fourth of the number of personnel required and that the total number of personnel for the Four-Party Joint Military Commission, to include its staffs, teams and support personnel, shall not exceed 3,300.

(g) The delegations of the two South Vietnamese parties may, by agreement, establish provisional subcommissions and joint military teams to carry out the tasks specifically assigned to them by Article 17 in the agreement. With respect to Article 7 of the agreement, the two South Vietnamese parties' delegations to the Four-Party Joint Military Commission shall establish joint military teams at the points of entry into South Vietnam used for replacement of armaments, munitions and war material which are designated in accordance with Article 7 of this protocol. From the time the cease-fire comes into force to the time when the Two-Party Joint Military Commission becomes operational, the two South Vietnamese parties' delegations to the Four-Party Joint Military Commission shall form a provisional subcommission and provisional joint military teams to carry out its tasks concerning captured and detained Vietnamese civilian personnel. Where necessary for the above purposes, the two South Vietnamese parties may agree to assign personnel additional to those assigned to the two South Vietnamese delegations to the Four-Party Joint Military Commission.

Joint Military Commission shall meet in Saigon so as to reach an agreement as soon as possible on organization and operation of the Two-Party Joint Commission, as well as the measures and organization aimed at enforcing the cease-fire and preserving peace in South Vietnam.

(b) From the time the cease-fire comes into force to the time when the Two-Party Joint Military Commission becomes operational, the two South Vietnamese parties' delegations to the Four-Party Joint Military Commission at all levels shall simultaneously assume the tasks of the Two-Party Joint Military Commission at all levels, in addition to their functions as delegations to the Four-Party Joint Military Commission.

(c) If, at the time the Four-Party Joint Military Commission ceases its operation in accordance with Article 16 of the agreement, agreement has not been reached on organization of the Two-Party Joint Military Commission, the delegations of the two South Vietnamese parties serving with the Four-Party Joint Military Commission at all levels shall continue temporarily to work together as a provisional two-party joint military commission and to assume the tasks of the Two-Party Joint Military Commission at all levels until the Two-Party Joint Military Commission becomes operational.

ARTICLE 12

(a) In accordance with Article 17 of the agreement, which stipulates that the two South Vietnamese parties shall immediately designate their respective representatives to form the Two-Party Joint Military Commission, 24 hours after the cease-fire comes into force, the two designated South Vietnamese parties' delegations to the Two-Party

ARTICLE 13

In application of the principle of unanimity, the Joint Military Commissions shall have no chairmen, and meetings shall be convened at the request of any representative. The Joint Military Commissions shall adopt working procedures appropriate for the effective discharge of their functions and responsibilities.

ARTICLE 14

The Joint Military Commissions and the International Commission of Control and Supervision shall closely cooperate with and assist each other in carrying out their respective functions. Each Joint Military Commission shall inform the international commission about the implementation of those provisions of the agreement for which that Joint Military Commission has responsibility and which are within the competence of the international commission. Each Joint Military Commission may request the international commission to carry out specific observation activities.

ARTICLE 15

The Central Four-Party Joint Military Commission shall begin operating 24 hours after the cease-fire comes into force. The Regional Four-Party Joint Military Commissions shall begin operating 48 hours after the cease-fire comes into force. The joint military teams based at the places listed in Article 11 (c) of this protocol shall begin operating no later than 15 days after the cease-fire comes into force. The delegations of the two South Vietnamese parties shall simultaneously begin to assume the tasks of the Two-Party Joint Military Commission as provided in Article 12 of this protocol.

ARTICLE 16

(a) The parties shall provide full protection and all necessary assistance and cooperation to the Joint Military Commissions at all levels, in the discharge of their tasks.

(b) The Joint Military Commissions and their personnel, while carrying out their tasks, shall enjoy privileges and immunities equivalent to those accorded diplomatic missions and diplomatic agents.

(c) The personnel of the Joint Military Commissions may carry pistols and wear special insignia decided upon by each Central Joint Military Commission. The personnel of each party while guarding commission installations or equipment may be authorized to carry other individual small arms, as determined by each Central Joint Military Commission.

ARTICLE 17

(a) The delegation of each party to the Four-Party Joint Military Commission and the Two-Party Joint Military Commission shall have its own offices, communication, logistics and transportation means, including aircraft when necessary.

(b) Each party, in its areas of control, shall provide appropriate office and accommodation facilities to the Four-Party Joint Military Commission and the Two-Party Joint Military Commission at all levels.

(c) The parties shall endeavor to provide to the Four-Party Joint Military Commission and the Two-Party Joint Military Commission, by means of loan, lease or gift, the common means of operation, including equipment for communication, supply and transport, including aircraft when necessary. The Joint Military Commissions may purchase from any source necessary facilities, equipment and services which are not supplied by the parties. The Joint Military Commissions shall possess and use these facilities and this equipment.

(d) The facilities and the equipment for common use mentioned above shall be returned to the parties when the Joint Military Commissions have ended their activities.

ARTICLE 18

The common expenses of the Four-Party Joint Military Commission shall be borne equally by the four parties, and the common expenses of the Two-Party Joint Military Commission in South Vietnam shall be borne equally by these two parties.

ARTICLE 19

This protocol shall enter into force upon signature by plenipotentiary representatives of all the parties participating in the Paris conference on Vietnam. It shall be strictly implemented by all the parties concerned.

Done in Paris this 27th day of January, 1973, in Vietnamese and English. The Vietnamese and English texts are official and equally authentic.

For the Government of the United States of America
WILLIAM P. ROGERS
Secretary of State

For the Government of the Republic of Vietnam
TRAN VAN LAM
Minister for Foreign Affairs

For the Government of the Democratic Republic of Vietnam
NGUYEN DUY TRINH
Minister for Foreign Affairs

For the Provisional Revolutionary Government of the Republic of South Vietnam
NGUYEN THI BINH
Minister for Foreign Affairs

Two-Party Version

Protocol to the Agreement on Ending the War and Restoring Peace in Vietnam Concerning the Cease-Fire in South Vietnam and the Joint Military Commissions

The Government of the United States of America, with the concurrence of the Government of the Republic of Vietnam,

The Government of the Democratic Republic of Vietnam, with the concurrence of the Provisional Revolutionary Government of the Republic of South Vietnam,

In implementation of the first paragraph of Article 2, Article 3, Article 5, Article 6, Article 16 and Article 17 of the Agreement on Ending the War and Restoring Peace in Vietnam signed on this date which provide for the cease-fire in South Vietnam and the establishment of a Four-Party Joint Military Commission and a Two-Party Joint Military Commission,

Have agreed as follows:
[Text of protocol Articles 1–18 same as above]

ARTICLE 19

The protocol to the Paris Agreement on Ending the War and Restoring Peace in Vietnam Concerning the Cease-fire in South Vietnam and the Joint Military Commissions shall enter into force upon signature of this document by the Secretary of State of the Government of the United States of America and the Minister for Foreign Affairs of the Government of the Democratic Republic of Vietnam, and upon signature of a document in the same terms by the Secretary of State of the Government of the United States of America, the Minister for Foreign Affairs of the Government of the Republic of Vietnam, the Minister for Foreign Affairs of the Democratic Republic of Vietnam and the Minister for Foreign Affairs of the Provisional Revolutionary Government of the Republic of South Vietnam. The protocol shall be strictly implemented by all the parties concerned.

Done in Paris this 27th day of January, 1973, in Vietnamese and

English. The Vietnamese and English texts are official and equally authentic.

For the Government of the
United States of America
WILLIAM P. ROGERS
Secretary of State

For the Government of the
Democratic Republic of Vietnam
NGUYEN DUY TRINH
Minister for Foreign Affairs

PROTOCOL ON CLEARING SEA MINES
Protocol to the Agreement on Ending the War and Restoring Peace in Vietnam Concerning the Removal, Permanent Deactivation or Destruction of Mines in the Territorial Waters, Ports, Harbors and Waterways of the Democratic Republic of Vietnam

The Government of the United States of America,

The Government of the Democratic Republic of Vietnam,

In implementation of the second paragraph of Article 2 of the Agreement on Ending the War and Restoring Peace in Vietnam signed on this date,

Have agreed as follows:

ARTICLE I

The United States shall clear all mines it has placed in the territorial waters, ports, harbors and waterways of the Democratic Republic of Vietnam. This mine-clearing operation shall be accomplished by rendering the mines harmless through removal, permanent deactivation or destruction.

ARTICLE 2

With a view to insuring lasting safety for the movement of people and watercraft and the protection of important installations, mines shall, on the request of the Democratic Republic of Vietnam, be removed or destroyed in the indicated area; and whenever their removal or destruction is impossible, mines shall be permanently deactivated and their emplacement clearly marked.

ARTICLE 3

The mine-clearing operation shall begin at twenty-four hundred (2400) hours G.M.T. on January 27, 1973. The representatives of the two parties shall consult immediately on relevant factors and agree upon the earliest possible target date for the completion of the work.

ARTICLE 4

The mine-clearing operation shall be conducted in accordance with priorities and timing agreed upon by the two parties. For this purpose, representatives of the two parties shall meet at an early date to reach agreement on a program and a plan of implementation. To this end:

(a) The United States shall provide its plan for mine-clearing operations, including maps of the minefields and information concerning the types, numbers and properties of the mines.

(b) The Democratic Republic of Vietnam shall provide all available maps and hydrographic charts and indicate the mined places and all other potential hazards to the mine-clearing operations that the Democratic Republic of Vietnam is aware of.

(c) The two parties shall agree on the timing of implementation of each segment of the plan and provide timely notice to the public at least 48 hours in advance of the beginning of mine-clearing operations for that segment.

ARTICLE 5

The United States shall be responsible for the mine clearance on inland waterways of the Democratic Republic of Vietnam. The Democratic Republic of Vietnam shall, to the full extent of its capabilities, actively participate in the mine clearance with the means of surveying, removal and destruction, and technical advice supplied by the United States.

ARTICLE 6

With a view to insuring the safe movement of people and watercraft on waterways and at sea, the United States shall in the mine-clearing process supply timely information about the progress of mine clearing in each area, and about the remaining mines to be destroyed. The United States shall issue a communiqué when the operations have been concluded.

ARTICLE 7

In conducting mine-clearing operations, the U.S. personnel engaged in these operations shall respect the sovereignty of the Democratic Republic of Vietnam and shall engage in no activities inconsistent with the Agreement on Ending the War and Restoring Peace in Viet-

nam and this protocol. The U.S. personnel engaged in the mine-clearing operations shall be immune from the jurisdiction of the Democratic Republic of Vietnam for the duration of the mine-clearing operations.

The Democratic Republic of Vietnam shall insure the safety of the U.S. personnel for the duration of their mine-clearing activities on the territory of the Democratic Republic of Vietnam, and shall provide this personnel with all possible assistance and the means needed in the Democratic Republic of Vietnam that have been agreed upon by the two parties.

ARTICLE 8

This protocol to the Paris Agreement on Ending the War and Restoring Peace in Vietnam shall enter into force upon signature by the Secretary of State of the Government of the United States of America and the Minister for Foreign Affairs of the Government of the Democratic Republic of Vietnam. It shall be strictly implemented by the two parties.

Done in Paris this 27th day of January, 1973, in Vietnamese and English. The Vietnamese and English texts are official and equally authentic.

For the Government of the
United States of America
WILLIAM P. ROGERS
Secretary of State

For the Government of the
Democratic Republic of Vietnam
NGUYEN DUY TRINH
Minister for Foreign Affairs

Appendix D: Text of the Final Declaration of the 1973 International Guarantee Conference on Vietnam

Reprinted from *Department of State Bulletin* 68, No. 1761 (26 March 1973): 345-47.

ACT
OF THE INTERNATIONAL CONFERENCE ON VIET-NAM

The Government of the United States of America;

The Government of the French Republic;

The Provisional Revolutionary Government of the Republic of South Viet-Nam;

The Government of the Hungarian People's Republic;

The Government of the Republic of Indonesia;

The Government of the Polish People's Republic;

The Government of the Democratic Republic of Viet-Nam;

The Government of the United Kingdom of Great Britain and Northern Ireland;

The Government of the Republic of Viet-Nam;

The Government of the Union of Soviet Socialist Republics;

The Government of Canada; and

The Government of the People's Republic of China;

In the presence of the Secretary-General of the United Nations;

With a view to acknowledging the signed Agreements; guaranteeing the ending of the war, the maintenance of peace in Viet-Nam, the respect of the Vietnamese people's fundamental national rights, and the South Vietnamese people's right to self-determination; and contributing to and guaranteeing peace in Indochina;

Have agreed on the following provisions, and undertake to respect and implement them;

ARTICLE I

The Parties to this Act solemnly acknowledge, express their approval of, and support the Paris Agreement on Ending the War and Restoring Peace in Viet-Nam signed in Paris on January 27, 1973, and the four Protocols to the Agreement signed on the same date (hereinafter referred to respectively as the Agreement and the Protocols).

ARTICLE 2

The Agreement responds to the aspirations and fundamental national rights of the Vietnamese people, *i.e.,* the independence, sovereignty, unity, and territorial integrity of Viet-Nam, to the right of the South Vietnamese people to self-determination, and to the earnest desire for peace shared by all countries in the world. The Agreement constitutes a major contribution to peace, self-determination, national independence, and the improvement of relations among countries. The Agreement and the Protocols should be strictly respected and scrupulously implemented.

ARTICLE 3

The Parties to this Act solemnly acknowledge the commitments by the parties to the Agreement and the Protocols to strictly respect and scrupulously implement the Agreement and the Protocols.

ARTICLE 4

The Parties to this Act solemnly recognize and strictly respect the fundamental national rights of the Vietnamese people, *i.e.*, the independence, sovereignty, unity, and territorial integrity of Viet-Nam, as well as the right of the South Vietnamese people to self-determination. The Parties to this Act shall strictly respect the Agreement and the Protocols by refraining from any action at variance with their provisions.

ARTICLE 5

For the sake of a durable peace in Viet-Nam, the Parties to this Act call on all countries to strictly respect the fundamental national rights of the Vietnamese people, *i.e.*, the independence, sovereignty, unity, and territorial integrity of Viet-Nam and the right of the South Vietnamese people to self-determination and to strictly respect the Agreement and the Protocols by refraining from any action at variance with their provisions.

ARTICLE 6

(a) The four parties to the Agreement or the two South Vietnamese parties may, either individually or through joint action, inform the other Parties to this Act about the implementation of the Agreement and the Protocols. Since the reports and views submitted by the International Commission of Control and Supervision concerning the control and supervision of the implementation of those provisions of the Agreement and the Protocols which are within the tasks of the Commission will be sent to either the four parties signatory to the Agreement or to the two South Vietnamese parties, those parties shall be responsible, either individually or through joint action, for forwarding them promptly to the other Parties to this Act.

(b) The four parties to the Agreement or the two South Vietnamese parties shall also, either individually or through joint action, forward this information and these reports and views to the other participant in the International Conference on Viet-Nam for his information.

ARTICLE 7

(a) In the event of a violation of the Agreement or the Protocols which threatens the peace, the independence, sovereignty, unity, or territorial integrity of Viet-Nam, or the right of the South Vietnamese people to self-determination, the parties signatory to the Agreement and the Protocols shall, either individually or jointly, consult with the other Parties to this Act with a view to determining necessary remedial measures.

(b) The International Conference on Viet-Nam shall be reconvened upon a joint request by the Government of the United States of America and the Government of the Democratic Republic of Viet-Nam on behalf of the parties signatory to the Agreement or upon a request by six or more of the Parties to this Act.

ARTICLE 8

With a view to contributing to and guaranteeing peace in Indochina, the Parties to this Act acknowledge the commitment of the parties to the Agreement to respect the independence, sovereignty, unity, territorial integrity, and neutrality of Cambodia and Laos as stipulated in the Agreement, agree also to respect them and to refrain from any action at variance with them, and call on other countries to do the same.

ARTICLE 9

This Act shall enter into force upon signature by plenipotentiary representatives of all twelve Parties and shall be strictly implemented by all the Parties. Signature of this Act does not constitute recognition of any Party in any case in which it has not previously been accorded.

DONE in twelve copies in Paris this second day of March, One Thousand Nine Hundred and Seventy-Three, in English, French, Russian, Vietnamese, and Chinese. All texts are equally authentic.

For the Government of the United States of America
The Secretary of State WILLIAM P. ROGERS

For the Government of the French Republic
The Minister MAURICE SCHUMANN *for Foreign Affairs*

For the Provisional Revolutionary Government of the Republic of South Viet-Nam
The Minister for NGUYEN THI BINH *Foreign Affairs*

For the Government of the Hungarian People's Republic
The Minister for JANOS PETER *Foreign Affairs*

For the Government of the Republic of Indonesia
The Minister for ADAM MALIK *Foreign Affairs*

For the Government of the Polish People's Republic
The Minister STEFAN OLSZOWSKI *for Foreign Affairs*

For the Government of the Democratic Republic of Viet-Nam
The Minister NGUYEN DUY TRINH *for Foreign Affairs*

For the Government of the United Kingdom of Great Britain and Northern Ireland
The Secretary ALEC DOUGLAS-*of State for Foreign* HOME *and Commonwealth Affairs*

For the Government of the Republic of Viet-Nam
The Minister for TRAN VAN LAM *Foreign Affairs*

For the Government of the Union of Soviet Socialist Republics
The Minister ANDREI A. GROMYKO *for Foreign Affairs*

For the Government of Canada
The Secretary of MITCHELL SHARP *State for External Affairs*

For the Government of the People's Republic of China
The Minister for CHI PENG-FEI *Foreign Affairs*

Notes

NIXON AND THE WORLD, *Alan M. Jones, Jr.*

1. See Goldwater's statements during the 1964 presidential campaign, as in John H. Kessel, *The Goldwater Coalition* (Indianapolis: Bobbs-Merrill, 1968), chap. 7, and in Theodore H. White, *The Making of the President, 1964* (New York: Atheneum, 1966), chaps. 9–11.

2. Senator McGovern's acceptance speech at the 1972 Democratic convention, quoted in *Congressional Quarterly Weekly Report* 30, no. 29 (15 July 1972): 1782.

3. Cf. the 1972 Democratic platform's section "VIII Foreign Policy," reprinted in ibid., pp. 1742–45. See especially Senator McGovern's Cleveland speech on foreign policy, reprinted in *New York Times*, 6 October 1972, p. 26.

4. "The Next Four Years," editorial in *New York Times*, 28 September 1972, p. 44; John V. Lindsay, "For a New National Balance," *Foreign Affairs* 50, no. 1 (October 1971): 1–14; Kingman Brewster, Jr., "Reflections on Our National Purpose," *Foreign Affairs* 50, no. 3 (April 1972): 399–415.

5. "Toward a Full Generation of Peace," 1972 Republican platform, reprinted in *Congressional Quarterly Weekly Report* 30, no. 35 (26 August 1972): 2152.

6. President Nixon's acceptance speech at the 1972 Republican convention, ibid., p. 2175.

7. "Foreign Policy," 1972 Democratic platform, reprinted in *Congressional Quarterly Weekly Report* 30, no. 29 (15 July 1972): 1742–45, quoted at 1742.

8. For an objection to Executive dominance of foreign policy on Vietnam, see J. William Fulbright, *The Arrogance of Power* (New York: Vintage, 1966), chap. 2. For the question of Executive vs. congressional powers in the May 1970 Cambodian crisis, see the selection from Senate debates in Eugene P. Dvorin, ed., *The Senate's War Powers* (Chicago: Markham, 1971).

9. U.S. Senate, Committee on Foreign Relations, *Foreign Assistance Act of 1972 Hearings*, 17–19 April 1972 (Washington, D.C.: Government Printing Office, 1972), pp. 16–17.

10. "Senate 'National Commitments' Resolution," *Global Defense* (Washington, D.C.: Congressional Quarterly Service, 1969), p. 79.

11. "Senate Passes Bill Defining Constitutional War Powers," *Congressional Quarterly Weekly Report* 30, no. 16 (15 April 1972): 827–30; the quotations are from the version of S. 2956 (*War Powers Act of 1971*) reprinted in Foreword to U.S. Senate, Committee on Foreign Relations, *War Powers Legislation Hearings*, March–October 1971 (Washington, D.C.: Government Printing Office, 1972), p. iii.

12. "War Powers," *Congressional Quarterly Weekly Report* 30, no. 34 (19 August 1972): 2102.

13. "Part I: The National Security Council System," *United States Foreign Policy for the 1970s: A New Strategy for Peace* (Washington, D.C.: Government Printing Office, 1970). This quotation is taken from the text as reprinted in *New York Times*, 19 February 1970, p. 20. This source is hereinafter referred to as the 1970 Nixon report.

14. "Part VI: The National Security Council System," *United States Foreign Policy for the 1970s: Building for Peace* (Washington, D.C.: Government Printing Office, 1971), pp. 225–32; "Part VII: The Policy-Making Process: The NSC System," *United States Foreign Policy for the 1970s: The Emerging Structure of Peace* (Washington, D.C.: Government Printing Office, 1972), pp. 208–12. These sources are hereinafter referred to as the 1971 and 1972 Nixon reports, respectively.

15. 1970 Nixon report (*New York Times* reprint), p. 20.

16. Various National Security Council memoranda of December 1971 were obtained by columnist Jack Anderson and reprinted in *New York Times*, 6 January 1972, pp. 16, 17, and 15 January 1972, p. 6.

17. McGovern acceptance speech at the 1972 Democratic convention, reprinted in *Congressional Quarterly Weekly Report* 30, no. 29 (15 July 1972): 1781.

18. Democratic platform, "Section VIII. Foreign Policy," reprinted in ibid., p. 1742.

19. The troop reduction to 27,000 was reported in *New York Times*, 30 August 1972, p. 1.

20. Nixon acceptance speech at the 1972 Republican convention, reprinted in *Congressional Quarterly Weekly Report* 30, no. 35 (26 August 1972): 2175.

21. Nixon address to the nation, 26 April 1972, reprinted in *Department of State Bulletin* 66, no. 1716 (15 May 1972): 685.

22. Cf. George McGovern, *A Time of War, a Time of Peace* (New York: Vintage, 1968), pp. 5–22 ("New Perspectives on American Security").

23. McGovern's experiences as Food-for-Peace director are related in George S. McGovern, *War Against Want* (New York: Walker, 1964).

24. The text of McGovern's speech is in *Congressional Record* 118, no. 5 (24 January 1972): S357–63, quoted at S358.

25. Ibid., p. S357.

26. 1972 Republican platform, reprinted in *Congressional Quarterly Weekly Report* 30, no. 35 (26 August 1972): 2154.

27. Nixon acceptance speech at the 1972 Republican convention, reprinted in ibid., p. 2176.

28. 1972 Nixon report, p. 155.

29. The 1972 Democratic platform is reprinted in *Congressional Quarterly Weekly Report* 30, no. 29 (15 July 1972): 1726–49, with the section on foreign policy at 1742–45; the 1972 Republican platform is reprinted in *Congressional Quarterly Weekly Report* 30, no. 35 (26 August 1972): 2151–71, with the sections on foreign policy and defense at 2151–56.

30. Senator McGovern's remarks as reported in *New York Times*, 4 November 1972, pp. 1, 14.

31. *New York Times*, 8 November 1972, p. 1, and 9 November 1972, p. 1.

32. Excerpts from the text of the interview with Senator McGovern are in *New York Times*, 14 November 1972, p. 36.

33. *New York Times*, 9 November 1972, p. 24.

34. *New York Times*, 12 November 1972, sect. 4, p. 1.

35. The text of the statement based on the interview with President Nixon by a reporter for the *Washington Star-News* is reprinted in *New York Times*, 10 November 1972, p. 20.

36. See note 32.

37. Gallup poll results as reported in *New York Times*, 26 November 1972, p. 18.

38. See note 35.

39. Podgorny telegram to Nixon as quoted in *New York Times*, 9 November 1972, p. 32.

40. John F. Kennedy, Inaugural Address, 20 January 1961, reprinted in Daniel J. Boorstin, ed., *An American Primer* (New York: New American Library, 1968), p. 939.

41. J. William Fulbright, *Old Myths and New Realities* (New York: Vintage, 1964), pp. 43–44.

42. The Fulbright-Cooper exchange is cited in U.S. House, Committee on the Armed Services, *U.S.–Vietnam Relations, 1945–1967, Study Prepared by the Defense Department* IV, c. 2(b) ("Military Pressures Against North Vietnam, July–October 1964") (Washington, D.C.: Government Printing Office, 1971), p. 14.

43. Fulbright, *Arrogance of Power*, p. 20. For a further elaboration of Senator Fulbright's altered views, see J. William Fulbright, *The Crippled Giant* (New York: Vintage, 1972).

44. Robert A. Taft, speech before the Senate, 5 January 1951, cited in David Rees, *Korea: The Limited War* (Baltimore, Md.: Penquin, 1970), p. 196.

45. Richard J. Barnet, "The Security of Empire," in Robert W. Gregg and Charles W. Kegley, Jr., eds., *After Vietnam* (New York: Anchor, 1971), p. 35.

46. John Foster Dulles, "Policy for Security and Peace," *Foreign Affairs* 32, no. 3 (April 1954): 358.

47. 1971 Nixon report, pp. 13–14.

48. Dulles, "Policy for Security and Peace," p. 359.

49. 1970 Nixon report (*New York Times* reprint), p. 20.
50. Dulles, "Policy for Security and Peace," pp. 355-58.
51. 1971 Nixon report, p. 14.
52. 1970 Nixon report (*New York Times* reprint), p. 20.
53. 1971 Nixon report, p. 26.
54. 1972 Nixon report, p. 46.
55. Ibid., p. 52.
56. Ibid., p. 58.
57. Ibid., p. 28.
58. 1970 Nixon report (*New York Times* reprint), p. 19.
59. 1971 Nixon report, p. 156.
60. 1972 Nixon report, p. 16.
61. Ibid., p. 25.
62. 1971 Nixon report, p. 130.
63. 1970 Nixon report, p. 27.
64. Ibid., p. 20.
65. Ibid.
66. Ibid.
67. 1972 Nixon report, p. 35.
68. *Department of State Bulletin* 66, no. 1708 (20 March 1972): 428.
69. "The Mutual Defense Treaty Between the United States and the Republic of China and Related Documents," reprinted in Ruhl J. Bartlett, ed., *The Record of American Diplomacy* (4th ed.; New York: Knopf, 1964), pp. 794-95.
70. See, for example, the accounts of the role of the treaty in the 1954-55 crisis as related in Dwight D. Eisenhower, *The White House Years: Mandate for Change, 1953-1956* (New York: Doubleday, 1963), chap. 19, and Sherman Adams, *Firsthand Report* (New York: Harper, 1961), chap. 7.
71. Excerpts from Ambassador Bush's speech as reprinted in *New York Times*, 19 October 1971, p. 12.
72. Ibid.
73. "Test of Joint Communiqué, issued at Shanghai, February 27," reprinted in *Department of State Bulletin* 66, no. 1708 (20 March 1972): 438.
74. 1972 Nixon report, p. 35.
75. Ibid.
76. "Text of Joint Communiqué." *Department of State Bulletin*, 66, 1708, 20 March 1972, p. 438.
77. Nixon acceptance speech at 1972 Republican convention, reprinted in *Congressional Quarterly Weekly Report* 30, no. 35 (26 August 1972): 2176.
78. See particularly "Part I. 1971: The Watershed Year—An Overview," 1972 Nixon report, pp. 2-13.
79. *New York Times*, 21 February 1972, pp. 1, 12.
80. A. Doak Barnett, *A New U.S. Policy Toward China* (Washington, D.C.: Brookings, 1972), pp. xiii-xv; *New York Times*, 16 July 1971, pp. 1, 3.
81. See various statements made during the China trip by Nixon and Chou, as well as Kissinger's news conference and the text of the joint

communiqué, as reprinted in *Department of State Bulletin* 66 (20 March 1972): 419–40.

82. *New York Times*, 23 February 1973, pp. 1, 14, 15; 13 March 1973, pp. 1, 10.

83. *New York Times*, 6 July 1972, pp. 1, 14.

84. The text of the U.S.–Japanese treaty restoring Okinawa to Japanese sovereignty is in *New York Times*, 18 June 1971, p. 10.

85. Excerpts from the speech by Ambassador Kiichi Aichi before the UN General Assembly, 19 October 1971, reprinted in *New York Times*, 20 October 1971, p. 12. Mr. Aichi's speech included the statement: ". . . it is beyond doubt that the expulsion or exclusion of the Republic of [Nationalist] China from the United Nations against her will will be a matter of great injustice . . . inconsistent with the purposes and principles of the Charter of the United Nations."

86. Excerpts from Tanaka television statement, July 1971, cited in *New York Times*, 6 July 1972, p. 14.

87. As reported in *New York Times*, 26 September 1972, pp. 1, 3.

88. For reports on the results and reactions to the Japanese Diet elections, see *New York Times*, 11 December 1972, pp. 1, 11. See also *Los Angeles Times*, 11 December 1972, pt. 1, p. 7; 12 December 1972, pt. 1, p. 7; and 15 December 1972, pt. 7, pp. 1, 3.

89. For a discussion of the background of North-South hostility in Korea and the prospects for change, see Morton Abramowitz, "Moving the Glacier: The Two Koreas and the Powers," *Adelphi Papers*, no. 80 (September 1971): passim.

90. As reported in *New York Times*, 5 July 1972, p. 16.

91. The text of the joint Korean communiqué is reprinted in ibid.

92. As reported in *New York Times*, 15 September 1972, p. 9; 10 April 1973, p. 9.

93. For an overview of Australian foreign policy during and after World War II, see Alan Watt, *The Evolution of Australian Foreign Policy, 1938–1965* (Cambridge: Cambridge University Press, 1967).

94. See, especially for Australian developments, *New York Times*, 3 December 1972, pp. 1, 29; 5 December 1972, p. 11; 6 December 1972, pp. 1, 3; 11 December 1972, p. 24; 12 December 1972, p. 13; 14 March 1973, p. 14; 1 April 1973, pp. 14, 15.

95. For reports that Nixon stressed the importance on maintaining Japanese ties to Taiwan in his talks with Tanaka, see *New York Times*, 3 September 1972, p. 16; and *Los Angeles Times*, 4 September 1972, p. 13. Despite the end of formal relations between Taiwan and Japan, trade between the two countries continued under nominally private auspices, actively assisted by both governments. Indeed, in the months immediately following the diplomatic break, Taiwan-Japanese trade expanded to an all-time high. Prospects for continued trade seemed favorable. See *New York Times*, 26 February 1973, p. 6; 28 March 1973, p. 17.

96. For Washington's surprise at the Korean unity talks, see the report

cited in note 90. Chinese–Japanese contacts in arranging the Tanaka visit were conducted semipublicly, so that Washington was aware for some time that such a trip was probable. Chou En-lai's invitation to Tanaka was reported in *Los Angeles Times*, 18 July 1972, p. 4; and Tanaka's acceptance in *Los Angeles Times*, 12 August 1972, p. 5. There is no indication that the United States was consulted beforehand. Indeed, the latter press report begins: "Foreign Minister Masyoshi Ohira Friday told two Peking officials that Prime Minister Kakuei Tanaka would accept an inviation to visit China and then, in effect, told the United States not to worry about it." The Tanaka trip was more fully discussed with Washington during the Nixon-Tanaka talks at the end of August 1972, as indicated in the reports cited in note 95.

97. "Text of Joint Statement," *Department of State Bulletin* 67, no. 1735 (25 September 1972): 331.

98. See note 95.

99. "Remarks by Prime Minister Tanaka" on his arrival in Honolulu, 30 August 1972, reprinted in *Department of State Bulletin* 67, no. 1735 (25 September 1972): p. 331.

100. "Agreements Signed at Moscow During President Nixon's Visit," *Department of State Bulletin* 66, no. 1722 (26 June 1972): 918–27.

101. For summary treatments of Soviet ABM developments, see Thomas W. Wolfe, *Soviet Power and Europe, 1945–1970* (Baltimore, Md.: Johns Hopkins, 1970), pp. 186–88, 437–41.

102. The text of the McNamara speech of September 18, 1967, is reprinted in *Bulletin of the Atomic Scientists* (December 1967): 26–31. For accounts of the processes leading up to this decision, see Morton H. Halperin, "The Decision to Deploy the ABM: Bureaucratic and Domestic Politics in the Johnson Administration," *World Politics* 25, no. 1 (October 1972): 62–95, and Edward R. Jayne II, *The ABM Decision* (Cambridge, Mass.: MIT Center for International Studies, May 1969).

103. The critical Senate vote (51–50) is reported in *New York Times*, 7 August 1969, pp. 1, 22. The House passed the ABM by a substantial margin (219–105), as reported in *New York Times*, 3 October 1969, p. 1. The 1970 Senate votes on ABM were also close, 52–47 on 12 August, and 53–45 on 19 August, both defeating amendments to kill the ABM program. See *New York Times*, 13 August 1970, p. 1, and 20 August 1970, pp. 1, 10. The 1970 House vote was overwhelmingly pro-ABM (308–57), see *New York Times*, 12 June 1970, p. 5.

104. Wolfe, *Soviet Power and Europe*, pp. 431–41; Thomas W. Wolfe, "Soviet Approaches to SALT," *Problems of Communism* (September–October 1970): 1–10; Lawrence T. Caldwell, "Soviet Attitudes to SALT," *Adelphi Papers*, no. 75 (February 1971): passim.

105. For a statement of the case against any ABM, see Abram Chayes and Jerome B. Wiesner, eds., *ABM* (New York: Signet, 1969); for the Nixon Administration's plans for the U.S. system (before the ABM treaty), see *Annual Defense Department Report, FY 1973* (Washington, D.C.: Government Printing Office, 1972), pp. 76–78.

106. The text of the ABM treaty is reprinted in *Department of State Bulletin* 66, no. 1722 (26 June 1972): 918–20; the Nixon speech to Congress is reprinted as "The Moscow Summit: New Opportunities in U.S.-Soviet Relations," ibid., pp. 855–59, cited at p. 856.

107. Articles IX, XII, and XV of the ABM treaty, reprinted in ibid., pp. 919–20.

108. As reported in *Los Angeles Times*, 4 August 1972, pp. 1, 16.

109. The interim agreement and its protocol are reprinted in *Department of State Bulletin* 66, no. 1722 (26 June 1972): 920–31.

110. "Strategic Policy and Forces," the 1972 Nixon report, pp. 156–62.

111. These figures for Soviet submarine strength are those contained in the "Protocol to the Interim Agreement," reprinted in *Department of State Bulletin*, pp. 920–31; for an elaboration of administration perceptions of the Soviet missile force, see *Annual Defense Department Report, FY 1973*, pp. 36–44.

112. As reported in *Los Angeles Times*, 16 August 1972, pp. 1, 28.

113. Ibid.; and *New York Times*, 16 August 1972, p. 3. Senator Fulbright denied this charge, as reported in *Los Angeles Times*, 17 August 1972, p. 29.

114. "Protocol to the Interim Agreement," reprinted in *Department of State Bulletin*, pp. 920–31.

115. For a discussion of the effects of technological advances on strategic forces, see Benjamin S. Lambeth, "Deterrence in the MIRV Era," *World Politics* 24, no. 2 (January 1972): 221–42.

116. The Jackson amendment is printed in the *Congressional Record*, 7 August 1972, p. S12946. This was a revised version of the original Jackson amendment, which had called for immediate abrogation of the ABM treaty if Soviet actions threatened the survivability of American strategic nuclear forces. In this form, the amendment was unacceptable to the White House, and Senator Jackson altered its wording to gain administration and Senate Republican support. See the reports in *New York Times*, 3 August 1972, pp. 1, 9, and 8 August 1972, pp. 1, 6.

117. *Congressional Record*, 7 August 1972, p. S12946.

118. As reported in *Los Angeles Times*, 15 September 1972, pp. 1, 11.

119. As reported in *New York Times*, 19 August 1972, pp. 1, 8; *Los Angeles Times*, 19 August 1972, pp. 1, 5.

120. As reported in *New York Times*, 1 October 1972, p. 18, and 4 October 1972, p. 3.

121. The texts of the statement of basic principles and joint communiqué are reprinted in *Department of State Bulletin* 66, no. 1722 (26 June 1972): 898–902.

122. As reported in *New York Times*, 20 June 1972, p. 7.

123. As reported in *New York Times*, 1 September 1972, p. 2; *Los Angeles Times*, 11 September 1972, p. 20.

124. See the reports in *New York Times*, 25 July 1972, pp. 1, 10, and 4 September 1972, p. 3.

125. The Soviet treaties with Egypt and India are reprinted in *Survival* 13, no. 10 (October 1971): 349–53. Soviet diplomatic aid to India was made

clear in its vetoes of UN Security Council resolutions calling for an Indo-Pakistani cease-fire, as reported in *New York Times*, 5 December 1971, pp. 1, 16, and 13 December 1971, pp. 1, 17.

126. As reported in *New York Times*, 7 December 1971, pp. 1, 16, 9 December 1971, pp. 1, 18.

127. *Department of State Bulletin*, 66, 1722 (26 June 1972) pp. 901-2.

128. The December 1971 Warsaw Pact and NATO communiqués are reprinted in *Survival* 14, no. 2 (March/April 1972): 78-82.

129. 1972 Nixon report, p. 25.

130. For negotiations during the Johnson administration, see Chester L. Cooper, *The Lost Crusade* (New York: Dodd, Mead, 1970), chaps. 13-15; and Lyndon Baines Johnson, *The Vantage Point* (New York: Holt, Rinehart, Winston, 1971), chaps. 11, 17, and 21, and appendix A, pp. 578-601.

131. See Rowland Evans, Jr., and Robert D. Novak, *Nixon in the White House* (New York: Vintage, 1972), pp. 75-81. See also presidential adviser Kissinger's focus on negotiations in his last published article before entering the Nixon administration: Henry A. Kissinger, "The Viet Nam Negotiations," *Foreign Affairs* 47, no. 2 (January 1969): 211-34.

132. President Nixon's 25 January 1972 report on the secret Vietnam talks is reprinted as "Indochina: An Equitable Proposal for Peace," in *Department of State Bulletin* 66, no. 1703 (14 February 1972): pp. 181-84. See also the text of the formal U.S. proposal and of Kissinger's news conference in ibid., pp. 185-98.

133. As reported in *New York Times*, 28 January 1972, pp. 1, 8, and 4 February 1972, pp. 1, 4.

134. *New York Times*, 24 March 1972, pp. 1, 5.

135. *New York Times*, 30 March 1972.

136. President Nixon's announcement of the decision to resume sustained American bombing of North Vietnam was made in an address on 26 April 1972, reprinted as "A Report on the Military Situation in Viet-Nam and the Role of the United States," *Department of State Bulletin* 66, no. 1716 (15 May 1972): 683-86.

137. *Los Angeles Times*, 27 April 1972, p. 22.

138. *New York Times*, 26 April 1972, pp. 1, 8.

139. *Los Angeles Times*, 5 May 1972, pp. 1, 7.

140. President Nixon's announcement of the decision to mine North Vietnamese ports and his new peace offer, 8 May 1972, reprinted as "Denying Hanoi the Means to Continue Aggression," *Department of State Bulletin* 66, no. 1718 (29 May 1972): pp. 747-50. See also Kissinger's news conference on the decision, reprinted in ibid., pp. 752-60, and Defense Secretary Laird's new conference, ibid., pp. 761-71.

141. *Los Angeles Times*, 30 June 1972, pp. 1, 11.

142. The North Vietnamese version of the secret talks through October 1972 and the nature of the draft agreement is reprinted in *New York Times*, 27 October 1972, p. 19. The American version of the talks described by Kissinger is reprinted as "Dr. Kissinger Discusses Status of Negotiations

Toward Viet-Nam Peace," in *Department of State Bulletin* 67, no. 1742 (13 November 1972): 549–58.

143. *New York Times*, 30 October 1972, pp. 1, 5, and p. 2.

144. *New York Times*, 28 October 1972, pp. 1, 10.

145. *New York Times*, 13 November 1972, pp. 1, 2, and 16 November 1972, p. 16.

146. See the text of Kissinger's news conference as reprinted in *New York Times*, 17 December 1972, p. 34.

147. Ibid.

148. *New York Times*, 31 December 1972, pp. 1, 3.

149. Excerpts from Brezhnev's address of 21 December 1972 are reprinted in *New York Times*, 22 December 1972, p. 10.

150. Report of an interview with Chou En-lai in *New York Times*, 29 December 1972, p. 4.

151. *New York Times*, 24 December 1972, sect. 4, p. 1, and 30 December 1972, pp. 1, 4.

152. *New York Times*, 30 December 1972, pp. 1, 6.

153. *New York Times*, 3 January 1973, p. 1, and 5 January 1973, pp. 1, 13. See also *Los Angeles Times*, 3 January 1973, p. 7, and 5 January 1973, pp. 1, 8.

154. Senator Fulbright's speech of 4 January 1973, as quoted in *Los Angeles Times*, 5 January 1973, p. 8.

155. *Los Angeles Times*, 15 January 1973, p. 1.

156. *Los Angeles Times*, 16 January 1973, pp. 1, 11.

157. Excerpts from remarks by Le Duc Tho as reprinted in *New York Times*, 7 January 1973, p. 4.

158. See reports of the Paris meetings in *New York Times*, 9 January 1973, pp. 1, 12, and 11 January 1973, pp. 1, 12; and *Los Angeles Times*, 9 January 1973, pp. 1, 10; 10 January 1973, p. 8; 11 January 1973, pp. 1, 6; 13 January 1973, pp. 1, 5.

159. *Los Angeles Times*, 16 January 1973, pp. 1, 12, 13, 14.

160. Texts of the Paris cease-fire accords are reprinted in the Appendix, together with a description of their contents by presidential adviser Henry Kissinger.

161. *New York Times*, 4 April 1973, pp. 1, 2, 7; 7 April 1973, p. 1; 30 March 1973, p. 17.

162. *New York Times*, 24 February 1973, pp. 1, 6; *Los Angeles Times*, 6 April 1973, pp. 1, 6.

163. *New York Times*, 30 March 1973, pp. 1, 16.

164. Transcript of President Nixon's news conference as reprinted in *New York Times*, 13 November 1971, p. 10.

165. "A Report on the Military Situation in Viet-Nam and the Role of the United States," *Department of State Bulletin* 66, no. 1716 (15 May 1972): 685.

166. 1970 Nixon report (*New York Times* reprint), p. 20.

167. 1972 Nixon report, p. 25.

168. Henry A. Kissinger, *A World Restored* (New York: Grosset & Dunlap, 1964 [1957]), p. 1.

169. Cited in ibid., p. 13.

170. Ibid., chap. 16.

171. 1972 Nixon report, p. 149.

172. 1970 Nixon report (*New York Times* reprint), p. 23.

173. On the background of U.S. relations with India and Pakistan, see William J. Barnds, *India, Pakistan, and the Great Powers* (New York: Praeger, 1972), chap. 5. For divergent views of the 1966 wheat crisis, see the account of President Johnson in Johnson, *Vantage Point*, chap. 10; and that of the American ambassador to India at the time in Chester Bowles, *Promises to Keep* (New York: Harper & Row, 1971), chap. 41.

174. Barnds, *India, Pakistan, and the Great Powers*, chaps. 8–9.

175. Ibid., pp. 233–36.

176. Ibid., pp. 237–47.

177. See the defense of administration policy in the December 1971 Indo-Pakistani war, contained in the section "South Asia" of the 1972 Nixon report, pp. 141–52.

178. 1971 Nixon report, pp. 127–28.

179. Ibid., p. 128.

CHINA AND THE NEW OPEN DOOR, *John B. Starr*

1. The text of the "Open Door Notes," written in 1899 by John Hay, secretary of state in the McKinley administration, is found in V. W. Rockhill, ed., *Treaties and Conventions with or Concerning China and Korea* (Washington, D.C.: Government Printing Office, 1904), pp. 185–200.

2. The wartime discussions in which Roosevelt pressed for China's being regarded as a major power in the postwar settlement in East Asia are treated in detail by Herbert Feis in his book *The China Tangle* (Princeton, N.J.: Princeton University Press, 1953).

3. A detailed treatment of the foreign relations of traditional China is found in Hosea Morse Ballou, *The International Relations of the Chinese Empire*, 3 vols. (London: Longmans Green, 1910–18). The conflict of rival systems of international relations involved in China's contact with Western nations in the nineteenth century is the subject of C. Y. Hsü's book *China's Entry into the Family of Nations: The Diplomatic Phase, 1856–1880* (Cambridge, Mass.: Harvard University Press, 1960).

4. The origins of Chinese nationalism are well treated in Chow Tse-tsung's book *The May Fourth Movement* (Cambridge, Mass.: Harvard University Press, 1965). The May Fourth Movement (1919) was a student protest against Japanese imperialist demands upon China and the failure of the Versailles Peace Conference, then in session, to support China in resisting these demands. It soon acquired the support of merchants in China's coastal cities and it is generally treated as the first movement in

China which can be called "nationalistic" in the modern sense of that term.

5. See Chün-tu Hsüeh, ed., *Revolutionary Leaders of Modern China* (New York: Oxford University Press, 1971).

6. See Maurice Meisner's biographical study of one of the founders of the Chinese Communist Party: *Li Ta-chao and the Origins of Chinese Marxism* (Cambridge, Mass.: Harvard University Press, 1967).

7. The argument is that of Joseph R. Levenson, from his book *Confucian China and Its Modern Fate* (Berkeley: University of California Press, 1966), 1:134–45.

8. The volution of these lines in Marxist-Leninist thought is discussed in the introduction to Stuart R. Schram and Hélène Carrère d'Encausse's collection of documents on the subject, entitled *Marxism and Asia* (Hammondsworth, England: Penguin, 1969).

9. Biographical studies of Mao are numerous. The best among them are Stuart R. Schram, *Mao Tse-tung* (Baltimore, Md.: Penguin, 1966); and Jerome Ch'en, *Mao and the Chinese Revolution* (New York: Oxford University Press, 1964).

10. Mao's principal political philosophical works are contained in the book *Four Essays on Philosophy* (Peking: Foreign Languages Press, 1966). It contains two articles written in 1937, "On Contradiction" and "On Practice"; the 1957 speech, "On the Correct Handling of Contradictions Among the People"; and a brief excerpt dated 1963 and entitled "Where Do Correct Ideas Come From?"

11. Mao Tse-tung, *Selected Works* (Peking: Foreign Languages Press, 1966), 1:13.

12. Ibid., 4:411–24.

13. A strong statement of the case against Stalin for his advice to the Chinese is found in Conrad Brandt's book *Stalin's Failure in China* (Cambridge, Mass.: Harvard University Press, 1958). The least sympathetic appraisal of Stalin's advice to the Chinese revolution to appear in the Chinese press is an article written by Mao and others shortly after the XXth Congress of the Communist party of the Soviet Union began the move toward "deStalinization" in the USSR in 1956. (*On the Historical Experience of the Dictatorship of the Proletariat* [Peking: Foreign Languages Press, 1956].) Soon thereafter the official Chinese view of Stalin was much more guarded in its criticism. See "On the Question of Stalin," one of the Communist party of China's nine comments on the "Open Letter" of the Central Committee of the Soviet Party of 14 July 1963 (*Peking Review* 6, no. 38 [20 September 1963]: 8 15]).

14. The text of Mao's speech is found in Center for International Affairs and East Asian Research Center, Harvard University, *Communist China, 1956–1958: Policy Documents with Analysis* (Cambridge, Mass.: Harvard University, 1960).

15. The course of this deterioration is well treated by Donald Zagoria, *The Sino-Soviet Conflict, 1956–61* (Princeton, N.J.: Princeton University Press, 1962); and by William E. Griffith, *The Sino-Soviet Rift* (Cambridge, Mass.:

MIT Press, 1964) and *Sino-Soviet Relations, 1964–65* (Cambridge, Mass.: MIT Press, 1967).

16. See John Gittings, *Survey of the Sino-Soviet Dispute: Commentary and Extracts from the Recent Polemics, 1963–67* (New York: Oxford University Press, 1968).

17. His arguments are summarized in the article "On Khrushchev's Phoney Communism and Its Historical Lessons for the World," written in 1964. It is translated and reprinted in A. Doak Barnett, *China After Mao* (Princeton, N.J.: Princeton University Press, 1967).

18. See Dennis Doolin, *Territorial Claims in the Sino-Soviet Conflict: Documents and Analysis* (Stanford, Calif.: Hoover Institution, 1965).

19. Mao's comments on Khrushchev are found in his interview with Edgar Snow in 1965 ("Interview with Mao," *New Republic*, 27 February 1965, pp. 17–23).

20. His view of Mao is contained in the book *Khrushchev Remembers*, trans. Strobe Talbott (Boston: Little, Brown, 1970).

21. The metaphor was advanced by Lin Piao in an article in which he compared the world revolution to the Chinese Revolution. The article, entitled "Long Live the Victory of the People's War," is reprinted in Barnett, *China After Mao*.

22. See, for example, George T. Yu, "Dragon in the Bush: Peking's Presence in Africa," *Asian Survey* 8, no. 12 (December 1968), 1018–26; and Bruce Larkin, *China and Africa, 1949–1970* (Berkeley: University of California, 1971); and, for a more general treatment, see J. D. Simmonds, *China's World: The Foreign Policy of a Developing State* (New York: Columbia University Press, 1971).

23. The clearest treatment of the meaning of Peking's "support" for wars of national liberation is found in Peter Van Ness's book *Revolution and Chinese Foreign Policy* (Berkeley: University of California Press, 1970) in which he studies in detail the treatment in the Chinese press of national liberation movements in Latin America. Other specific cases are treated by Daniel D. Lovelace, *China and 'People's War' in Thailand, 1964–1969* (Berkeley: University of California, Center for Chinese Studies, 1971); and by Jay Tao, "Mao's World Outlook: Vietnam and the Revolution in China," *Asian Survey* 8, no. 5 (May 1968): 416–32.

24. A case study is found in Charles Neuhauser, *Third World Politics: China and the Afro-Asian People's Solidarity Organization, 1957–67* (Cambridge, Mass.: Harvard University Press, 1969).

25. An especially clear statement of this new view is found in the Chinese article commemorating the centenary of Lenin's birth in 1970: "Leninism or Social Imperialism?" *Peking Review* 13, no. 17 (24 April 1970): 5–15.

26. Barbara Tuchman has described the period in her book *Stilwell and the American Experience in China* (New York: Macmillan, 1971). Two other Americans have written recently of their impressions of the Chinese Communists during this period: see John S. Service, *The Amerasia Papers:*

Some Problems of U.S.–China Relations (Berkeley: University of California: Center for Chinese Studies, 1971); and David Barrett, *The Dixie Mission: U.S. Army Observer Group in Yenan* (Berkeley: University of California Center for Chinese Studies, 1970).

27. Barbara Tuchman, "If Mao Had Come to Washington: An Essay in Alternatives," *Foreign Affairs* 51, no. 1 (October 1972): 44–64.

28. Sino-American relations during the Korean war are treated at length by Allen Whiting in *China Crosses the Yalu: The Decision to Enter the Korean War* (New York: Macmillan, 1966). A very different assessment of the events leading up to a major rupture in U.S. relations with China during the Korean war is found in I. F. Stone, *The Hidden History of the Korean War* (New York: Monthly Review Press, 1969).

29. A detailed treatment of the course of Sino-American relations in the post-Liberation period is found in Roderick MacFarquhar, *Sino-American Relations, 1949–1971* (New York: Praeger, 1972).

30. See Union Research Institute, *The Case of P'eng Teh-huai, 1959–1968* (Hong Kong: Union Research Institute, 1968).

31. See Franz Schurmann, "What Is Happening in China?" *New York Review of Books* 7, no. 6 (20 October 1966): 18–25.

32. The relationship between the three is discussed in Donald Zagoria, *Vietnam Triangle: Moscow, Peking, Hanoi* (New York: Pegasus, 1967).

33. Melvin Gurtov, "The Foreign Ministry and Foreign Affairs During the Cultural Revolution," *China Quarterly* 40 (October–December 1969): 65–102.

MOSCOW'S OPTIONS IN A CHANGING WORLD,
Vernon V. Aspaturian

1. *Rinascita* (Rome), 4 August 1967.

2. For a discussion of the broad implications of the Brezhnev Doctrine, see Vernon V. Aspaturian, *Process and Power in Soviet Foreign Policy* (Boston: Little, Brown, 1971).

3. For further elaboration see Vernon V. Aspaturian, "Soviet Aims in East Europe," *Current History* (Philadelphia), October 1970.

4. Full texts of the treaties with Egypt and India can be found, respectively, in *Pravda* (Moscow), 28 May 1971, and *Izvestia* (Moscow), 10 August 1971. The chief distinction between the two treaties is that the Egyptian treaty contains provisions relating to "cooperation in the military field." Article 8 reads: "Such cooperation will provide, in particular, for assistance in the training of UAR military personnel and in mastering the armaments and equipment delivered to the United Arab Republic for the purpose of increasing its capability for eliminating the consequences of aggression, as well as for increasing its ability to withstand aggression in general." There is no counterpart to this article in the treaty with India. Otherwise, the two treaties share the following significant provisions: Each

party pledges not to enter or participate in military alliances directed against the other, or to allow its territory to be used militarily by another party attacking the other; each pledges to refrain from giving assistance to a third party involved in armed conflict with the other; in the event of attack or threat of attack upon one of the parties, mutual consultations are provided for to deal with it; and finally, each side pledges not to make commitments to third states incompatible with the treaty and declares that no existing commitments to third parties are incompatible with the treaty. Significantly, however, the treaty with India covers secret as well as open commitments to third parties, reaffirms India's "policy of nonalignment," and also includes the specific phrase "will not make any commitments that may be militarily detrimental to the other side," whereas none of these provisos is in the treaty with the UAR.

The most recent of the three treaties, that with Iraq (full text published in *Pravda*, 10 April 1972), embodies some noteworthy variations from the treaty with Egypt. Article 2 of the Egyptian treaty defines the UAR as a state "which has set as its goal the socialist reconstruction of society," whereas socialism is not mentioned in the Iraqi treaty; on the other hand, Article 4 of the latter pledges "a steadfast struggle against imperialism and Zionism," whereas Zionism is not mentioned in the UAR treaty. The most notable difference, however, is in the military provisions, which are more precise and elaborate in the Egyptian treaty than in the treaty with Iraq. In contrast to the detailed provisions of Article 8 of the UAR treaty, already quoted above, Article 9 of the Iraqi treaty merely states that both parties "will continue to develop cooperation in strengthening their defense capabilities."

5. See, for the most recent data, *The Military Balance, 1971–1972* (London, Institute for Strategic Studies, 1971); and for a trenchant analysis, Walter D. Jacobs, "Soviet Strategic Effectiveness," *Journal of International Affairs* 26, no. 1 (1972): 60–72.

6. While the Soviet leadership shows an awareness of this new state of affairs, Soviet military writers continue to stress the expansion of U.S. strategic capabilities. For a recent example, see Col. V. Kharich, "The Strategic Arms Race in the USA: Reliance on Nuclear Might," *Krasnaia zvezda* (Moscow), 16 July 1971.

7. For example, in what might be considered a cautionary warning that a policy based on achieving Soviet superiority might simply refuel the arms race and backfire, Georgi Arbatov, director of the Soviet Academy of Sciences' Institute of the U.S.A. points out that during "the very alarming experience of the previous decade, the 1960's . . . the USA's strategic arsenal increased by 10 to 12 times. An aggressive war against the Vietnamese people was started. Israel launched aggression against the Arab states. . . . And in 1962, as a result of the Carribbean crisis, the USA and the USSR found themselves rather close to the brink of war. . . . If the 1970's are merely a repetition of the 1960's . . . peace may be seriously jeopardized." "A Step in the Interests of Peace," *SShA—Ekonomika, Politika, Ideologiia* (Moscow), November 1971, p. 56.

8. *Pravda*, 7 April 1971.

9. The conflicting views of these opposed interest groupings have found frequent expression in Soviet writings. For example, an exponent of the consumptionist viewpoint, commending Soviet efforts to lower international tensions and check the arms race, wrote in 1969 that "experience has proven that only under conditions of a relaxation of tensions is it possible to concentrate a maximum of resources for accomplishing plans for the building of communism" (K. P. Ivanov, *Leninskie osnovy vneshnei politiki SSSR* [Leninist Fundamentals of the Foreign Policy of the USSR], Moscow, 1969, p. 50). On the other hand, a military spokesman, writing in the official organ of the Soviet Defense Ministry, paraphrased Lenin in an effort to imply that no ceiling should be placed on military spending. "Everyone will agree," he wrote, "that an army that does not train itself to master all arms, all means and methods of warfare that the enemy possesses, *or may possess*, is behaving in an unwise or even criminal manner." A. Lagovsky, "The State's Economy and Its Military Might." *Krasnaia zvezda*, 25 September 1969.

10. See H. S. Dinerstein, *War and the Soviet Union* (New York: Praeger, 1959).

11. See Andrei Sakharov, *Progress, Coexistence and Intellectual Freedom* (New York: W. W. Norton, 1968).

12. "The Soviet Military-Industrial Complex—Does It Exist?," *Journal of International Affairs*, no. 1 (1972): See also Vernon V. Aspaturian, "Foreign Policy Perspectives in the Sixties," in A. Dallin and T. Larson, eds., *Soviet Politics Since Khrushchev* (Englewood Cliffs, N.J.: Prentice-Hall, 1968); "Soviet Foreign Policy at the Crossroads," *International Organization*, no. 3 (1969); and "Internal Politics and Foreign Policy in the Soviet System," in R. Barry Farrell, ed., *Approaches to Comparative and International Politics* (Evanston, Ill., Northwestern University Press, 1966) 212-87.

13. G. A. Arbatov, "American Foreign Policy on the Threshold of the 1970's," in *SShA—Ekonomika, Politika, Ideologiia*, January 1970, as translated in *Soviet Law and Government* 9,1 (Summer 1970): 3-27.

14. Ibid., p. 10.

15. See Richard M. Nixon, "Asia After Viet Nam," *Foreign Affairs*, 46,1 (October 1967): 111-25.

16. Arbatov, "American Foreign Policy on the Threshold," p. 17.

17. "American Imperialism and New World Realities," *Pravda*, 4 May 1971.

18. Ibid.

19. "A Step in the Interests of Peace," *SShA—Ekonomika, Politika, Ideologiia*, November 1971, p. 55.

20. Ibid., p. 56.

21. *New York Times*, 23 May 1972 (emphasis added).

22. "A Step in the Interests of Peace," p. 56.

23. Ibid., p. 57.

24. Ibid.

25. A. Lagovsky, "The State's Economy and Its Military Might,"

Krasnaia zvezda, 25 May 1969 (emphasis added). See also Thomas W. Wolfe, *Soviet Interests in SALT; Political, Economic, Bureaucratic and Strategic Contributions and Impediments to Arms Control*, Rand Paper P-4702, Santa Monica, Calif., Rand, 1971; and Uri Ra'anan, "The Changing American-Soviet Strategic Balance: Some Political Implications" (Memorandum prepared for the US Senate Committee on Government Operations, 92nd Congress, 2nd sess. [Washington, D.C., Government Printing Office, 1972]).

26. For a detailed discussion of these matters, see the author's "Soviet Aims in East Europe," *Current History* 59, no. 350 (October 1970): 206–11.

27. I. Aleksandrov, "Slogans and Deeds of the Chinese Leadership," *Pravda*, 4 September 1971.

28. These Soviet perceptions were undoubtedly reinforced by a Chinese attack on both the Soviet Union and the United States during President Nixon's visit to Moscow, when the central Chinese party organ *Jen-min Jih-pao* (People's Daily) let loose with a blast condemning both powers as the "archcriminals" of the modern world who "are colluding and at the same time contending with each other" for the purpose of dividing the world into spheres of influence. The paper assured its readers that "despite the baring of their fangs and showing of their claws today, the US and Soviet overlords are very weak by nature and nothing but paper tigers," and predicted that both would be swept "into the garbage heap of history." See *New York Times*, 22 May 1972.

29. G. Kadymov, "Class Betrayal is the Essence of the Maoists' 'Superpower Domination' Thesis," *Krasnaia zvezda*, 14 December 1971.

30. Ibid.

31. *Pravda*, 2 September 1964.

32. Thus, one Soviet commentator petulantly notes that Chinese rhetoric about the "two superpowers" is merely a smokescreen behind which "the Peking leaders are trying to create an independent ideological and political center (a 'third force') . . . [and] they hope that, relying on this center, they can turn China into a global power and make up for its military and economic potential, which is insufficient for the purpose." Kadymov, "Class Betrayal."

33. The distinction between "nuclear powers" and "global powers" has been clearly though implicitly drawn in Soviet commentaries. E.g., see the commentary on the Soviet-proposed conference of the five nuclear powers, in *Pravda*, 30 July 1971.

U.S. FOREIGN POLICY TOWARD EASTERN EUROPE,
A. J. Groth

1. See Robert Littell, ed., *The Czech Black Book* (New York: Avon, 1969); Harry Schwartz, *Prague's 700 Days: The Struggle for Democracy in Czechoslovakia* (New York: Praeger, 1969); A. J. Groth, *Eastern Europe After Czechoslovakia* (New York: FPA, 1969); Philip Windsor and Adam Roberts, *Czechoslovakia*

1968: Reform, Repression and Resistance (New York: Columbia University Press, 1969); and Robin A. Remington, ed., *Winter in Prague* (Cambridge, Mass.: MIT, 1969).

2. See Robin A. Remington, "Czechoslovakia and the Warsaw Pact," *East European Quarterly* 3, no. 3 (September 1969): 315–36, and Robert L. Pflatzgraff, Jr., "The Czechoslovak Crisis and The Future of the Atlantic Alliance," *Orbis* 13, no. 1 (Spring 1969): 210–22.

3. Richard F. Staar, *The Communist Regime in Eastern Europe* (rev. ed.; Stanford, Calif.: Hoover Institution, 1971), p. 225.

4. See Wolfgang Klaiber, "East European Relations With the West," in *The Changing Face of Communism in Eastern Europe*, ed. Peter A. Toma (Tucson, Ariz.: University of Arizona Press, 1970), pp. 313–36.

5. See Hermann Gross, "East-West Trade Policy and Economic Cooperation," in *Western Policy and Eastern Europe*, ed. David S. Collier and Kurt Glaser (Chicago: Regency, 1966), pp. 186–87. Harold B. Scott, "The Outlook for U.S.–East European Trade," *East Europe* 19, no. 2 (November 1970): 9–12. ". . . in 1968, Eastern Europe excluding Russia, purchased $2.7 billion from the West. Of this only $158 million or 6 percent was of U.S. origin. . . . The Comecon countries sold $2.6 billion to western countries and only $140 million or 6 percent, to the United States." Ibid., p. 9.

6. Staar, *Communist Regime in Eastern Europe*, p. 255.

7. Ibid., p. 252.

8. See Scott, "Outlook for U.S.–East European Trade," p. 11.

9. See Henry L. Roberts, *Eastern Europe: Politics, Revolution and Diplomacy* (New York: Alfred A. Knopf, 1970), pp. 216–17, for a view that Eastern Europe's relations with the USSR not only constitute a balance of power situation, but that its adhesion to the USSR substantiates a "wave of the future momentum" for Soviet expansionism.

10. United Nations, *Statistical Yearbook, 1970* (New York, 1971), pp. 410–14.

11. Gross, "East-West Trade Policy and Economic Cooperation," p. 187.

12. Scott, "Outlook for U.S.–East European Trade," p. 11.

13. United Nations, *Statistical Yearbook, 1970*, pp. 398–400.

14. These frontiers (unlike those of the United States) are, in any case, only from two to three hundred land miles from Bonn, Paris, Amsterdam, and Brussels. See Pierre Hassner, "The Implications of Change in Eastern Europe for the Atlantic Alliance," *Orbis* 13, no. 2 (Spring 1969): 237–55, and Robert Legvold, "European Security Conference," *Survey*, no. 76 (Summer 1970): 41–52.

15. See Peter Bender, "Inside the Warsaw Pact," *Survey*, no. 74–75 (Winter-Spring 1970): 253–68.

16. NATO Information Service, *NATO, Facts and Figures* (Brussels, 1969), p. 227.

17. John Erickson, *Soviet Military Power* (London: Royal United Services Institute for Defense Studies, 1971), p. 100. According to the NATO source,

the Soviets were using between 25 and 35 percent of GNP for defense. NATO, *Facts and Figures*, pp. 77. See also American Security Council Committee, *USSR vs. USA, the ABM and The Changed Strategic Military Balance* (Washington D.C.: Acropolis Press, 1969). According to Secretary of Defense Melvin Laird in 1969 the USSR was outspending the United States on offensive weapons by a ratio of 3 to 2 (p. 23). See also pp. 24 and 27 on Soviet advantages in spending on research and development and on the so-called strategic forces, including missiles and nuclear submarines. By 1968 the USSR had trained and deployed 2.1 million engineers and scientists; the United States 1.05 million (pp. 33–34). See also Hanson W. Baldwin, *The Great Arms Race* (New York: Praeger, 1958), pp. 37–38, for an appraisal of Soviet troop reduction announcements in the 1950s.

18. Bela Kiraly, "Why The Soviets Need the Warsaw Pact," *East Europe* 18, no. 4 (April 1969): 16.

19. Erickson, *Soviet Military Power*, p. 103.

20. Kiraly, "Soviets Need Warsaw Pact," pp. 12–13.

21. Ibid., pp. 15–16.

22. Edgar M. Bottome, *The Balance of Terror* (Boston: Beacon Press, 1971), p. 100.

23. *NATO, Facts and Figures*, pp. 77–78.

24. Bottome, *Balance of Terror*, pp. 101–2.

25. *NATO, Facts and Figures*, p. 80. Cf. Eugene Hinterhoff "The Soviet Presence in the Mediterranean," *Orbis* 14, no. 1 (Spring 1969): 261–69. He concludes that: "If the Soviets could force the withdrawal of the U.S. Sixth Fleet, the Mediterranean would become a Soviet lake with the Soviet Navy in charge" (p. 269).

26. Bottome, *Balance of Terror*. This argument recognizes that NATO has, in fact, a greater concentration of forces in North-Central Europe than elsewhere; hence an all-out attack here could be met *still more* effectively than a less likely Soviet assault upon, for example, Greece or Norway. See the International Institute for Strategic Studies, *The Military Balance 1971–1972* (London, 1971), pp. 13, 76–78. See also T. W. Stanley and D. W. Whitt, *Detente Diplomacy: United States and European Security in the 1970's* (New York: Dunellen, 1970), pp. 109–12, for an examination of factors that might possibly help "right the balance" toward NATO. One of these is superior quality and firepower of some NATO weapons, including tanks and aircraft. Also, should a European crisis develop rather slowly, NATO deployment vis-à-vis WTO could be markedly improved. Given little time for mobilization, however, Warsaw Pact forces "would have a superior reinforcement capacity derived from their geographical situation" (p. 116). Cf. IISS, *Military Balance*, p. 78.

27. Klaiber, "East European Relations," p. 334; see also J. F. Brown, "Rumania Today: The Strategy of Defiance," *Problems of Communism* 18, no. 2 (March–April 1969): 32–38.

28. Robert G. Livingston, "East Germany Between Moscow and Bonn," *Foreign Affairs* 50, no. 2 (January 1972): 297–309.

29. Cf. e.g., Edward Taborsky, *Communism in Czechoslovakia 1948–1960* (Princeton, N.J.: Princeton University Press, 1961), pp. 361–467.

30. A Report to the Congress by President Nixon, *U.S. Foreign Policy For the 1970's, The Emerging Structure of Peace* (Washington, D.C.: Government Printing Office, February 1972), p. 50.

31. Ibid.

32. The Polish regime was blaming the outbreak of the December 1970 riots against Gomulka on the alleged instigation of the RFE. See A. J. Groth, *People's Poland: Government and Politics* (San Francisco: Chandler, 1972), p. 123.

33. See Francois Fejto, *A History of The People's Democracies* (New York: Praeger, 1971), especially "The Lure of The West," pp. 207–12, and "Forces of Cohesion," pp. 213–34; see also Ilie J. Smultae, "Ideology and Political Continuity in Eastern Europe: The Case of Rumania," *Eastern European Quarterly* 4, no. 4 (December 1971): 505–36.

34. See, e.g., Sidney I. Ploss, "Politics in The Kremlin," *Problems of Communism* 19, no. 3 (May–June 1970): 1–14; see also Lewis S. Feuer, "Intellectual Opposition," and Maurice Friedberg, "Soviet Jewry Under Pressure," *Problems of Communism* 19, no. 6 (November–December 1970): 17–26, respectively.

35. "European Security: Prospects and Possibilities for East Europe," *East Europe* 19, no. 2 (November 1970): 2.

36. Ibid., pp. 3–4.

37. For tendencies in the direction of particularism, see Wolfgang Klaiber, "Security Priorities in Eastern Europe," *Problems of Communism* 19, no. 3 (May–June 1970): 32–44.

BRITAIN JOINS EUROPE, *Robert J. Lieber*

* Support from an International Affairs Fellowship of the Council on Foreign Relations is acknowledged with appreciation.

1. For an extremely lucid treatment of this nuclear relationship, see Andrew J. Pierre, *Nuclear Politics: The British Experience With an Independent Strategic Force, 1939–1970* (London and New York: Oxford University Press, 1972), pp. 141 ff.

2. For a useful and more detailed discussion of these efforts see Uwe Kitzinger, *The Politics and Economics of European Integration* (New York: Praeger, 1964).

3. The Council remains in operation and has expelled the Greek regime because of violations of human rights by that country's military government.

4. This complex period is treated in Robert J. Lieber, *British Politics and European Unity: Parties, Elites and Pressure Groups* (Berkeley: University of California Press, 1970). See especially chaps. 5, 7.

5. A report by the EEC Commission essentially refuted the position of de Gaulle and found that the negotiations could have succeeded, particu-

larly with a further move by the British government. See European Economic Community Commission, *Report to the European Parliament on the State of the Negotiations with the United Kingdom* (Brussels, 26 February 1963), pp. 110 ff.

6. Quoted in *New York Times*, 21 January 1972.

7. Former Labour ministers such as George Thompson (the government's negotiator in 1967), Lord George Brown, and Lord Chalfont argued that the Heath terms would have been acceptable to the previous Labour Cabinet. See, e.g., *New Statesman*, 6 October 1972, p. 453. See also Kitzinger, *Diplomacy and Persuasion: How Britain Joined the Common Market* (London: Thames & Hudson, 1973), pp. 190–93.

8. E.g., a prominent Labourite and close associate of Harold Wilson threatened that the Rome Treaty would not be accepted by a future Labour government (Peter Shore, *New Statesman*, 11 February 1972, p. 173).

9. See the *Times* (London), 4, 5, and 6 October 1972.

10. The agreements, signed at Brussels on 22 July 1972, provide for a sixteen-country grouping (the six original members of the EEC, plus its new adherents: Britain, Denmark, Ireland, and Norway were linked to five of Britain's former partners in the EFTA—Austria, Iceland, Portugal, Sweden, Switzerland—and one associate EFTA member—Finland. Norwegian voters rejected EEC membership in a September 1972 referendum, but Norway then negotiated an associational status like that of Sweden). By the end of a transition period, free trade will apply to about 90 percent of the trade between the EEC and these outside countries.

11. The October 1972 clash between Sicco Mansholt, then president of the EEC Commission, and Harold Wilson, leader of the British Labour party, over the feasibility of Rome Treaty renegotiation provides an example of this political involvement.

12. During the 1960s, younger strata of the European population were clearly more pro-European than their elders. See, e.g., Ronald Inglehart, "An End to European Integration?" *American Political Science Review* 61 (March 1967): 91–105. While there is no firm evidence to contradict the continuation of this pattern, the autumn 1972 referenda on Norwegian and Danish membership in the EEC appeared to reveal a strong anti-Common Market sentiment among many younger voters of these two Scandinavian countries.

13. However, massive majorities in the original six EEC countries (though not Britain) favored the evolution of the Common Market to a political United States of Europe. See J.–R. Rabier, "Europeans and the Unification of Europe," in *The New Politics of European Integration*, ed. Ghita Ionescu (London: Macmillan, 1972), pp. 157–60.

14. See, e.g., criticisms of recent U.S. policy by Robert Schaetzel, former U.S. ambassador to EEC, in "A Dialogue of the Deaf Across the Atlantic," *Fortune*, November 1972.

15. The nature of this lowering of tariffs may be seen by comparing the average British ad valorem 10 percent to 11 percent tariff on imported

manufactured goods with the comparable EEC figure of 7 percent to 7.5 percent. See e.g., N. Kaldor, *New Statesman*, 12 March 1971. There have been a few cases of discrimination against American exports, as for example during the "chicken war" of the early 1960s.

16. Victor Basiuk, "Perils of the New Technology," *Foreign Policy*, no. 2, (Spring 1971): 51–68, at 54 ff.

17. The Brookings Institution report slightly overstates the case against troop reductions, but the considerations it raises are significant. See John Newhouse et al., *U.S. Troops in Europe: Issues, Costs, and Choices* (Washington, D.C.: Brookings Institution, 1971).

18. Alastair Buchan and his associates delineate six possible futures for Europe: Evolutionary Europe, Atlanticized Europe, Europe des États, Fragmented Europe, Partnership Europe, and Independent Federal Europe. But their assumptions are somewhat different from those set out here. See Alastair Buchan, ed., *Europe's Futures, Europe's Choices: Models of Western Europe in the 1970's* (New York: Columbia University Press for the Institute for Strategic Studies, London, 1969).

19. Among the sweeping and a priori assumptions underlying this ranking scheme is that each mention of an obstacle or "unlikelihood" should be weighted equally.

THE MIDDLE EAST CRISIS, *Shahrough Akhavi*

1. For a recent Arab interpretation, see Ibrahim Abu Lughod, ed., *The Arab-Israeli Confrontation of June 1967: An Arab Perspective* (Evanston, Ill.: Northwestern University Press, 1970). On the colonial danger to the Arabs, see, for example, Maxime Rodinson, *Israel and the Arabs* (Baltimore, Md.: Pelican, 1968).

2. For the Israeli viewpoint, see Nadav Safran, *From War to War: The Arab-Israeli Confrontation, 1948–1967* (New York: Pegasus, 1969); and Walter Z. Laqueur, *The Road to War: The Origin and Aftermath of the Arab Israeli Conflict, 1967–68* (Baltimore, Md.: Pelican, 1968).

3. See the two volumes by William Langer: *European Alignments and Alliances, 1871–1890* (2nd ed.; New York: Alfred A. Knopf, 1950), and *The Diplomacy of Imperialism* (New York: Alfred A. Knopf, 1935) for discussion bearing on the Eastern Question.

4. Leonard Binder, "The Middle East as a Subordinate International System," *World Politics* 10, no. 3 (April 1958): 408–29.

5. For an excellent analysis, see Bernard Lewis, *The Emergence of Modern Turkey* (London: Oxford University Press, 1961).

6. For an account of the Nizam-e Cedid period, see Stanford J. Shaw, *Between Old and New* (Cambridge, Mass.: Harvard University Press, 1971); on the Tanzimat, see Roderic H. Davison, *Reform in the Ottoman Empire, 1856–1876* (Princeton, N.J.: Princeton University Press, 1963).

7. Ben Halpern, *The Idea of the Jewish State* (2nd ed.; Cambridge, Mass.:

Harvard University Press, 1969) for the development of Zionist theory and action.

8. The classic, though controversial, Arab interpretation is George Antonius, *The Arab Awakening* (New York: G. P. Putnam, 1946).

9. The McMahon-Hussein correspondence has been reprinted in various sources. See, for example, J. C. Hurewitz, ed., *Diplomacy in the Middle East*, II (Princeton, N.J.: D. Van Nostrand, 1956), pp. 13–17.

10. Cited in Fred J. Khouri, *The Arab-Israeli Dilemma* (Syracuse, N.Y.: Syracuse University Press, 1968), p. 360.

11. Richard Cottam, "The United States and Palestine," in *The Transformation of Palestine*, ed. Ibrahim Abu-Lughod (Evanston, Ill.; Northwestern University Press, 1971), pp. 391 ff.

12. *Nazi-Soviet Relations 1939–1941, Documents from the Archives of the German Foreign Office*, Department of State Publication 3023 (Washington, D.C., 1948), p. 257. In a clarification 13 days later, Molotov recorded "that the area south of Batum and Baku in the general area of the Persian Gulf is recognized as the center of the aspirations of the Soviet Union." Ibid., p. 259.

13. William B. Quandt, "United States Policy in the Middle East: Constraints and Choices," *Rand Corporation Memorandum RM-5980-FF* (Santa Monica, Calif.: Rand, 1970), pp. 6–9.

14. Cited by Arthur M. Schlesinger, Jr. "Origins of the Cold War," *Foreign Affairs* 46, no. 1 (October 1967), reprinted in *The Conduct of Soviet Foreign Policy*, ed. Erik Hoffmann and Frederic Fleron (Chicago: Aldine-Atherton, 1971), p. 235.

15. See J. M. Mackintosh, *Strategy and Tactics of Soviet Foreign Policy* (New York: Oxford University Press, 1963), p. 44.

16. For a systematic treatment of Soviet policy toward Israel, see Avigdor Dagan, *Moscow and Jerusalem* (London: Abelard-Schuman, 1970).

17. Cited in J. C. Hurewitz, *Middle East Politics: The Military Dimension* (New York: Praeger, 1969), p. 70.

18. Ibid., p. 83.

19. Quandt, "United States Policy in the Middle East," pp. 10–12.

20. This story was originally told by Muhammad Hasanayn Haykal, editor in chief of *al-Ahram*.

21. For an illuminating glimpse of Egyptian negative opinion on the Soviet Union prior to the arms deal, see the series of articles by *al-Ahram's* international affairs specialist, George 'Aziz, during the period 1954–55.

22. Anouar Abdel-Malek, *Egypt: Military Society*, trans. C. L. Markmann (New York: Vintage, 1968), p. 97 ff.

23. Hurewitz, *Middle East Politics*, p. 94.

24. See, for example, Haykal's innuendo in "Khrushchev Qala Li," [Khrushchev Told Me], *al-Ahram*, 22 November 1957, p. 1, where he tells the erstwhile Soviet leader: "Some people in Egypt feel that your final warning to Britain, France and Israel was somewhat [!] late. If this warning had been advanced on time, if it had been prior to the actual aggression, as happened

with Syria [in 1957], then this aggression would have stopped before it began."

25. See Geoffrey Kemp, "Strategy and Arms Levels, 1945–1967," and Lincoln P. Bloomfield and Amelia C. Leiss, "Arms Transfers and Arms Control," both in *Soviet-American Rivalry in the Middle East*, ed. J. C. Hurewitz, Proceedings of the Academy of Political Science, 29, 3 (New York: Columbia University, 1969), pp. 21–54. Also, Uri Ra'anan, *The USSR Arms The Third World* (Cambridge, Mass.: MIT Press, 1969); and Hurewitz, *Middle East Politics*, pp. 438–88.

26. William B. Quandt, "Domestic Influences on U.S. Foreign Policy in the Middle East: The View From Washington," *Rand Corporation Study P-4309* (Santa Monica, Calif.: Rand, April 1970), pp. 2–5.

27. Quandt, "United States Policy in the Middle East," pp. 34 ff.

28. Malcolm H. Kerr, *The Arab Cold War: Gamal 'Abd al-Nasir and His Rivals* (3rd. ed.; New York: Oxford University Press, 1971), p. 115.

29. Yehoshefat Harkabi, "Ending the Arab-Israeli Conflict," in *People and Politics in the Middle East*, ed. Michael Curtis (New Brunswick, N.J.: Transaction, 1971), pp. 258–77.

30. See, for example, *New York Times*, 9 October 1971 and especially 26 October 1971.

31. *New York Times*, 6 February 1972.

32. *New York Times*, 14 January 1972.

33. *New York Times*, 24 November 1971.

34. *New York Times*, 24 September 1972, sect. IV; also 30 December 1971, 1 January 1972, 3 December 1972.

35. As reported in *al-Nahar* (Beirut), 5 August 1972.

AFRICA: THE CHOICES FOR AMERICA, *Donald Rothchild*

1. Ali A. Mazrui, "The Kennedy-Johnson Era of Afro-American Relations," mimeographed (Cambridge, Mass.: Center for International Affairs, Harvard University, n.d.), p. 1.

2. "American Interests in Africa and African Development Needs," *Issue* 2, no. 1 (Spring 1972): 44.

3. Andrew W. Kamarck, "The African Economy and International Trade," in *The United States and Africa*, ed. Walter Goldschmidt (New York: American Assembly, 1958), pp. 118–19.

4. "Remarks by Senator Edmund S. Muskie," *Issue* 1, no. 1 (Fall 1971): 29.

5. *New York Times*, 30 December 1967, p. 28.

6. "Remarks by Senator Edmund S. Muskie," p. 29.

7. Program of African Studies, Northwestern University, *United States Foreign Policy: Africa*, a study prepared at the request of the Committee on Foreign Relations, U.S. Senate, 23 October 1959 (Washington, D.C.: Government Printing Office, 1959), p. 2. Statement by J. C. Satterthwaite.

8. *Congressional Quarterly* (May 1970): 134.

9. *Department of State Bulletin* 66, no. 1707 (13 March 1972): 366.

10. "The New Africa: A Guide and a Proposal," *Harper's* 220, no. 1320 (May 1960): 49.

11. *New York Times*, 24 November 1958, p. 7.

12. *Times of Zambia* (Ndola), 19 March 1971, p. 1.

13. *The Peace Negotiations: A Personal Narrative* (Boston: Houghton Mifflin, 1921), p. 97.

14. *Daily Nation* (Nairobi), 29 July 1968, p. 6.

15. "United States and Africa in the Seventies," Statement submitted by Secretary of State William P. Rogers to the President on 26 March 1970, *Issue* 1, no. 1 (Fall 1971): 24.

16. "Southern Africa: Constant Themes in U. S. Policy," *Department of State Bulletin* 67, no. 1726 (24 July 1972): 121.

17. William Minter, "Allies in Empire," *Africa Today* 17, no. 4 (July–August 1970): 28–32.

18. *Los Angeles Times*, 8 April 1973, p. 1.

19. Kamarck, "African Economy," p. 118.

20. United Nations Association, *Southern Africa: Proposals for Americans*, a report of a National Policy Panel (New York: UNA–USA, 1971), p. 18.

21. *Times of Zambia* (Ndola), 10 February 1972, p. 1.

22. *Times of Zambia* (Ndola), 8 January 1972, p. 1.

23. Vernon McKay, *Africa in World Politics* (New York: Harper & Row, 1963), p. 249.

24. Editorial, *Nationalist* (Dar es Salaam), 25 February 1969, p. 4.

25. *Southern Africa: Proposals for Americans*, pp. 44, 48.

26. Ibid., p. 52.

27. *Times of Zambia* (Ndola), 12 May 1971, p. 1.

28. *Daily Nation* (Nairobi), 16 February 1970, p. 6.

29. "American Interests in Africa," p. 45.

30. *Daily Nation* (Nairobi), 11 July 1972, p. 11.

31. *People* (Kampala), 19 July 1972, p. 1.

32. *Daily Nation* (Nairobi), 19 October 1972, p. 18.

33. By contrast, Senator George McGovern asserted in his foreign policy statement that "we will show our concern for the racist expulsion of Asians from Uganda." *New York Times*, 6 October 1972, p. 26.

34. Ibid., 15 September 1972, p. 1.

35. Ibid.

36. *Daily Nation* (Nairobi), 22 November 1972, p. 28, and 20 December 1972, p. 44.

37. Ibid., 21 December 1972, p. 9.

38. It is interesting to note that Newsom, in making such denials, attributes the policy on channeling the bulk of aid to ten selected countries to the need for a regional and multilateral aid approach and the desire to reduce large American missions abroad. See David D. Newsom, "Aid to Africa—A Moral and Economic Necessity," *Department of State Bulletin* 66, no. 1703 (14 February 1972): 203–4.

39. *Daily Nation* (Nairobi), 22 June 1972, p. 15.

40. Donald Rothchild, "America's Regionalism-in-Aid Policy," *East Africa Journal* 5, no. 4 (April 1968): 19; and *Times of Zambia* (Ndola), 3 July 1971, p. 1.

41. Charles de Gaulle, *Memoirs of Hope: Renewal and Endeavor*, trans. Terence Kilmartin (New York: Simon & Schuster, 1970), p. 131.

42. *New York Times*, 13 April 1972, p. 7.

43. Tom Mboya, *The Challenge of Nationhood* (London: Andre Deutsch, 1970), p. 191.

44. Segun Durosola, *Dollar Pressure in Africa* (Lagos: Nigerian Study Circle, n.d.), p. 7.

45. Ibid., p. 19. For a discussion of Tanzania's emphasis upon self-reliance, see Donald Rothchild, "Kenya's Africanization Program: Priorities of Development and Equity," *American Political Science Review* 64, no. 3 (September 1970): 751–52.

ENVIRONMENTAL QUALITY, *Geoffrey Wandesforde-Smith*

1. I have in mind here the kind of doomsday prophet that Curt Gentry describes in *The Last Days of the Late, Great State of California* (New York: Ballantine, 1969), pp. 8–13.

2. Donella H. Meadows et al., *The Limits to Growth* (New York: Universe, 1972). This book is a nontechnical report of a research project undertaken by an international team of researchers at the Massachusetts Institute of Technology. It examined five basic factors that were held to determine, and in interaction ultimately to limit, growth. The factors were population increase, agricultural production, nonrenewable resource depletion, industrial output, and pollution generation. The research was sponsored by an organization called the Club of Rome which is financed in large part by Italian industrialist Aurelio Peccei. The book has been the subject of considerable controversy both because of its methodology and its sponsorship (see, e.g., reviews by Lester Brown and Larry Fabian in *Saturday Review*, 22 April 1972, pp. 65–70).

3. Richard A. Falk, *This Endangered Planet: Prospects and Proposals for Human Survival* (New York: Random House, 1971).

4. Lynton K. Caldwell, *In Defense of Earth: International Protection of the Biosphere* (Bloomington, Ind.: Indiana University Press, 1972).

5. Lord Ritchie-Calder, "Mortgaging the Old Homestead," *Foreign Affairs* 48 (January, 1970): 207–20.

6. George F. Kennan, "To Prevent a World Wasteland: A Proposal," *Foreign Affairs* 48 (April 1970): 401–13.

7. Kenneth E. Boulding, "The Economics of the Coming Spaceship Earth," in *Environmental Quality in a Growing Economy*, ed. Henry Jarrett (Baltimore, Md.: Johns Hopkins Press, 1966), pp. 3–14. For use of the same metaphor, see also Barbara Ward, *Spaceship Earth* (New York: Columbia

University Press, 1966), and R. Buckminster Fuller, *Operating Manual for Spaceship Earth* (Carbondale, Ill.: Southern Illinois University Press, 1969).

8. Harold Sprout and Margaret Sprout, *Toward a Politics of The Planet Earth* (New York: Van Nostrand Reinhold, 1971), p. 31.

9. Caldwell, *In Defense of Earth*, pp. 148–54.

10. For an interesting portrait of Strong, see Sally Lindsay, "Cleanup Man Maurice Strong," *Saturday Review*, 7 August 1971, pp. 43–47.

11. In four meetings between the fall of 1970 and the spring of 1972 a broad agenda was developed consisting of the following topics: (1) planning and management of the environmental quality of human settlements; (2) environmental aspects of natural resource management; (3) identification and control of environmental pollutants and nuisances; (4) educational, informational, social, and cultural aspects of environmental issues; (5) economic development and the environment; and (6) international organizational implications of proposals for action.

12. Extracts from the address to the conference by the chairman of the delegation from the People's Republic of China are printed in *Bulletin of the Atomic Scientists* (September 1972): 54–55.

13. Hans Landsberg, "Can Stockholm Succeed?," *Science* 176 (19 May 1972): 749.

14. Public Law 91-190, National Environmental Policy Act of 1969, sect. 102(E).

15. U.S. Council on Environmental Quality, *Environmental Quality: Second Annual Report* (Washington, D.C.: Government Printing Office, August 1971), p. 334.

16. Ibid.

17. For a general and controversial treatment of this subject, see Paul R. Ehrlich and Anne H. Ehrlich, *Population, Resources, Environment: Issues in Human Ecology* (2nd ed.; San Francisco: W. H. Freeman, 1972).

18. For a brief critical review of the literature on the climatic effects of man's activities, see *Man's Impact on the Global Environment: Assessment and Recommendations for Action* (Cambridge, Mass.: MIT Press, 1970), pp. 39–112. This is the report of the Study of Critical Environmental Problems (SCEP), and is hereinafter referred to as SCEP Study.

19. SCEP Study, pp. 126–66.

20. Fairfield Osborn, *The Limits of the Earth* (Boston: Little, Brown, 1953).

21. National Academy of Sciences, *Institutional Arrangements for International Environmental Cooperation*, a Report to the Department of State by the Committee for International Environmental Programs, Environmental Studies Board (Washington, D.C.: National Academy of Sciences, 1972), pp. 7–8. The plan of this paper in exploring the implications of world environmental problems for American foreign policy follows that of the report.

22. Ehrlich and Ehrlich, *Population, Resources, Environment*, chap. 12.

23. The consequences of American policy toward international pollu-

tion control for existing patterns of international trade have been of particular interest to several groups in the United States. See U.S. President's Commission on International Trade and Investment Policy, *United States International Economic Policy in an Interdependent World* (Washington, D.C.: Government Printing Office, 1971), pp. 129–39, and the comments of the United States Chamber of Commerce in U.S. Congress, Senate, Committee on Foreign Relations, *Hearings, U.N. Conference on Human Environment: Preparations and Prospects*, 92nd Cong., 2nd sess., 1972, pp. 146–63 (hereinafter referred to as Congress, *Preparations and Prospects*). The OECD has also taken great interest in this subject and the text of its guiding principles concerning the international economic aspects of environmental policies is reprinted in U.S. Council on Environmental Quality, *Environmental Quality: Third Annual Report* (Washington, D.C.: Government Printing Office, 1972), pp. 102–4 (hereinafter referred to as CEQ, *Third Annual Report*).

24. Philip R. Pryde, *Conservation in the Soviet Union* (Cambridge, Mass.: Cambridge University Press, 1972). See also Philip P. Micklin, "The Baykal Controversy: A Resource Use Conflict in the USSR," *Natural Resources Journal* 7 (October 1967): 485–98.

25. Andrei D. Sakharov, *Progress, Coexistence and Intellectual Freedom* (New York: W. W. Norton, 1968).

26. The text of the cooperative agreement on environmental protection between the United States and the USSR signed during the May 1972 summit meeting is reprinted in CEQ, *Third Annual Report*, pp. 105–7.

27. For a review, see Caldwell, *In Defense of Earth*, chap. 3.

28. The data in this paragraph are from Ehrlich and Ehrlich, *Population, Resources, Environment*, pp. 72, 406.

29. Lynton K. Caldwell, "An Ecological Approach to International Development: Problems of Policy and Administration," in *The Careless Technology: Ecology and International Development*, ed. M. Taghi Farvar and John P. Milton (Garden City, N.Y.: Natural History Press, 1972), pp. 927–47.

30. SCEP Study, pp. 253–54.

31. Farvar and Milton, *Careless Technology*, is a massive compendium of recent studies on this subject.

32. Sprout and Sprout, *Politics of Planet Earth*, pp. 9–11 and 361–70. See also Harold Sprout and Margaret Sprout, "National Priorities: Demands, Resources, Dilemmas," *World Politics* 24 (January 1972): 293–317.

33. See, e.g., Kermit Gordon, ed., *Agenda for the Nation* (Garden City, N.Y.: Doubleday, 1969).

34. This account of the Arusha Conference is summarized from Max Nicholson, *The Environmental Revolution: A Guide for the New Masters of the World* (New York: McGraw-Hill, 1970), pp. 202–3 and 226–28.

35. U.S. Council on Environmental Quality, *Second Annual Report*, pp. 29–30.

36. Nicholson, *Environmental Revolution*, chap. 9. See also Caldwell, *In Defense of Earth*, chap. 3 and pp. 119–44.

37. Congress, *Preparations and Prospects*, p. 76.

38. Ibid., pp. 76–77. There is support for Gardner's point elsewhere in the hearing record. In response to an inquiry from Senator Claiborne Pell as to why the Nixon administration refused to grant recognition to East Germany as a full-fledged participant in the Stockholm Conference, the State Department made clear its view that such participation might jeopardize final negotiations on a Berlin Agreement. Ibid., pp. 10–11.

39. For a discussion of the potential role of the United Nations, see David A. Kay and Eugene B. Skolnikoff, eds., *World Eco-Crisis: International Organizations in Response* (Madison, Wis.: University of Wisconsin Press, 1972).

40. The discussion at these meetings is summarized usefully in *Conservation Foundation Letter* (November 1971).

41. National Academy of Sciences, *International Environmental Cooperation*, pp. 25–26.

42. Congress, *Preparations and Prospects*, p. 89.

43. Although the conference approved the concept of a fund, no monetary goal was adopted. The United States proposed a total of $100 million over five years with the United States contributing $40 million. Other specific contributions were promised by Canada, $5 million to $7.5 million; Australia, $2.5 million; and the Netherlands, up to $1.5 million. Fifteen other countries also pledged support without indicating amounts.

44. For insight into the frightening complexity of international arrangements to deal with environmental problems, both inside and outside the United Nations, and for an assessment of the difficulties standing in the way of meaningful institutional change, see Brian Johnson, "The United Nations' Institutional Response to Stockholm: A Case Study in the International Politics of Institutional Change," in Kay and Skolnikoff, *World Eco-Crisis*, pp. 87–134. For a discussion of alternative international organizational arrangements to those discussed in the present paper, see International Institute for Environmental Affairs, *The Human Environment: Science and International Decision Making*, Workshop Report No. 1 (New York, 1972); Albert E. Utton, "International Aspects of Environmental Policy," *Natural Resources Journal* 11 (July 1971): 513–17.

WEIGHING THE BALANCE OF POWER, *Stanley Hoffmann*

1. See Stanley Hoffmann, "Will the Balance Balance at Home?" *Foreign Policy*, no. 7 (Summer 1972): 60–87.

2. See Robert O. Keohane and Joseph S. Nye, Jr., eds., "Transnational Relations and World Politics," *International Organization* 25, no. 3 (Summer 1971): 329–50.

Index